Exploring the Internet

A Technical Travelogue

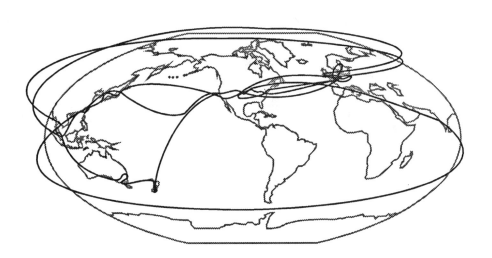

Exploring the Internet

A Technical Travelogue

Carl Malamud

PTR Prentice Hall

Englewood Cliffs, New Jersey 07632

Library of Congress Cataloging-in-Publication Data

Malamud, Carl, 1959-
  Exploring the Internet: a technical travelogue/Carl Malamud.
      p.   cm.
  Includes bibliographical references and index.
  ISBN 0-13-296898-3 :
  1. Internet (Computer network)   I.Title.
TK5105.875.I57M36   1993
384.3—dc20   92-16450
                                                  CIP

Acquisitions editor: Mary Franz
Jacket design: Bruce Kenselaar
Cover design: Joe DiDomenico
Prepress buyer: Mary E. McCartney
Manufacturing buyer: Susan Brunke

Copyright © 1992 by Carl Malamud

 Published by Prentice-Hall, Inc.
A Simon & Schuster Company
Englewood Cliffs, New Jersey 07632

The publisher offers discounts on this book
when ordered in bulk quantities. For more information, write: Special Sales/Professional
Marketing, Professional & Technical Reference
Division, Prentice Hall, Englewood Cliffs, NJ
07632.

All products are the trademarks of their respective manufacturers. Carl Malamud is a trademark of Carl Malamud.

Printed in the United States of America
10 9 8 7 6 5 4 3 2 1

ISBN   0-13-296898-3

Prentice-Hall International (UK) Limited, *London*
Prentice-Hall of Australia Pty. Limited, *Sydney*
Prentice-Hall Canada Inc., *Toronto*
Prentice-Hall Hispanoamericana, S.A., *Mexico*
Prentice-Hall of India Private Limited, *New Delhi*
Prentice Hall of Japan, Inc., *Tokyo*
Simon & Schuster Asia Pte. Ltd., *Singapore*
Editora Prentice-Hall do Brasil, Ltda., *Rio de Janeiro*

Contents

Foreword and Preface, in which we secure funding for a voyage which will take us three times around the world in six months and give new meaning to the phrase "many fine lunches and dinners."

Prologue: The Document Liberation Front, in which we delve into the abyss of international politics and wade through hordes of Jehovah's Witnesses to examine a Bulgarian FEP.

    Geneva • Prague • Zürich • Geneva • Paris • Boulder

Round 1: From INTEROP to IETF, in which we meet the Internet Samurai and the Uncle of the NSFNet and go to the zoo to witness the birth of EBONE.

    San Jose • Honolulu • Tokyo • Fujisawa • Akihabara
    Hong Kong • Macau • Singapore • Dublin • Amsterdam
    London • Tampere • Paris • Geneva • Nice • Geneva
    Ithaca • New York • Washington, D.C. • Santa Fe • Boulder

Round 2: From Christmas to Cleveland, in which we encounter a massively parallel bicycle in Mt. View, find magic boxes in Oz, and go swimming in the Sea of Acronyms in Europe.

    Berkeley • Mt. View • San Francisco • Moffet Field
    Wellington • Dunedin • Auckland • Melbourne • Sydney
    Canberra • Adelaide • Singapore • Kuala Lumpur • Bangkok
    Amsterdam • Utrecht • Bonn • Brussels • Paris
    Washington, D.C. • Cleveland • Chicago • Boulder

Round 3: In Search of a Standards Haven, in which we meet the world's most intelligent building, try to convince people to do the bloody obvious, and learn the origins of the Internet.

    Marina del Rey • San Francisco • Tokyo • Seoul
    Taipei • Hong Kong • Bombay • Madison • Boulder

Index

In July 1991, Carl Malamud flew out from Boulder, Colorado, a place he describes as "closer to Kansas than I'd like." He had just finished writing *STACKS*, which we were distributing as The IN-TEROP Book to conference attendees, and wanted to present us his latest proposal.

He met me at breakfast and presented me with a pith helmet plastered over with Interop logos. "What Interop Company really needs," he explained, "is an Official Internet Explorer."

His proposal was to fly three times around the world, visit as many sites as possible, and write what he was calling "a technical travelogue." The catch, of course, is he wanted me to foot the bill for travel expenses.

Exploring the Internet is the result of this odyssey. This book demonstrates what many of us have long felt: the worldwide network is here. Interoperability is not some imaginary goal at vendor briefings, but a concrete part of networks all over the world.

This book is more than just a series of case studies—it is truly a technical travelogue. As we read about the worldwide spread of the Internet, we get to appreciate its diversity and its usefulness to millions. This is not some experimental research environment, some academic toy, it is a real tool used by real people.

At that breakfast in 1991, Carl confided his hidden agenda. After going on about "global infrastructures" and other nice phrases designed to impress my senior managers, he turned to me and gave me the executive overview. "Actually, this is a very simple project," he explained. "Buy my airplane tickets and I'll try to get into as much trouble as I can. Then I'll write a book."

Here it is.

Dan Lynch
Founder and President
Interop Company

The reason I visited 21 countries in six months, embarking on a technical voyage of discovery, can be traced back to an encounter I had with a platoon of bureaucrats. In June, 1991, I struck a deal with the Secretary-General of the International Telecommunication Union (ITU), coordinators of the very formal process which eventually results in standards such as the Blue Book: 19,000 pages of international recommendations which define the operation of data networks, telephone systems, and other aspects of communication.

The deal was that the ITU would give me a copy of the standards in the antiquated online format they used for text processing and that I would convert the standards into something the rest of us could deal with and publish the standards on the global Internet. Instead of charging obscene amounts of money for this information, the standards would be available to anybody at no charge.

Organizations, rhetoric notwithstanding, don't work for such lofty goals as the dissemination of knowledge. The real reason for this breakthrough in standards distribution was that the ITU couldn't figure out how to convert their own data from the proprietary box they had built around themselves. My offer to do the conversion seemed an easy way out of a job they had estimated at U.S. $3.2 million. In return for converting the data and giving them a copy, I could publish on this Internet thing, this academic toy.

The ITU gave me half the data they promised and conveniently lost half the documentation to their Byzantine (both in age and in complexity) formatting system. Then, after a mere 90 days, the ITU abruptly cancelled distribution on the Internet. The academic toy, to the bureaucracy's horror, turned out to have over seven million people. They were shocked to see hundreds of thousands of ITU documents being accessed by thousands of people in dozens of countries.

Despite their abrupt cancellation of the project, the ITU still demanded a report. They wanted a certified bureaucracy document they could input into their process, analyzing possible scenarios and deliberating impacts.

This is that report.

At first glance, this report looks like it would get the bureaucratic seal of approval. It is thick, for example. However, this book is something different than the bureaucrats might expect. My research methods were unorthodox: I spent most of my time talking to people.

In fact, I talked to lots of people. In three trips around the world, I talked to people on the front lines: people who make computers, people who create networks, and people who use them. To explain to the bureaucracies facts that are painfully obvious to the rest of us, I had to leave the confines of meeting rooms and fancy hotels and go into the research laboratories, network operating centers, and bars and restaurants where real work happens.

This report is thus a travel book, a book of exploration in the tradition of classic writers ranging from Captain Sir Richard Francis Burton, author of over 50 books and master of 29 languages, to Dr. Hunter S. Thompson, author of careful documentaries about political campaigns and police conventions.

Instead of exploring the Nile or Las Vegas, I looked at the emerging Global Village. This isn't a comprehensive atlas, nor is it a definitive history. *Exploring the Internet* really is a technical travelogue, a narrative description of the people and networks I encountered during my travels. In my visits, I saw something the ITU and the rest of the standards bureaucracy seem to have missed. The Internet is here and it is not an academic toy.

While I saw many people, I should add that even in three circumnavigations, I couldn't see everybody. This is one walk through the forest, and there are many trails one can take. This book is a selective look at some of the people, laboratories, and institutions that help illustrate the diversity and the scope of the Internet.

This voyage would not have been possible without the support of Interop Company which helped finance my travel expenses. Be aware, though, that this book is mine, not theirs. There are many opinions which are not shared by Interop Company and it is a great credit to Interop Company that they felt it important to finance this kind of work.

This book would not have been possible without the help of the hundreds of people I talked to and particularly those who opened their laboratories, homes, and CPUs to me. The hospitality I encountered was truly gratifying and I am thankful for the time given to me by the people you will read about throughout this book.

This book owes a great deal to logistics, and I want to thank the Boulder office of United Airlines for their infinite patience. Infinite patience is an understatement when it comes to David Brandin, Stephanie Faul, Mary Franz, Ole Jacobsen, Martin Lucas, and Yvette Ozer, the editors who worked on this book, and it is to them that I give the biggest thanks.

Carl Malamud
Carl@Malamud.Com

Prologue

The Document Liberation Front

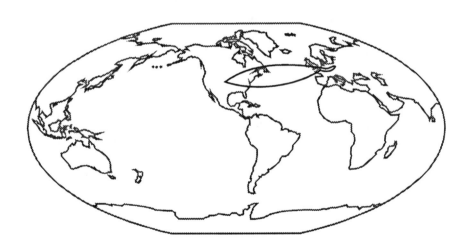

It was August 1991, and I was sitting in a café in Geneva, Switzerland, having lunch with Tony Rutkowski, a man who was a senior official in the International Telecommunication Union (ITU) but whom nobody could seem to pin an exact title on. While many called him the General Counsel of the ITU (for reasons that will become apparent), Tony prefered to refer to himself as "Counsellor to the Secretary-General," a title with enough ambiguity to serve his purposes.

Tony and I were celebrating a minor palace coup, a year in the making and the result of a bizarre partnership. How all this came to be can be traced to my propensity to flame.

For several years, I've been complaining about the high cost of international standards documents published by the ITU and other international standards groups. After all, I write professional reference books for a living and these documents are my raw materials.

At first the flames started as simple whining, but soon they grew to full-fledged diatribes in publications running the gamut of technical sophistication from *Data Communications* to *ConneXions*. I got lots of quotes from illustrious people like Jon Postel, Editor of the Internet Request for Comments (RFCs), who explained that keeping international standards away from "random people" was hurting their acceptance. The gestation time for software based on Open Systems Interconnection (OSI) serves as ample illustration of Postel's point.

The fabled power of the press produced an effect about as pronounced as, say, an editorial in favor of truth and beauty. An occasional nod from a passing reader, but no cries of outrage.

As a sanity check, I posted a note on the Internet asking if anybody else thought that the inaccessibility of international standards was hindering technical progress. This hit a nerve. In fact, the resulting firestorm surprised even survivors of historically notable dialogues such as "should pornography be distributed on the net?"

Exploring the Internet

The Internet has a wide community of users, but a convenient taxonomy splits them into flamers and firefighters. Flaming is easy to explain. You send a message and bingo, you've made 1,000 people all hit the delete key in their mail readers. The power to make so many people twitch is seductive and some people occasionally succumb. In fact, some succumb all too often.

The firefighters have a different motivation. Their happiness is inversely proportional to the size of their electronic inbox. Not everybody was terribly happy when their inboxes started filling with "me too," "I agree," and "another minor yet trivial point" variants on the first wave of reaction.

Dan Lynch, the founder of Interop Company, is a firefighter. He didn't want to see this situation continue forever, so he sent me a copy of a memo written by Tony Rutkowski at the ITU. Turns out Tony was doing the same sort of complaining I was, but was directing his comments internally to the huge ITU bureaucracy.

Tony and I exchanged a few e-mail messages and found we were in violent agreement: standards have to be widely available or the standards are irrelevant. We started trying to figure out what could be done about it.

Turns out that we agreed on another point. We both feel that the ITU has a fairly dubious basis for asserting copyright protection on standards, since a standard spends months (often years) wandering around the public domain as a working-group document before it ever becomes blessed as an official standard and is "published."

You can't make a speech to a crowded room and then, one week later, tell people that your speech contained valuable trade secrets. You can't publish a newspaper and then unpublish it. Once you give something away, it stays given away.

The lack of valid copyright protection is one argument for making standards more widely available, but there is a much more important one. If you believe, like Tony and I fervently did, that the ITU does valuable work, then the standards are an essential public good. Standards are laws and laws must be known to be observed.

Failing to make the standards widely available was, in the long run, going to make the work of the ITU irrelevant. Other standards-making bodies were promulgating standards, and despite its official

United Nations treaty status, the ITU had to compete with other groups for the attention of implementors and users.

I sent Tony a note and suggested that since we both agreed that the ITU really had an indeterminate legal basis for asserting copyright, I would simply take all 19,000 pages of the Blue Book, scan it, run it through OCR software, and post it on the Internet for distribution by anonymous FTP, a service that allows a site to give the public access to file archives using the File Transfer Protocol to any user who logs in as "anonymous." (The Blue Book is the massive set of 1988 standards developed by the ITU's Consultative Committee on International Telephone and Telegraph to govern the operation of everything from telephone signalling systems to packet data networks to ISDN to high-speed modems.)

Now, there are a couple of points worth keeping in mind. Tony was a senior lawyer for a powerful United Nations group that made lots of money selling these documents. While Tony certainly sympathized with my goals, I wasn't quite sure how he was going to react to this form of standards terrorism. Putting a lawyer on notice that you plan to relabel his corporate assets with a $0 price tag is kind of like putting Honda stickers on the motorcycles parked outside a Harley bar.

The other point is that the Blue Book is over 19,000 pages long. Scanners and OCR are great technology, but it would take an awfully long time to carry out such a project on my little home PC. In fact, in a world of finite resources, you might even call my plan an idle threat.

Idle threat or no, this message caught the ITU's attention. One year later, in June of 1991, after endless messages back and forth to Tony, I had received a fax from the Secretary-General asking me to post all ITU standards on the Internet on an "experimental" basis. I promptly booked a plane ticket to Geneva for August to pry the data out of the cold, clammy hands of the bureaucracy. Next thing I knew, I was in Geneva, ready to go to work.

❒

I was sitting in Tony's office reading a book while he went off to clear political barriers. In the other room, Julie Butterfield, his assistant, was busy typing away when the phone rang. Julie raced in with a pad of paper and answered the phone.

"Mr. Rutkowski's office." She scribbled some notes on a pad.

"I'll give him the message," Julie said, hanging up the phone.

Something wasn't right with this picture. As she walked out, I inquired why she didn't just have the phone roll over to her desk if Tony doesn't pick it up.

"We have nothing that sophisticated here at the ITU," she responded with a smile and a strong dose of sarcasm.

A few minutes later, Tony came back and we started talking while Julie ran some errands. Her phone rang and Tony sprinted out to the outer office to take the call.

The ITU was using a very old donated Siemens PBX. This PBX was actually quite advanced for its time, but its time had long passed. This was a feature-rich PBX, but most of the features were so difficult to use that people didn't use them. Tony brought in his AT&T phone from home just so he could have a few stored numbers.

Until recently, in fact, the entire ITU had one fax machine for over 900 employees. A single fax machine was more the result of bureaucratic desire to limit outside communications than a cost factor. The fax machine was in the Secretary-General's office. This meant that sending a fax could require approval right up to the Secretary-General. To get the Secretary-General's approval, you had to go through the Deputy Secretary-General, which would require recursive approval right on down the food chain. Needless to say, to communicate through this medium you would have to be pretty strongly motivated.

What is really funny about all this is that ITU, as part of its enabling treaty, has the right to free telecommunications throughout the world. This perk is meant to allow easy communication to the 160 member countries, and even goes so far as to allow the ITU to set up terminal clusters at off-site meetings with X.25-based links back to Geneva.

Geneva

I'm not quite sure what I expected at the ITU, but I kind of figured a modicum of computer literacy. Nothing fancy, mind you, but at least things like basic phone tricks, fax machines, and maybe even electronic mail. After all, this is the home of X.400, the message handling system to end all message handling systems. Was the ITU using X.400, though? Not a chance! They had Digital's proprietary Message Router and the infamous All-in-(N)One as a user interface. X.400 connectivity was achieved by a poorly functioning gateway.

This lack of computer literacy at the ITU was what made Tony Rutkowski such an odd duck. When he came to Geneva he saw that none of the international bureaucracies had Internet hookups. So, Tony did what any self respecting technocrat would do and called up the nearest Internet provider, in this case the CERN physics laboratory, and asked for a guest account. Several years later, Tony was still the only ITU employee with access to the Internet.

Tony had taken a rather strange career path to his position at the ITU (a position he left at the end of 1991). After studying engineering at the Florida Institute of Technology, he became quite active in civil rights. Eventually, he landed himself a seat on the city council, getting further involved in policy and politics.

From there, through a roundabout road, his interest in telecommunications drew him to Washington, D.C., where he went to work for the chief scientist at the FCC. The chief scientist was also an Internet old boy, and the FCC was promptly installed as part of the Internet. While working at the FCC by day, Tony put himself through law school at night at American University.

Eventually, Tony went up to Boston to become the publisher of *Telecommunications*. In Boston, he alleviated the drudgery of punching out a magazine by working as a Research Associate at MIT's Media Laboratory.

Altogether, this mix of lawyer, regulator, and engineer was just the combination needed when Pekka Tarjanne took over the helm of the ITU. A physicist by training, Tarjanne was determined to bring the ITU into the telecommunications age and asked Tony to work as his personal assistant.

◻

My first face-to-face meeting with Tony, after countless e-mail messages, was in August when I took the train in from Paris and went to the twelfth floor of the ITU tower. As I got off the elevator, a short man with a beard darted in after me, posted a piece of paper in the elevator and jumped back out again just as the doors slammed shut.

This was Tony. He was trying to get into every elevator to post a notice of my lecture the next day. The lecture was news to me, so I read the notice. Along with the obligatory hype, the notice explained that I would be lecturing about a host of topics ranging from the future of networking in the civilized world to how more bandwidth would lead to world peace.

After catching the last elevator, Tony and I wandered across the street to the International Organization for Standardization (ISO). It is ironic that the acronym used by this global standards organization is a dyslexic variant of its real name.

ISO is a rather strange group. Unlike the ITU, ISO is a private organization. Like ANSI in the U.S., ISO's lack of real legitimacy to carry out its quasi-governmental functions makes the organization a bit insular and very conservative. Located in a squat, drab building, ISO occupies the dimly lit corridors of the third and fourth floors. The halls are almost always empty, but occasionally one can see a functionary dart out of one office and flit into another.

Tony and I wandered around the halls to find people to invite to my lecture. The purpose of our visit was to make sure everybody at ISO knew about the ITU experiment. I was a bit worried that putting ISO on notice would be considered confrontational, but Tony assured me that there was "nothing wrong with pushing forward the state-of-the-art a bit."

My lecture, by the standards of public bureaucracies, was a stunning success. Aside from the obligatory ITU contingent trying to figure out what their management was up to, there was a large crowd of functionaries from diverse UN contingencies interested in the Internet. Only a few people fell asleep, and a few even asked questions. This was described by several people as a "dynamic" performance.

I described how the standards would be posted on the network, how different access protocols would be used, and how making standards widely available had been so successful for the TCP/IP protocols. I explained how, once the data was digital, we could all start using advanced services, write better code and how, when all was said and done, we would enter a state of standards equilibrium, a nirvana of documentation.

Unbeknown to us at the time, the audience included an operative from ISO, sent over to keep tabs on the radical goings-on across the street. When my own spies informed me of this the next morning, I placed a call to Dr. Zakharov, head of the ISO computer group. I explained who I was and said that, at the request of ITU management, I would be happy to come over and give them a courtesy briefing on our little project.

"That sounds mighty exalted. Come over Thursday morning."

❐

Two days later, I donned my suit and dashed through the rain to the other side of Rue Varembé. I bypassed the obligatory visit to ISO reception and went straight to the third floor and back through a warren of offices, where I was ushered into the inner sanctum of Dr. Zakharov.

Walking in, I saw an older man behind the desk wearing the sort of safari suit that the British favor. "You are Malamud?" he asked. "I have asked McKenzie to join us" he said, beckoning to a young man wearing a shirt and tie who nodded at me with a glum gaze.

"McKenzie is our database expert. I have asked him to be here because what we have here is a database issue, not a network issue."

"Let me first say that I know all about this Internet of yours," he continued. "I used the Internet even before it was the Internet. In fact, before it was the ARPANET. This Internet of yours may be fine for researchers, but here at ISO we have real clients to serve, so enough about this Internet."

I was still standing. A pause introduced itself, so it seemed an appropriate moment for a few formalities.

"Glad to meet you," I said, holding out my hand.

McKenzie continued to glance at the floor and Dr. Zakharov grunted in what I took to be an amiable fashion so I gathered my courage and made a little speech about how my efforts with the ITU were experimental, provisional, something we could learn from, temporary, and any other non-threatening platitudes I could think of.

My little speech contained a fatal flaw. I had used the pronoun "we." Now, "we" is not totally inappropriate as this effort was based on the efforts of several interested parties, but I must admit that the corporate offices of Me, Inc. do not actually teem with corporate retainers.

"We?" Zakharov pounced. "Who is 'we'?" he demanded. "How many members are on your team, anyway?"

Like many corporate types, my lack of a formal institutional affiliation did not sit well with him. I sidestepped his question and explained that, in my view, the question of publishing standards was, rhetoric notwithstanding, just not that hard. After all, there were hundreds of ways to get data on-line, ranging from Wordstar to bitmaps to SGML (an ISO standard).

To say that ISO viewed my little project as a threat was an understatement. Zakharov let slip that the Secretary-General of ISO had sent a letter to his counterpart at the ITU protesting the experiment. Zakharov made it quite clear that he viewed my approach as simplistic, misguided, and naive.

I gently tried to make the point that there were positive aspects to this project that should not be overlooked, such as increasing the public awareness of the vital work that groups like ISO were undertaking by making primary resource documents available to a wider audience.

Once again, my diplomatic efforts seemed less than successful. "People don't need to read the standards," Dr. Zakharov snapped. Indeed, he felt that ISO standards were basically unreadable and that normal people shouldn't even bother to try. What was apparently needed was some guru to write a book, and that these second or third-generation digested versions of standards were more appropriate for the general public. Turns out that Zakharov had himself written such a book ("a monograph, actually") on some long-forgotten CAD standard.

I'm all in favor of promoting book sales, but there is still no substitute for the original documents. A programmer working on an implementation should be required to RTFM ("Read the F***ing Manual" or, in the staid company of standards potatoes, "Read the FTAM Manual"). There is no excuse for second-hand knowledge of something as vital as international standards.

So far, we had spent 45 minutes of a one-hour meeting about databases, and the subject of databases still had not come up. It didn't look like it was going to. McKenzie still hadn't said anything and didn't appear to be about to burst into action.

As I paused to gather my forces, Zakharov jumped in. "Another thing, young man. Do the people in charge of the Internet know about your efforts?"

He seemed convinced that when some appropriate official learned that I would be distributing documents—"with graphics, no less"—on the network, my renegade activities would be quickly stopped.

(Let's put this into perspective. The NSFNET backbone transfers well over 14 billion packets per month. Even if my server was wildly popular, the backbone could handle it. Just to be sure, I was going to send the big computer companies archive tapes so they didn't need to FTP the entire file store into their internal networks.)

I told him that indeed my activities were supported by appropriate officials. The chairman of the Internet Activities Board (IAB), for example, had offered to be one of the anonymous FTP sites for the standards. I didn't tell Zakharov that the incoming chair of the IAB, who had also chaired several ISO committees, had on his home computer many ISO documents and had half-seriously offered them to be posted along with the Blue Book.

"It's not that we're against the Internet," Zakharov explained. "We just want to make sure that all the issues are properly considered. In fact, we are using the TCP/IP protocols here at ISO." ISO had been unable to find enough OSI software to keep their internal network going, so they used a combination of Novell and TCP/IP.

My allotted hour was nearing the end, so I once again began mumbling conciliatory phrases about experiments, cooperation, and similar appropriate fin-de-meeting noises.

"So what do you want from us?" Dr. Zakharov cut in, ever the diplomat.

I pulled out my extra large shovel and explained that since ISO obviously had concerns about the experiment, I was simply here to explain my efforts. "By the way," I continued, "ISO is welcome to join in our little experiment. I have plenty of disk space left."

Zakharov grunted. McKenzie sat.

Zakharov rose. McKenzie rose.

Our little meeting was over.

Back at the ITU, the machinery had swung into action and, with a few false starts, my tapes were being cut.

With a week to kill before my plane left to go back to the States, I decided to try and get in a little fun. Sitting in Tony's office using Telnet to read my mail in Boulder, I looked next to his mouse pad and saw a disorderly stack of business cards. On top was the card of one Jan Gruntorad, head of data communications at the Czech ~~Technical University~~ in Prague.

With the opening of Eastern Europe, this seemed an appropriate omen. I picked up the phone and gave him a call. On Sunday morning, after an all-night train ride, I arrived in Prague. In addition to the usually high ratio of tourists to infrastructure, I had timed my visit to coincide with an international congress of 100,000 Jehovah's Witnesses. Every hotel was full. Each clerk in an endless parade of hotels grunted the same explanation: "We have Jehovah Congress today."

"They've always caused me problems, too" I cracked to one surly reservations clerk, attempting to inject a little levity into my fruitless tour of hotels. The clerk stared at me, giving me the same blank look she would give a moldy potato. My sense of humor was evidently not appreciated.

Most hotels in Prague are privately run, but Cedok, the state tourist agency, still books most of the rooms. In one hotel, for example, 80 percent of the rooms were controlled by Cedok. Cedok, which advertises itself as "the biggest travel agency in Czechoslovakia" (until recently the only travel agency, so it had a long head start), doesn't believe in reservations. When I asked to make a reservation for the next day, they told me to come back the next day and they would see what they could do.

After 8 different hotels, I found a room. No wonder. The Prague Palace, at U.S. $230 per night (payable in foreign exchange) would be no bargain in London or New York. In Prague, it might be considered extortionate.

I had the day off, so I slipped into the mob of Jehovah's Witnesses and set off to see the sights. For lunch, I stopped at one of the overcrowded, spartan restaurants and ordered the house special, a pizza topped with ham, eggs, and peas. The beverage menu also featured "Bois Avocat," a French drink which could be translated either as the blood of a lawyer or some form of avocado nectar. I had a beer.

With relief, I finished my sightseeing and went back to my room. The number of tourists in Prague was staggering, but they didn't seem to have anything to do. With few restaurants, most milled around in the streets. The Jehovah's Witnesses smiled a lot. It was as if Walt Disney had taken over the country, but had named Kafka managing director.

The next day, I went over to the Czech Technical University. Jan Gruntorad ushered me into his office wearing a Hawaiian shirt, having come in from his holiday a day early to see me. His office was piled high with papers, computer boxes, a huge 3270 terminal, and books. An ancient TV was on top of one cabinet, and on the other were dozens of empty bottles of various kinds. In other words, my kind of office.

For many years, Czechoslovakia had suffered a technology embargo due to COCOM regulations and, like other Eastern bloc countries, concentrated on reverse-engineering IBM mainframes. Jan took me into their computer room and showed me a Russian mainframe clone, together with a Bulgarian-made front end processor (FEP). The MVS-like operating system had been written locally and it had taken two years to integrate it all into a semi-working system.

The Bulgarian FEP and the Russian mainframe were right out of an episode of "Lost in Space." Full of knobs and mechanical registers, it reminded me of early computers like the ENIAC, which can be seen at the Smithonian's American History Museum in Washington, D.C. In a corner were a pile of removable disk packs, each the size of a keg of beer.

Forcing designers to reverse-engineer systems and to serve as super-systems integrators had produced one positive effect. Many of the engineers at the school were quite sophisticated. Unfortunately, however, the operating system had never quite run right and the users never had enough confidence to invest their time learning to do useful work.

Prague

In 1989, with the revolution, things changed dramatically. Czechoslovakia was able to put in a 9,600 bps leased line to Linz in Austria and join the European Academic Research Network (EARN), the European BITNET. In Bratislava, another school started using UUCP links over dial-up lines to Vienna and became part of EUnet.

An important breakthrough for Gruntorad came in 1990, when IBM donated a 3090 mainframe as part of the IBM Academic Initiative. Starting with Czechoslovakia, but later including other countries such as Hungary and Poland, plunking supercomputers down in key locations gave an important boost to Gruntorad's networking efforts (you can't build a shopping mall without upgrading the roads around it).

EARN had expanded to include seven other facilities in Prague. Efforts were underway to extend the national backbone to Bratslava and other cities. From zero users in 1989, the system grew to over 1,500 users by the summer of 1991.

Gruntorad is much more than just the BITNET manager, however. He was leading the effort to install a national networking infrastructure. He wanted to see UUCP, NJE (for BITNET), and TCP/IP protocols all sharing an infrastructure of leased lines.

Leased lines, as in many European countries, are quite expensive in Czechoslovakia. A 9,600 bps line from Prague to Brno, for example, costs 36,000 crowns per month (U.S. $1,242/month). With monthly salaries averaging 3,000 crowns, a leased line becomes a major line item in the budget. The PTT didn't have the infrastructure in place to properly support digital lines, so a 64 kbps line would be provided by ganging up six 9,600 bps line.

Although I managed to time my departure with what appeared to be the majority of the Jehovah's Witnesses, some other deity must have been on my side. Not having bought a ticket allowed me, through some mysterious bureaucratic rule, to bypass the hundreds of people waiting to check in and report to the excess baggage window.

The burly representative from Czechoslovakian State Airlines who sold me my Swissair ticket even smiled when I suggested she should feel free to close the airport after I had gone—a sure solution to overcrowding. They even allowed me to change my crowns back into dollars without the obligatory official receipt proving that I hadn't used the black market.

Zürich was a real contrast to Prague. I settled into an expensive hotel with small rooms and crossed the street to a beer house, where I feasted on three kinds of sausages, each accompanied by a large frothy mug of local beer.

The next day, I went to meet Urs Eppenberger, a technical manager at SWITCH who explained how the Swiss research network was being established. SWITCH, which stands for Swiss Telecommunication System for Higher Education and Research, was established six years ago by the federal government and the cantons of Switzerland to start and maintain a university research network and a national supercomputer center.

Urs works in the SWITCH network office, which consists of eight engineers, an administrator, and lots of computers. SWITCH is a network infrastructure with services like e-mail. The infrastructure consists simply of leased lines and Cisco boxes installed at 11 sites around the country, plus links into the X.25 Telepac network. The interface between the campus and SWITCH is clearly defined at the Ethernet plug. SWITCH maintains its own system, including configuring the routers.

Originally, the network was going to be religiously OSI, using services such as X.400, FTAM, VTP, and any other OSI services available. The system quickly switched over to a more pragmatic approach, supporting TCP/IP, X.400 over OSI, and even DECnet.

The network is very Swiss. It is carefully planned and carefully implemented. Impeccably engineered, not too adventurous, and focusing on offering a reliable production service, SWITCH is an orderly addition to the carefully manicured Swiss landscape.

I took the train back through the rolling hills of the Bernese Ober-
land and Fribourg to Geneva. There, I went to see Brian Carpenter,
head of networking for CERN, the European physics laboratory.

CERN is one of the major centers for the study of high-energy
physics in the world. The laboratory has over 5,000 visiting scientists, plus another 3,000 permanent staff members. CERN is funded
by 17 European countries, including a substantial East European
membership. The laboratory is mission oriented, a place to do serious, world-class research. It has, as have many other physics laboratories such as Fermilab in Chicago, been on the forefront of
networking as a way of allowing physicists to exchange data.

A typical CERN experiment in high-energy physics might involve 400 scientific staff from 20 to 40 different institutions. For example, one of the experiments on the Large Electron-Positron (LEP),
the new 27-km accelerator, involves physicists from seven CERN
members working alongside scientists from China, India, Israel,
Hungary, the U.S., and Russia.

Because of CERN's constituency, it has become one of the global
Internet hubs. Much of the connectivity to Eastern Europe funnels
through CERN. The CERN mail gateway routes messages for hundreds of networks.

Internally, the CERN network runs the usual motley assortment
of technologies, including gigabit Ultra networks, FDDI, and over
3,500 stations on 60 different Ethernets. Over 400 gigabytes per
month are transferred on the FDDI backbone alone. Over 1,000 stations on a 4 Mbps token ring are used to control the accelerator.

WAN links at CERN are equally impressive. Over 150 gigabytes
per month are transferred out of the laboratory over wide area networks. The laboratory has a 384 kbps link to MIT, a T1 line to Cornell, an E1 line to Bologna, and an 8 Mbps feed to the CHEOPS
satellite. Francois Flückiger, deputy head of networking, estimated
that of the total 15 Mbps of international bandwidth devoted to research networking, 11 Mbps terminate at CERN.

I went back to Paris to accomplish the more serious business of eating and drinking until my plane left to take me back to the U.S. In August, Paris transforms itself. The French all leave on their annual four- to six-week holidays. The absence of Frenchmen contrasted sharply with the surge in the American presence.

It seemed like the entire population of New Jersey had come to see the Eiffel Tower. They had brought with them a large portion of Sony's Camcorder output for the past few years. This called for guerilla tourism on my part, avoiding the Champs Élysées and concentrating instead on seedy cafés on the Left Bank. Before leaving, however, there was one bit of business I wanted to accomplish.

On my last day in Paris, I called Gerard Poireau and arranged to visit his office, located in the shadows of what used to be the Bastille. Poireau is an evangelist for videotex. One of the original marketing managers for the French Minitel system, he is active in efforts to spread this underrated technology into the U.S.

When you get a telephone, France Telecom gives you the choice of a phonebook or a computer terminal. As a result, over 3 million people have, free of charge, one of the squat brown Minitel terminals in their home. Of these 3 million terminals, France Telecom estimates 80 percent are actually used. Even if the number is inflated, this was still, until very recently, the largest single network in the world.

The core of Minitel is directory assistance, however. Poireau had a formidable memory, rattling over a dozen phone numbers off the tip of his tongue. When his memory failed, however, he reached over to his Minitel terminal and tapped the two digits to connect him to directory assistance. He typed in the last name and the city, and the fax, voice, and audiotext numbers all appeared on the screen. (Audiotext is the French word for phone-based services like stock reports or voice mail.) Gerard picked the menu item for the voice line, and the number was automatically dialed for him.

Minitel is much more than just directory assistance. The usual bulletin board services—pornography, dating services, IQ tests, and sports results—were all present, but with a few additional surprises.

For example, Nynex had the New York Yellow Pages up on Minitel. Prohibited from offering electronic yellow pages services in the U.S. by Judge Greene's restraining order, Nynex had no such restraint in France and was evidently testing their U.S. system for future deployment. Gerard and I looked up the names of all Bangladeshi cafés in Manhattan and jotted down their locations for reference on subsequent trips to the Big Apple.

Most access to Minitel was based on the French X.25 network, Transpac. With over 300 X.25 switches connected at speeds of up to 2.048 (E1), Transpac and Minitel have a symbiotic relationship. A service like Minitel does no good if there is no access path to it. Likewise, an X.25 network is a road to nowhere without useful services on it.

Minitel was a case study in providing useful information services. By the beginning of 1990, Minitel had over 12,000 service providers. Even intra-company transactions, incuding banking, insurance, and order processing, occurred on the network. The directory service alone received well over 10 million calls per day and train reservations received over 1.5 million calls per day.

Leaving Gerard Poireau, I went to catch my plane back to the U.S. Through some fast talking, I managed to get my no-refund, nochange, economy ticket upgraded to a first class seat. It's amazing what you can get, if you just ask.

I sat munching my Beluga caviar and drinking my Dom Perignon champagne and decided that travel wasn't so bad if you just get the right seat. By the time the single malt scotch, the vintage port, and the freshly-peeled kiwi fruits had come and gone, I even became optimistic about the weeks ahead converting ITU data. Drink can certainly cloud your judgment.

At the New York airport on the way back to Denver, I sat in the bar. Over in the corner was a motley assortment of people that could only be a rock and roll band on tour. Leather pants, nose rings, orange hair, and a half-dozen drinks in front of each person were just a few of my clues.

At the check-in counter, the band members stood around making the agents nervous. Evidently, they had booked their seats late and were not pleased with their assignments of middle seats. As I was in the same boat, I stood with this crew harassing the ticket agent. I surreptitiously flashed my frequent flier card and she took my ticket and gave me an aisle seat.

Getting on the plane, I saw that I was next to one of the disgruntled musicians, this one adorned with shoulder length hair and various martial adornments on his leather jacket. He squeezed over me and sat down.

"You have to be with a rock and roll band," I ventured.

He grunted, presumably in confirmation.

When we got into the air, he called the flight attendant over and ordered two double screwdrivers ("hold the orange juice") and began methodically going at them. I drank a beer and started reading *The Chinese Screen*.

To my great surprise, he leaned over and asked "Is that Somerset Maugham?" I said it was, and we sat there discussing late nineteenth century English literature.

His name was Würzel and he was in Motörhead, the quintessential British loud rock band. They were on tour with Judas Priest and Alice Cooper in a heavy metal extravaganza. Würzel's job was lead guitarist.

"Basically, I try and play as loud as I can," he said, explaining his job.

"Well, somebody's got to do it," I replied.

This comment pleased Würzel so much he waved to the flight attendent to bring two more double vodkas for himself and a beer for me, simultaneously repeating my new rationale for his existence to his mates scattered a few rows up. The flight attendent was treating this crew quite gingerly lest they mistake the plane for one of their hotel rooms, and promptly brought the drinks.

Before landing, Würzel handed me his business card and invited me to the big show at some location he couldn't remember. Alas, I was still reading my mail by that evening and let this opportunity for cultural enrichment pass me by.

❒

Although I got back in late August, it was into the second week of September before my tapes from the ITU finally arrived, leaving us about 20 days to convert the tapes before the hooptedoodle began.

At INTEROP 91 Fall, on October 11, a live video link to Geneva had been arranged. Pekka Tarjanne and Tony Rutkowski would make the big announcement about the newly freed Blue Book to a packed and hushed audience in San Jose.

My job was to get the standards converted and on the network before the announcement so there would be no turning back. Until we actually let the documents loose on the Internet, there was always the possibility that the bureaucrats would somehow gain the upper hand and stop the experiment.

A week spent trolling the halls of the ITU had produced documentation on about half of the proprietary, in-house text formatting system they had developed many years ago on a Siemens mainframe. The computer division had given me nine magnetic tapes, containing the Blue Book in all three languages. Despite repeated tries, we had gotten nowhere on trying to also get the CCIR radio recommendations and reports, even though the Secretary-General and the head of the CCIR had both appeared anxious to see this data online.

Along with the magnetic tapes, we had half a dozen TK50 and TK70 cartridges from the ITU VAXen. The cartridges contained PC files that were stored on a VAX using DEC's PC networking products. We had two types of files, one of which was known to be totally useless.

Boulder

The useless batch was several hundred megabytes of AUTO-CAD drawings, furnished by the draftsmen who did the CCITT illustrations. Diagrams for the Blue Book were done in AUTOCAD, then manually assembled into the output from the proprietary text formatting system. The draftsmen were very helpful and quickly said I could have any data I needed.

On my way out of meeting with the draftsmen, however, one of them starting asking some questions about scanners and babbling on about TIFF files. I was puzzled. Why should I care about scanners and TIFF files when I had the diagrams in the original formats?

Turned out that AUTOCAD was indeed used for the diagrams, with the exception of any text in the illustrations. The textless diagrams were sent over to the typing pool, where people typed on little pieces of paper ribbon and pasted the itsy-bitsy fragments onto the illustrations. Come publication time, the whole process would be repeated, substituting typeset ribbons for typed ribbons. A nice production technique, but the AUTOCAD files were useless.

The rationale for this bizarre document production technique was that each diagram needed text in each of the three official languages that the ITU published. While AUTOCAD (and typing) was still being used, the ITU was slowly moving over to another tool, MicroGrafix Designer. There, using the magical concept of layers, they were proudly doing "integrated text and graphics."

The second batch of DOS files looked more promising. Modern documents, such as the new X.800 recommendations, were being produced in Microsoft Word for Windows. My second batch of tapes had all the files that were available in the Word for Windows format, the new ITU publishing standard.

To do the conversion, I was quite lucky to be working with Sun Microsystems on a research grant. They had sent over two large servers for a research program I was participating in and graciously agreed to allow us to use one server to post standards on the network. Without their help, we wouldn't have had the resources to do anything.

❐

Step one was to begin tackling TPS, the ITU wonder program developed years ago. I brought the tapes over to Mike Schwartz, a professor at the University of Colorado and my partner on the Sun research grant.

The ITU had documented the format we could expect the tapes to be in. Each file had a header written in the EBCDIC character set. The file itself used a character set seemingly invented by the ITU, known by the bizarre name of Zentec. The only problem was that the header format wasn't EBCDIC and the structure the ITU had told us would be on the tape wasn't present.

Using Captain Crunch Decoder Rings, we finally figured out a collating table for the mystery header character set and managed to hack the files off the tape. There were large amounts of data at the beginning and end of files which seemed useless and was simply deleted. We crossed our fingers that the deleted information would not be needed later and indeed, it wasn't.

Next, we had to tackle TPS. This text formatting language was as complicated as any one could imagine. Developed without the desire for clarity and simplicity I had come to expect from the UNIX operating system and its tools, I was lost with the Byzantine, undocumented TPS.

The solution was to take several physical volumes of the Blue Book and compare the text to hexadecimal dumps of the files. I then went to the Trident Café and spent a week drinking coffee trying to make sense of the data I had, flipping between the four files that might be used on any given page of text trying to map events in the one-dimensional HexWorld to two-dimensional events in the paper output.

Inbetween trips to the coffee house, I was trying to take care of diagrams and the PC files. Diagrams were simple: I sat down every morning for a few hours and scanned in diagrams. The diagrams were saved as TIFF and EPS files, then uploaded to our Sun server.

The PC files were all unloaded onto a VAX, then moved over to the Sun, then downloaded at 9,600 bps to my home network. There, the files were loaded into Word for Windows, and then exported as Rich Text Format, the Microsoft proprietary standard for open document interchange. The RTF files were then converted to Word Perfect and ASCII, and all four file formats were sent back up to the Sun.

All told, it wasn't unusual to be downloading and then uploading 10 to 20 megabytes per day, all using a 9,600 bps modem. Still, this was the easy part. It was TPS that almost killed us.

Finally, after pages and pages of PERL code, we had the beginnings of a conversion program. We had tried to use the software developed at the ITU to convert from TPS into RTF, but the code had been worse than useless.

The day before leaving for INTEROP, I was still working desperately away on the conversion program. Tables and equations were still not coming out the way I had wanted them to, but finally, it came time to start hand editing. Any tables that couldn't convert properly were thrown out. Same with equations.

At 2 A.M., with the SuperShuttle coming at 6 A.M., it was finally time to pack for INTEROP (and the six weeks of travel that would immediately follow INTEROP). The data wasn't perfect, by any means, but the Blue Book was on the Internet ready to be distributed. The Bruno project was ready to roll.

As I packed, I reflected on what had been an awful 20 days, programming like a madman to do the conversion. It was amazing how the ITU had been doing a conversion, with lots of people available, but had reportedly estimated that it would take a total of 10 years, and roughly U.S. $3.2 million, to complete the job. By my calculations, if it would have taken 40 days to make the conversion perfect, my time would have been worth, on the ITU scale of reality, U.S. $10,000 per hour. My only hope was that I might be able to use this data to justify an increase in my consulting rates.

As I was going to sleep, I tried to figure out how bad a case of bureausclerosis one would have to have to in order to turn a 20 day (40 to make it perfect) conversion effort into 10 years of agony. Over the next few months, as I visited Geneva again and saw the experiment run into the famed international bureaucracy, I was to learn how it could easily take 10 years, or, more likely, never get done at all.

Round 1

From INTEROP to IETF

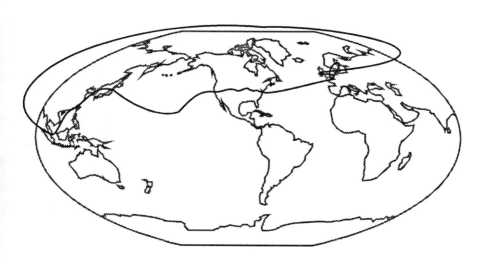

When people ask me to explain how INTEROP is different from other trade shows and conferences, I like to describe it as resembling a circus, but not a zoo. A circus appears to be all chaos, but it is carefully managed chaos. A zoo, on the other hand, puts the animals into cages and lets them do what they want.

Networld—referred to by one wag as "Notworld"—is the trade show equivalent of a zoo. Each little cage has its own independent little show. In some cages, exuberant marketing types reach out to touch you with their brochures. In others, they stand listlessly around. The visitors to Networld stroll from one cage to another, feeding their name tags to the animals, hoping that one of them will do something interesting.

INTEROP, on the other hand, is a show. Granted, there are also cages, but those are a small part of what is going on. There are tutorials, a conference, and, most importantly, a huge, operational network.

When I arrived on Saturday, October, 5, 1991, people were just beginning to descend on San Jose. After checking into the luxurious Holiday Inn, I wandered over to the Fairmont Hotel. In a meeting room, about 50 volunteers, engineers from all over Silicon Valley and from around the world, were gathering.

All were quite bleary-eyed. Most of them had been up all night stringing cable in the Diamond Pavilion, one of the auxiliary exhibit halls being used by INTEROP. This gathering was getting ready for the real work that lay ahead that night: installing the network at the San Jose Convention Center.

All of the vendors (with a couple of minor exceptions like my publisher) were connected to a real operational show network, which in turn was connected to the Internet. This was no coaxial cable down the center of an exhibit hall. The network used over 35 miles of cable and connected 300 vendors together with what one observer estimated would be the equivalent of the components needed to wire a 20-story high-tech skyscraper.

The organizing principle for the network was a series of ribs. Each rib ran through a physical area, such as an aisle in the convention center or the Diamond Pavilion. Each rib had an Ethernet based on unshielded twisted pair and a 16-Mbps token ring. Each of the 25 ribs had a 19-inch equipment rack at the end with the electronics to drive the subnets and routers to be connected to the backbones.

Two different backbones connected the 50 subnets, one based on FDDI, the other on Ethernet. A T1 line connected the Diamond Pavilion to the Convention Center. A microwave link went to two terminal clusters nearby in the Fairmont Hotel. Yet another T1 link linked the show network to the NASA-Ames Research Center, which in turn provided links to the Bay Area Research Network and out to the NSFNET backbone.

This entire network was put in by a semifanatical team of volunteers, overseen by two INTEROP staff members frantically trying to keep some sense of order. The challenge to this network is that you don't get convention centers a month ahead of time to put in your network. In fact, as we met Saturday afternoon, they were still tearing down the booths from the previous week's Seybold Publishing Conference.

At midnight, the Convention Center would be turned over to the Interop Company. At 8 A.M., just eight hours later, dozens of 18-wheel tractor trailers would roll onto the convention floor to start setting up the vendor exhibits. By that time, all the cable needed to be off the floor: try telling a teamster on a forklift to take the long way around because he might crush the fiber.

Between midnight and 8 A.M., 35 miles of cable had to be rolled out and hung from the ceiling with cherry pickers. Equipment racks had to be moved safely into place, and equipment for the Network Operations Center (NOC) had to be moved up into the control booth overlooking the convention floor.

To make this all happen, a core team of a half-dozen volunteers met with Interop all year to plan the network. In July, the company got the convention center for a day and hosted a cable laying party. All the cable was laid out and connectors added. Then, the cables were tied together and carefully rolled onto drums and moved into a warehouse. Before the show, there was a hotstaging in the warehouse, where the cables were connected to equipment racks to be tested. Then, everything was packed up onto pallets to await the teamsters.

At midnight, a group of about 50 had gathered in the lobby of the convention center. Each member of the core team had a different colored shirt, each with the words "Do Not Disturb" stencilled on the back.

I was assigned to the teal team, under the leadership of Karl Auerbach. Karl was one of the founders of Epilogue Technology and a long-time participant in the INTEROP ShowNet. He's also a lawyer, which makes him a formidable rabble rouser at IETF meetings.

With a loud bellow, we were all called over for a briefing by Stev Knowles. (The ending "e" in "Steve" got left off of a mail message once, and Stev decided he preferred it that way.) Stev is vice president of engineering at FTP Software and is widely acknowledged as the loudest member of the ShowNet team.

Stev's briefing was, as usual, direct and to the point. "Do what you're told and if you have a question, ask."

Stev is an interesting character. Rumor is that he got involved in the very first ShowNet because he couldn't read his mail. The network wasn't working, so he marched into the show and commandeered the ShowNet team until things started working.

By sheer force of will, he and the other core team members do this every year, staying up for several days straight to get the network up and running. For this, everybody gets a t-shirt. Of course, the core team got put up by INTEROP at the Fairmont, but even the impressive bar bills they ran up didn't quite explain why they did this.

A few minutes after midnight, the doors opened and we all stood on the cavernous convention floor, clustered around our leaders. Two tractor-trailers were driven into the center of the floor and began to dump their contents. Equipment racks, spools of cable, and various other network paraphernalia were all hustled to their proper locations.

The barrels of cable began to be unspooled. Teams of volunteers, spaced every few feet, would march a string of cable across the hall. A few ties holding cable were cut and the feeds that would hang down from the ceiling were separated from the main rib.

Then, five cherry pickers started a slow march down the convention floor. At each rib, the cherry pickers descended, then in unison (or some ragged semblance of unison) lifted the cables to the rafters.

Hanging down at intervals were coils of cable. These feeds were left about 16 feet off the ground, high enough to clear the semis coming in the next morning but low enough to reach without a cherry picker.

By 5:30 A.M., most of the ribs were successfully up, so I went back to the luxurious Holiday Inn for two hours sleep before I started my day of meetings. The volunteers were still working when I left and would continue to do so for the next two days straight. Getting the cables up was the most time-critical task, but plenty of work still remained. Cables had to be connected to equipment racks, connectors tested, the backbone had to be tested, vendors had a million questions, the Internet link needed to be initialized, and a million other details had to be finished before the show opened on Wednesday.

The volunteers that put in this network are an amazing bunch. Some of the best network managers from all over the country come just to help out. When they are done, they have a complex internetwork up and running and connected to the rest of the global mesh. Three days later, it is torn down.

While the ShowNet is operational, it supports some fairly heavy-duty applications. Groups of vendors get together to demonstrate the interoperability of standards such as Frame Relay, SMDS, X.400, SNMP, and many others. In marketing-speak, these are called Solutions Showcases. As you walk through the exhibits on the convention floor, different booths have little signs indicating which showcases they are part of.

The Solutions Showcases are certainly useful as a marketing tool. Lots of users come to the show to see what works and who sells the equipment. However, the showcases are equally important to the engineers that design and make the technology.

I spoke to one engineer who says he gets more bugs worked out in one week at INTEROP than he can in six months in the lab. By testing his implementation with those of other vendors, he can quickly hone in on ambiguities in the standards and figure out what to do to make the standard an interoperable reality.

□

The INTEROP week passed by quickly. The first two days, I sat in on a few of the tutorials, hearing people like Craig Partridge talk about gigabit networks or MIT's Jeffrey Schiller talk about network security and Kerberos. On Wednesday, the show officially began and the pace picked up. The plenary address was via T1 video link from Geneva. I was particularly interested in this address since I was going to need the same satellite link on Friday.

Things went smoothly Wednesday morning, mostly because the previous two days had been spent in frantic preparation. The video link was donated by Sprint. Coordination of this part of the show at INTEROP was handed to Ole Jacobsen. Ole had worked long hours with Sprint technicians, watching the line go from Geneva to Atlanta until, the day before, it had reached Kansas City. By Tuesday night, video was finally making it all the way from Geneva to San Jose.

Ole was the perfect choice to handle anything telephone related. Officially, he is editor and publisher of the *ConneXions* journal. Unofficially, he is a phone junkie. For example, he has a PBX in his house. Of course, the PBX is a small one with only 6 lines and 16 extensions, but how many houses do you know with their own PBX? His wife Susan still can't get used to dialing "9" for an outside line.

After the plenary, I dove into the exhibition and conference. Most people were in high-speed data acquisition mode, trying to work out optimal patterns for navigation of the floor, or flitting from one conference session to another hoping that time division multiplexing would enhance their information intake.

My personal favorite, as it had been the year before, were the SNMP demonstrations. In 1990, John Romkey had developed the

Internet toaster. The toaster was hooked up to the ShowNet with a PC running TCP/IP and SNMP software. Workstations around the show floor had network management software, complete with a toaster Management Information Base (MIB). By setting variables on the toaster MIB from a network management station, people could make the toaster start toasting.

The problem everybody immediately saw with the 1990 demonstration was that you had to put the toast into the toaster. This was suboptimal from the point of view of the network engineer, who wanted to stay in bed while breakfast was made.

This year, the FTP Software booth sported the new, enhanced Internet toaster. Using the latest Lego technology, they built a little crane that would pick up a piece of bread and deposit it into the toaster slot.

What made this demonstration especially funny is a bit of an inside joke. If you read Marshall T. Rose's *The Simple Book*, you will see that he feels strongly that people should make better use of the get-next operator for efficiently using the network and the remote management agent.

To get his point across, Marshall always refers to the get-next operator as the "powerful get-next operator." The INTEROP audience was truly impressed that the powerful get-next operator was being used to make toast.

◻

Friday morning was the official unveiling of the activities of the Document Liberation Front. I got up early and went over to the Center for the Performing Arts, the biggest hall at the INTEROP show, seating 2,701 people. This hall is so big that it even has enough room to hold the hundreds of students that show up for the tutorial taught by Doug Comer of Purdue, a researcher well known for his explanations of TCP/IP fundamentals through his tutorials and books.

The members of the panel started to show up. Dr. Vinton Cerf, chairman of the Internet Activities Board, was there to lend his support to the announcement. Richard desJardins, head of a training group called The GOSIP Institute, was there to provide his commentary on the different models of standards making.

We finally got through to Geneva. Although neither Tony Rutkowski nor Dr. Tarjanne was present yet, we held our breath and got ready to start the session. Looking out into the audience, which contained no more than 50 people who had bothered to get up for the early morning session, I was very glad that the cameras couldn't beam back to Geneva.

We made our announcement and the one member of the press to show up furiously took notes. The announcement went well, but I was worried that nobody would care and that all this effort had been in vain.

Over the next two months, I was to discover how wrong I was. Leaving INTEROP and travelling around the world, I got more news at every stop on how popular Bruno and the Sons of Bruno had become. I thought the choice of Giordano Bruno (1548-1600) as the namesake for my server in Colorado had been an appropriate one.

The Greeks, in those days before the printing press, used a mnemonic method for remembering verse or other forms of knowledge. The Dominican order had kept alive these secrets during the dark middle ages, but had kept them tightly guarded. Bruno joined the Dominican order in 1565 and mastered the Dominican secrets. Then, he revealed the secrets to the rest of the world in his classic, Shadow of Ideas (1582).

Bruno was expelled from the Dominican order, and was later denounced to the Inquisition in Venice for acts of heresy, including telling jokes in poor taste about God. He was burned at the stake in 1600.

Would Bruno's secrets help the world? Would the ITU Inquisition kill our server? These and other questions were on my mind as I boarded a plane Sunday, bound for Hawaii and then onwards, three times around the world in the next six months.

I came to Hawaii to learn more about packet radio. Really.

The fact that I spent most of my time on the beach drinking Mai Tais was an accident.

Honolulu is the home of Torben Nielsen, a man who has played an important role in helping to spread the Internet into the Pacific Rim. The University of Hawaii provides the Internet link for several Asian countries, particularly Korea and Japan.

He is also known for starting up the University of Hawaii network. Networking was not originally considered to be a high priority at the University. In fact, it was such a low priority that nothing was happening. Torben enlisted a few of his colleagues (including four department chairmen), rented power tools, and started digging trenches.

For a total of U.S. $1,500, lots of hard work, and the extreme displeasure of the facilities management group, the renegade professors managed to get four buildings linked together in a network. The project was done so cheaply that they even salvaged refueling lines from military aircraft to use as conduit.

Nielsen's laboratory is a windowless room lined with foam padding and absolutely stuffed with computers. The Blue Book, Sun documentation, and various other books line the wall. Sitting inside this room, it is hard to imagine that nearby is a world of beaches and drinks decorated with paper umbrellas.

I arrived at 8:30 A.M. and Torben had already been there for two and a half hours. When he mentioned this, I made the appropriate polite noises of amazement. Torben looked at me like some shirker. "I'll be here till 9:00 tonight and we do this seven days a week," he patiently explained to me.

Needless to say, a leisurely lunch was probably not going to be in the works here. I realized that my time slot in Torben's scheduling algorithm was going to be limited, so I tried to learn quickly what I could about his work.

Honolulu

Getting lines up and running is what Torben is best known for, but he is rapidly tiring of keeping pipes open and bits flowing. Instead, his interests are higher up the stack in areas like videoconferencing, the Andrew File System (AFS), interactive books, and a wide variety of other applications.

The topic of the day appeared to be SGML and ODA, so we talked about revisable form document architectures. In Torben's view, the Office Document Architecture is basically useless. To him, SGML tagging is the appropriate internal format for a document.

As evidence he cites a commercial program that uses SGML as the internal representation of documents. The SGML document is then moved through TeX, which processes the tags. TeX is thus a formatting engine for SGML, which in turn produces output in a language such as PostScript for final form representation.

In Torben's view, ODA fills the same intermediate role as TeX. You can use SGML source and use it to produce ODA, which is then sent to some ODA reader for display on the screen or the printer.

After this brief flurry of discussion on revisable form formats, Torben dismissed me and switched context to some other work. I borrowed a terminal to read my mail.

When I left the cocoon of Nielsen's lab, it was still only 10 A.M., much too early to return to the Waikiki tourist ghetto. I swung my car over the mountains to the other side of the island.

After driving around the sugar plantations, I arrived in the little town of Haleiwa. There, I spotted a sign saying "Best Lunch in Haleiwa." Afraid that this might also well be the only lunch in Haleiwa, I pulled onto the back lawn of the building, almost ran over a dozen cats and parked next to the outhouse.

After a wonder lunch of Mahi Mahi and eggs smothered in a hot sauce made with lilikoi flowers, I felt much better. I spent the rest of the day in exhaustive research looking for the perfect Mai Tai.

Arriving at Tokyo's Narita airport ahead of schedule, I waited two hours for my bus into town. After an hour on the bus, we were still wending our way through the Tokyo suburbs, passing Disneyland, the docks, and threading through ever larger mazes of freeways.

Looking down, I realized the freeway was built on top of a river. Next to us, only a few feet away, were rows and rows of office buildings. Looking inside each, I could see rooms and rooms filled with row after row of desks all crowded together. Below us, but above the river, ran the railway tracks, above us another freeway.

The next morning, I ventured forth on the subway system to find the University of Tokyo, known as Todai. There, I met Professor Haruhisa Ishida, a professor at the Computer Centre. Professor Ishida proceeded to give me an excellent introduction to networks in Japan.

Japan, like the U.S., has many different networks. BITNET, as in most countries, was initially funded by IBM, but is now member supported. What membership fees don't cover is provided by the main sponsor, the Science University of Tokyo. Japan's BITNET has a 56 kbps link to CUNY and provides tail links to Korea and Taiwan.

N-1net is an older, proprietary network to tie together mainframe systems with services like remote job entry and remote login. N-1net was managed by the National Center for Science Information Systems (NACSIS). NACSIS, a research institute funded by the Ministry of Education, also maintains a link to FIX-West, with two other links continuing on to NSF and in Washington and the British Library.

NSF uses a portion of the line to search several large databases maintained by NACSIS. A small part of the line is available for BITNET and TCP transfers and is used mostly for mail exchange from their X.400 messaging system. NACSIS plans to upgrade the U.S. link to 192 kbps in 1992, at which time it will become one of the key international links for Japan.

A third network is the Todai International Science Network (TISN, pronounced "Tyson"). TISN uses the DECnet protocol suite and is used by physicists and chemists. TISN maintains a 128 kbps link between Todai and the University of Hawaii. Due to political walls between organizational fiefdoms, Japan also maintains HEP-net connectivity at the High Energy Physics Laboratory (KEK) to the Lawrence Berkeley Laboratory in California.

One last network is JAIN, a TCP/IP-based university network that links the university LANs together. This whole plethora of networks is tied together by JUNET, based on UUCP, and WIDE (Widely Integrated Distributed Environment), the Japanese Internet.

There are two paths between the Japanese Internet and the rest of the Internet. WIDE maintains a 192 kbps link from Keio University in Fujisawa to the University of Hawaii. In addition, the 128 kbps link between Todai and Hawaii, used primarily for DECnet traffic, acts as an automatic backup in case the 192 kbps link has problems.

WIDE is an interesting network in the Japanese system. All the other networks are funded by the Ministry of Education or another group. Officially, WIDE doesn't exist. Even more amazing, in the tightly segmented world of Japanese politics, commercial and educational users are all mixed together.

I asked Professor Ishida how such a situation could come to be. His answer was quite simple.

"Jun Murai."

Jun Murai used to be a research associate at Todai, working with Ishida, but recently moved south to his alma mater, Keio University. In the staid world of academics, Jun is a fairly remarkable character.

Just for starters, he wears blue jeans. Failing to dress in the regulation dark blue suit has caused no small amount of comment among senior faculty members. Jun gets away with it because he really knows what he is doing. He commands a loyal following among students, has the respect of all his peers, and has even won the grudging respect of his seniors.

The WIDE network is based on donations of money from corporations and labor from graduate students. The network lives almost hand to mouth. Money is funnelled into Murai's "research programme" and is used to pay for the network. It was not unusual at times to have the coffers get down to 1 or 2 months of operating costs, forcing Murai into perpetual fundraising.

After this introduction to Japanese networks, Professor Ishida gave me a tour of the Todai facilities. The main campus is wired with three FDDI backbones, one for TCP/IP, one for DECnet, and a third for administrative computing. A fourth 400 Mbps backbone is used for video. Fanning out from each of the backbones are UTP-based Ethernets. These local networks form the point of connection for terminal clusters, workstations, and even the supercomputers.

Professor Ishida led me past a peopleless room stuffed with Hitachi mainframes and supercomputers into a terminal cluster. The cluster was divided up into cubicles and was dead quiet. At the entrance was a color video display with a map of the cluster. The occupied cubicles had red dots inside and the empty cubicles were marked in green, allowing people to find an available workstation or terminal without disturbing the people already working.

Off to the side was a glass-lined room with 9-track tape and cartridge drives. Each drive had a terminal in front of it with a menu system to help users do their own tape work.

Another room was filled with printers. When a user prints a job at Todai, it automatically spools to disk. Each printer has a card reader attached to it (magnetic card, not punch card, that is). A user walks up to the reader, slides an ID card through, and the job is retrieved from disk and printed. A terminal in front of each printer indicates how long the current queue is.

Leaving the cluster, we went down to the first floor where Professor Ishida pointed to a large electronic signboard on the wall. The board displayed the current status of the mainframes, including the number of jobs and the expected delay before a new job would begin processing. No need to walk upstairs and log in if the system is slow.

Walking outside, I felt a little whir under my feet as the automatic brushes on the doormat came to life, cleaning my shoes. I headed down to the subway.

◻

Coming off the subway, I ducked into a tiny, dark noodle shop where a line of salary men all sat hunched over the counter slurping noodles. Hoping my neighbor hadn't chosen chicken lips, I pointed to his dish and was promptly handed a steaming bowl of delicious miso soup.

Feeling refreshed and refurbished, I went back to my hotel, entering at the same time as LaToya Jackson and a very large entourage. I fell in with the entourage and smiled graciously at the hotel reception committee.

On the way to the elevators, we were waylaid by a group of six American tourists all bearing labels to identify their tour group and all armed with cameras. Figuring LaToya could handle this one alone, I slipped into the elevator that three hotel staff members had been guarding for her. Before they could say anything, I punched my floor number and the startled attendants went jumping out in search of another elevator.

I spent the afternoon in the Pub Misamu, waiting for an evening dinner engagement with Tomoo Okada, general manager of Fujitsu's Value Added Group. My appointment with Tomoo Okada was at 7 P.M. At precisely 7:01, my phone rang. I descended to the lobby to meet what was obviously a very senior manager, a distinguished-looking executive in his early 50s. Okada supervised more than 700 people, including Fujitsu's Value Added Network division, two wholly owned subsidiaries, and a collection of divisions of other subsidiaries. His main responsibility was running a network used by both Fujitsu and its customers.

The network is essentially an X.25 network with 144 local access nodes spread throughout Japan. Over 250 leased lines running at speeds from 128 kbps to 6 Mbps form the network backbone. Running on the network are classic protocols for asynchronous terminals, such as X.28 and X.29, and synchronous protocols for 3270 and Fujitsu terminals. As a general rule, full protocol stacks aren't run on the network, although an insurance company has begun deploying an OSI CONS-based service over X.25. International links include 64 kbps lines to Sydney, Singapore, Korea, Hong Kong, and Malaysia. Higher-speed links are available to the U.K., the U.S., and Germany.

Exploring the Internet

Perhaps the most interesting project Okada supervised is NiftyServe, a wholly owned subsidiary that acts as the licensee to the U.S. CompuServe. NiftyServe preserves the famous CompuServe user interface, but the software was entirely rewritten to run on a UNIX platform and to support Kanji characters.

To make NiftyServe start off with a bang, 32,000 Fujitsu employees were given accounts. Over 70 percent of those accounts are active users. The reason for this high utilization is quite simple—important meetings, such as promotion reviews, are posted there.

Some of the most devoted users are overseas Japanese employees. In addition to providing things like daily Japanese language news, the service has proved important in another respect. In Japan, when family or friends die, it is considered very important to *immediately* express condolences. With Fujitsu or any large corporation, of course, fellow employees *are* family. Before the bulletin board service started, it could take days for the postal service to deliver the news overseas, forcing Fujitsu employees into the unwilling position of appearing impolite.

NiftyServe has added a few other interesting twists to the classic bulletin board. For example, you can instruct the system to redirect your mail to a fax machine. You can even go to a pay phone and have your mail read to you.

All this information about Fujitsu was imparted to me with rapid-fire delivery over a seemingly infinite parade of dishes in a dim sum restaurant. After polishing off a half-dozen large bottles of beer, Okada suggested we switch to a Chinese aged wine, similar to sake, but darker in color (and at least as potent).

Even with all these drinks, Tomoo Okada kept up a steady delivery of information on Fujitsu. With my head swimming and my stomach stuffed, I stumbled back to my hotel to await the next day's pilgrimage to Fujisawa to visit Jun Murai, the Internet Samurai.

The next morning I was up early, having heard horror stories of how hard it would be to navigate the succession of subways and trains in the middle of rush hour.

Yes, there were packers to get more people into the subways. Since the density was only about equivalent to a crowd leaving a football game, however, the packers weren't yet needed. They sat watchfully by, wearing white gloves and ready to jump into action when the time came.

The density of the crowds was amazing. Passing the Tokyo suburbs, I expected the crowds to disperse, but the Yokohama commute brought even more people onto the trains. Even outside of Yokohama in Fujisawa, the density remained constant.

Arriving at Tsujido station, I waded through huge crowds until I got outside the station. There, I started waving Jun Murai's card around and mispronouncing "Keio," my destination, until a kindly old gentleman in an indeterminate uniform pointed me to the stop for bus number zero.

I queued up and boarded. We passed through Fujisawa and started to head into the countryside. Throughout the ride, every time we passed a cluster of university-like buildings, I would accost some hapless passenger, mumble "Keio," and wave the business card around. One by one, the passengers waved for me to sit down.

Finally, we reached the end of the line. Rising out of the countryside, sitting on a hill, was a futuristic clump of buildings, surrounded by empty fields. I made my way up a long set of stairs into the central courtyard. In marked contrast to the subways, trains, and streets, constantly teeming with people, the Fujisawa campus of Keio University, Japan's best private university, was absolutely deserted.

Feeling like I was in some futuristic ghost town, I wandered around random buildings until I chanced upon a group of administrators hidden away in a back office. Waving Jun's business card produced a flurry of whispered consultations until a map of the campus suddenly appeared and I was pointed towards building number zero.

Going to the third floor, I knew I was in the right place when I saw an office with a pile of empty computer boxes piled outside. I parked myself on the boxes and waited for Jun. It was an eerie feeling, sitting there in this deserted building on this deserted campus listening to the building creak and groan. Occasionally, a door would open and a person would scoot out of a room and scamper away, leaving only the echoes of their footsteps.

I was to find later that the deserted campus was merely an illusion. Being a self-employed idler, I had arrived well past 9, by which time everybody was already hard at work.

Jun Murai's secretary soon arrived. Known worldwide as "Junsec," her e-mail address appears on all WIDE literature, posters, stickers, and the like. Junsec let me onto an X terminal to read the several hundred mail messages that had accumulated since Honolulu. Most of the mail was about Bruno, the standards server.

Evidently, word had gotten out. Bruno was running 24 hours a day, with load averages of 35 packets per second not uncommon. So many mail requests had come into the infoserver software that the batch queue had over 150 unfulfilled jobs. The amount of FTP traffic was so heavy that we had become a serious user of bandwidth on the transatlantic links.

This posed a delicate problem. On the one hand, we wanted lots of people to use the server in Colorado so that we could prove to the ITU that the service was needed. On the other hand, being good network citizens meant setting up mirrored servers, putting replicas of the data on other machines to avoid having too much redundant traffic cross the backbone.

Offers to provide mirrored servers were pouring in from all over the world. Comparing notes with Tony Rutkowski, it appeared that every country in Europe had volunteered to maintain a set of the standards. Several hundred hosts had already received files from Bruno and it looked like we were getting FTP traffic from over 25 countries.

❐

When I was almost done plowing through my mail, Jun Murai came bursting in. Disheveled, animated, and wearing his trademark blue jeans, he greeted me enthusiastically. Taking me into the obligatory conference room, we began talking while Junsec brought in cups of tea (she had already brought me two cups of coffee).

I presented Jun with a copy of *STACKS* for his boss, Dean Aiso. He presented me with a handsomely bound copy of the WIDE annual report, several hundred pages of kanji with gold-embossed lettering on the cover. My manners being better than my Japanese, I thanked him while mentally trying to figure out how to get this heavy and, to me at least, cryptic tome back to the States.

Formalities duly dispensed with, we started talking about WIDE. Jun is only 36 years old and I was curious how, in a stratified society like Japan, somebody like him had ended up running the Japanese Internet.

In 1984, NTT still had a throttle on all telecommunications. Putting alien devices (e.g., modems) on the telephone lines would be considered about as proper as greeting the Emperor by slapping him on the back. However, it was widely known that in April, 1985, NTT would deregulate.

All the senior researchers had been debating how to take advantage of deregulation to put in networks. Meetings were held to debate the subtleties of various OSI architectures. To Jun, this was a waste of time. As he puts it, "I was young and that was boring."

He took two modems, scammed a phone line from university administrators (no easy feat), and started running UUCP transfers. That was the start of JUNET. While the establishment continued to attend OSI meetings, JUNET continued to grow. Links were set up to a machine named mcvax in Amsterdam (the precursor to EUnet) and to seismo in Washington, D.C. (the precursor to UUnet). By 1986, a domestic IP network had started and by 1989, Jun Murai and Torben Nielsen had established a link to Hawaii. Larry Landweber helped to hook up Japan to CSNET.

Meanwhile, the powers that be continued to debate OSI. When they finally looked up from their deliberations, Jun already had several hundred nodes on his network. As in much of the world, while committees waited for OSI, a few people turned TCP/IP networks into a reality. Japan, like other countries, had many people trying to legislate networks into existence while a few people rolled up their sleeves and installed cable.

By the 1991 school year, WIDE had grown to the point where it had an annual budget of U.S. $1 million raised totally by donations. WIDE was officially a research project, involving 57 researchers, roughly half from the university community. The operational requirements of WIDE became so demanding that Jun was actually turning away requests to be connected until a suitable infrastructure could be set up to run the net.

During our conversation, Jun repeatedly referred to a desire to stop running networks and get back to his real research. Even with the demands of running WIDE, he has compiled an impressive record.

When JUNET was first being put into place, Jun noticed "we had a network but nobody was using it." Networks are like a fine dinner: the whole effort is wasted if nobody comes. The reason in the case of JUNET was quite simply that e-mail and USENET used the Roman alphabet and Japan uses kanji characters. Jun changed that. He and others added kanji support to the X Window System, kanji character handling for RFC 822 mail, and multibyte character handling for the C programming language.

He also helped design a font server. This software lets users start spelling out characters in romanized Japanese. As the words begin to be formed, Kanji characters start appearing on the screen. When the right character shows up, the user points to it and proceeds to the next word.

When I visited Fujisawa, Jun was involved in fascinating projects to support mobile hosts and mobile people. One of the more interesting projects was the Phone Shell. The Phone Shell is a fully functional UNIX shell which takes input from a 12-key telephone pad instead of a keyboard or a mouse. Typically, users execute scripts, such as having mail messages redirected into a voice synthesizer.

As Jun explains it, "I can go to the bar and drink beer. I go to a phone and ping my routers, and if they are still working, I go back and drink more beer."

Another project brought ISDN into the TCP/IP protocol suite. Unlike other countries, which are still demonstrating the viability of demos, Japan has deployed ISDN as an operational service. In fact, WIDE uses ISDN lines to supplement leased lines in case of congestion or failure.

The WIDE ISDN module is fully integrated into TCP/IP. When a datagram for an ISDN-reachable source is encountered, a call is placed. The delay to set up the circuit ranges from 800 ms to 3 seconds. Once established, the line stays up until it has been idle for a user-configurable period, at which point it is taken down.

ISDN can be used for more than just routers, however. Jun has TCP/IP on his laptop. Tokyo has ISDN pay phones. He can bring a laptop into a phone booth and be a fully functioning member of the Internet. Even Superman would be jealous.

Another project close to operation when I visited was the use of satellite circuits for home PCs. Japan has deployed satellites as an alternative to cable TV. Dishes cost as little as U.S. $100 each. Satellites for TV signals are a one-way data channel, but they operate at high bandwidth. A PC with an ISDN card can use 64-kbps "B" channels to send commands. Data coming back to the PC can use up to the 8 Mbps wide-area bandwidth of the satellite dish.

Ethernet cards are used to give the PC a 10 Mbps interface in a LAN environment. Jun and his staff had linked the Ethernet card to the satellite receiver to give the home user the ability to do WAN-based multimedia, large file transfers, and other operations requiring large amounts of bandwidth.

We went from Jun's laboratories to tour the campus. Fujisawa was a brand new campus of Keio University. In sharp contrast to other Japanese (and most U.S.) universities, senior researchers at Keio teach freshmen and sophomores. Jun delighted in telling how he would instruct a class of freshmen, "now we will ping Switzerland."

At the Fujisawa campus, all entering freshmen are required to learn UNIX, to operate workstations, and to acquire other basic skills. Although laptops are not required, they are very strongly encouraged.

Exploring the Internet

We walked into the library where students run an ID card through a reader to enter. Of course, Jun forgot his card, so we crawled over the barriers. We walked into a lounge area where groups of students sat clustered around HDTV sets watching assignments.

Around them, students were at workstations, each equipped with a cassette tape drive and a headphone, doing language exercises. Other students were debugging programs.

Finally, it dawned on me.

"Jun, there are no books in here."

"You still have books?" he asked with a smile. The books were up one floor, but it still gave the library a strange feeling.

Walking outside, we spotted Junsec patiently waiting for us in a car. We all went into Fujisawa where we were ushered into a private tatami room for an exquisite lunch of many courses, each beautifully arranged and delightfully prepared.

As I was gulping down the tenth course, a delicate broth with a single tiny mushroom and a little piece of fish, Jun started explaining to me how the spindly little mushroom I had just inhaled was handpicked in the forests and only available for a few weeks each year. Each mushroom cost as much as 5,000 yen (U.S. $35). I puffed out my cheeks as if I were still rolling the mushroom in my mouth to savor the delicate flavor, while Jun went on to explain how rare the fish was.

Akihabara is a district of Tokyo devoted to consumer electronics, where building after building is stuffed with everything from 2 by 2 foot stalls specializing in diodes or resistors to full-fledged, multi-floor shops, each so full of devices that Marconi would have thought he was hallucinating.

I knew I had reached Akihabara proper when I looked down on the sidewalk and saw a street vendor selling oscilloscopes and microchips. In a stall behind him, 60 different kinds of laptops were on sale, ranging from plain vanilla clones to full-fledged 80386, 60 Mbyte, 6-pound notebooks.

Thinking I must have died and gone to geek heaven, I knew that this district was going to take a while to visit. I ducked into a noodle stand and used my two-word Japanese vocabulary to order a beer and a bowl of miso soup. As I noisily slurped my noodles, I could hear dozens of stereo systems, all playing different brands of disco at full volume.

Suitably fortified, I spent the next two hours trooping up and down stairs in building after building. I had to keep reminding myself that I had many more weeks on the road, lest I yield to the temptation to buy a home satellite dish (only $100) or a personal computer that weighed only 980 grams and ran on AA batteries. The computer was only available in a kanji model, but I figured I could always learn. Even more tempting were DAT drives, high-definition TVs, global positioning system receivers, and three-inch color televisions.

Feeling somehow unsatisfied, yet still solvent, I tore myself away and headed back towards the subway. On the way, I passed a group of young women all dressed up in natty uniforms bearing the somewhat cryptic label "With Me" and all walking in a line. The women at the head and tail of the column carried banners which matched their uniforms. The rest of the "With Me" girls each jauntily carried the new two-pound Hitachi notebook, shamelessly displaying their VDTs for all to see.

Every ten minutes or so, the conga line would go out into Akihabara and walk for a few blocks, dragging along a sound system guaranteed to attract lots of attention. They would wend their way back towards the With Me store and disappear inside, luring a portion of the mob in with them. Somehow, I suspected the short skirts had more to do with the crowd's loyalty than any desire to purchase Hitachi's latest and greatest.

I arrived at 11 P.M. at Hong Kong's Kai Tak airport, thinking that the God of Aviation must have been guarding me. A new gate opened up at customs just as I walked up, and my luggage was the first off the chute.

But, this apparent good fortunate was only to set me up for a cruel joke by the Aviation Deity. Once outside the airport terminal, I saw a line of several hundred people at the taxi stand. It was the end of the long weekend that marks Ching Ming, the Grave Sweeping Ceremony, and all the planes from the mainland had just returned.

I jumped the barrier to get out of line and walked up the road to where taxis were letting off customers. Standing with my baggage, the temptation proved too much for one driver. We both looked furtively around for police and I jumped in.

There were only two problems. He knew no English and he looked like he had been driving for at least 48 hours. We circled the freeways for 20 minutes until it was established that I was going to "Number One Hotel, Happy Valley." Actually, Happy Valley had only one hotel, so number one didn't mean much, but it did get us heading the right direction.

The sleep problem was a bit scarier. Every time his head would start to nod, he would jerk up suddenly and then wave his arms around in spasmodic circles, presumably to get the circulation going. I know it certainly kept me awake.

❒

The next morning, I strolled over to see Edwin Yeung, an MIS manager at the Royal Hong Kong Jockey Club. The Jockey Club is to Hong Kong what the Louvre is to Paris. Gambling is the national pastime and the Jockey Club is the national icon.

Officially, the Jockey Club is the only place you can bet in Hong Kong. In practice, of course, all sorts of other gambling takes place ranging from bookies to mahjong parlors. In theory, though, if you want to gamble you go to the neighboring island of Macau. If you want to bet you go to the Jockey Club.

Founded in 1884, the club is run as a non-profit organization. It makes so much of a non-profit that it is, by far, the largest charity in Hong Kong. In the 1990-91 season, for example, the club handed over HK $1.04 billion (U.S. $138 million) to charity.

The club conducts 67 racing days a year, either in Happy Valley or at the mammoth new Shah Tin racetrack. A Diamond Vision system, like that used in U.S. football stadiums, shows the race at the track not being used, allowing overflow crowds to go to the alternate location to watch the races and, of course, place bets.

This is what you might call a serious transaction processing application. In the 1990-1991 season, over 187 million bets were placed for over HK $47 billion (roughly U.S. $8 billion). On a typical race day, 2.8 million bets were placed. To make this especially challenging, the vast majority of bets were placed within the last 10 minutes before a race, yielding a transaction processing rate of over 600 per second.

Like a bank, this is a system that better not make mistakes. Unlike a bank, this was a system that you really don't want going down (or even slow) right before a race. A bank can afford a few minutes' delay, but bettors don't appreciate having to wait until the race has started to have their money refused.

To funnel these bets into their coffers, the Jockey Club uses two main systems. Cashbet is for people handing over cash, and Telebet handles people who maintain accounts with the club.

Cashbet consists of terminals that accept money, or debit cards which lift money right out of a bank account using electronic funds transfer. The Jockey Club operates 127 off-course betting counters. These have roughly 2,900 terminals staffed by operators. Another 2,900 operator-staffed terminals are at the two race tracks. In locations throughout the city, people can place their own bets at 144 Electronic Funds Transfer (EFT) terminals and 700 cash-based terminals.

Off-course centers use 275 leased lines to connect to a series of 12 PDP 11/44s that act as front-end processors. Another 16 PDPs handle the terminals at the race tracks.

The Telebet system allows customers who maintain an account with the club to place their bets remotely. Bettors can place bets using a telephone or using a special custom terminal developed by the club.

The telephone system is quite simple. You place a call and are routed to one of 1,600 operators at Sha Tin or 388 operators at an off-site facility on Tsing Yi island. The incoming lines are all connected to a bank of over 2,000 voice recording lines to resolve any later disputes. An average of ten times each race day, a particular conversation has to be located.

Each operator on the Telebet system has a terminal which is connected to a series of VAX 3100s and PDP 11/44s. Operators enter the bets into the system and the bets make their way through the Jockey Club network.

Rather than continuing to add operators to service increased demand, the Club decided to design a custom portable betting terminal, known as the Customer Information Terminal (CIT). Bets are entered using a series of menus on a touch screen. Then, the device is plugged into a nearby phone jack where it autodials the Jockey Club network, using banking-standard cryptographic security to protect the line. The bet is placed, the customer's account debited, and the line cleared, all in a few seconds. A voice transaction could easily take a minute.

The amount of time per transaction is a real issue for this application. Ten minutes before race time, the number of calls completed on the phone network spikes to 20 to 30 times over normal levels. In fact, the telephone system was so overloaded that it was estimated that only one in eleven call attempts actually got through to an operator queue. In other words, to handle the Jockey Club load at race time would require a telephone network designed to handle more than 200 times the normal load.

To alleviate the load, a dollar minimum on bets was imposed five minutes before race time, but even this didn't solve the problem. The key was reducing the connect time per transaction to funnel more transactions into the available capacity.

The typical CIT customer could be described as a Hong Kong Yuppie. The devices requires a deposit (the interest from the deposit covers the unit cost in five years) and a service fee. Over 30,000 CIT terminals are in the field. Higher numbers had not been shipped, the Jockey Club said, because of a bottleneck in manufacturing which had limited production to only 400 units per month.

Once a bet makes it through the front-end systems, it hits the Jockey Club back-end network, based on lots of VAXen. In fact, the Jockey Club is Digital's largest customer in Asia. It has struck quite a few people as ironic that such a major customer for the straight-laced Digital should be a major betting operation.

The club maintains 10 VAX Clusters at the two race tracks, with a total of over 30 large systems, 22 HSC controllers, and 100 Gbytes of disk space. In addition to the VAXen, special data security modules on the network provides authentication for Telebet based on a 6-digit PIN code. Other systems control the video display and provide links to disseminate race results to other networks, including a paging system, newspapers, X.25 networks, and Hutchison Mobile Data's packet radio network.

On race day, the two sites share processing and back each other up in case of failure. Transactions are logged at both sites. Connecting all this together are dual Ethernets at each site and an FDDI backbone that spans more than 20 km, using single-mode fiber provided by the telephone company.

The club has an aggressive policy towards vendors and technology, often telling the vendors what to make instead of being content to choose from glossy brochures. When their first network went in, John Markwell who would later become the Head of Information Technology (the senior MIS position), designed a custom data link protocol. For the CIT terminal, the Club participated heavily in the design.

While this heavy involvement caused occasional grumbles from vendors and caused the staff to have a bit of NIH (Not Invented Here) syndrome, you couldn't argue with success. The system worked, and worked well enough that it has been licensed to similar operations in eight countries.

After my briefing, I was taken on a tour of the facilities. In the machine room, I was asked to put on a white lab coat. Lots of technicians with windbreakers, baseball caps, and tennis shoes were walking around inside the machine room, making my medical outfit a bit superfluous, kind of like smoking a cigarette in the clean room of a semiconductor factory.

After the tour, I suggested that we all go out to lunch. I suggested (rather strongly in fact) that Chinese food was in order. A worried look crossed my hosts' faces who had evidently been planning on taking me out for Western food just to be safe, but they led me through the lunchtime throngs to a place jammed with people. We had a nice lunch of noodles, sesame shrimp cakes, and Peking-style chicken, and I grabbed a pair of chopsticks and dived in, to the evident relief of my hosts.

◻

After lunch, I left the Jockey Club and boarded the subway to Sham Shui Po to visit the Golden Shopping Center, the red-light district of the computer industry. The Golden Shopping Center is like a sleazy version of Akihabara, all packed into three floors of an immense building crammed with warrens of shops. There are three reasons to go to the Golden Shopping Center: cheap hardware, pirated software, and counterfeit books. Whenever I go, I make three passes through the place.

First, I look to see if any of my books have been pirated into Chinese. Figuring that my descriptions of DECnet Phase V (a book I like to think of as "paperware about vaporware") wouldn't be any more popular in Chinese than in English, I searched instead for my Novell book.

To tell the truth, I always kind of hope to see my books. Van Nostrand Reinhold, the legitimate publisher, had kept my books such a tightly guarded secret that I would have welcomed having somebody read them, even at the cost of no royalties.

I soon became convinced that I was not a celebrity in this district, so I made my second pass to look at software piracy. Stopping in stalls with names like Dream Maker and Ultimate System Company, I perused the lists. Each shop maintained a master list, a menu du jour of illicit data, if you will.

Software here was priced by the disk. Low-density disks were HK $15 (U.S. $2) each, high-density disks are HK $25 (U.S. $3). To see how much your favorite software would cost, simply count how many disks it is distributed on. Each list had several hundred software titles, each title with the number of disks written next to it. In the U.S., I had just purchased Microsoft Word for Windows under an extra-special rebate program for U.S. $129. The Golden Shopping Center was having a special sale for U.S. $12.50.

Particularly impressive were programs like AUTOCAD (15 high density disks) or even a full distribution of SCO's Open Desktop, a wonderful combination of UNIX, Ingres, Motif, and a DOS emulator, available on 46 high density disks for U.S. $138. In the U.S., the price was U.S. $1,000 and was, quite frankly, a great deal even at that price. In Hong Kong, it was literally a steal.

As I walked from shop to shop, I watched locals and foreigners queuing up. Business was booming, despite the Hong Kong government's assurances that piracy had been stopped. A year ago, there had been a crackdown of sorts. Then, you could buy your software at the flat rate of U.S. $2 per disk, but the goods had to be delivered to your hotel in a brown paper bag. Things were back to normal now, and you only had to wait for "copy a: b:" to complete its magic.

Going from stall to stall, I turned the corner to face a 3 by 9 foot stall called Macrosoft. It featured a sign that caught my attention: "Licensed Software Available Here." This was highly unusual. In fact, it was downright miraculous.

Crowded in this booth were three young men, several dozen PCs, and an attractive display of shrinkwrapped software. The specialty of the stall was "Booky," a three-pound computer with a 40 Mbyte drive and a 9 inch VGA monitor, all packaged in a box small enough to fit under an airplane seat. It was a desktop system, but the unit was smaller (and much more useful) than my DECnet book.

There was a bit of a language barrier, so I spent 10 minutes establishing the fact that I didn't want to make copies of their legitimate software. I wanted to know if they sold many copies, and they kept insisting that I couldn't make copies, sorry, please.

Finally, the boss, who couldn't have been more than 18 years old got off his mobile phone. We talked for a while, and I delicately brought up the fact that he was selling software for an order of magnitude more than his neighbors.

"Do you sell much software?" I asked.

A long pause.

"No," he said.

"Why don't you make copies like other stores?"

Another pause.

"Some things are right, some things are not."

As he said this, I noticed a beatific glow arising from him and realized that I was looking at one of the first computer engineers destined for sainthood.

Leaving the hallowed grounds of Macrosoft, I turned the corner to find myself at the administrative offices of the Golden Shopping Center. Inside, two very large men sat smoking cigarettes and drinking tea. Outside the office were posted the financial reports of the center, detailing gross rentals, overhead, and other items of interest to the pirates that ran the stalls. I took out my camera and started snapping pictures of the financial reports, feeling a bit like a spy.

As I was snapping the last picture, I noticed one of the secretaries who had come back from lunch, standing there and staring at me. She scurried inside, yelling something I couldn't understand (but could guess). It was evidently time to explore other areas, so I made myself as inconspicuous as a foreigner wearing a suit can be in such a situation. I felt a bit like a marketing executive trying to hide at an IETF meeting.

I then started my third pass through the center, looking at hardware. This is always the most enjoyable part. I put my self righteousness aside, put away my investigative cloak, and became just another digital tourist.

The selection is not as unusual as in Japan, but the prices certainly were wonderful. This is the place to come if you are looking for the latest 486 motherboards, fax modems, cheap disk drives, or other components. My favorites are the little shops that sell commodities at good prices, perfect for people building clones.

One shop, for example, featured a box of XT motherboards for U.S. $12 each. Inside the store was every conceivable part from solenoids to keys to keyboards. Definitely the place to come if you wanted to make your own generic PC.

❐

Leaving the bowels of the Golden Shopping Center, I decided it was time for a beer. I threaded my way through the noodle stands and incense vendors and bought a can of San Miguel in a nearby pharmacy.

I tried to sit at a table next to a noodle stand, but quickly discovered no noodle, no chair. I perched atop a crate of empty bottles and watched the vendors cut up chicken giblets and toss them over bowls of steaming noodles. It reminded me of when I lived in Bangkok, where I would have one of these bowls everyday for lunch.

Wearing my going-to-meeting clothes and sitting on a box furiously scribbling notes, I fit in about as well as an Elvis impersonator in the Senate Caucus Room, but I met the bemused stares of the noodle cooks with my own noncommittal look. Finishing my beer, I went back up Fuk Wing street, past the snake shop (great for soups) to the subway. One interesting attribute of the Sham Shui Po area, where the Golden Shopping Center is located, is its proximity to the Hong Kong airport landing pattern. As you walk along, it is not at all unusual to look up and see a Boeing 747 appear to be landing on the building in front of you.

I took the subway to Tsim Sha Tsui, right on the edge of the Kowloon side of the bay. It was still too early for my dinner appointment, so I strolled by the bay and watched dozens of boats scurrying about their business, then went to the lobby of the Peninsula Hotel to await my friends.

Hong Kong

The Peninsula is one of those grand old hotels of the Orient. It is the kind of place that sends a Rolls Royce Silver Shadow to meet you at the airport and has the chauffeur phone ahead with your cocktail order so it is waiting for you when you alight.

The lobby is a place where you can nurse a gin and tonic (or a beer if you happen to be uncivilized) and watch the beautiful people act genteel. The thirty-foot ceiling is ornately decorated with golden ceiling ornaments, angels, and other remnants of the 1920s.

Going up to the concierge, I asked if I could borrow the display copy of "The Peninsula, Grand Old Lady of the Orient," explaining that I was a journalist and wished to include some information about his establishment in a story I was writing.

"Could I borrow the book for a few minutes for a story I'm working on? I'll be at that table right over there," I said, pointing three feet away.

"$160," he said without looking up. My journalist disguise evidently was not working.

☐

Tuesday morning, my assignment was to meet Dr. Nam Ng (pronounced just as it looks), director of Hong Kong University's computer center. The university is one of six in Hong Kong and I had gotten Dr. Ng's name out of John Quarterman's classic guide for the digital tourist, *The Matrix*.

To get to Hong Kong University, you go up winding streets steep enough to make San Francisco look like Kansas. Not an inch of space is wasted in Hong Kong, a city with one of the highest population densities in the world and built on islands that are nothing more than the tops of submerged mountains. The university is no exception, carved into a hill that most countries would call a cliff.

After a 45-minute expedition from my hotel, I ended up spending only 20 minutes with Dr. Ng. Yes, they had a 9,600 bps BITNET link. No, they didn't connect to the Internet. The PCs were based on Novell's Netware.

All this was obviously useful to the students (the microcomputer labs were well equipped and full of intent-looking undergraduates), but this didn't fulfill my dual aims for the day: finding material worthy of a technical travelogue and reading my mail, which was accumulating at the rate of fifty messages per day back in Colorado.

It was still early in the day, so I called over to the Chinese University in the New Territories. I started with the operator, and after several false starts, ended up connected to Michael Chang, a lecturer in Information Engineering (lecturers are the equivalent of U.S. assistant and associate professors). He offered to let me dial in from Wanchai on the main island, but I didn't relish the idea of reading 200 messages at 2,400 bps on my prehistoric excuse for a notebook. Besides, I'd never been over to the New Territories, having confined myself on previous visits to Kowloon and Wanchai.

I tumbled down the hill from Hong Kong University, crossed under the bay on the MTR subway, and boarded a train for the New Territories. I passed the huge Shah Tin racetrack and got off at the stop for Chinese University. There, I took a shuttle bus up an even steeper hill, finally stopping at the Lady Shaw building, right across from the Run Run Shaw Building. I asked a couple of students on the bus who the Shaws were, but nobody seemed to know. (I found out later that Run Run Shaw produced kung fu movies and was the man who brought Bruce Lee to America.)

Michael Chang turned out to be young, competent, and very friendly. He ushered me into a room full of DECstations and PCs, and started up a guest account for me. As I plowed through my mail, I noticed students around me confidently working their way through the Internet, reconfiguring systems, and otherwise acting like normal undergraduates. I found out a little later over lunch that Chinese University had only received its Internet link two months previously.

❐

After lunch, I crossed back over the bay to find Waleed Hanafi, Managing Director of Hutchison Mobile Data. Hong Kong has the highest concentration of mobile phones in the world. It is not surprising, therefore, that this is where the world's first public radio data network sprang up.

Hong Kong

Waleed started the company, a subsidiary of the Hutchison conglomerate, in 1987, and by 1989 Hutchison had fielded its first network. When Federal Express contracted with Hutchison for communication with its trucks, the network achieved a firm financial footing.

Hutchinson's network is based on 35 transmitters, strategically posted around Hong Kong using 20 different channels of the radio spectrum. The architecture of 20 channels and 35 stations allow expansion by stacking. In the financial district, one site already had two transmitter/receivers. There is no reason why 20 couldn't be stacked up at one site.

When a radio modem powers up, it checks the 20 different channels. Each transmitting site continually transmits a signal and the modem scans until it receives a signal with an acceptable bit error rate, set at the time I visited at 0 percent.

At that point, the modem sends a "here I am" message to the transmitter/receiver, which logs the unit ID. All units sharing a channel with a particular station use an arbitration scheme to decide when to send data. When the receiver is occupied, the transmitter sends a busy bit. When the channel clears (i.e., a modem is done sending a packet), the busy bit is dropped.

At this point, each modem backs off for a random period of time, then listens again. If the signal is still free, that modem gets to send. Otherwise, somebody else got the channel.

Collisions are theoretically possible, though highly unlikely because of the short packet transmission time. The key to this arbitration scheme is a very fast attack time by the modem—if the line is available after the backoff, the modem sends very quickly.

One thing that makes radio modems much simpler than cellular phones is the fact that handoff from one cell to another is not an issue. A packet is sent to one station. When necessary, the modem simply gives a "here I am" message to a new station, and the ID for the unit is moved. There is no need to keep a continuous circuit going as there would be for isochronous voice traffic.

Once a packet hits a transmitter/receiver, it is then routed into the Hutchison computer systems, which are simply two μVAX 3500s running the Ultrix operating system. The two μVAXen keep track of individual units and routed packets out to other sites. For example, Federal Express packets go back out via an X.25 link to the Federal Express host system.

A unit called a Develnet acts as a sort of LAN bridge, taking a radio packet and translating it into X.25, Ethernet, or Asynch-based formats. The Ethernet packets could go over a Hughes WAN bridge into a Novell LAN; the X.25 packets out over the Hong Kong public data network called Datapak, or even out via X.75 links from Hutchison's network to reach Sprint's X.25 network.

The biggest problem with a service like this is convincing people that it is worth using. "Great features" doesn't usually convince procurement agents. To spur demand, Hutchison took an 80386 and made it into a fancy BBS. Waleed founded the first Hong Kong BBS in 1982, so this was certainly a natural tack to take. The system on Hutchison's network links to several information sources, including weather servers and the Knight-Ridder news service.

Using your radio modem and a laptop, you could sit in your car and read the news wires. More importantly, in Hong Kong at least, you could check out stock prices.

One other link on the network which has proven quite popular is connection to the Royal Hong Kong Jockey Club's Telebet system. Customers hooking a CIT portable betting terminal up to a Hutchison radio modem can place bets from anywhere in Hong Kong.

For the outlying islands, this is often how bets are placed on race day. One old gentleman on the island of Ping Chau habitually sets up a unit next to the ferry depot. Islanders come to him to place their bets. At construction sites, the foreman often sits in a minivan and places bets on race days, thus keeping his crew from disappearing.

Mobile radio networks are big business. Hutchison is a world-wide conglomerate and hopes to expand the data network into other countries. Hutchinson is putting a network into England and several other companies are putting in systems in other countries. In the U.S., IBM and Motorola have joined forces to put in the Ardis public data network. In Sweden, Ericson is putting its own Mobitex system in.

Hong Kong

Although the service has potential, it is taking a while to get started with consumers. Hong Kong, with the high concentration of cellular phones and small area, is certainly an ideal place to start. Yet, even in Hong Kong, less than 1,000 radio modems are being used.

❐

I left Waleed's office and took the subway back to Happy Valley. Actually, that's not quite true. I took the subway to the wrong stop, walked around lost for 30 minutes, and then, after asking directions several times, took a taxi to Happy Valley.

There, I strolled through the market past piles of smoked oysters, dried mushrooms, fish heads, and jackfruit, and finally parked myself on a stool at a duck stand. After a few minutes of pantomime, a cold beer was produced and I spent the next few hours eating duck giblets smothered in chili sauce and drinking San Miguel. The cooks couldn't figure out why I was scribbling frantically in a notebook, but decided after a while that anybody who liked duck innards couldn't be all bad.

One interesting thing I noticed, between bites of giblets, was that people would come in off the street and, without asking, pick up the phone and place a call. Hong Kong Telephone has a flat monthly fee throughout the islands, so it is not considered at all rude to just walk in and pick up a phone. Try that in your average New York deli.

An outgrowth of the flat fee has been some interesting value-added services. Datapak, for example, offered a free ASCII-Fax service to its customers, since the marginal cost of doing so was zero. Flat-rate pricing, if properly designed, can be an ideal way to spur emerging industries. Commercial IP service providers in the U.S., for example, often used this strategy to encourage customers who might be scared of per-packet, per-hour, or other volume-based pricing schemes. Waleed Hanafi was using the same strategy to get his radio modem service off the ground.

Once an industry matures, more sophisticated pricing structures become possible. At first, however, customers don't have any idea what their use of a new service might be and don't want to assume the risk that their users might accumulate infinite service fees. Setting engineers loose on a volume-priced Internet is equivalent to leaving a dozen teenagers in a room with a list of 976 numbers posted next to the phone.

I finished my duck guts, drank up my last beer, and returned to my hotel.

Wednesday morning, with the day to kill before the flight down to Singapore, I took the hydrofoil down to the island of Macau. Settled by the Portuguese in 1554, Macau is now known for its casinos. It is also one of the few places that the government of North Korea maintains contact with the western world.

I took a cab down the stately Rua da Praia Grande to the Commercial Building. On the 23rd floor, I got off at the Talented Dragon Investment Company, Ltd., where I asked for Mr. Cho.

I ended up in this situation as a result of my dinner the previous evening with my friend Harry Rolnick, a writer who, among his many other accomplishments, is the music critic for the South China Morning Post.

"What's new?" I asked.

"Nothing much," Harry responded. He paused and took a drink of his Mekong whiskey.

"Oh," he added, "I'm writing a tourism guide to North Korea."

I laughed. Harry has a great sense of humor.

"Really, I am," he insisted.

The week before, he had noticed a small want ad in the Post which read "Tours to DPR Korea - Inquire Mr. Gpu." So he inquired.

Over a long lunch of rice wine and kim chi, Mr. Gpu had told Harry that of course Americans were welcome in North Korea. He could issue a visa on the spot. And, by the way, did Harry know perchance where to get large quantities of American cigarettes?

Harry had introduced Mr Gpu to a distributor in Hong Kong and presumably somebody is now smuggling cigarettes into North Korea, because Harry got his visa. I figured nothing ventured, nothing gained, so I asked Harry to tell Mr. Gpu that I would pay him a visit.

I was ushered into a paneled conference room and presented Mr. GPU with a copy of *STACKS*, dutifully inscribed "To the Democratic

People's Republic of Korea, with best wishes." I had never inscribed a book to a country before.

I explained the idea behind *Exploring the Internet* and my desire to visit Kim Il Sung University in Pyongyang to see the status of networking under the Great/Dear Leaders. I had heard that the complete works of Kim Il Sung, the Great Leader, were available in digital form and wished to meet the people behind the software.

Mr. Gpu abruptly got up and left the room. I wondered if he was going to get my visa. He returned a few minutes later with a shopping list of equipment which included a strange device called a "down converter" which, as best as I could make out, translated radio waves from one frequency to another. I confessed I had no idea what a down converter did, let alone why anybody would want one. I had this funny feeling that I didn't really want to know.

My ignorance appeared to have blown my credibility as a computer expert. The interview quickly ended. No offers of rice wine or kim chi. No visa.

I strolled back on the Avenida Do Doutor Rodrigo Rodrigues, stopping on the way for a fine lunch of Galinka Piri-Piri, a grilled chicken Macanese style smothered in spices.

The hydrofoil on the way back to Hong Kong was almost empty, with no tourists taking snaps of the boat floor or pointing to each island and asking "is that China?"

The tourists must have known something. We hit rough seas and the hydrofoil started to resemble a rollercoaster ride. I closed my eyes and hung on tight, finally arriving at the hydrofoil dock. I collected my bags from Harry's friends at the Macau Tourist Office and headed across the bay to the airport.

My plane arrived after 1 A.M. in the morning at Changi airport and I steeled myself for waiting in long lines while customs officials woke up and ambled over. To my amazement, from the time I came off the plane to the time I got into a taxi, including clearing customs and getting my bags, a total of seven minutes passed.

My taxi hurtled into town on a wide, immaculate freeway lined with flowers and trees. We passed a Pizza Hut and a bowling alley. This is Asia? Cars even pulled over to the side of the road to let an ambulance through.

Getting to the hotel, I found that the five copies of *STACKS* sent over by Interop had not arrived. I placed a call to David Brandin, the Vice President for Programs, who assured me they had been sent over a week ago by Federal Express.

The next morning, we found out that the books had in fact arrived five days earlier, but had been intercepted by the Undesirable Propagation Unit, one of the government censors. I knew that pornography and communism were not welcome, but I hadn't figured my descriptions of SMDS would offend anyone other than Frame Relay manufacturers. After pointing out that the books were engineering manuals, Federal Express eventually sprang them loose.

I spent the morning at the National University of Singapore (NUS) talking to Dr. Thio Hoe Tong, director of the computer center. NUS, with 17,000 students, is the largest university in Singapore. The university had just installed a 64 kbps link to JVNCnet in Princeton and joined the Internet.

The campus internet had recently caught the attention of the National Science and Technology Board (NSTB), which decided that the experiment should be expanded. Dr. Thio's deputy, Tommi Chen, had been delegated to develop TECHnet, a project with the aim of developing a national research IP network.

Technically, TECHnet was simple. For SG $300 per month, an organization got a port on the NUS router. Politically, however, it was a big step forward. TECHnet involved both commercial and educational users. As long as the NSTB determined that a company is a "bona fide" research and development group, it could join the network.

This may seem a bit pale to some readers, but the idea of multiple users sharing a single leased line (which is what TCP/IP does), runs contrary to a long-established tenet of international communications, the infamous Recommendation D.1.

Recommendation D.1 of the CCITT established the principle that multiplexing multiple users over a single international line should be the province of the "network provider," a code word signifying the single monopoly, the PTT. In this parlance, a "value-added network" was anybody who was forced to buy services from the telephone company. By defining multiplexing over international lines as the proper function of the network, not the value-added network, competition never even got out of the gates.

Recommendation D.1 has been defanged for most of the world. When you think about it, D.1 and similar barriers to entry run counter to the Treaty of Rome, the GATT, and any other principles of fair trade and antitrust ever promulgated in international law. While most organizations and some countries ignore it, there are a few places where D.1 still rears its ugly head. Although the recommendation itself is rarely cited specifically, it has certainly established itself as part of the telephone company mentality.

Rumors were that Singapore Telecom was not pleased by the idea of TECHnet. After all, if a company uses the Internet to communicate with the U.S., the reasoning went, they wouldn't be placing phone calls.

This reasoning had been applied before to networks. In Singapore, BITNET was not available to undergraduates. The rumor was that Singapore Telecom objected because if undergraduates could use electronic mail to reach brothers and sisters studying in the U.S., they wouldn't place international voice calls.

In the case of TECHnet, the government had exerted enough pressure so that the system moved forward despite the objections of more conservative elements. However, as a safety check, CEOs of companies joining TECHnet had to sign a certification that the employees of a company would only use the network for R&D, strenuously avoiding commercialistic or even (save us) personal purposes.

After describing TECHnet, Dr. Thio explained the rather unusual approach to campus networking at NUS. A mere 18 months before, several thousand PCs and Macintoshes had been isolated islands with no connectivity. Rather than phase in networks over a long period of time, NU.S. adopted a "big bang" theory of network design.

An RFP was issued which was won by a consortium that included Hewlett Packard and Fibronics. In two stages, six months apart, 3,000 machines went on the network. Most of the network was based on HP9000s and PS/2s acting as LAN Manager servers. An FDDI backbone and Ethernet subnets tied it all together.

Needless to say, with several thousand users going live at the same time, training and support became, as Dr. Thio put it, "an issue."

That night, I was scheduled to give a talk to the local IEEE chapter. I gave my usual rambling discourse on "our friend, the Internet." Afterwards, I was presented with an attractive pewter dish and we went out for a dinner of hairy crabs and garlic prawns.

❐

I had agreed to be a guest lecturer Friday morning at the Information Communication Institute of Singapore (ICIS). ICIS, a cooperative program between AT&T and the Singapore government, offered a postgraduate degree in telecommunications.

I was picked up by Don Stanwyck, an ICIS faculty member and AT&T employee. Don had been one of AT&Ts representatives to various CCITT and ANSI study groups and had served as editor for several key ISDN recommendations.

Don took me down to Little India, where we had a breakfast of roti prata, Indian fried bread which you dip into a bowl of spicy mutton curry. Don explained how he had ended up on the expatriate circuit in Singapore. As a CCITT delegate, he had logged well over a million frequent flier miles, travelling 70 to 80 percent of the time. He finally decided "enough is enough," and told AT&T he wanted to live in Singapore. In addition to Singapore, Don had lived in Japan, and speaks proficient Mandarin and UUCP.

With a love-hate relationship to Singapore, he was typical of many of the expats who live in Asia. He knew more about Singapore than many locals, yet remained very much a visitor here. After two years, he had kept an intellectual detachment and alternated between wild praise and cynical criticism.

At ICIS, I lectured to a packed room with several classes meeting together. It was a typical lecture in some ways. The students laughed at my jokes and seemed to enjoy the talk. Yet, when I was done and asked for questions, not a single person raised their hand.

I had experienced this in the past, so was not as disconcerted as I might have been. In many Asian countries, it is considered bad manners to ask a question. To do so implies either that the teacher did a bad job explaining or that the student wasn't paying attention. Risking either implication would be a loss of face for somebody.

Instead, questions are best asked in a more informal setting. After the lecture, sitting in the lounge, I spent a half-hour answering detailed questions on everything from namespace administration to exhaustion of the 32-bit address space.

❐

I spent Friday afternoon with Singapore Telecom. Singapore Telecom is one of the classic PTTs, controlling every aspect of telecommunications, as well as the postal system. For many years, local telephone service in Singapore had been essentially free, with a flat annual equipment rental of SG $190 for homes and SG $250 for businesses. (The Singapore dollar was trading at 1.694 to the U.S. dollar at the time.)

When I arrived in Singapore, the flat rate was about to be abolished in favor of a straight usage-based system of 1.4 cents per minute during peak periods and 0.7 cents per minute during off-peak periods. "Rentals" would decrease to SG $100 for homes and SG $150 for businesses.

This change was causing such an uproar that the Prime Minister, travelling in Zimbabwe, had called a press conference to discuss the subject, and his comments were front page news in the *Singapore Straits Times*. For Singapore, this was a major political flap. A newspaper columnist felt compelled to write a piece debunking the theory that the entire social fabric would disintegrate because children would place fewer calls to their mothers. Singapore Telecom issued a study saying that 66 percent of bills would go down and that the scheme would be revenue-neutral. Of course, recent year-end results by Singapore Telecom of profits of SG $1.2 billion didn't help matters.

In order for a residential bill to go down, a residential customer had to make less than 107 hours per year of peak, or 214 of off-peak, calls. It boiled down to a situation where families with teenagers and modems were going to face higher bills.

Singapore Telecom contended that the previous flat rate policies had made it difficult to sell some new services. ISDN was a key example. Singapore was quite proud in 1989 of being the first country to have nation-wide availability of ISDN.

ISDN cost 10 cents per minute in Singapore. With variable pricing on regular phone lines, Singapore Telecom hoped to increase the demand for data services. I asked Chew Mun Chun, manager of the Network Technology Group at Singapore Telecom how successful ISDN had been. He smiled bravely and said, with all the positive spin he could muster, "today we have close to 300 subscribers." Needless to say, most businesses had found it simpler to use high-speed modems on dialup lines.

While ISDN had not been a raging success, Singapore Telecom had been more successful in other areas. It teamed up with British Telecom and the Norwegian Telecom to offer Skyphone, a service that allowed airplanes anywhere in the world to place calls. Each of the three telephone companies provides a ground station that covered a certain geographic area: Norway covered the Indian Ocean, Singapore the Pacific, and British Telecom the Atlantic.

Skyphone is built on top of a network of eight satellites run by INMARSAT, a consortium headquartered in London and sponsored by 60 member countries. INMARSAT provides a generic satellite service which members then use to build value-added services such as Skyphone. An airborne user communicating with an INMARSAT satellite indicates which service she is trying to use. When a call reaches one of the earth stations, such as the one that Singapore Telecom operates on Sentosa island, it is routed through the local telephone network and then out to the International Direct Dial (IDD) links. Since Skyphone is a telephone link like any other (albeit, an expensive one at U.S. $6.70 per minute), it can be used for fax and data as well as voice traffic. It is even possible to place ground-to-air calls, although the caller would need to know the aircraft ID in order to do so.

The first customer for Skyphone was the Sultan of Brunei. Singapore Air was the first commercial airline to install the service. Other airlines quickly followed suit.

❐

Another interesting Singapore Telecom project I saw was Teleview, a videotex system that went into field trials in 1988 and went public in 1990. The government had very ambitious plans for the system, but by late 1991 there were only 6,500 subscribers.

Teleview was an unusual videotex system in that it supported high-quality photographic images. Commands to Teleview went in via normal asynchronous dialup lines. Photos returned at 2,400 bps would not be very effective, however, so a return data path was provided via a television channel dedicated to Teleview.

Each frame on the television channel had a subscriber ID on it, directing it to the appropriate system. The signal had a 4.5 Mbps data throughput rate, allowing frames for lots of users to share the single television channel.

Your average PC is not set up to handle either photographic quality displays or to receive RF signals. To provide these capabilities, the original Teleview terminal was a specially developed device which could be seen in many shopping centers and public facilities.

Dedicated terminals, especially fairly expensive, single-purpose terminals, were not an ideal way to penetrate the home market. PC users were able to access Teleview by adding an RF card for receiving data, a modem for sending commands, and a photo display card to drive a monitor at 480 by 280 pixels with 18 bits per pixel for a total of 256,000 simultaneous colors.

While photographic display was a unique feature of Teleview, it was possible to bypass the feature and access the system simply with a modem for an 80 by 40 character display. It appeared that many, if not most, of the users were content with the character-only displays and used the system for things like stock quotes.

As videotex systems went, Teleview had a fairly good selection of information available. In addition to the obligatory stock prices, it also had the Reuters news service, airline information, real estate listings, and even record and book shops.

Some of the more unusual applications reflected the influence of a strong government involvement. Mandarin tutorials, for example, proved quite popular as an instructional tool. Always sensitive to the cultural makeup of the island, the government added Malay lessons soon after the Chinese.

The initial architecture for the system was a single proprietary computer system with X.25 links to service providers and asynchronous and RF links to users. The next generation system was an attempt to vastly expand the functionality (or at least the capacity). Teleview officials were still in the middle of the procurement process and could not discuss details, but interviews with an anonymous source established that the contract for the system had been won by Digital.

The front-end to the new network was going to be a series of modem racks, presumably connected to VAXen, which are in turn connected to a series of front-end Ethernets. Each front-end Ethernet would then be connected, via a bridge, to an FDDI backbone. Other bridges would connect to a back-end Ethernet. On the back-end Ethernet would be another series of VAXen, which would contain a cache of recently accessed frames.

The cache VAXen would be connected by a mystery net (presumably Ethernet and LAT) to a series of VAX Clusters, which would serve as data repositories. Other VAXen would act as X.25 links to other information sources.

As one of my anonymous sources said, "they're throwing VAXes around like water." Singapore had, as of October 1990, invested SG

$50 million in the system and it was likely that current investment was an order of magnitude higher.

The government placed great importance in Teleview. When it was deployed commercially, Yeo Ning Hong, the Minister for Communications and Information said "beginning today, Teleview will bring the Information Age into every home and workplace." Like France, Singapore saw videotex as the way to bring widespread computing into every home.

◻

Saturday morning, I went back to Science Park and entered yet another ultra-modern office building, this one housing the offices of Singapore Network Services, developers of the Tradenet EDI system.

I was met by two individuals wearing the international marketing uniform of business suits, business cards, and business-like smiles. They whisked me into the board room and sat me down at a table the size of a golf course. They sat down far away on the other side of the table, yet still close enough that I could see them.

I knew I was in trouble when the slide projector came out. The junior of the team, bearing the title of "Executive Marketing" got up and started smiling broadly and talking about "increasing productivity" and similar concepts that we could all agree on as being positive.

Singapore Network Services (SNS) was formed with very strong government support as a joint venture between the Civil Aviation Authority of Singapore, the Port of Singapore Authority, the telephone company, and the government.

Although Tradenet, designed to clear cargo through customs by using EDI, was the first application, SNS was branching out into other EDI applications. The slide presentation was meant to illustrate a grand vision of the world, and words like "network hub" and "information services" kept getting tossed out.

A bit of inquiry established the fact that the "network hub" was in fact an IBM 9000 which traders accessed via dialup or leased lines. Not being familiar with the IBM 9000, I naively asked what operating system was being used.

Singapore

"That is a very technical question," my presenter responded. "We were not told you would want such technical information."

It is the bane of marketing the world over that successful projects, such as a massive application of EDI in Tradenet, gets papered over with superficial nonsense like "information services for productivity." Instead of simply describing the success and how it came to be, which would certainly be very impressive, marketing feels compelled to invent silly catch phrases.

Tradenet had in fact been quite a successful system. Traders used the EDIFACT standard to format documents which were uploaded to the IBM 9000. SNS didn't use X.400 to transfer the document, although Executive Marketing agreed with me that X.400 was a good thing. Once the files were uploaded OfficeVision mail was used to move the documents between different groups.

The system linked traders in Singapore to customs, the Trade Development Board (TDB), and to what was euphemistically referred to as "other controlling agencies." An example of the latter was the Undesirable Propagation Unit, the government agency that had held my books for inspection.

Typical transactions were import/export declarations, certificates of origin, and other documents. Many of these operations, such as customs clearance for a shipment, were semi-automated. An answer from customs on whether clearance is automatically granted or an inspection is needed, could be returned in a few hours instead of the few days required in a manual system.

Tradenet was launched in 1989 and at the time the government had hoped that by 1993, 90 percent of the traders would be using the system, at which time it would become mandatory. By 1990, 90 percent of traders were already on the system and it became mandatory in 1991.

After Tradenet, Singapore Network Services started branching out into other EDI applications. Medinet was used for automated processing of medical claims. $Link was an electronic funds transfer application. OrderLink was a system developed to allow the government to issue Requests for Quotation and receive bids from suppliers.

Executive Marketing finished his slides and I escaped the plush confines of the Singapore Network Services board room into the refreshing humidity of the street. I flagged down a taxi, which managed to decelerate from 50 mph to 0 in a little under 1 second. I jumped in with a bit of trepidation and the tires squealed as he took off.

"Where you from?" the cabbie asked.

"Colorado, U.S.A.," I replied.

"Ah, Chicago!" he replied. He seemed to find this hilarious and laughed furiously. After laughing for a few minutes, he would quiet down, then repeat the word "Chicago" again and start laughing. I occupied myself with pressing my foot against an imaginary brake pedal.

◻

Saturday night, Michael Yap from the National Computer Board picked me up for drinks. After a couple of beers in a generic pub in one of Singapore's huge entertainment developments, we went for a ride and ended up in Chinatown.

There, we went into a traditional tea house, Tea Chapter. After taking off our shoes, we walked up narrow stairs two stories into a large room filled with low tables and pillows.

"This is a Singapore Chinese Yuppie joint," Michael explained. It had been started a few years ago by a few friends as a place people could sit and relax. Around the room, people were sitting at tables. At a corner, a young couple sat on cushions on the floor while their two young children bounced off the walls.

Tea Chapter was part of a growing trend in Singapore to rediscover ethnic roots and to allow ethnic diversity. Originally, the country pursued an aggressive melting pot strategy, but it had since taken an about face. Malays, Indians, and Chinese all have distinct ethnic communities in Singapore.

Tea arrived with an elaborate array of devices. A big pot of boiling water was used to feed another tiny pot where the tea steeped for a few minutes. The tea from the first batch was thrown away and more water added. Then, a few batches from the tiny pot were used to fill a medium-sized serving pot. From there, the tea was poured into teacups so small they held only a swallow. The tea was accompanied by eggs which had been preserved in green tea leaves, a delicious snack.

Along with the teapots was a container filled with mysterious implements: miniature shovels, tongs, picks and the like. I asked Michael to explain the purpose of all these devices.

"I'm not quite sure," he confessed sheepishly.

Michael Yap is typical of the technocrats who run Singapore. His education at the University of Maryland was paid for by the government as part of an elite scholars program for fast-trackers. In return, he is bonded for eight years of government service, although it is likely that he will stay much longer.

Michael is passionately devoted to the joint causes of technology and Singapore. He continually steers the conversation back to one of the two topics (and preferably both at once), always accentuating the positive aspects of Singapore society.

Michael's job is Programme Manager for IT2000, Singapore's effort to build an "intelligent island" by the year 2000. The scope of IT2000 is vast, one of the most encompassing visions ever formulated by a government to build a network infrastructure for a society.

First and foremost, IT2000 is a symbolic commitment by the government to use technology. It is an effort to find a way to maintain the stunning economic growth that Singapore has managed in the last 20 years through shipping, finance, and hi-tech manufacturing.

As a vision, it starts with high-level goals, such as increasing productivity and well-being. At the next level down, it moves on to the applications that can help achieve these goals. Only at the very end is specific technology considered.

Thus, unlike many national plans, fiber to the home or use of ISDN are not the goals. Instead, the vision of IT2000 is to maintain productivity increases of 3 to 4 percent per year for a population of 2.65 million people for a sustainable period of time.

Singapore is one of the few countries that could seriously advance such a goal. Known as Singapore, Inc. to the financial press, the country is run much like a big corporation. It is not unusual for senior management (i.e., government ministers) to give direction to corporations, citizens, and the civil service.

Throughout its history, Singapore has been run with this combination of broad consensus and top-down direction. IT2000 is not the first large scale plan. In 1984, there was "Vision 1999," in 1986, the "Agenda for Action." In 1990, the government issued a beautiful coffee-table book produced by Times Editions called *Singapore— the Next Lap.* The book contained a series of broad goals, such as the following:

> "we must encourage more Singaporeans to marry, to do so earlier, and to have three children, and more if they can afford it."

Pictures of smiling children and happy families were accompanied by specific goals, in this case a target population of 4 million people. These goals were then used to guide government policies, such as tax policies, or even housing assignments.

In the area of information technology, which the Singapore government refers to as IT, policy was spearheaded by the National Computer Board (NCB). The NCB coordinates government computerization efforts, and is also charged with creating a "National IT Plan." In consensual Singapore, the NCB shuns the term "create," preferring instead to "lead to the realization" of a National IT Plan.

In the civil service computerization area, NCB had deployed over 800 of its staffers into government offices. An example of a system developed by the NCB is the immigration system, which claims to be able to check passports for foreigners in 30 seconds and residents in 15. My own experience at the airport, even though in the middle of the night, certainly bore this out.

Other examples of government automation efforts are an automated card catalogue for the national library, a computerized registry of companies, and automated production of birth certificates. No one of these applications was particularly unique; what was interesting was the breadth and focus of the computerization effort.

NCB had been slowly trying to tie these different systems together to allow data sharing among government bodies, an effort known as IDNet. I met with employees of NCB to learn more about IDNet. The meeting took place in the vast NCB headquarters located in Science Park. On the walls were posters of people looking very modern, sporting slogans like "Success Through Partnership" and "Fulfillment Through People Orientation."

I was met by an NCB public relations officer and ushered into a conference room. "Help yourself to coffee," she said, pointing to a device called the Café Bar and leaving to get the people I would be meeting with.

The strange looking contraption had different buttons you pushed to dispense various powders (coffee, milk, soup) into a cup. You then pressed the water dispensing bar to put hot water into your own personal mix of soluble powders. After a few false starts, I figured out the apparatus and made myself a cup of fresh, steaming Nescafé.

Being the curious type, I had the cover off the Café Bar and my head buried inside when the door opened and a group of NCBians (as the posters downstairs referred to employees) were ushered in by the PR officer. I slammed the cover on my finger and sat down to learn about IDNet.

The network is fairly simple. It consists of an IBM 3090 at the Ministry of Finance acting as the hub for a multidomain SNA network. The basic service allows a user on one net to send and receive 3270 data streams to another net. A few custom applications are also available.

To use cross domain services requires a special ID. One thousand IDs had been granted, each tied to a user profile detailing which services that particular user could access. IDNet has 31 sites, 90 machines, and 40 applications.

The IDNet architects didn't seem particularly adventuresome technically, as is often the case with people whose job is to keep a network running. They grudgingly acknowledged that token ring networks might play a role in the future, but more for terminal access based on PCs than for peer-to-peer networks. Protocols like TCP/IP and OSI were acknowledged, but with a notable lack of enthusiasm.

In a distinct twist from many large organizations, NCB was centralizing its servers into four very large data hubs, each devoted to a particular type of data. Centralizing the location of computers would, hopefully, save on overhead and permit better control over operations. The four centers would have data about land, people, legal establishments, and finance. While each data center might have many computers, the NCB staffers didn't rule out the possibility of replacing many systems with a single mega 3090 running DB2.

The guiding principle for computerization of government was the slogan "one stop, non stop." This meant that a citizen ought to be able to go anyplace and do all government business at once (and quickly). As one official pointed out, no matter how comfortable you make the chairs in a government waiting room, people will still want to leave. Of course, it is worth pointing out that reality does not always meet the lofty goals of slogans, but it was encouraging to see that Singapore policy makers had a policy they were trying to communicate.

Data sharing among government agencies was one aspect of one stop, non stop. The other was delivery of services. Systems like Teleview videotex were envisioned as the delivery vehicle for many government services. Some services were already available on Teleview, such as listing of government tender notices and awards.

Other systems were not on Teleview but did show the effects of data sharing. For example, the census bureau tapped into existing databases and preprinted census forms, allowing people to verify data instead of reentering it.

One stop, non stop was part of the broader vision of IT2000. Singapore had had a national IT plan for several years, but in 1990, Dr. Tay Eng Son, the Senior Minister of State for Education unveiled the IT2000 concept which greatly increased the scope (and the stakes).

IT2000 is being called a "national masterplan for an information infrastructure." When I talked to Michael Yap in late October 1991, the NCB had just finished the first phase of feasibility studies. Based on that first phase, NCB had received significant government funds to develop an architecture to make it all happen.

The feasibility phase divided the economy into 11 sectors, ranging from construction to health care to transportation. Each sectoral study group was chaired by a "captain of industry."

NCB staffers assisted each study group. The staffers led the groups through top-down analyses such as trends analysis and wish lists and through bottom-up planning procedures such as dependency graphs and functional decomposition.

The goal was a set of strategic applications: things that people should be able to do on an intelligent island. Many of the projects that fell out of this planning are truly ambitious, ranging from a national multi-function smart card and an intelligent vehicle highway system, to a queueless, counterless government services system.

Altogether, the planning process involved 200 industry leaders and 50 NCB staffers. This resulted in the goals for IT2000. The next step will be to begin defining a series of target applications. Underlying the applications will be a set of common network services (e.g., authentication) which in turn use the national telecommunication network. Tying all this together is a series of technical standards and a legal framework.

Defining each of these pieces is the challenge. When Michael Yap talks about a legal framework, for example, he includes such difficult issues as copyright for intellectual property. When he talks of common network services he means everything from transport connections to "look and feel" to application tool kits.

Will it work? When NCB decides an item is a priority, it can achieve impressive results. For example, it developed a ship planning system for the Port of Singapore Authority that reduces the planning time for each ship by half. Together with the massive use of EDI in TradeNet, there is no doubt that the port is a highly efficient, automated enterprise.

The real challenges will be the common network infrastructure and the legal framework. In the U.S., such issues are still in the very early conceptual stages. The Corporation for National Research Initiatives has attempted to address both issues in their Knowbot architecture, but Knowbots are still at the early prototype stage.

Michael and I finished our tea and he dropped me off at my hotel. I was off the next day to Dublin to learn more about a key U.S. infrastructure, the NSFNET, which had come into being because of an Irishman.

The next morning, I stood in long lines at the Singapore airport and read the Singapore Straits Times. I noticed a story that had an interesting mix of old Asia and high-tech. In the Taoist religion, when people die, paper models of important things in their life are burned in a ceremony, allowing the newly departed to take the good things they enjoyed in life with them. Typically, these paper models are things like houses and cars. On Sin Ming Drive, however, paper models of portable phones, VCRs, and even karaoke sets were available. No ISDN handsets were on sale yet, though.

I arrived in Dublin on Monday. I had heard that it was a holiday, so I asked the cabbie what the occasion was.

"Nobody knows," he replied.

And there goes your tip, I thought to myself.

Checking into my hotel, I caught a bus into town to find a true Irish pub. I must have walked five miles before I found one that was open.

"Never thought I'd have trouble finding an open pub in Dublin," I remarked to the bartender.

"Ah, it's the holiday, you know," he replied.

"What's the occasion?" I asked.

"Nobody knows," he replied.

I left him a tip. Always tip your bartender is what my mother told me as I left home, and the advice has never failed to serve me.

The next morning, feeling a combination of Guinness and jet lag, I met Dennis Jennings, who picked me up in an ancient BMW and drove me across the street to University College, Dublin, where he runs the Computer Centre.

A tall, affable Irishman, Dennis set me down in his office, filled with mountains of paper and wall-to-wall binders on a wide range of networking topics.

"I understand you're the father of NSFNET?" I asked.

He laughed.

"More like an uncle," he said. For the rest of the morning he proceeded to tell me the story of how the NSFNET was born.

When all is said and done, Jennings certainly qualifies as the father (or at least one of several fathers) of the NSFNET. One must ask, of course, if the child turned out as hoped, but that is a different issue from its paternity.

Jennings started working on research networks in 1979 when he started the Irish Universities Network linking the two major Dublin schools. At the time, X.25 was considered a network and for two years, from 1979 to 1981, the Irish Universities Network consisted of X.25 and "higher level" protocols such as X.28 and X.29.

In 1982, he proposed a national star-based network centered around University College Dublin. After a year of discussion, negotiation, and consideration, the Higher Education Authority funded HEAnet.

The original HEAnet was based on the JANET Coloured Book protocols. When I visited Jennings at the end of October 1991, HEAnet 2 was beginning to be operational. Based on X.25 with a 64 kbps backbone and multiprotocol routers, the network was rapidly becoming TCP/IP-based.

In 1983, with funding for HEAnet approved, Jennings heard a rumor at Yale that IBM would be bringing BITNET to Europe. Although the European Academic Research Network (EARN) was going to be based on the big six European players, Jennings managed to turn that into seven countries.

The initial EARN meetings were chaotic and, as I found out over the next couple of days, Dennis Jennings is not shy about grabbing the white board and jumping in. He did, and ended up becoming the first president of the EARN board.

The EARN position started bringing him to the continent on a frequent basis. On one trip, he attended a Landweber networking symposium. At the symposium, Jennings and his wife had dinner with many of the participants. Jennings' wife mentioned to Larry Landweber that Dennis had always wanted to work in the States. You know, one of those polite things you say over dinner.

"Would you like to be director of CSNET?" Landweber asked, not one to let such offers pass idly by.

Dennis had a trip scheduled to California anyway. While he was in California, he phoned Larry Landweber. Next thing Dennis Jennings knew, he was flying to Washington, D.C. to meet with the head of the CSNET board.

"By the way," Larry added, "I'm also going to Washington. The NSF is considering a new initiative. Want to sit in?"

Landing in Washington after a red-eye flight, Dennis took a cab straight to the NSF, where he meekly took a seat in the back while network luminaries like Dave Farber, Ira Fuchs, and Vint Cerf came in. "Frankly," Dennis explained, "I was a bit awed. After all, this was America." Among some Europeans at the time, America had the reputation as some sort of super technology haven.

He didn't stay awed for too long. In fact, he soon found himself at the white board again.

Eventually, he was offered two jobs: Director of CSNET and the NSF Program Director in charge of networking. He played hard to get for a bit, until NSF upped its offer to include considerably more money.

Back in Dublin, he was sorting out his affairs when NSF called.

"Any chance you can be English?"

Asking an Irishman to be English is a bit like asking an IBM account executive to sell camels.

"I beg your pardon?"

In order to work for NSF, you had to be a citizen of an allied nation. Ireland didn't cut it. Luckily, Dennis had been born in England. He got an English passport, and on January 2, 1985 he started work at NSF.

At the time, NSF wasn't thinking in terms of building a national network. It had funded four supercomputer centers and merely wanted to give scientists access to them. The original thinking, in fact, was to have four networks, one for each of the centers.

A technical advisory group was formed, chaired by Dave Farber and including such people as the ubiquitous Larry Landweber, Tony Lauck (head of the DECnet architecture group), Frank Kuo from SRI, and several others.

The first big issue to tackle was standards. The computer scientists quickly honed in on TCP/IP. Others were not so sure. At the time, there were several higher-performance proprietary networks such as DECnet and MFEnet (sardonically referred to by some as MuffyNet).

The argument was framed in terms of openness versus efficiency. Protocol suites like DECnet or MFEnet were thought to be significantly more efficient than TCP/IP. Another issue was freedom of choice. Some supercomputer center directors didn't want to be constrained. Significant populations of users, especially in the physics community, preferred DECnet.

Eventually, TCP/IP won out. It was decided, however, that a network could start out as something else as long as it would migrate to TCP/IP. An interesting side note was the role of OSI. Everyone envisioned that OSI was five years away and would provide a migration path to a world of openness, truth, and beauty. More than five years later, OSI was still five years away and had become the canonical example of the sliding window.

Even more fundamental a choice than the protocol suite was the structure of the network. Jennings felt very strongly that this should be a general purpose internetwork. General-purpose meant that it was not specifically aimed at the current supercomputer user.

The argument was made that a general-purpose internetwork would best serve the goal of promoting science and engineering, the mandate of the NSF. The internetwork part of the structure was fundamental: this would be a network of networks. The lowest unit was the campus network.

From the present vantage point, this doesn't sound like a radical requirement, but at the time there were many major universities without campus networks. As Jennings explained it, "networking was the private domain of individual researchers." By refusing to extend the internetwork to the desk or the department, Jennings hoped to help fuel an expansion of the internet.

In 1985, many of today's mid-level networks got their start. Some, like the San Diego Supercomputer Center's SDSCnet, were run by the centers. Others, like the Bay Area Regional Research network (BARRnet) were independently formed.

Looking back, one thing that Jennings regrets is that the NSF did not make a long-term funding plan explicit to these regional networks. Funding was based on a simple year-to-year allotment. A better model would have told the regionals that they would be funded at 100 percent for three years, with a two-year falloff. This is the same model, of course, that IBM used with BITNET and EARN.

Making the funding model explicit would have had two benefits. First, NSF would have been freed from continuing funding obligations with the regionals, allowing NSF to move on to other infrastructure projects. Second, and more important, the regionals would have had a very strong incentive to find alternative funding, from their members, consortiums, or the states in which they did business. The Jennings model of infrastructure is thus to have government start off the project and then have the users take it over. This leaves the government free to move on to the next building block.

In addition to funding the regionals, NSF ended up putting in a backbone, the NSFNET. In August of 1985, Jennings attended a two-day meeting in Boulder, Colorado with the directors of the four supercomputer centers and the director of the National Center for Atmospheric Research (NCAR).

Jennings presented his model of regional networks connected by a national backbone. The directors were not pleased. After all, this was a way for one of their local researchers to use the facilities of another center.

The next morning, however, the directors did an about face. True, their local researchers could use somebody else's system, but the converse was also true. An Internet would make one center's services available to the entire country. If you think your center is better than the others (and all the directors did), a backbone is a wonderful idea.

As Jennings related the story, not only did the directors change their minds, they started pounding the table asking why this wasn't already in place. The group adjourned to a picnic table up on Table Mesa, in the shadow of the Rocky Mountains, and sketched out the backbone on a piece of paper. Jennings still has the piece of paper, dated September 17, 1985. He had been on the job nine and a half months.

The backbone would consist of 56 kbps lines linking NCAR and the four centers. It was immediately labeled the "interim backbone" since everyone agreed a T1 network would soon be needed.

Events were moving very quickly. At times, Jennings was cautioned by the NSF bureaucracy that he was "sailing close to the wind." For example, Bill Schrader and others at Cornell went ahead and ordered all the 56 kbps lines before NSF had formally approved the project. Cornell then took the lead in putting in the interim system.

In addition to lines, there was a crucial decision on the selection of routers. Major and minor router vendors were asked to make presentations. BBN had a wonderful system, but their routers cost U.S. $180,000 each. Cisco and Proteon came close, but didn't have nationwide support structures in place.

Ultimately, attention focused on the Fuzzball, a device based on the PDP-11 and developed by David Mills. Everybody was reluctant to depend on a homegrown system developed and maintained by one person. As reluctant as anybody to have the national network based on the Fuzzball was David Mills himself.

David ended up spending the next two years maintaining and modifying his Fuzzball. Some of the changes were simple bug fixes, but others reflected some significant architectural flaws in the original TCP/IP.

For example, the TCP/IP protocol suite implied a single backbone: the ARPANET. Now, with the addition of the NSFNET, there were two backbones and the Exterior Gateway Protocol (EGP) broke. Mills was forced to periodically hack up his Fuzzballs to handle this, and other, situations.

Jennings felt that the decision to go with the Fuzzball was one of the major successes of the NSFNET project. It forced the Internet community into a formal examination of routing, leading to specifications of router requirements and the development of new protocols such as the Border Gateway Protocol (BGP).

Common, open specifications for routing in turn led to the immense growth of companies like Cisco, Proteon, and Wellfleet, as well as substantial product lines for larger companies such as DEC and Sun Microsystems. Low-cost routers allowed the creation of ad hoc internetworks, which in turn led to the creation of companies like PSI and AlterNet.

In March 1986, Dennis Jennings brought to a close his 15 months at NSF. Just 15 days later, the 56 kbps backbone went live. Jennings was replaced at NSF by Steve Wolff, who began the difficult job of formulating the solicitation for the T1 backbone and then later, a T3 backbone.

If Dennis Jennings is the uncle of NSFNET, then Steve Wolff would qualify as the nanny, expanding the network from an ad hoc, interim system into a mature, production network transferring over 14 billion packets per month. Wolff deserves a great deal of the credit for the rapid growth of the Internet by agressively expanding the backbone, funding international links, and encouraging the growth of the regional and campus networks.

After a morning learning the history of NSFNET and a chance to view the tattered piece of paper that served as the original architecture document, we went out to lunch with the directors of the other two university computer centers. Over a glass of wine, the conversation turned to the question of European backbones. How would Dennis, if he had the power, accomplish the same thing in Europe that he did in the U.S.?

Dennis quoted a classic Irish proverb given when a tourist asks a farmer for directions: "I don't know, but if I were going there, I certainly wouldn't be starting from here."

In the United States, a government agency, the NSF, was charged with promoting research and education. Within the European Commission, however, there was no such group. There was no mention of education in the Treaty of Rome, the enabling legislation for the European Community. Instead, funding for research networks was funnelled through groups like the infamous 13th directorate.

DG XIII was responsible for promoting things like competitiveness and standards. In practice, this led to a strong focus on the PTTs and OSI. What it did not lead to was an operational, pan-European backbone, either commercial or research. Everybody was waiting for the Commission to act and the Commission was waiting for OSI to be commercially available.

After lunch, Dennis told me about an extraordinary meeting that was to be held the next day to try and bootstrap a European Backbone (EBONE). We quickly rearranged my plane tickets to route me to Amsterdam and Dennis drove me back to my hotel for a glass of Guiness.

My wakeup call came at 5 A.M. I found my way into a cab, met Dennis at the airport, and flew to Amsterdam. We hailed a cab to the EBONE meeting being held in the Tiger Room at the Artis Zoo. En route, our cabbie regaled us with obscene animal jokes.

When we arrived at the Tiger Room, the meeting had started already, with 35 deadly serious people sitting around a large square formed by long tables. Kees Neggers, co-managing director of SURFnet, chaired the meeting, which included most of the major networking players in Europe.

The idea behind EBONE was quite simple. Until the Commission got its act together, people would pool existing resources and form a voluntary, interim consortium. If and when the EC or some other body started operating a more formal backbone, the consortium would disband.

A consortium like this was an incredible balancing act. Deep religious barriers divide Europe. Some people insisted that any workable network must be based on OSI, the Connection Oriented Network Service (CONS), and X.25. Others prefered TCP/IP and leased lines. To make a workable backbone, enough of these players had to be convinced to sign up to the EBONE concept.

Kees Neggers and a few others had formulated a memorandum of understanding which would form the "gentlemen's agreement" to put EBONE into being (the word "gentlemen" being appropriate for this almost exclusively male enclave). The gentlemen were walking through the draft word by word.

The basic concept behind EBONE was that all organizations signing the memorandum would make some form of contribution in return for being able to use the backbone. Some would contribute lines or routers, others would contribute people, and a few would even contribute money.

All the resources would be a loan to EBONE. At the end of 1992, everything (except the money, of course) would revert back to the contributors. The hope was that by the beginning of 1993 some formal group would be in place to handle the pan-European backbone and EBONE would be unnecessary.

One of the biggest items of debate was who would or should be the parent organization that would replace EBONE in 1993. Some wanted the Réseaux Associés pour la Recherche Européenne (RARE), the association of research networking groups in Europe, to play a role. Others wanted no such thing. Kees Neggers continually refocused the discussion on 1992, emphasizing that EBONE was making no decisions about anything past the one-year interim ad hoc network.

The EBONE backbone, like the NSFNET, would have no directly attached users. It would be connected to regional systems, such as SURFnet, which in turn would be connected to users. The backbone would be a diamond, connecting four major European cities. On at least two points on the diamond there would be links to the U.S. (A few months later, the initial 1992 topology was finally determined to be five major hubs—London, Montpellier, CERN, Amsterdam, and Stockholm—connected with 256 kbps to 512 kbps links and with three links to the U.S.)

The network, unlike NSFNET, would have no restrictions on the content of traffic. Although targeted for the benefit of academic and research use, commercial traffic could pass over the backbone and it was up to each regional network to determine an appropriate use policy. Likewise, although EBONE was envisioned primarily as a TCP/IP backbone, it was explicitly multiprotocol. An OSI "pilot service" was listed in the draft memo as one type of traffic, and others were alluded to.

Much of the wording of the memo was quite delicate. For example, EBONE was described as providing "value-added open networking services." Why these particular words?

Well, networks are the domain of PTTs in Europe. If you leave out the word "value-added," you tread on the turf of the PTT. Likewise with the word "open." Many countries had decided that open networks (i.e., OSI) were crucial and they would not participate in EBONE unless the word open was used.

Other types of wordsmithing at the meeting reflected the cultural differences of the 35 participants. For example, the backbone had been described as being "redundant." In England, when you fire somebody, you "make them redundant." "Resilient" proved to be a better word.

Lunch at the zoo consisted of frantic huddles among various factions. While I enjoyed a delightful buffet of eel and paté, others were desperately trying to forge a consensus.

Issues like the role of DECnet proved to be especially tough. Some people wanted to allow DECnet Phase IV traffic across the backbone. Others said that this wasn't necessary as DECnet Phase V would be able to use the ISO CLNS service. It was finally decided not to decide. DECnet traffic could cross the backbone if the two ends of a link decided it was allowed and it didn't adversely impact the operation of the backbone.

Carrying DECnet traffic was in some ways a foregone conclusion. Some of the links being contributed to EBONE were multiplexed into underlying lines. These underlying lines were not an EBONE issue and could carry DECnet, SNA, and any other kinds of traffic.

EBONE was clearly a chicken-and-egg situation. Many organizations would be unable to persuade their management to join until the consortium existed. The consortium wouldn't exist until enough organizations joined.

At the end of the day, with all the words finalized, Kees Neggers went around the table and asked people to tell the group if they would join, and, if so, what their contribution would be. To start things off, SURFnet would donate ECU 300,000 (U.S. $369,000) worth of lines, routers, and people.

Others joined in. The Spanish network would help the line costs of the backbone and would donate 35 percent of a person. Telecom Netherlands, if the EC approved, would provide a gateway to IXI, the large European X.25 network funded by the Commission.

Dennis Jennings at UCD would use the IXI links to reach EBONE, as would many of the smaller countries. Dennis also had an unusual contribution of money. He offered ECU 10 per full time academic staff member at University College Dublin, for a total of ECU 8,000 (U.S. $9,840). Not a huge sum, but Dennis pointed out that if every university in Europe adopted his formula, the network would have a budget of ECU 10 million per year.

Many groups were unable to commit immediately. Brian Carpenter, head of networking at CERN, the international physics laboratory, had to get approval from all his member countries and would ultimately end up "supporting" EBONE instead of formally signing the memorandum. The European BITNET, EARN, wanted to commit a line to CUNY in New York, but had to wait until its board met to commit formally.

On the opposite side of the room from Kees Neggers was Harry Clasper, the representative from IBM. IBM ran EASInet, a large European network. Its contribution of lines would be a significant addition to EBONE.

Throughout the day, Harry Clasper had been a vocal participant. Dressed in a regulation IBM pinstripe suit, he had been carefully tracking the proceedings. When the question of contributions reached him, he began speaking in a quiet voice and the room strained to hear him.

" I'm disappointed that this is not as open as it could be, and therefore IBM Europe is reserving its position at this time." IBM had substantial SNA traffic in EASInet and was clearly worried that if they joined the EASInet, sites might have problems.

Even with IBM sitting on the fence, however, it was clear that there was enough to make EBONE work. After IBM, groups like EUnet and NORDUnet added substantial contributions.

Finally, the end of the table was reached. The last person to speak was Bernhard Stockman from NORDUnet, also an active participant in the IETF. NORDUnet had already made known its contribution, but Bernhard had one thing to add.

"I will take everything you contribute and turn it into something that works." Bernhard would help form the Ebone Action Team, the engineers who would try to rationalize the contributions into a network.

With EBONE becoming a virtual reality (it would still take several months to get all the pieces in order), Kees Neggers made one more round around the table to see if anybody would be interested in being on the management committee. Harry Clasper from IBM raised his hand.

"If IBM were to commit, I would like to be on the management committee."

Everybody laughed and the meeting was adjourned. A half-dozen of us took a tram to the railway station to have a few beers and conduct a post mortem. Kees Neggers, Harry Clasper, Dennis Jennings, and myself sat with some beers while Kees and Dennis worked on the IBM position. Harry Clasper, like some pin-striped corporate Buddha, sat quietly and drank his beer.

Finally, Kees left to catch his train to Belgium and Harry, Dennis and I all boarded the express train to the Schiphol airport. We were cutting it a bit close, but the 18:26 train left us just enough time.

"Don't worry," Dennis reassured us, "you can set your watch by the Dutch trains."

I looked out the window as 18:26 came and went. Finally, ten minutes later, an announcement came across the intercom in Dutch and people start gathering things and got off the train.

A mob of 100 or so people all sprinted over to another track to catch the local train. On the local, we began doing mental arithmetic. The conversation quickly went from European infrastructure to travel horror stories then to nervous silence.

Arriving at the airport train station at 7:10 for 7:30 flights, the three of us took off in three separate directions, each of us doing an O.J. Simpson imitation. Despite an airline clerk who gave new meaning to the term lethargic (although that was certainly not the word I used at the time), I made it to my plane for London.

Thursday morning I strolled from my seedy hotel room through soot-blackened streets to University College London to meet Steve Hardcastle-Kille. Steve is one of the two guiding lights behind the ISO Development Environment (ISODE), the other of course being the eminent Dr. Marshall T. Rose.

While Marshall concentrated on making a public-domain OSI implementation of the middle layers that can run over both TCP/IP and OSI stacks, Steve focused on the application layer. Through a prodigious string of Internet Drafts and RFCs, Steve helped to turn the X.400 and X.500 standards into workable services.

It is somewhat ironic that some of the best work on ISO standards (and the most popular implementation) should have come out of the TCP/IP world. By providing public-domain OSI code, Hardcastle-Kille and Rose had pushed these standards from paper and theory to things that people use in their day-to-day work.

If you want a standard that works in the real world, it needs to interact with the existing base of services. Some of the early work Steve did was to define the functionality for X.400/SMTP gateways. Later, Steve focused on X.500.

UCL, under Steve's leadership, integrated X.500 into ISODE in an implementation known as Quipu, after the fringes of knotted cords used to keep numerical records by the Quechuan Indians of the Incan empire. It was traditional to name each country's master Directory Service Agent after an animal, preferably one found in South America. Finland's DSA is the jaguar, Germany the puma, and Marshall T. Rose contributed the alpaca for the U.S. In a historic decision, however, as a tribute to X.500's growing maturity, South American animal names were abandoned in favor of monikers marketing could pronounce.

X.500 directories are structured as a tree. Each part of the tree is managed by a DSA (although it is important to note that the directory and the DSA are carefully defined as separate concepts allowing a particular part of the tree to be provided by multiple vendors).

The root for the world is the Giant Tortoise at UCL. In addition to being the world root, this DSA is also the root DSA for the United Kingdom.

The United Kingdom had been aggressively deploying X.500. The Joint Network Team (JNT) began funding X.500 by giving universities a Sun/4 to act as a DSA. By November 1991, 40 organizations in the U.K. had DSAs serving them with a total of 54,387 registered entries. By the end of 1991, all 55 universities in the U.K. were scheduled to have their Sun workstations.

UCL also functions as the coordinator for the PARADISE ES-PRIT project. PARADISE stands for Piloting an International Directory Service. (A cute acronym is one of the prerequisites for European Commission funding.)

Under the coordination of PARADISE in Europe and similar projects in the U.S., the global directory had grown by November 1991 to reach 1,212 organizations, 144 DSAs, and 421,552 directory entries.

The DSA is the X.500 component responsible for some part of the directory tree. To access X.500, users have a Directory User Agent (DUA). A couple of dozen user interfaces have been defined to interact with Quipu, ranging from a simple white pages lookup utility (FRED) to a full-fledged management interface (DISH) to Macintosh and X-Windows based graphical interfaces.

To make X.500 work in the real world, several extensions were needed from the standards as originally defined. The X.500 specification assumes a homogenous OSI-based network where any DUA can set up an application layer association over a worldwide network to reach any DSA.

In many places, a homogenous network is not realistic. The U.K., for example, had long supported the Coloured Book protocols, although TCP/IP support had recently been added. Many ISODE implementations run on top of TCP/IP, adding another important environment. It is interesting to note that many places that use ISODE on top of TCP/IP still have as an official policy a "migration" to true OSI. They have yet to learn that birds migrate, not corporations.

London

One of the first requirements for the deployment of X.500 was a relaying mechanism. If a DUA in the TCP/IP world needs to reach a DSA in the OSI world, it can ask a DSA connected to both worlds to relay the request.

A second key area addressed was replication. X.500 assumes one DSA is responsible for one piece of data. If a DUA needs to reach a DSA in another country, it is possible that many intermediate DSAs must be contacted as the user climbs the name tree to the root and then back down towards the target (although an intelligent DSA implementation would presumably cache some of this information). Replicating some of that upper-level information makes it much easier to find target organizations and is a significant performance enhancement.

In addition to replication and relaying, Steve has been especially active in helping to forge a consensus on a common schema for the directory. After all, it doesn't do much good to find an organization if the information it keeps is non-standard. A common schema contains the definition for standard objects, such as a person, and standard attributes common to those objects, such as a person's favorite drink or e-mail address.

Just before I arrived in London, the Internet Activities board had issued a carefully drafted RFC endorsing X.500 as a strategic direction for the Internet community. If that stragtegy took hold, it would be a significant shift away from the Domain Name System (DNS).

The transition between older name systems, such as DNS and the venerable WHOIS service, would certainly be the key to the success or failure of X.500 on the Internet. DNS adherents cite two problems with X.500: the complexity of the namespace and the slowness of implementations.

X.500 structures names in a well-defined tree, with objects typically going from country to management domain to organization to organizational unit to name. Some feel that a rigid hierarchy is a key flaw. Steve argues strongly that the opposite is true.

One rigid hierarchy is indeed the basis for X.500; however, alternative hierarchies can be defined on a local or regional basis with pointers into the basic tree. An alternative tree, based on the Domain Name System, for example, can be used to point to X.500 objects.

A single rigid hierarchy does have some advantages, particularly in the area of management. With a well-defined schema, people know exactly where to put an object, making management of the namespace similar in different areas.

Before X.500 can operate as a truly global directory, it needs much better performance. One of the major problems for performance is that X.500 implementations must carry around the baggage of the fully general middle layers of OSI. Although a skinny stack has been defined, most X.500 implementations support all the features of the session, presentation, and ACSE services, including those developed for other networking paradigms such as transactions processing. For example, X.500 makes no use of the checkpointing and synchronization features of the session layer.

A light-weight Directory Access Protocol could go a long way towards providing faster DSAs. The lightweight protocol would map OSI down to a needed subset. If you need full generality, as in the case of communicating with a DUA or DSA that doesn't support the lightweight protocol, a separate process can provide the translation.

After spending a morning with Steve, I started making the rounds at UCL. UCL is highly unusual among computer science departments in that it emphasizes networks as a valid area of research. In fact, networking takes prominence at UCL (the school was the first international member of the ARPANET).

UCL's prominence is due in no small part to the influence of the department chairman, Peter T. Kirstein, known around the world by his login name of PTK. An old joke in the networking community is that when in Europe you have to deal with the PTTs, but in England, you have to deal with the PTK.

No visit to UCL would be complete without a courtesy call to Peter, so I left Steve's office at one end of the building to pay my visit to Peter Kirstein. Peter's current passion (and a source of substantial funding) was the Office Document Architecture (ODA), so we spent a half-hour talking about his testing of ODA packages, and his cooperative projects with groups like Bellcore and the American

Chemical Abstracts to convert large databases into ODA to help spur the standard forward.

UCL is also active in many other areas of networking. Jon Crowcroft described his efforts to run video conferencing over the Internet. One researcher showed me his work on ISDN Primary Rate interfaces; another showed me new X.500 user interfaces running on soot-blackened terminals.

With my head swimming from networking vertigo, I left UCL to get a drink. I stepped into an old pub near the university, with some appropriately quaint name like The Queen's Foot or the Tam and Mutton. Settling down with my pint of bitter, I looked up to see that a karaoke competition was scheduled to start soon. Feeling that I could miss this particular event, I finished my pint in record time and went off for some Indian food.

Friday morning, I headed north to Tampere in Finland. With three hours to kill in the Helsinki airport before my plane left, I idled away the time trying to decide between the sauteed reindeer with lingonberries and the elk pate with rowanberry gelatin. It was 4 P.M. and the sun had just set.

I was met at the Tampere airport by Vesa Parkkari, a man I often refer to as the Finnish Bill Gates. Of course, Vesa has a much more effusive personality than Bill Gates, although I confess my only contact with Mr. Bill has been through interviews in the trade press, which could make anybody look boring.

The next morning, I got up early enough to watch the sun rise at 7:30, then had a leisurely breakfast of pickled herring and brown bread. It was Saturday morning and evidently some sort of holiday in Finland. Of course, nobody had any idea what the holiday was for, but it was enough to close most of the shops in town.

It wasn't enough, though, to slow down Vesa. At 10 A.M., he brought me down to the company he founded, Mikrokonsultit Oy. The name is a bit of a misnomer, as they didn't have anything to do with microcomputers and didn't do any consulting. (Since my visit, they changed the name of the company to Relevantum Oy.)

In the late 1970s, however, Vesa was heavily involved with both microcomputers and consulting. He took early Motorola chips, made them into microcomputers, and then used the systems to design custom applications. One system was developed by Vesa for NESTE, the state monopoly oil company. Involving 2 square meters of electronics (and lots and lots of assembly language programs), the system coordinated the weighing of all lorries coming into the refinery to load oil, printing all the necessary lists and other documents.

Another, system, developed by Raimo Harju, his copartner, was still being used. The system takes raw timber and figures out the most efficient way to saw up the log to produce the most lumber. In an economy where 30 to 40 percent of GNP is based on forestry, this system proved quite popular.

Vesa had the same problem with consulting that others all over the world face. He did the programming, and thus bore the risk when a job took an order of magnitude more time to complete than planned. A fact of consulting, however, is that you often end up several subcontracts deep in order to get a job. Vesa bore the risks, but others higher in the food chain were making all the money.

Vesa decided instead to give seminars about putting microcomputers together. He gave a few at the Tampere Institute of Technology, and the demand quickly overwhelmed the university facilities. This was obviously a worthwhile business to be in.

Vesa and his colleague Raimo Harju went into business. At first there was no company, just a couple of guys in a hotel conference room. The hotel couldn't handle the idea of a meeting without a company name, so they made one up: Mikroboys.

Mikroboys became the more dignified Mikrokonsultit and business flourished. In the early 80s, however, the prepackaged PC came into being and Vesa saw that there would be a limited future for very low-level courses like his. In 1982, they switched the company to an exclusive focus on data communications seminars.

Seminars are a funny business. Almost everything is a fixed cost. You spend a month or two (or more) to develop the seminar. Then you print and mail brochures. Then you wait.

If enough people sign up, usually something like 15 to 20, you break even. Everything after that is gravy. Well, in 1983, the gravy began for Vesa. Finland had just started up two different public X.25 networks and Mikrokonsultit had a hands-on practical X.25 course. They began teaching seminars to 70 people or more on a regular basis.

Based on the early success, the company expanded and now has 13 different seminars. Finland, with a population of 5 million people, is a small country. Yet it is big enough to support Mikrokonsultit.

There are two keys to the early X.25 seminar success, and both factors hold for the later courses. First, courses are based on technology that is available and cost effective. In the X.25 realm, for example, Finland has two public data networks in heavy competition with each other supporting over 3,000 hosts. Leased lines are cheap enough in Finland that it is estimated that there are another 3,000 hosts on private X.25 networks.

The second key to Mikrokonsultit's success is that the seminars are hands-on. In a 5-day X.25 course, for example, users not only learn the theory of X.25 but how to configure Packet Assembler/Disassemblers (PADs) and hosts and how to run applications.

Vesa took me through some of the exercises that the instructor does in the X.25 class. We took a PC X.25 card, installed it, configured it, then loaded up the X.25 and PAD software. We then set up links to Russia, China, the U.S., and the United Arab Emirates. We looked at a network analyzer to analyze PAD and X.25 parameters. We looked at tariff tables and calculated breakeven points for leased lines versus packet networks. We ran SNA 3270 and X.400 over X.25 to real hosts.

Other courses on subjects such as X.400, TCP/IP, internetworks and routers, and SNA all take the same hands-on approach. Dragging Cisco routers, PCs, analyzers, and other equipment along means that you can't just slap an instructor on a plane and have him read the words on slides to the class. You need people who can both teach and use the technology and, in the case of Mikrokonsultit, are fluent in Finnish.

All day Vesa led me from one room to another and from one topic to another.

"Now we will do X.25 demonstration."

"Now we will discuss DECnet Phase V."

"Now you can use the Internet to read your mail."

At the end of the day, with my eyes glazing over, he had a new assignment.

"Now we will go to my castle and do Finnish sauna."

The training market had been kind to Vesa and he had recently bought a castle. Much as I wanted to see this castle, I was torn. I had visions of being thrown naked out of a scalding sauna into a moat filled with ice.

We arrived at the Parkkari castle, and Vesa showed me around from room to room. While his wife Pirjo Sistola and their three year old daughter took their sauna, we polished off a bottle of champagne. Finally, the fateful moment arrived.

Tampere

"Now we will do Finnish sauna."

I tried to demur, but Vesa made it quite clear that failing to participate would be considered a grave form of national insult. After a shower, I entered a very, very hot room.

Vesa picked up a bucket and threw ladles of water onto the stones, producing blasts of steam. What I had thought of as very, very hot became an order of magnitude hotter. While Vesa kept throwing ladles of water onto the rocks, he explained the seven levels of the Finnish Sauna Reference Model.

I was experiencing level 1. Level 2 seemed to have something to do with more water on the coals. In level 3, you exit the sauna periodically and rub ice cubes over your body, then jump back in. Level 4 consists of whipping yourself with strips of birch bark to stimulate the skin. In level 5, you leave the sauna and run outside to the lake. Level 6 has you roll around in the snow. Level 7 was some form of Finnish national secret and, quite frankly, I didn't really feel I needed to know.

□

Sunday morning was spent discussing the Internet with Vesa's staff. We speculated on the motives of ANS and the fate of the NREN, after which I spent the afternoon taking a walk around the Tampere lake.

That evening, I was met by Juha Heinänen, one of the creators of the Finnish Internet and an important technical influence for the whole Nordic region. Juha took me to "Salud," a Spanish restaurant, where we feasted on a carpaccio of wild boar and an entree of alligator served with a coconut and papaya sauce.

Juha began setting up UUCP links in Finland in 1982. At the time, Finland had a large X.25 network for connecting the University VAXen, and UUCP was used to transfer mail and news over phone lines within the computer science community.

In 1984, having finished his doctorate, he went to the University of Southwestern Louisiana for a postdoctoral fellowship. While there, he helped set up a TCP/IP network for Louisiana and, as he tells it, enjoyed many Cajun parties.

Coming back to Tampere, he spent four years as an Associate Professor at the Tampere University of Technology. At the University, he was asked to join the steering committee for FUNET, the Finnish University Network.

There was a problem, though. FUNET was basically DECnet running on X.25 and Juha had a Sun workstation. He persuaded FUNET that their role should be to connect LANs together, not VAXen.

At the time, there were no multiprotocol routers, so FUNET became a network based on wide-area bridges. A year later, however, Juha went to a USENIX conference and saw a couple of guys standing behind a small table.

This was the Cisco booth and the company had just added DECnet support to their boxes. Juha came back to Finland ready to buy Cisco boxes, but couldn't find a distributor. He convinced a salesman at a local company to start carrying Cisco and two months later FUNET had become a multiprotocol network based on routers.

After his success with the University network, Juha became a consultant. His clients include FUNET, as well as Telecom Finland, the country's nominal PTT.

Finland, unlike most European countries, has considerable competition in telecommunications. At one point, in fact, there were over 700 telephone companies. In 1991, there were over 50, each serving a small area. In addition, there was Telecom Finland.

Telecom Finland was state owned when I visited, but was soon to be incorporated. It had two functions. It served as the local telephone company in areas where there are no others. It also functioned as the long distance telephone company. Even in the long distance market, it already had competition in data and would soon have so for voice traffic.

In all cases, Telecom Finland received no special treatment and competition was encouraged by the Ministry. Data networking was especially competitive. Finland had two commercial IP networks: Datanet, run by Telecom Finland, and Lanlink, run by a consortium of the smaller companies.

Both Datanet and Lanlink had connections to FUNET. FUNET, in turn, was part of NORDUnet, the regional academic network linking five Nordic countries. Datanet had another link into Infolan, an international IP service owned by a consortium of PTTs. Infolan, in turn, was connected to PSI's commercial network in the U.S.

All told, Finland had over 10,000 Internet hosts. This was 10 percent of all European hosts on the Internet, far in excess of Finland's proportion of the European population.

Both Datanet and Lanlink differed from their commercial American cousins in a very important respect. PSInet, CERFnet, and other U.S. networks were open networks. When you joined, you could talk to any other IP host. Of course, that host might not want to talk to you, but the backbone delivered packets up to the customer router or host.

In the Finnish commercial networks, access was explicitly controlled in the backbone. When a customer started up service they explicitly identified a set of hosts. Routers at the edge of the backbone enforced the policy with access control lists.

Datanet and Lanlink were thus more than just IP networks. They actually formed a sort of multiprotocol, LAN interconnection service. When I went to talk to Juha, Datanet was in transition. It was just beginning to provide the generic LAN interconnection service in a different way.

The old model consisted of a border router at the edge of the backbone, which in turn was connected to a router at the customer site. The backbone itself consisted of a large number of E1 lines running at 2 Mbps. As Juha explained it, "no need to scrimp on backbone capacity. After all, we are the telephone company."

The new model of Datanet was based on Frame Relay. The Cisco router at the customer site, equipped with a Frame Relay interface, established a permanent virtual circuit (PVC) to another router on the edge of the network. If a user wanted to send TCP/IP traffic onto the Internet, for example, a permanent virtual circuit would be set up to either the FUNET or Infolan router. Traffic from Novell, DECnet, or any other protocol could use the same PVC to send data.

Juha saw a number of advantages in moving the public network down from the network layer into a level 2 data-link service. First, bridges can be supported on a multi-user network. Bridges broadcast all packets to the other side. Since Datanet supports multiple private virtual networks, in the old model there was always the question of where to broadcast the packets. With permanent virtual circuits, the customer answers that question.

Subnetworks are equally difficult to support in a general-purpose Internet, like the old model. If a customer had a single class B address split over multiple sites, an IP-based internetwork would not be able to figure where to route the packets.

There is an even more difficult problem with a level 3 network, the question of policy routing. Let's say that there are two Datanet customers, one commercial and one a researcher, wishing to set up a connection to the same destination in the U.S. The researcher would want to use the FUNET route and, in theory, the commercial user would need to go over the Infolan path.

When a packet from the first user comes in, a route to the destination would be cached in a router. Subsequent packets, regardless of the source address, would all go by the same route. Under the Frame Relay model, the user would set up a permanent virtual circuit to the edge of either FUNET or Infolan. Note that the policy routing dilemma may show up further down the road, but as far as the local (or national) data network is concerned, policy routing decisions have been eliminated.

Policy routing protocols are one of the most difficult issues in the Internet. Many are advocating the solution that Juha chose of simplifying the network layer topology in favor of a general, public data link service such as Frame Relay or SMDS. Others would argue that moving the public network down to the data link solves problems today, but is a solution that will not scale well as the scope of the network increases.

For Juha's employers, Frame Relay certainly solved several immediate needs. It avoided the policy routing dilemma for TCP/IP, it supported a variety of non-TCP protocols over the same infrastructure, and it did away with access control lists.

Monday morning, I stopped by Juha's laboratory at Telecom Finland to see the network and read my mail. Finland is so well connected that I got better response time reading my mail on a Telnet session back to Colorado than I got when I went in locally over a

9,600 bps dialup line. In fact, Vesa Parkkari had demonstrated FTAM file transfers on top of TP4 and the CLNS providing end-to-end performance from California to Tampere of 38,000 bytes per second.

I then spent the rest of Monday making my way from Tampere to Helsinki to London to Paris, with the obligatory many-hour layover at London Heathrow. It was a relief to arrive at my familiar hotel in Paris.

Tuesday morning, I took the Paris Métro over to the offices of *Communications Week International*. The one editor I knew let me in, showed me his boss's office, then promptly left for the U.S. The rest of the morning, I furiously banged away at a PC, trying to get enough columns written to stave off my editors in New York (and pay for some dinners in Paris).

After finishing enough pithy columns to pay the Maitre d', I went to the nearby bistro for a lunch of chicken Riesling, ratatouille, and a bit of wine. Sauntering back to the office, I had only to figure out how to submit the columns to the head office.

Of course, the menu option on the PC labeled "MCI Mail" did absolutely nothing. I knocked on a few random editor's doors, but was met by frantic stares and hurried brushoffs. My problem, of course, was that I was wearing a suit and was thus mistaken for one of the all-too-frequent employees from the U.S. that came in to use the office for a day in order to write off their trip to Paris on their income taxes.

Needless to say, the editor with a deadline to meet has no time to work with these corporate junketeers who come in to do some "work." The only work these visits involved would be for the locals. Finally, I convinced an editor that I was only masquerading as a respectable person and actually did write for a living. I couldn't quite bring myself to take on the identity of "trade press" or "journalist" but it was finally established that I was a "guest columnist/consultant."

The editor became quite helpful and took my disk and disappeared into her office to perform some magic submission ritual into the Atex system in New York. I asked her why any PC couldn't perform the same operation.

She explained that a team of consultants had been working assiduously on the problem, but some mysterious incompatibilty problem had prevented fully operational capabilities from being attained. Since I had a couple of hours to kill while waiting for a call from London, I decided to take a look at this mysterious modem malady.

I went back to the PC I had been working on and started up Procomm. It seemed to be installed correctly, although, frankly, it is just about impossible to install it incorrectly. I then pulled up the dialing menu and picked MCI from the directory.

Nothing. Next step was to pull up a simple terminal emulation screen and type "AT."

"OK," the modem responded.

Hmm. Obviously there was either a fully functioning modem or a pretty good modem emulator on this system.

Walking around to the back of the desk, my highly trained eye spotted the problem. The modem wasn't plugged into the wall. Sure enough, a few minutes later, I was reading my MCI mail.

Why would an Internet explorer keep an MCI Mail account? There are two reasons. First, the telex gateway on MCI Mail is wonderful. It allows me to communicate with people in countries like China, which have very limited e-mail capabilities. The telex gateway actually allows me to send and receive telexes.

There is a more important reason, however. There are a few people with whom I correspond, mostly members of the trade press who haven't figured out how to reach my Internet mailbox from their MCI Mail accounts. If I don't keep an MCI Mail account, I'm reduced to sending faxes back and forth to these people.

It has often puzzled me how people who spend their life covering computers can know so little about how they work. There are some exceptions of course. The editor of *Communications Week*, for example, has both Internet and MCI mailboxes, and knows the difference between them.

People like him are, unfortunately, very much the exception in the trade press. The features editor of one prominent networking newspaper, for example, was unable to figure out how to use MCI Mail, yet persisted in editing "in-depth" articles about Broadband ISDN, NFS, and a host of other technically sophisticated issues.

So how does the trade press write in-depth pieces? All too often, the articles are simply a rehash of brochures and briefings. I remember a time I did a feature piece on DECnet Phase V for one of the monthly publications.

I met the senior editor assigned to "work with me" in Boston. Wearing a yellow power tie and driving a Detroit muscle car, he told me that the piece lacked "punch." So he rewrote it. Close to deadline, somebody decided I ought to have a look at it. The new and improved lead explained how DECnet Phase V would be available on systems ranging from VMS and Ultrix to the Macintosh and PDP.

Macintosh and PDP?

Running DECnet Phase V on a PDP is kind of like trying to simulate the weather on a PC/AT. Running on a Macintosh, though highly unlikely, was theoretically possible, but in my stacks and stacks of reading on the subject, I had not heard of any such project.

In a not so gentle manner, I explained to my senior editor that having read a stack of functional specifications five feet high, it was my considered technical opinion that running on a PDP was unlikely if not impossible. Did my esteemed editor have a source for his information.

"I was briefed by marketing," he replied.

I called up the Senior Executive Technology Editor and told him he was free to run the DECnet piece, but I would prefer, indeed insist, that my name not be on it.

So he fired me and killed the piece.

Technical knowledge is considered to be of minimal importance, indeed often a liability by the computer and communications trade press. Again, there are exceptions. For example, Kelly Jackson, formerly with *Communications Week*, is known for insightful coverage of data communications issues. There are others, but they are too rare.

People with degrees in journalism are often hired straight out of school, and are given no time to acquire any technical knowledge. Frequent contact with senior executives gives junior journalists a feeling that they are "part of the scene." All too often, though, they are simply manipulated and fed a carefully composted salmagundi of marketing manure.

The cycle feeds itself. The executives get used to getting good press based on marketing hype instead of real information. The journalists keep feeling like they are getting the real story and feel increasingly confident and powerful.

There are two solutions to this quandary. First, technically astute people need to write more. People like Marshall T. Rose, who devotes part of his time to writing books, are all too rare. The technology does no good if people don't know how it works and it is the responsibility of the developers to document their work.

The second answer is for the trade press to acquire a bit more knowledge. Being able to use electronic mail, for example, should be a prerequisite to getting a piece published and certainly won't cause a writer to transform into a technogeek.

❐

Wednesday morning, I sat outside my hotel and waited to be picked up by Pascal Renaud, head of the computer group at ORSTOM, a national research institution in France.

ORSTOM's mission is to work with researchers in developing countries. It is an unusual institution in that half of its permanent staff are outside France, scattered over 41 sites around the world.

Twenty minutes late, early for Paris, a tiny car zipped up on the sidewalk outside of my hotel. Pascal jumped out and we introduced ourselves. As we darted through the streets of Paris, I handed him a copy of STACKS. He was pleased.

He was so pleased, in fact, he commenced to leaf through the book as he drove. I had visions of my own book causing my death. While this sort of untimely morbid vision had certainly occurred to me before, I had always assumed I would meet my end at the hands of an OSF hit squad, not in a ten horsepower Renault. Of course, the OSF would use different tactics, probably boring me to death.

As we passed the Louvre, Pascal finished my book and we started talking about ORSTOM. ORSTOM was founded right after World War II as a think tank devoted to the French colonies. While much of the research concerns questions such as agriculture and health, it is nonetheless not a development agency. It focuses instead on basic research issues, such as how to stop the spread of diseases like malaria and sleeping sickness.

Many of the ORSTOM research centers are located in former French colonies. For example, most of the 17 African centers are located in French West Africa, in countries like Niger and the Ivory Coast. A typical research center, such as the ones in Niamey, Niger, and Lomé, Benin, employs 50 people. Others, such as the center in Dakar, Senegal, employs 100 French and 200 African researchers. All told, the institute has a budget of FF 900 million (U.S. $150 million), employs 880 researchers and 720 support staff, and has offices in Africa, South America, Asia, and Oceania.

So how do you provide computing support to such a group? In 1985, Pascal Renaud was brought in to head the computer support group. At the time, resources consisted of a motley assortment of systems like an HP1000 and a Honeywell mini.

"I tossed out everything," Pascal said with a smile. "It was a bit of a fight, but I got rid of it all."

The basic applications needed for ORSTOM were typical of many scientific institutions, including statistical analysis, a bibliographic database, and analysis of satellite images. There were, however, two quite unusual requirements. First, with 41 locations all over the world, communication was vital.

To make the communication issue even more important was the issue of support. Many ORSTOM sites were located in places with some of the world's worst telecommunications. In addition, most sites didn't have trained personnel. Setting up and maintaining equipment in such locations was a real challenge.

After a bit of digging around, ORSTOM settled on Sun workstations. Within France, the systems were hooked together using TCP/IP over X.25 and were part of the French Internet.

Keeping links up 24 hours a day to Africa would not be practical. Some countries turned off electricity at night. In addition, tariffs were high enough that a call to Paris 24 hours per day would be prohibitive. TCP/IP also had some problems in such an environment. Running TCP/IP over a 2,400 bps link, the wizardry of Van Jacobson notwithstanding, just doesn't work.

The solution was UUCP. In some countries, such as Togo, X.25 networks were available and were often much newer than the voice network. A SunLink board connected the workstation to Togopac at 1,200 bps. An X.75 link hooked Togopac to the French Transpac. The UUCP F protocol ran on top of X.25 and calls were placed once or twice a day to transfer mail.

The normal UUCP G protocol, designed for very bad lines, is highly resilient but also inefficient. The F protocol has one checksum per file and is thus more appropriate for the relatively high-cost, high-quality X.25 links.

Other places didn't have X.25. In Ouagadougou, for example, ORSTOM simply placed a daily call to the Montpellier hub in France. The UUCP G protocol was used to transfer mail over the dialup link.

This network was called RIO, which stood alternatively for Réseau Informatique de l'ORSTOM or Réseau Intertropical d'Ordinateurs. Connectivity to the rest of the Internet was provided through a TCP/IP link into France's FNET and UUCP links to EUnet.

The service on the network (at least the UUCP portions) was simply e-mail. A pre- and post-processor for mail allowed accents to be included in 7-bit ASCII. UUENCODE allowed transfer of PC and Macintosh binary files.

When a new site was added to the network, Pascal Renaud and local researchers would host a conference. Conferences were typically well attended and typically included government officials, PTT staff, any local non-governmental organizations (e.g., the UN), and university researchers.

ORSTOM had a policy of allowing any of these people to use RIO. This open policy helped make ORSTOM part of the local community and helped spread mail access to many new parts of the world.

Invariably, Pascal relates, somebody at one of these conferences would want to know if they could access RIO from the PC in their office instead of walking over to the ORSTOM offices. As far as Renaud was concerned, he had no problem with remote access.

Unfortunately, placing a telephone call in many of these countries can be a torturous experience. After Pascal would explain that remote access was possible, but would involve a modem and a call, most researchers would shrug their shoulders and say "thanks anyway, I'll walk in."

Supporting scientific computing in such a far-flung network is quite a challenge. Only a few sites had real computer support people. Dakar, for example, had one staffer to support the 15 Suns at that site. For other facilities, ORSTOM had an interesting support structure.

In France, military service is compulsory. An alternative, however is a system somewhat like the U.S. Peace Corps. ORSTOM, as a national laboratory, receives an annual quota of young engineers and puts them to work maintaining computers in far-away places.

With several hundred users and an open-door policy, RIO is evidence that some of the most important work in the Internet community is done far on the periphery, removed even from the TCP/IP protocols that many use to define the core.

At the core of the Internet, the issue is one of adding new classes of users, such as recent K-12 initiatives. RIO serves an equally vital, if not more important role of adding new countries to the global village.

Leaving Pascal, I went to a café near my hotel and had a fine cassoulet of snails for lunch. There, over a half bottle of Beaujolais Villages, I pondered the immense difficulty of spreading the Internet into some of the places Renaud had to work.

A few years ago, I travelled to a some of these sites: Niamey in Niger, Lomé in Benin, and Abidjan in the Ivory Coast. In the cities, such as Niamey, there is a passable infrastructure. Phones work much of the time and with a UPS, power regulators, and security guards you can keep a computer system going much of the day. In regional cities in Niger, however, things were much tougher. Yet, these regional cities have universities, international aid groups, hospitals, and research centers.

Some would argue that high technology, such as computer networks, are inappropriate in countries where per capita income is measured in the hundreds of dollars and the basic infrastructure, like roads, is crumbling.

In such an environment, technology should be appropriately used, not avoided. Agricultural aid workers, for example, need to consult their colleagues overseas. Likewise, doctors should be able to work as part of a global community instead of being left alone in an isolated outpost.

Voice communication over a telephone system is not an effective technology in these circumstances. International telephone calls take a very long time to place and are often terminated abruptly. Calls are expensive, and you never know if your party will be there. Voice calls are a point-to-point communications technique and do not allow appeals to large groups.

It is precisely in these outlying areas that the Internet is most needed. Messages can be prepared at any time and then batched for transmission. In many countries, the X.25 networks are far superior (i.e., far newer) than their voice counterparts.

Technologies like electronic mail are important in the developed countries by helping us do better research or provide better education to children. In countries like Niger, electronic mail can support education and research, but it can also do something much more important. It can help save lives.

Thursday morning, I got up early so I could reach the Gare de Lyon in time to take the 7:25 Train à Grande Vitesse (TGV) to Geneva. The TGV is the French high-speed train, taking only three hours to get to Geneva, compared to six hours on a normal train and four on a plane (by the time you get to and from airports).

I soon found myself on the Rue de Mont Blanc in Geneva with plenty of time to spare before my long-awaited audience with Dr. Pekka Tarjanne, Secretary-General of the ITU. The purpose of my meeting was two-fold: to keep the standards server alive and lobby for further changes. This was the only day of the month he would be able to see me, hence the special visit.

Calling on people like the Secretary-General is a funny kind of affair. You typically get only a few minutes, most of which is spent in pleasantries, and I don't ever expect much to be decided. Yet, it is a vital step to take in an international bureaucracy like the ITU.

First, I went up to the 12th floor to see Tony Rutkowski. While he finished sending out some mail messages, I wandered around his office looking at the stacks of paper lying all over the place. Occasionally, I would see multiple copies of some interesting report and grab a copy.

Meanwhile, Tony had assembled his own stack of paper for me, including copies of the slickly produced "Friends of Bruno" newsletter. The newsletter was rife with references to the Digital Resource Institute and "Project Leader Malamud." This institute thing was certainly taking on a life of its own. Even worse, I had been stuck with a title. The only title I usually get is "Mister" (and even that is somewhat rarely employed).

Finally, the time came for the meeting with Dr. Tarjanne. Tony ushered me up to the 14th floor. Now, I've been in some impressive offices before, but this one certainly took the cake.

The secretary's office and adjacent waiting rooms could easily have rented as a SF 15,000 (U.S. $10,000) per month apartment. The main office had a beautiful view of Lake Geneva and the Alps. It was lined with Persian rugs and was big enough to fit all 400 attendees at an IETF meeting.

Dr. Tarjanne came striding over from the other side of the office. While he walked over, I did mental calculations trying to figure out how many miles per day he must put in simply greeting visitors at each meeting.

Dr. Tarjanne was trained as a Finnish physicist. Active in politics, he rose to become head of the liberal party in Finland. As a member of the coalition government, he secured the appointment as head of Telecom Finland, the Finnish PTT and he was able, through an adroit political sense, to parlay that into his position at the ITU.

After reviewing the progress of Bruno and the 21 Sons of Bruno servers, we talked about the steps that would be needed to realize a truly global network that included developing countries and had a solid, well-managed infrastructure. Perhaps the ITU could play a role in helping that come about?

Tony and I then paid a similar visit to the Deputy Secretary-General to brief him on our visit with the Secretary-General. Mr. Jipguep, a former high official in Cameroon and considered the dean of the African telecommunications community, appeared to support the Bruno experiment.

Returning to Tony's office, we discussed who I should meet and brief on my return visit back to the ITU the next week. I suggested to Tony that he call across the street and extend an offer to have me brief them on the "experiment."

He called Mike Smith, an Irishman who heads up the information systems area. Tony relayed my offer, and hung up.

About five minutes later, Mike Smith called back. Tony listened for a minute and hung up the phone laughing.

"Larry Eicher *very much* wants to talk to you," he said, "I said you'd be delighted." Eicher was Secretary-General of ISO. I laughed and asked if I should bring my bulletproof tie.

I left Tony to take care of an important personal matter. No visit to Switzerland is ever complete without a stop at the Mercure chocolate shop. Picking up a nice assortment of champagne truffles, bittersweet bars filled with 90-proof Cognac, and various other forms of adult candy, I resisted the temptation to buy the 4.5 kilo-gram bar of Toblerone.

With the chocolate safely mailed back to the U.S., I took the TGV back to Paris, arriving after midnight at my hotel in Montparnasse. I ordered a taxi for 6, set my alarm for 5, packed my things, and went to sleep.

Friday morning, I took the first plane down to Nice to meet Christian Huitema, the first European member of the Internet Activities Board. One parochial American had referred to him as the first "alien" on the IAB, but in my view that title had long since been taken by one of the American members.

In Nice, I picked up my rental car and joined the morning grand prix doing at least double all posted speed limits. In Antibes, I took the turnoff for Sophia-Antipolis, the "French Silicon Valley." Sophia-Antipolis was founded 20 years ago as a joint venture between nine local towns, a regional government, and the Nice chamber of commerce. The regional group, the Departement des Alpes-Maritimes, contributes over half the money.

By 1991, the park had grown to over 700 firms, the majority in computers and communications. Air France keeps its central reservation system here, Digital keeps a major research center, and the EEC has the European Telecommunications Standards Institute (ETSI).

Sophia-Antipolis is also the site of one of the major centers of the Institut National de la Recherche en Informatique et Automatique (INRIA), the premier French computer science research institute and the home base of Christian Huitema.

Travelling too fast, I zoomed out of a roundabout and didn't see the INRIA sign. A few kilometers later, I saw a sign for INRA and turned in. The place was full of greenhouses. I had arrived at the Institut National de la Recherche Agronomique. Woops.

After a few more diversions, I found INRIA. INRIA, like OR-STOM, is a national research institution. It specializes in computer science and numerical methods and employs 900 staff in 5 locations. Each location is organized into a series of research projects.

At the Sophia-Antipolis site, there were a couple of dozen projects employing a little over 300 staff members. Three projects were in robotics, including work for the European Space Agency's Mars mission. Occasionally, the robot would take a tour around the building to test its navigation skills.

Christian headed a project in computer networks. When I finally made it into his office, he was explaining his work to a young German who was considering starting a Ph.D. at a nearby university and working at INRIA to do his research.

I spent the day with Christian, and by the end of the day I began to see why he had been named to the IAB. At the age of 22, Christian had no definite career plans, so he became a consultant. He did quite well, but found he was always doing the same thing and got bored.

He then joined the Centre National d'Etudes de Telecommunications (CNET). By 1985, he had received the Doctorate d'Etat, roughly equivalent to an assistant professor at a U.S. university. His thesis, part of the NADIR project, dealt with transport protocols for satellite links.

He had by then moved on to GIPSI, a French effort to build a workstation. CNET made the hardware, there was a port of UNIX, and the system even sported a graphical interface.

As part of the team working on GIPSI, Christian concentrated on networking. He invented an NFS-like remote disk protocol that worked directly on Ethernet. He also designed a version of X.25 that ran over Ethernet.

This modified X.25 was implemented by removing HDLC, since 802.3 already provided a satisfactory data link. Any transmission necessary was moved up into the link layer of X.25. The software even did call setup using an ARP-like mechanism. The calling station broadcast a call setup and the target station would respond.

The result was an X.25 running at over 500 kbps, matching the performance of TCP on the test platform, a Motorola 68010. Not bad, to say the least. Christian, backed by the French PTT, brought this idea to the international standards table. This was his first, but certainly not his last, encounter with what he sardonically calls the "classical" standards process.

The opposition camp, led by the English and the Germans, felt that if you did X.25, you should do so by the book. This meant that sending datagrams into the ether was out. Instead, they wanted the use of Logical Link Control class II, a connection-oriented version of Ethernet which has been widely standardized but rarely used.

The whole thing degenerated into a religious stalemate. As with many talented people, this encounter with the standards world moved Christian more firmly into the TCP/IP camp.

In 1986, Christian was brought on as an INRIA staff member. In an unusual move, INRIA immediately named him a project leader. One of the first projects in Christian's group was an X.400 over X.25 implementation. Christian's work on X.400 led to other projects such as an X.400/SMTP gateway. That gateway is still up and running at INRIA and is used by several groups. SWITCH, the Swiss Research Network, used a leased line to INRIA to link their X.400 services to the Internet SMTP base for several months. Over time, that mail link migrated into a 64 kbps IP line from SWITCH to IN-RIA.

Related to the X.400 project was an X.500 project called The Obviously Required Name Server (THORN), run under the auspices of the European Community Esprit project. THORN led to a DSA implementation called Pizarro. Naming it after the Spanish conqueror was a takeoff on the UCL's Quipu, an Incan name.

Working on all these OSI-based systems gave Christian's group considerable experience in coding the OSI middle layers. One outgrowth of that experience was an ASN.1 compiler.

ASN.1 is a very powerful, very general specification for the presentation layer in OSI. The problem is that most people write programs in C, not ASN.1.

When an application receives data from an OSI network, as in the case of an incoming X.400 message, that message is encoded in ASN.1. An ASN.1 compiler starts with the ASN.1 specification for a message and generates the encoding and decoding routines that allow an application to interact with the network.

The INRIA compiler, known as MAVROS, was a fully general system, accepting any ASN.1 specification. It also handled variants of ASN.1, such as the X.509 standard used for digital signatures. It supported a lightweight version of the presentation layer, quite useful when similar machines send lots of integers and floating point numbers back and forth.

An outgrowth of the compiler effort was an ASN.1 benchmark. To test the compiler, and to compare ASN.1 to other presentation paradigms such as the Sun XDR specification, the benchmark provides a basis for measuring performance.

Christian's group started by examining a typical X.400 message. Based on that message, a tree was developed with a depth of 8 and a total of 400 ASN.1 elements. As per the typical X.400 message, 80 percent of the elements were octet strings, 10 percent strings, and 10 percent integers.

Next, they started comparing the code generated by the ASN.1 compiler with basic lightweight methods. They looked at the amount of time to encode and decode data as well as the amount of data transferred on the network.

Needless to say, the initial performance was slow. The results from the benchmark were used to start optimizing the compiler. For example, decoding is slow in ASN.1 because of the tag, length, and value encoding for each element. In a technique similar to Van Jacobson's TCP work, the ASN.1 routines began using header prediction techniques. If the next tag can be predicted from the current context, header prediction can greatly speed up decoding.

Running the ISO layers over TCP/IP and FDDI on two DEC 5000s, the INRIA group was able to achieve presentation layer throughput of 8 Mbps. By contrast, TCP throughput on the same configuration was 17 Mbps, UDP 25 Mbps. The bottleneck in all three cases appeared to be the CPU.

In addition to his research efforts, Christian has been active in helping to link the French infrastructure to the Internet. As with many international connections, this one can be traced back to the ubiquitous Larry Landweber. Christian was invited to attend one of Landweber's networking conferences, this one hosted by Dennis Jennings in Dublin in December 1986.

Larry and Christian started talking and decided that INRIA should be linked to the Internet. Larry went to NSF, Christian to INRIA and each got half the link funded. Before the link was up, UUCP mail to the U.S. could take anywhere from hours to days. With an initial link speed of 56 kbps, mail started taking just minutes, or less. The INRIA link to the U.S. gave Christian more involvement with the Internet community and led to his appointment to the IAB.

I had a wonderful meal of foie gras and veal, hoping there were no animal rights activists lurking outside. To drink, we had a nice Bordeaux followed by an even better Beaujolais. One thing I've noticed is that one of the qualifications for membership on the IAB seems to be a exquisite taste in wines (many of which come with exquisite prices). IAB members such as Stephen Kent, Vinton Cerf, Lyman Chapin, Dan Lynch, and Christian Huitema are all renowned in the Internet community for their technical abilities in this area.

Saturday morning, I retrieved my car and drove along the coast of the Mediterranean back to the Nice airport. Arriving back at Hertz 26 hours after I had picked up my keys, I was handed an invoice for U.S. $300.

"Thank you very much," I said, picking up my bags and heading towards the terminal. You know you've been travelling too long when a U.S. $300 bill for one day in a Renault "Junior" seems acceptable, even if only momentarily.

By the time I got to the terminal, my currency conversion process got swapped into memory and I promptly turned around and walked back to Hertz. Using a few choice words remembered from my high school days in Switzerland, along with some universally understood hand gestures, I convinced the station chief that I felt that a fee of $300 was not totally appropriate. Through some hard negotiating, I got the rate down to U.S. $125. What a bargain.

Sunday night, I took the TGV back to Geneva. Feeling refreshed after a day in the south of France and a weekend in Paris, I was ready to sink into the bureaucratic abyss of Geneva.

Sink I did. I spent the next three days battling the ITU bureaucracy, trying to stop a rear guard action that was threatening to kill the Bruno project.

In four weeks, the Bruno server had been a remarkable success. Twenty-one servers on four continents had cloned the file system and were distributing the Blue Book. Bruno was getting as many as 35 packets per second. Over 500 hosts in 27 countries had retrieved over 65,000 files. We had no statistics from the other servers, but it was not unreasonable to think that several hundred thousand files of the Blue Book had made their way out to people who were actually reading them.

How did this compare with paper copies? This was hard to say, as profits from documents had served as a sort of discretionary fund for the previous Secretary-General of the ITU. Knowledge of publications was highly dispersed; only finance seemed to have sales data, and they kept this information closely guarded.

Nonetheless, it appeared that the Bruno experiment had increased the distribution of the Blue Book by at least one order of magnitude, and probably two or more. Tony had documented all this in his "Friends of Bruno" newsletter and had papered the ITU—paper being the only medium that appeared to work there.

Yet, despite all this, the high-level Information Systems Steering Group had met the previous Friday to decide the future of Bruno. Rumor had it that the outcome of the policy group was that the experiment had not been successful and was over.

Stopping the experiment was, of course, not an option. The server was in Colorado in a locked room and I had no intention of stopping operation. Besides, twenty-one other servers had the data. Tony and I had carefully structured this project so there would be no turning back.

There were, however, some important factors at stake. I had hoped to begin putting other ITU documents on the servers. A policy decision that the experiment was over would mean that we might have to bypass the ITU and start scanning paper copies.

More importantly was the role of the ITU in dissemination of standards over the network. The logical outcome of the Bruno experiment was to have the ITU put itself on the Internet and take over this function.

Tony had set me up for three days packed with meetings. Many of these people were division directors or other Very Important Bureaucrats (VIBs) who sat on the Information Systems Steering Group.

One meeting, in particular, stood out over all the rest. I was scheduled to meet with Walter Richter, director of something important. He was 45 minutes late, so I spent the time looking at the stacks of file folders on his secretary's wall-to-wall bookcase.

They had wonderful labels such as "The Preparatory Committee on Restructuring of Subsidiary Machinery" or "The Administrative Committee on Coordination." One was simply labeled "High Level Committee" and took up several folders high up on the top shelf. The committee that seemed to take the most wall space was the "Consultative Committee on Substantive Questions."

Finally, Richter strode in. Speaking with a heavy Austrian accent, he preceded to tell me how my experiment "was not a success and has been terminated."

He seemed very certain that the experiment had not been a success, so I asked why. It appeared that this Internet of mine (the ITU considered the Internet to be some private project run by Tony Rutkowski and myself) just didn't reach the right sort of people. By the right people, he seemed to mean those who were on the Administrative Council of the ITU or those that worked on the consultative committees like the CCITT or the CCIR.

The conclusion that the Internet had the wrong sort of people was odd, since I had not analyzed the data on who was accessing my server. In fact, anecdotal evidence was pointing to just the opposite conclusion. I had received personal messages from places like AT&T, Bell Labs, and Telecom Finland.

I found out later how Richter came to this view. Richter had a buddy on the radio side of the ITU, the CCIR. His buddy had a pal in Canada to whom he had spoken.

"Ever hear of this Bruno thing?"

"Nope."

"Ever hear of this Internet business?"

"Yeah, but we checked it out a few years ago and it was too expensive."

Well, there you go. Can't argue with a few personal anecdotes when making a high-level policy decision. I tried trotting out a few of my own anecdotes, but Richter had already assembled the data he needed.

Richter had something in common with most of the other VIBs that I met in three days at the ITU. He was very, very sure of himself. For example, he was absolutely convinced that the entire ITU network architecture was fatally flawed.

I must confess, this was certainly my working assumption when starting to deal with the ITU computer group, but the reality turned out to be that they had a fairly decent network architecture in place. Not what I would have chosen, but adequate for the job.

I asked Richter to tell me what was wrong.

"The Ethernet," he replied. When his PC had first been installed, it was a diskless machine. A mistake, of course, but it had been fixed. He was convinced that all ITU network problems had at their root Ethernet saturation, because it had once taken several hours after pressing a key to see the character appear on his screen.

Based on this anecdote, he was ready to completely micromanage some fairly talented engineers that worked at the ITU computer department. Rather than set broad policy (an area that had been sorely lacking), he was convinced that the answer was to roll up his sleeves and dig into the bits and bytes.

Another curious aspect of the three days of meetings was this idea of the Internet as some academic toy that real people didn't use. I met with one staff member who expressed this view and waved a piece of paper at me that had the names of delegates he was working with as proof.

I picked up the piece of paper and started going through the list. Many of the places, such as the Centre National des Etudes de Telecommunications in Paris, were clearly on the Internet. In fact, the vast majority of institutions on the list appeared to be connected in one form or another.

There was another more fundamental issue that started to focus and helped explain this reluctance among the VIBs. Printing documents was a big empire at the ITU, and building empires was the name of game. My project was not a good way to build big empires (efficiency never is).

The printing department at the ITU was truly an impressive place. I walked past the "keep out" signs and gave myself a private tour. There were seven offset presses, four state-of-the-art, top-ofthe-line Xerox 5090 copiers, and a dozen or so other large copiers. The ITU's own facility generated only a fraction of the total output. Swiss printers had a long and cozy relationship with the ITU bureaucracy.

Things would be printed with no relationship to demand under the assumption that larger print runs meant a lower per-unit cost. True, of course, but if you throw away most of the units, your average costs can be considerable.

One of my underground sources gave me an example. For several years, the ITU had produced a beautiful four-color "charts in profile" document. Each time, 10,000 copies would be printed at a cost of several hundred thousand dollars.

Of this print run, 2,000 copies would be given away and roughly 100 sold. Yet, every few years, a new edition would be put together and 10,000 new copies would be printed. Strolling around basements and subbasements, I saw enough paper to start a firestorm. Pallet after pallet was loaded with boxes and boxes of documents that nobody would read.

This being the decade of the environment (or was it the children?), I naively asked about the ITU recycling program. Needless to say, one didn't exist.

The Bruno experiment directly threatened this paper empire. The bureaucracy had framed its argument very cleverly. Every year, the ITU had received several million Swiss Francs in revenue from selling documents. The official "profit" from the Blue Book had gone to fund programs in the developing world.

In other words, Bruno was depriving the ITU of revenues that would fund vital infrastructure. My selfish little project meant that people who needed to call a doctor wouldn't be able to. Project Bruno, baby killer.

Nobody actually accused me explicitly of killing babies, but I certainly felt that undercurrent. After donating several months and several thousand dollars to putting ITU standards online, I had somehow not expected this type of reaction.

The donation was the single most difficult concept for the VIBs to understand. Why was I doing this? What was my motive? What was in it for me?

Of course, donations to the common infrastructure are how the Internet was built. Even formal standards bodies like the ITU run on donations. Corporations work in the standards process as a volunteer effort.

In the Internet community, volunteer efforts are the norm. The IETF has many people who attend as private citizens, paying for the privilege three times per year out of their own pockets. Paying for the privilege of getting the Blue Book online was not remarkable, but VIBs didn't know what to make of it.

The "Bruno, baby killer" aspect was a difficult one. Profits from document sales were virtual at best, and the simplest solution would be to redo the accounting system to look at the total costs of the inefficient document production process, but that proved to be dangerous.

I thus attacked the widespread unease with giving away copies on the Internet. Tony was advancing the novel theory that by giving copies away, you increased the market and thus increased sales. Such an argument, although bearing a few logical flaws, seemed to stop the VIBs, at least for a few minutes.

While the ITU was criticizing the Bruno experiment, they were attempting to move forward on their own electronic document handling system. Evidently, the Bruno situation had impressed the Secretary-General enough that he had presented himself at the meeting of the Information Systems Steering Group and suggested that they should do something.

The committee had thus spawned a task force. The task force had formed a small working group. Their initial inclination was to start using X.400 as a way to send out working documents, but only to members of the committees.

Tony and I tried valiantly to switch the focus to getting the ITU on the Internet and sending the documents out to as wide an audience as possible. This was not meeting with much success. The computer department was worried about the resource implications of such a move and wanted two additional staff members (in addition to their current network staff) to support the effort.

Basically, the bureaucracy desperately wanted to get back to a world they could control. In order to control documents, however, you need to own them. Nobody at the ITU wanted to admit that there was a possibility that the ITU didn't own its own documents.

Tony Rutkowski had made an analysis of the issue of copyright and had come to the conclusion that the ITU didn't have a sustainable basis for asserting copyright protection. Many of the other VIBs, however, felt that the issue was cut and dried.

There are no apparent legal cases in which somebody has challenged copyright on a standards document. There are many factors that must be weighed before a court will uphold a copyright claim, and it was naive to think that the issues are so simple that the ITU could confidently claim they would win in a court of law.

In order for a document to have a copyright applied to it, it must, among other criteria, be original and not previously published. Since almost all standards start out as public domain working documents, even this fundamental requirement is not often met.

Many jurisdictions do not allow protection to be granted on official or governmental works. Even a private standards body might be considered by the courts to be quasi-governmental. Many places, such as the U.S., make standards a procurement requirement, making copyright enforcement questionable at best.

Even if standards are copyrightable, only the representation of the standard, not the contents, can be protected. Tony's conclusion was that in almost any jurisdiction, running the paper through a scanner and OCR software and posting ASCII text would be defensible.

Many standards do have graphics, of course. The graphics have a stronger basis for copyright, since the representation is everything. As we had seen with the Blue Book, though, in many cases the graphics were not absolutely essential, at least for getting a rudimentary understanding of the standard.

With these factors in mind, Tony and I walked across the street to meet Larry Eicher, Secretary-General of ISO. My feeling was that even if there was no copyright on standards, it was certainly easier to work with ISO than against them.

The fact that Tony accompanied me was meant to send the message that my efforts enjoyed at least some support from the ITU. I brought along a copy of *STACKS*; Tony brought the slides from his presentation to INTEROP in which he concluded that it was unlikely that any standards organization could assert copyright on documents.

"Do you think that's diplomatic?" I asked.

"Nothing wrong with pushing forward the state of the art," he said with a smile.

We met Eicher and Mike Smith, one of the leaders of the task force which supports the OSI effort. Both turned out to be very reasonable people.

I gave a little speech about the moral necessity of disseminating standards. I advanced the view that the reason that OSI had taken so long to come to market was simply because it cost so much to find out about it.

We then started talking about applying Bruno to the ISO world. Eicher was quite frank: 25 percent of ISO revenues came from the sales of standards documents. How did I propose to replace that revenue? Even more importantly, ISO was controlled by its member organizations, which also made much money from standards sales. How did I propose to convince groups like ANSI that posting standards for free would help them?

Simply put, it was a question of financial survival. Interestingly enough, Eicher was clearly unwilling to argue his case on copyright grounds. When I ventured the theory that copyright protection for

ISO documents was legally weak and that some radical might just go ahead and post the standards, Eicher said "it's not a question of copyright protection, it's a question of fair business practices."

We began searching for a potential solution. I proposed my high resolution/low resolution compromise. The plan would post low resolution versions of documents for free on the network and allow ISO and ANSI to continue to sell the high resolution versions, either on paper or electronically.

Low resolution might mean ASCII text and 200 DPI bitmaps of graphics, formulas, and other elements not well suited to representation as ASCII text. Some document format such as ODA could be used to tie the pieces together. Using ODA would help ISO by spurring the development of the standard by giving people a substantial base of documents worth reading.

The crucial assumption was that people with the free version would then pay for documents. I argued that free distribution of standards would increase the base of people who read documents by at least a factor of 10, maybe even more. Many of these would want the paper documents. Giving away standards would lead to increased revenues.

I then offered to test this theory on Bruno at no cost to ISO. Eicher agreed to at least consider a formal proposal, so we went back to the ITU and dashed off a formal letter. Kind of a long shot, I figured, but certainly a first step. (I never received a response to my letter, but that was no suprise. I did, however, publish the offer in *Communications Week* just in case ISO had misplaced my letter and needed a reminder.)

Tony and I had one more item of business to attend to. A seminar had been scheduled for Monday morning to give people at the ITU a briefing on Bruno. Tony had sent electronic mail on Friday, but by Monday, none of the mail had arrived and therefore nobody showed up at my lecture.

Turned out that the entire ITU mail system was running off a VAXmate with a very limited amount of memory. If you sent mail to everybody at the ITU (only a few hundred people), the system crashed.

Rather than remove the offending mailing list or even move the message handling system up to an appropriate host, the issue of the "mail server situation" had entered the bureaucracy and a heated debate had begun, focusing on whether or not to expand memory on the VAXmate. I was a bit incredulous. Running a mail system for 900 professional bureaucrats off a VAXmate is kind of like using a Volkswagen Beetle to haul timber out of the Amazon jungle.

We rescheduled the seminar, booking Tarjanne's personal conference room for the occasion. The secretaries were worried that the room would be too small (it could only hold 50 people or so), but Tony and I insisted that the venue had the appropriate symbolism and that having to turn away people wouldn't be all bad.

Since electronic mail wasn't going to do the trick, we had only one alternative: ElevatorNET. Posting notices in the elevators was about the only effective means of communication at the ITU, the organization that invented X.400.

The ITU has some of the strangest elevator manners in the world. When you enter a lift, custom requires you to greet everyone. Everybody then choruses back a hearty "bon jour."

When you leave, you say goodbye and everyone responds with their own "au revoir." Nice custom, but what it means is that during a busy period, it can cost you a dozen hellos and goodbyes to go up just a few floors.

Tony and I pushed the button for the elevator and caught the first one, respecting the elevator protocol. Every time we caught an elevator, we rode a few floors, long enough to post the notice. We then got off, pushed the button again, and hoped that a different elevator would start. Finally, dozens of bon jours later, we had caught the last elevator and posted the last notice.

Wednesday morning, Tony had prepared all sorts of handouts for the eager crowds. I nervously sat in the corner and prepared my talk.

Two people came. One was our ally in the computer department, another a gentleman I had already briefed. Nobody else bothered to show up.

We all chatted for a few minutes, had a cup of coffee, then went back to Tony's office. I bid Tony goodbye.

Geneva

Thursday, I took a series of four flights from Paris to London to New York to Ithaca, home of Cornell University. Sitting on the planes, I had plenty of time to reflect in wonder at the ITU. Many people were grateful that Tony Rutkowski had put the time into the bureaucracy, but you had to wonder how somebody that talented could survive in such a labyrinth. (He didn't for very long. Tony is now an employee of Sprint International and Vice President of the Internet Society.)

Thursday night, I arrived at New York's Kennedy Airport and took a commuter flight to Ithaca. USAir decided that 15 cities with no luggage lost was tempting the fates and obliged me by sending my bags to Syracuse. My request for extra frequent flier miles, based on the route my bags took, was greeted with a blank stare.

While negotiating with the lost luggage functionary, H. David Lambert, my host in Ithaca, arrived to pick me up. He smiled knowingly when he saw that I was looking for my bags. Evidently, USAir uses some stochastic routing algorithm for luggage in upper New York state.

Dave brought me to his house, with a stop en route for massive quantities of Chinese take-out. There, David, his wife Carol, and I caught up on old times.

Dave Lambert operates on the front lines of computing: he manages academic computing centers. I got to know him when I was a graduate student at Indiana University and Dave was Assistant Director of the Academic Computing Services.

In those days, Academic Computing meant a CDC 6000, punch cards, and two terminals for the entire campus. My first word processor was on that machine. We would use punch cards and a homegrown text formatter written in FORTRAN to input our formatting directives, with the results sent to a line printer.

Dave brought me into the student consulting pools, rescuing me from yet another semester teaching a required class in economics to drooling undergraduates. My job was to sit in a cubicle and answer any and all questions. In the summer, I continued to do my consulting, but we had only a few students and most of them spent their time at the abandoned quarries swimming.

We did, however, have 6 VAX 11/780s that had just been delivered. My consulting cubicle was a designated receptacle for one of the sets of documentation, which filled up most of a wall. Having nothing else to do, I started at one end of the wall and read manuals. It was then that I learned the key to a successful consulting practice was to Read The FMS Manual (RTFM).

Under Dave's leadership, the Indiana University network grew from a few hundred to several tens of thousands of active users. He introduced a wide variety of programs that dramatically changed how computers were used on campus. An example was the so-called MBA Experiment.

The word "experiment" is a way of labelling some project to get over strenuous objections from people opposed to anything new (hence the use of the word "experiment" at the ITU). The experiment gave permanent accounts to all MBA students, instead of doling out resources as part of some specific class, as had been the case previously.

A single, over-worked VAX was loaded up with 1,200 students, along with tools to do e-mail, financial modelling, and even access external data sources such as the Dow Jones News Service. Noncredit seminars were held to familiarize students with the tools, and a consulting cubicle and terminal room were put into the business school.

The project met strong resistance from two places. First, the systems group in the computing center were aghast at this wild, uncontrolled use of resources. What if everybody started using the system at once? One system manager actually went so far as to say putting users onto the system would make it run inefficiently.

The second source of opposition was the business school faculty, who felt all this new-fangled nonsense would take away from a serious academic atmosphere. Behind the scenes, of course, was the unspoken fact that if the students learned the tools, the faculty would have to also.

Despite these objections, the experiment started up. The results were dramatic. Students started using sophisticated modelling tools to solve case studies, forcing the professors to learn the same tools in order to grade the assignments. Electronic mail became such a part of the culture that one professor even gave his exams by mail.

Eventually, the entire nature of the MBA Program changed. The obligatory Fortran class was dropped in favor of a computer skills seminar emphasizing tools like e-mail and Lotus. Many other classes in the curriculum were radically changed. Students left the program computer literate, with a noticeable change in placement success.

The MBA Experiment was one of dozens of projects that Dave Lambert started, usually over the strenuous objections of one or more factions. He helped wire dormitories, develop educational software in fields like English, obtain cheap PCs for students, and hooked the campus to the Internet.

What Dave started, Carol Lambert had to help finish. Carol specializes in setting up support structures for computing services. At Indiana University, this originally meant writing the reports on how to use the CDC mainframe. This matured over time to a highly trained, highly service-oriented operation, providing everything from a help desk (with people who had answers) to a problem tracking and escalation system, extensive user documentation and classes, and standardized procedures for obtaining resources.

The computing service that Dave and Carol helped build was so successful that it won the first INTEROP Achievement Award for excellence in education. By then, Dave and Carol had moved on to Ithaca, where they were part of a team trying to expand and develop the Cornell campus network.

Cornell is the largest Ivy League school, with a population of 17,000 undergraduates. It is also one of the key Internet hubs. The Cornell Theory Center was one of the original NSF supercomputer centers. Cornell is also the site of the Network Operations Center, supporting Sprint's role as international connection manager for the NSFNET. Cornell monitors international links to NORDUnet and INRIA in France and is part of both the T1 and T3 backbones.

Cornell is also one of the key sites in the Internet for work on routing protocols. In fact, the campus network is run over routers developed at Cornell and running on a PC/AT. These multiprotocol routers support, along with many other networks, over 284 separate AppleTalk networks. The Cornell routers are managed by a set of bootservers. When new software is developed, Trivial FTP is used to send the new boot images down to over 100 routers.

Some of the more interesting routing work at Cornell was done by the team of Scott Brim and Jeff Honig. Scott, quiet by nature, is a bit of an anomaly in the raucous world of routing. Meetings about routing protocols at places like the IETF tend to be full of histrionics and hysterics, routing being the original religious issue in the Internet, but Scott talks in a whisper.

Scott and Jeff are the developers of the Gateway Daemon (*gated*), a widely available piece of routing software for UNIX and other operating systems. The *gated* software has its origins in the period when regional networks started coming into being and hooking themselves up to the NSFNET.

TCP/IP has two kinds of routing protocols. Interior protocols are used to communicate reachability information within a routing domain. On UNIX systems, the Routing Information Protocol (RIP) was the quintessential interior protocol and was implemented in a software module called the Route Daemon (*routed*).

Reachability between routing domains, as in the case of a regional announcing its networks to the backbone NSFNET, uses a protocol such as the Exterior Gateway Protocol (EGP), or its more modern successor, the Border Gateway Protocol (BGP).

In the early days, both *routed* and EGP received reachability information. Each would take that information and update a master routing table in the UNIX kernel. As long as each routing protocol handles a separate set of target networks, having two modules update a single routing table sort of works.

What started happening, however, was that a target network might be reachable through two different routes. Information about one might arrive via RIP, the other via EGP. The update by one protocol would be walked all over by the other.

The *gated* software took the two separate modules and put them into a single daemon, allowing coordinated updates to the routing table in the kernel. Over time, *gated* was revised to make it very modular, allowing new routing protocols to be quickly added.

The *gated* software has become one of the standard platforms for prototyping new routing protocols. Current *gated* modules include the OSI IS-IS and its TCP/IP cousin OSPF, the Border Gateway Protocol (BGP), the old RIP-like Hello protocol, and the policy routing twins, IDPR and IDRP.

An interesting aspect of *gated* is the way it is distributed. Cornell maintains the reference implementation, which people can download from anyplace in the Internet. This makes it perfect for small organizations that have a UNIX box and want to connect to the Internet.

Vendors that incorporate *gated* in their products sign a redistribution agreement. This agreement requires the vendor to feed any enhancements to *gated* back into the reference implementation, making any improvements available to the entire community.

❐

Next, I met Steve Worona, who escorted me through the gorges of Ithaca to find some lunch while he told me about CUINFO. In the world of Cornell, replete with supercomputers, optical disk juke boxes, and other paraphernalia of high technology, CUINFO is certainly one of more impressive services on campus.

CUINFO is a low-tech information service. It started nine years ago when Steve was an IBM systems programmer working on special projects for the academic computing group. He noticed that there were exam schedules and class rosters available online to administrators.

Why not make this information available to students? He wrote a program and put a terminal in the lobby of the administration building and CUINFO was born.

Pretty soon, somebody suggested they put up the daily headlines from the campus paper. Sounded good, so that was added. Pretty soon, the information on the system started growing exponentially.

Perhaps the best known service is "Dear Uncle Ezra," started by Worona and Jerry Feist, the head of counseling services at Cornell. Uncle Ezra is a Dear Abby-like service named after Ezra Cornell, the founder of the school. It provides a way for students to ask questions, anonymously if they wish, of counselors.

Answers to questions are usually posted in a bulletin board format, allowing everyone to benefit. Individual responses are often sent directly to the student for more serious inquiries.

Questions range from the very serious, such as suicide counseling, to the inane. My favorite question, of course, is on the inane
side of the spectrum: "Dear Uncle Ezra, I always wonder why Carl
Sagan is so famous. I mean he doesn't have any personality and he
speaks funny."

Contrary to the well-written, precise, to-the-point answers usually provided by counseling services, this one got a fairly evasive,
noncommittal response.

Uncle Ezra has spawned a host of other answer-line services.
The Career Services group started Auntie Em, Mr. Chips handles
issues related to instruction, and NutriQuest provides information
on nutrition and food.

All of these services run on an IBM using the VM operating system. TCP/IP support on the IBM extends the services to the campus network and out to the rest of the Internet. Users can access the
service by using Telnet to CUINFO.cornell.edu, specifying that port
300 should be used instead of the default Telnet port.

CUINFO has grown to the point where it receives over 100,000
accesses per month. It contains information on local restaurants and
a wide variety of the other types of information you might expect
from a high-tech videotex service. It proves that if you give people
very simple tools to publish information and a bit of support, a
videotex system can be quite successful at very low cost.

❐

That night, Dave and Carol Lambert and I started swapping user
services horror stories. We started with the simple ones, like the
IBM staffer who couldn't figure out how to get the command
prompt on his Macintosh. Carol brought out the old war horse of
the PC user who transformed a 5.25-inch disk in to a 3.5-inch disk
using scissors so it would fit into the slot.

Finally, Dave trotted out the ultimate user story, attributed to
Ken King, former Vice Provost at Cornell and then President of
EDUCOM.

Ken King was sitting in his office at Cornell one day when he
got a call from the machine room. There was a crazy man down

there waving a knife around and threatening operators. Some Fortran bug or something.

King promptly called security then went sprinting down the hall towards the machine room. Halfway down the hall, his secretary shouted after him that he had an important call. Thinking it might be security, he raced back to take the call.

It wasn't security. It was an irate user who proceeded to yammer on about some problem with the service he was getting. Ken tried to cut in and finally succeeded.

"I'm sorry, but I have to run. There's a crazy man in the machine room waving a knife around," he explained.

"Oh," the user replied, "but this will just take a minute."

Monday morning, my publisher Paul Becker got up at an ungodly hour to pick me up at 7 A.M. and bring me to breakfast. One of the secrets to supporting yourself as a writer is to get your publisher to buy you as many meals as possible, although with Prentice Hall this is certainly no guarantee of fine dining.

Paul drove me up towards Harlem, near my first appointment at Columbia University. We found a cheap diner and I had my first American breakfast in weeks, greasy eggs and limp bacon.

I grabbed my bags and carried them across the street to the Seeley W. Mudd building, home of Columbia's Center for Telecommunications Research (CTR). CTR is one of six NSF-sponsored Engineering Research Centers and specializes in optical networks.

The main CTR project is called Acorn or Terabit, depending on whom you ask. The Terabit name aptly summarizes the goal of the project, to develop a scalable optical network providing gigabits to the user and terabits of aggregate bandwidth by exploiting the full capacity of optical fiber.

I rode up to the 12th floor of the Mudd building, thinking what a silly ring the name had, and reminding myself never to allow a building to be named after me. Not that the subject has come up frequently.

Since I was early, I went into the office of W. Clayton Andrews to wait for him, resisting the temptation to walk over to the workstation and Telnet to Boulder to read my mail. A few minutes later, Clayton Andrews came in.

A distinguished-looking professor, Andrews was formerly director of an important IBM laboratory in Switzerland. He had joined CTR as an associate director, working alongside such optical luminaries as founder Mischa Schwartz and the current director, Anthony Acampora.

Acorn had been successfully deployed in the laboratory when I visited, and Andrews and others were making plans for further deployment into the real world. They were pursuing two different sites to test the hardware and software.

One would use the dark fiber that Teleport had deployed in lower Manhattan. The other use was on the Columbia campus network, which was getting ready to lay multimode fiber around campus. CTR was trying to get some single-mode fiber pulled at the same time, because of the minuscule marginal cost.

Acorn is based on the linear lightwave network (LLN) concept developed by Thomas Stern, another Columbia professor. The LLN uses different wavelengths of the fiber for different signals. By combining wavelength multiplexing with a star-like topology, circuits can be set up between different nodes on the LLN.

The architecture is scalable, allowing stars of stars to be built, potentially supporting a network of a million or more nodes. Circuit establishment is provided by electro-optical filters located throughout the LLN which establish a path from a source to the destination.

Networks that actually do something are certainly more useful than those that run test patterns, so Acorn is pursuing a half-dozen test applications to help shake out the network. At the edge of the LLN network is a Network Interface Unit (NIU). The NIU links up to the user workstation using local interfaces such as HIPPI.

Andrews brought me into the laboratory to see the prototype network. The entire network was on a single laboratory table, with a few racks of electronics located nearby to test and drive the network. The system had been tested with the transmission of High Definition TV over the network, using ATM cells to move data at 800 Mbps. The network has also been tested at the full speed of 1 Gbps.

The Acorn project would deliver this gigabit capacity to the door of several organizations on campus, who would then work with CTR to try and exploit the bandwidth to do something useful.

The applications included classical gigabit projects such as medical imaging and quantum chemistry. It would also bring bandwidth to places like the law school, which was trying to move large amounts of data around for full text search and retrieval. Of course, the bottleneck in the law school application would probably be the complicated keyword searching of large optical jukeboxes, not the network.

Another application, possibly the most useful, was a proposal by the Teacher's College at Columbia University to use computers more in K-12 programs. Teachers College hoped to link two schools in New York, one in the inner city and the other an exclusive private school, to multimedia resources.

In 1990-91, a prototype of the system was put in at the private school, allowing sixth-graders to communicate with a CD-ROM containing a data base on ancient Greek culture called the Perseus Project. The software allows groups of students to perform a group excavation of a hypothetical site in Greece.

The Acorn project would set up a library of resources at Columbia and make them available to students at the schools. The project would buy as many off-the-shelf resources as possible and store them in the library. When a user wanted to access a resource, the data would be retrieved, compressed, and sent over the network to the user's workstation.

Throughout the twelfth floor, we saw laboratories filled with esoteric-looking hardware. This was definitely a hands-on research center. In one room was a molecular beam epitaxy system, in another a testing laboratory for HDTV, and in a third an experiment to provide different guaranteed classes of service on complex, high-speed networks.

❑

The real, operational nature of CTR was a sharp contrast to many computer laboratories, where hands-on usually meant typing on a keyboard. It was an even sharper contrast to my afternoon appointment at the Columbia Institute for Tele-Information (CITI), located in the Business School.

CITI, as you might guess from a place with Tele-Information in the name, is not the kind of place with lots of computers. Instead, the offices are stuffed with paper, books, and loads and loads of reprints of CITI publications.

CITI is an economist think tank about networks. The founder is Eli Noam, a lawyer and an economist. A former member of the New York State Public Service Commission, his is one of those ubiquitous figures in the discussions that hover around the FCC and set much of our policies for public networks.

CITI had been trying to drag me into one of their policy studies, a grandiose project called Private Networks and Public Objectives. My contact was an ebullient young Irish Marxist, Áine M. Ní Shúilleabháin, an able policy analyst putting in time at CITI to pay the rent.

Public Networks and Private Objectives is characteristic of the studies conducted at think tanks like CITI. Lots of people attend a few conferences and seminars and some papers are prepared. The papers are then sold as part of the huge Working Papers series. Then, after a little massaging, some of the papers are collected together and published as a book.

This particular study was going to look at a taxonomy of networks, develop a general research framework, turn that into a conceptual model of networks, and finally come up with a policy agenda for the future.

The problem CITI was having was that they were getting lots of speakers, but very few of them knew much about networks. Granted, many were specialists in networks, but most were economists specializing in issues like public utility pricing models. Occasional terms like "star topology" or "coaxial-fiber hybrid system" would enter the conversation, but the general discussion was a bit removed from reality.

Áine was certainly aware that in discussing the policy fate of technical networks, it helped to know a bit about the technical nature of those networks. She had been trying hard to recruit some more technical people to participate and help lend a note of reality to the process.

I ended up waffling out of the study. Having been trained as an economist and then escaped, I was not anxious to get back into the world of simplistic theoretical models based on unrealistic assumptions. Besides, I had to finish my trip and then get ready for two more circuits around the world.

Tuesday morning, I got up early for a D.C. power breakfast of the *Washington Post* and black coffee. The black coffee on an empty stomach helps counteract the nausea you get reading the latest goings-on on Capital Hill, a subject the *Post* covers in excruciating detail.

I then strolled down 16th Street, past the White House and the Old Executive Office Building to the nondescript, generic federal-issue offices of the National Science Foundation. There, I went up to the 4th floor to find Steve Wolff, the Director of the Division of Networking and Communications Research and Infrastructure.

I was shown into a dark office. Steve strode over out of the shadows and introduced himself.

"I hate fluorescent lights. If you want, I can turn them on."

I demurred and groped around for my notepad. There was just enough light coming in from the hall to take notes.

Steve Wolff took over the position of program manager from Dennis Jennings, the Irishman. Wolff helped formalize the NSFNET, supervising the shift from an interim 56 kbps backbone to a professionally managed T1, and later T3, network.

The solicitation for the T1 network had been won by a group that included the Michigan state network (Merit), IBM, and MCI. Later, a non-profit company was founded by MCI and IBM. This company, Advanced Network and Services (ANS), built a T3 nationwide network. ANS was inserted into the organizational chain with NSF and Merit.

When Steve Wolff and I talked in November, these organizational details had been ironed out and a nationwide T3 network, run in parallel with the older T1 network, was slowly becoming operational. Wolff was turning his attention to the next phase.

After numerous public hearings, Wolff was about to recommend to the National Science Board what the next phase of the network should look like. Needless to say, Wolff was not going to give me his formal recommendations before he told his bosses. Since I wasn't trying to scoop *Network World*, we discussed more general issues.

Wolff explained the theory of network infrastructure as a pyramid. You could grow it by adding to the top or by broadening the base. Adding to the top was being done in areas like the national gigabit testbeds, intended to make the core run faster. Gigabit networks were still being tested, but it was evident that in some form they would soon allow researchers to start using higher bandwidth.

Adding to the base of the pyramid was equally important. Every year, NSF helped another 100 schools get on the Internet. This connections program was really quite simple. The school received U.S. $20,000, enough money to buy a router, pay for some telephone calls, and enslave part of a graduate student. After the initial U.S. $20,000, the school was on its own. To Wolff's knowledge, not a single school had dropped off the network after the initial money ran out.

Seeding activities and leveraging investment are the fundamental strategies the NSF uses. They view their job as one of getting things started, not providing ongoing support. Most of the regional networks, for example, started off with exclusive or extensive NSF funding. By 1991, many of the regionals were self-sufficient. Even the core, NSFNET, received only a portion of its funds from the federal government.

My next stop that day was the Office of Technology Assessment where I raided the document room and even found a copy of a study I had contributed to several years ago, but had never seen the final results. I then headed out to Dulles Airport for my last stop of the trip, the Internet Engineering Task Force meeting in Sante Fe, New Mexico.

Late Tuesday night, I arrived in Santa Fe. I checked in and walked down to the terminal room that had been set up for the IETF. After reading several dozen mail messages, and with over 100 still left to wade through, I didn't have the heart to continue and called it quits.

Standing in the hall was Paul Mockapetris, the inventor of the Domain Name System. Paul and I left the hotel to go find some dinner, choosing a restaurant stochastically. The waitress came over, and gave us the introduction obligatory in such chi-chi places.

"Hi, I'm Foo and I'll be your waitress this evening."

She handed us each a flimsy little card. On the card were the words "fish," "chicken," "beef," and "lamb." A little icon was next to each word. There were a couple of other icons signifying potato and onion ring. No prices. No prose.

"What is this," Paul asked, "a RISC menu?"

I decided to see what the wine list would look like in a place like this. Foo came back a few minutes later carrying four bottles of Chardonnay and plopped them on the table. We pointed to our desired icons, Paul pointed at a bottle of wine, and our point-and-click supper was on its way.

◻

The next morning, suitably fortified with a breakfast of a burrito stuffed with Chipolte cactus and eggs, I followed a stream of what were obviously computer engineers to the morning plenary.

The IETF differs from most other industry meetings in that it is not a show or a conference. It is a place where people come to work. The plenary was very short and consisted of a technical presentation on ATM. Then, people went off to their working groups. Working groups are the main business of the IETF. It is in these meetings that people get together to develop the standards that make the Internet work.

The standards that have come out of the IETF have been impressive. They are produced quickly, and they work. In the area of network management, for example, the IETF produced an object identification hierarchy, management information bases for a wide variety of modules, and the Simple Network Management Protocol.

The IETF has been remarkably successful, but as it grows in size, its ability to accomplish work appears to diminish. Veterans of the IETF, like Marshall T. Rose, are vocal about the negative impact of success on the ability to accomplish real work. Marshall likes to distinguish between two types of attendees: the "goers" and the "doers." The goers are those who like to go to conferences, forgetting that the IETF is a working group, not a conference.

The basic difference is one of self-definition. Somebody like Marshall T. Rose defines himself in terms of accomplishments: "the father of ISODE" or "a leader in the development of SNMP." Others, however, define themselves by position: "head of a working group" or "member of the ACM."

This conflict has a fundamental impact on groups like the IETF. The goers try to get themselves named as working group chairs, and all of a sudden committees for the sake of committees start to flourish. The number of working groups topped 60 by the time of the Atlanta meeting in Summer, 1991. Stev Knowles, the most vocal minority of the IETF, suggested a working group be formed with the purpose of reducing working groups. Somebody else suggested that a working group be formed to study the question.

Meanwhile, it keeps getting harder to get real work done. People attend meetings who have not done the preliminary reading. Working group sessions get stalled with naive questions. Even posting required reading lists to the net doesn't seem to get people to do their homework (or to attend and keep quiet if they hadn't done the reading).

Marshall T. Rose grew tired enough of the "goers" that, over a drink, he suggested a radical system of Certified Protocol Engineers. By Marshall's scheme, in order to attend a working group meeting and participate, you must be certified by a board of your peers in that area. Network management, routing, and mail systems, are all examples of possible areas.

The board in an area would be bootstrapped by two people of unassailable quality, who would draft the oral and written exams. Once certified in the area, you would be part of the governing group. The system would be quite similar to that used in the medical profession.

Working group participation would thus be limited to certified protocol engineers. Anybody could attend a meeting, but to participate you must either be certified or be invited by the chair. This fairly radical proposal would probably never get passed—and was certainly proposed with tongue planted firmly in cheek—but it makes one think about how such a technocratic priesthood might function.

❐

Aside from the usual work of readying router requirements and massaging management information bases (MIBs), the IETF has a ritual bloodletting plenary session on the penultimate day. The plenary always starts very slowly, with IETF chair Phill Gross uttering the obligatory platitudes of introduction.

While he is speaking however, you can look around the room and see people positioning themselves at the microphones, waiting for the meeting to open to the floor. Usually, if the controversy will be especially loud, you can hear rumors in the halls in the days before the plenary.

The Sante Fe meeting, however, had seemed fairly quiet and nobody was expecting a major controversy. Lack of real issues, however, will not always stop people from speaking.

As soon as Phill Gross stopped speaking, one engineer stepped to the mike and started raving about the Internet Activities Board. His proposal was to abolish the board as superfluous.

I was sitting in the back of the room, looking over the shoulder of Jon Postel, editor of the RFCs and a long-time member of the IAB. Jon has a habit of scrunching down in his seat as he gets more and more disgusted. As the engineer continued to rave, Jon was almost sitting on the floor.

Finally, people started to chime in with the monologue, interrupting the mad ravings of the lunatic engineer and reminding him that the IAB may have problems but it certainly had played a valuable role in the development of the Internet. Jon Postel slowly started sitting up in his seat.

The IAB doesn't always get accolades at the IETF meetings. The role of the IETF is technical advisor to the IAB, which goes ahead and makes policy decisions. In the previous IETF meeting, held in Atlanta in July, tempers had flared as high as the humidity.

The story of that firestorm helps illustrate some of the inherent conflicts in the process. The IETF had developed an MIB for SNMP-based management of Ethernet modules. The working group that developed the MIB included many of the standard IEEE-developed management variables, but also included a few optional variables that the group felt were necessary.

After several meetings and much e-mail correspondence, the working group forwarded the MIB to the general IETF. At a plenary meeting, the MIB was put on the table and no objections were voiced. It then went to the IETF Steering Group (IESG), composed of leaders from each of the main areas the IETF works in.

The IESG examined the MIB, saw no objections, and forwarded the document up to the IAB with a recommendation for approval. This is the normal process that any recommended standard originated by the IETF takes.

Once the document hit the IAB however, it sat. People were busy and had lots of things to do. Finally, it came time to act on the document. Tony Lauck, the chief network architect for Digital Equipment Corporation and a member of the IAB, looked at the MIB and thought that some existing Ethernet vendors would not be able to easily implement the standard. He felt that it was different from the IEEE standard and that this was not necessarily a good thing.

This is all well and good. The role of the IAB is technical arbiter of the TCP/IP protocol suite and Tony Lauck had identified what he saw as technical issues. He marked up the document, crossing out some variables and adding detailed instructions for revision of the MIB. The IAB then sent it back down to the working group.

The working group exploded. They felt that there had been many opportunities to provide technical input into the process and that the MIB reflected a technical consensus consistent with the network management framework that had become an Internet standard. They saw the IAB as making a crassly commercial decision, caving in to the wishes of a few vendors instead of providing leadership in the standards arena.

In Atlanta, everybody came to the microphone and started giving their views. Why hadn't the IAB attended the working group meeting if they had concerns? Why had the IAB made technical edits instead of providing policy guidance?

Karl Auerbach of Sun Microsystems got up to speak. A lawyer by training and an accomplished engineer, he is a vocal participant in the IETF and an active SNMP developer. The rewritten MIB had been discussed at an unscheduled working group meeting the previous evening, and Karl was concerned that this violated the open, consensual nature of the IETF.

Others got up and complained that the IAB had issued several different explanations of what had happened, each different. Others were concerned that the IAB had tried not to tread on the IEEE turf, neglecting technical leadership for politics.

Finally, members of the IAB admitted they had fumbled the question. The issue was not technical, it was procedural. How to run an informal standards process like the IETF, yet preserve due process safeguards, has been a continuing problem as the body grew in size from the original 13 participants to the several hundred attending at Atlanta.

The issue of due process was certainly a crucial one. It appeared to some members of the IETF that Digital Equipment had sabotaged a standards action on commercial grounds. Karl Auerbach raised the question of the potential legal liability of the group.

The questions of accountability and liability had not escaped the attention of people like Vint Cerf, then chair of the IAB. He was actively working to promote a new professional society, the Internet Society, which would sponsor the activities of the IAB and appoint the members.

The IETF was fun, but by the time an angry mob got around to putting Jordan Becker, vice president of ANS, on the grill about the transition from the T1 to the T3 NSFNET backbone, I was ready to leave. Seven weeks on the road had certainly been enough for me.

Getting off the plane in Denver, I found myself in the middle of a minor blizzard. I collected my bags and fought my way through the snow to find the shuttle bus back to Boulder.

On the bus, I struck up a conversation with the clean-cut young man sitting next to me.

"What do you do?" I asked with some apprehension.

"I install custom industrial equipment," he replied.

Well, I thought to myself, that's not too bad. In Boulder, I hesitate to ask that question because more often than not the person is a professional aromatherapist, an astrologer, or a trance-channeler for mythical beings.

"What kind of equipment?" I asked.

"Large-scale bean sprout growing machines," he replied.

The Boulder version of heavy industry. At least he didn't work for Wholebrain Technology, the prototypical Boulder boutique, a business establishment specializing in "light and sound technology for mind expansion and brain development."

The next four weeks were spent reading mail, paying bills, and sorting out hotel reservations in 43 cities. About half-way through my stay at home, I came home from the travel agent to find a fax from Pekka Tarjanne of the ITU.

The letter congratulated me for the wonderful work I had done and terminated the Bruno experiment as of December 31, 1991, a mere 90 days after it went operational.

The letter disingenuously said that although the experiment was terminated, "measures are in progress for a similar service to be made available under ITU auspices."

I had talked in Geneva to Robert Shaw, the technical staff member working on an Electronic Document Handling System. His vision, still very much in the conceptual stage, was to put a PC with X.400 software on the ITU network and offer only working documents to a tightly controlled group of people.

The letter from Tarjanne also insisted that I somehow convey to "all those who are operating info-servers with copies of the ITU standards that IT's authorization for distribution of this material ceases after December 1991."

Kind of like publishing a newspaper and then asking people to return the copies. Even worse, many of the 21 sites around the world had invested money in upgrading their equipment to handle the ITU standards. A 90 day experiment was a farce. Pekka Tarjanne, despite his good intentions, had finally been beaten down by the bureaucracy.

I tried to find out what had happened from Tony Rutkowski. He had been called in (but only after the letter was dispatched to me), sat down at a table, and read the letter. He had protested vainly that once the cat is out of the bag, there is not much you can do, but his arguments fell on the unwilling ears of a bureaucracy threatened by any sign of innovation.

Meanwhile, I sent out notes to the Internet community, informing them of the ITU's decision. Even if the ITU had not kept its commitment, we didn't want to expose any of the other sites to an unwitting legal liability.

Of course, chances were highly unlikely that the ITU would sue anybody. A strong legal argument could be made that by allowing uncontrolled dissemination of its standards, the ITU had given up any claim to a copyright it might have once had.

One problem with undoing distribution on the Internet was that I had no idea where all the copies were. Just to make sure that I reached all the servers, I dashed off a piece for *Communications Week*, letting Tarjanne's office know that I was performing this service for him.

Round 2

From Christmas to Chicago

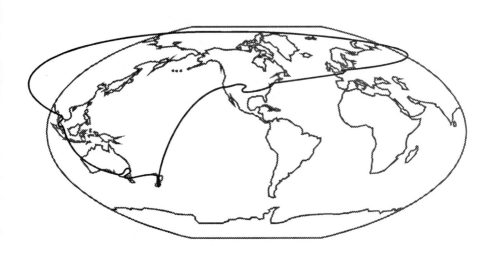

I didn't realize that traveling on Christmas day would be such a novelty, but it was in the Wonderbread world of Boulder. Being Jewish, I long ago learned that travel was optimal on Christian holidays. While the silent majority practiced their rituals, I was able to travel in peace. The flight attendants feel sorry for you and feed you champagne, which you can enjoy with plenty of elbow room.

In Boulder, though, the news that I would be traveling on Christmas was inevitably met with great remonstrations of pity.

"It's OK, I'm Jewish," I would try to explain.

"Oh, but still," they would sigh.

Boulder is a cowboy version of California. It sports an uneasy mix of starry-eyed new-agers and redneck wannabees, with an odd combination of the intensely mellow and the highly midwestern. This is the kind of place where, when you tell a joke, people thank you for sharing it with them. It's the kind of place where everybody eats organic sprouted bran breads, but they go to mini-malls to get it. Its the kind of place that thinks it's the center of the world, but in reality is simply too close to Kansas and not nearly far enough away from Marin County.

❏

You know you've come from an island when Berkeley seems real and down-to-earth. I picked up my car from the airport and drove up the Bay, past the hole where the Embarcadero Freeway had been torn down, and over the Bay Bridge to Berkeley.

Thursday morning, with a day to kill, I walked down to Telegraph Avenue. Although increasingly littered with junkies and winos, the street still has some charm left from its heyday in the 60s.

First stop was the Café Mediterraneum, a cavernous coffee shop where you can sit for hours nursing a café latte and watching the passing parade of residents sporting "proud to be weird" buttons and teenagers dressed like Hippies. On the wall of the Café Med is a "no soliciting or dealing" sign. It was on the second-floor terrace of this café that I wrote two of my books, typing every day until my café latte and laptop batteries ran out.

The only problem with typing in Bay Area cafés is the questions you must periodically field. At the Café Med, every day that I typed I would receive several inquiries about the feasibility of calculating astrology charts on my device.

The astrologically-inclined would-be cyberpunks were an interesting diversion from trying to decipher vendor manuals. Some of the queries were even more basic, such as the one I received while working on another book in the Café Picarro, located in the heart of San Francisco's Mission district. I was busily typing away, trying to wax poetic on master-slave replication when I realized that somebody had been standing staring at me for a good ten minutes. I looked up and saw one of the local bums, a benign psychotic who wrote random ravings on a piece of paper, xeroxed a dozen copies, and sold them as a newsletter to buy a U.S. $1 bottle of wine. Feeling that we had something in common, I always tried to be nice to him.

He had a very puzzled look on his face, staring at my notebook computer. Seeing me look up, he seized his chance.

"Uh, excuse me, but, like, how do you print on this thing?"

"You don't," I replied in a matter-of-fact tone of voice, and went back to typing.

He stood there for another ten minutes watching me and scratching his head, trying to figure out what the point was to this write-only memory device.

I wasn't sitting in the Café Med, however, to answer any existential questions. I had been gone from the Bay Area for several months and I was stoking up on caffeine to get myself ready for a tour of the bookstores.

My standard tour has three stops and takes all day. It starts with Cody's in Berkeley, one of the best general purpose bookstores in the country and one of the places bombed for selling Salman Rushdie's Satanic Verses.

After stocking up on obscure travel literature (and making sure my own books were in stock), I headed out of the Berkeley sun, over the Bay Bridge, and into the mist of San Francisco. The city hadn't yet fully recovered from the earthquake yet and instead of being dumped in the middle of North Beach, I took a round-about route through the warehouses and the financial district.

In previous years, I had taken this route every day, but on a scooter instead of in a car. Then, I had blasted through traffic, doing the messenger slalom across the lanes. This time, I had a rental car and had to resist the temptation to treat the gas pedal as a digital device.

Finally, I found myself on Columbus avenue and darted into a parking space across from the City Lights bookstore. On the top floor is the publishing house that, in 1953, became become famous for being the only house willing to publish beat authors like Jack Kerouac. The first floor and the basement are stuffed with a wonderful collection of literature, communist propaganda, and the like.

After spending my allowance, I walked up into North Beach. First stop was Molinari's deli. In a few weeks, I would be in Bangkok visiting the restaurant critic of *The Bangkok Post* and it was unthinkable to arrive without an appropriate sausage. I debated the merits of diverse salamis with the clerks, purchased a few of the better specimens, popped a few prosciutto-and-mozzarella stuffed peppers into my mouth, then headed back to the car for the trip to the South Bay. On the way, though, I received a shock. The Condor, San Francisco's first topless bar and a sleaze magnet for the entire state, had become the Condor Bistro, a fern-and-cappucino establishment.

On the way to the South Bay, I made a diversion to the Mission for lunch. La Tacqueria Menudo is named after their specialty, tripe tacos. No tripe tacos for me, though. I prefer lengua, beef tongue.

La Menudo is no ersatz chimichanga joint. Tacos are the real thing here, served on soft tortillas with lots of salsa and cilantro, washed down with a can of Tecate beer. Rubbermaid containers on the tables hold fresh radishes, pickled hot peppers, and more salsas. Mexican MTV booms out over the speakers, unless a soccer match is on.

Suitably refurbished, I took the I-280 freeway down to the South Bay to Computer Literacy, the largest and definitely the best computer bookstore in the world. With 20,000 different titles, this store is a mecca for the computer literate. For the first two years I wrote, I calculated that I spent as much money buying books here as I earned from writing them.

With a new collection of reading matter, I continued playing the digital tourist and headed up to Fry's. Fry's is to Silicon Valley what the Louvre is to Paris. This is a supermarket for hackers.

The doors to this store are labeled Enter and Escape. Over 20 full-duplex aisles, each 100 feet long, are stacked with every conceivable piece of software, peripheral, chip, and cable. People wield shopping carts up and down the aisles and then report to 35 checkout stands that can easily process several thousand people per day. On your way out with your new peripherals, you can pick up twinkies and Jolt to fuel the creative process.

After picking up a new fax modem, I headed next door to browse in the Weird Stuff Warehouse, a store that specializes in used and surplus equipment. This is the kind of place where you can pick up a VAX 11/750 for $50 or a Symbolics 3600 for $125, always useful if you are remodelling your recreation room and want to put in a bar.

After a stop in Los Altos Hills for the best wine I've ever tasted, courtesy of Dan Lynch of Interop, I headed back to the hotel to sort out my modems, books, and salamis.

Saturday afternoon, I headed down to Mountain View, the home of Sun Microsystems. I was going to visit Steve Roberts, better known as "the guy with the bike."

In 1983, Steve decided that a life of consulting and writing books on the subject of microprocessors was not for him. He tallied up the things he liked to do, and decided on a short list of writing, meeting people, and riding bikes. He sold his home in Columbus, Ohio, and invested everything he had in a recumbent bicycle, an early laptop, solar panels to power his ham radio and other devices, and then hit the road.

For 10,000 miles, he kept on pedaling, going through Florida, the Rockies, the deserts of Utah and California, and the bleak desolation of San Clemente. On the way, he used CompuServe as his electronic mailbox and wrote articles for any publication that would send him money. The bike was certainly a natural conversation opener, helping to fulfill his most important ambition of meeting lots of people.

The original "Winnebiko" was only a couple of hundred pounds and had 18 gears. Over time, that original frame has grown to support 105 gears, 580 pounds, and an incredibly sophisticated collection of on-board computers.

Sun Labs lent space to Steve to let him work on the latest incarnation of the Bike, called the Big Electronic Human-Energized Machine . . . Only Too Heavy (Behemoth). I reported to Sun's Building 4, and was met by Steve, a tall bearded man in his late thirties, wearing a "Peace" T-shirt. He led me through dark empty corridors to a locked door bearing a neatly labeled sign which read "Nomadic Research Labs."

"Labs" was an understatement in this case. Under one of the desks was a futon and scattered throughout were other signs that the lab doubled as a home. Walking in the first time, though, I didn't immediately notice the futon, the flute, or the cereal bowl. My eye naturally turned to the huge bike in the middle of the floor.

At first glance, I saw a recumbent bicycle with a storage unit mounted behind the seat and an aerodynamic hood up front. Behind the bike is a trailer, covered with 72 watts of solar panels used to charge 45 amp-hours worth of batteries.

Sticking up from the rear of the trailer is a big yellow pole containing ham radio antennas. The pole is six feet tall and can be extended to 12 feet for even better reception. Another antenna on the back is a little Qualcomm satellite dish, similar to what you would use on a delivery truck. Roberts keeps a Sun 4/260 at Qualcomm headquarters and runs 165 bps UUCP-based transfers into the bike.

The satellite dish provides coverage anywhere, but 165 bps isn't really optimal for true connectivity. A high-speed modem and a cellular phone allows high-speed IP access to a server located at Sun.

The bike has a variety of different computers. A Sparcstation, a Macintosh portable, and a DOS portable had all been ripped apart and mounted onto the bike. The screens were mounted on the bike console, with one screen flipping up to expose another.

Another laptop is in a removable carrying case, allowing Steve to compute in diners and other places where the bike is not welcome. The carrying case is, of course, in constant communication with the bike.

Input to computers while riding is provided by a handlebar keyboard and a head mouse. The handlebar device is based on an Infogrip BAT chord keyboard which has 7 keys. Force-sensing resistors are built into the handlebar grips and are linked to the BAT keyboard controller.

The chord keyboard allows Steve to type at roughly 35 words per minute, not an optimal rate when you make your living being paid by the word. Once the keyboard controller generates characters, the data is sent to a macro package on a DOS machine that expands the data. Through careful use of macros, the data hitting the target computer appears to be a typist working at 100 words per minute.

The head mouse is the other major form of input. Three transducers are mounted on Steve's helmet and they are used to sense an ultrasonic beam generated from the console. The resulting motion detected is fed into the controller of a Macintosh ADB mouse.

The helmet has a few other features to help the digital nomad. A 720 x 280 pixel red image floats in front of him on a little display mounted on the helmet and acts as a console. A heat exchange system built into an inner liner for the helmet acts as an air conditioner, using the refrigeration unit on the bike to cool fluids which travel up and remove heat from the helmet.

The helmet also has a little microphone on it which connects to a serial cross-connect bus. The bus can set up connections to cellular phones, the ham radio, or even the voice recognition unit on the bike. The cross-connect bus also links modems to serial ports and any other serial links that need to be established. The audio bus can handle up to 8 simultaneous events and the serial bus can handle up to 4 simultaneous events.

Just as the serial bus goes throughout the bike, so does a power bus. Power is distributed in a series of batteries. The main power source is three 15 amp-hour batteries, plus there are various other special purpose batteries scattered about.

On sunny days, photovoltaic cells recharge the system. Additional power is provided by a regenerative braking controller, which transforms the heat generated by braking into power. If there are no hills and no sun, a cable connected to a car's cigarette lighter will do the trick.

A Motorola 68HC11, programmed in Forth, acts as the power controller, sending power where needed and monitoring usage. The controller signals the main bicycle control unit when power is low, which in turn tells Steve so he can take corrective action. Two other 68HC11 controllers handle the serial and audio buses.

The audio bus allow sound output from many sources to be mixed. Two 4 inch Blaupunkt speakers are mounted behind the driver and connected to an automotive stereo amp. Data from the CD player, the cellular phone, the ham radio, or the speech synthesizer can all be mixed. Steve carries over 100 CDs with him on the road, removed from their original packaging to save space.

This entire contraption is worth over $300,000 in parts alone. If you added in time, it is easily worth over $1 million. Security naturally becomes an issue with an asset of this magnitude.

Security for the Behemoth is provided on several levels. At the most basic level, a microwave doppler motion detector reports any motion within 8 to 10 feet. Other detectors signal when a person touches the bike or sits on the seat. A Global Positioning System (GPS) receiver on the bike hood reports bike movement and speed.

Different responses can be set to security events depending on the circumstances. The voice synthesizer can use the speakers to utter an appropriate phrase if somebody touches the bike, such as "do not touch, or you will be vaporized by a laser beam!" A siren can be activated, or Steve can be paged.

If the bike starts moving without a password, more drastic actions are possible. The wheel can lock, a call can be placed to 911 and the speech synthesizer can request help, the siren can be activated, and, most effective of all, a wild-eyed digital nomad is programmed to come automatically bursting out of his tent in a mad frenzy.

The Behemoth and its previous incarnations attracted the media from the word go. CBS, *USA Today*, and even the trade press quickly realized that this was a story. Being "the guy with the bike" has made Steve instantly recognizable throughout the U.S.

For the first 17,000 miles of journeys, Steve simply wandered. An office manager at home base took care of things in return for a cut of the revenue. Over time, though, Nomadic Research Labs has grown into quite a business. Steve publishes a somewhat quarterly journal called *Nomadness* and is in frequent demand on the lecture circuit, providing an interesting alternative for groups that can't afford Oliver North.

To meet the demands of speaking engagements and trade shows, the bike had just added a mother ship, a large trailer pulled by a nice van. The bike went inside the mother ship and hooked up to the antennas in the trailer and a console in the van. The bike continued to operate as the communications hub, even though it was inside a trailer.

I thought that my three round-the-world trips for this book were quite a journey, but I felt like a digital dilettante compared to Steve's wholehearted commitment. His lifestyle was different from that of your usual commute-to-cubicle engineer, but he has certainly proved that you can have fun and put together a technical tour de force at the same time.

I left Steve to drive up the peninsula to meet Ole Jacobsen, my editor at *ConneXions*. Over a dinner of pasta with garlic, olive oil, and anchovies, we plotted how we could get Steve Roberts to pedal around the INTEROP show floor, hooking, of course, into the ShowNet. How about remote SNMP bike management? A Behemoth MIB? The possibilities were endless.

Monday morning, I headed into the Mission district. With an hour to kill, I walked past El Pollo Loco and the Carlos Club ("commuters welcome"), to the Café La Bohème, one of my old haunts. I threaded my way through the couches and tables with derelicts playing chess to get a cup of coffee.

In the corner of the café, I spotted something new. There was a computer terminal with a sign saying "SF Net" and a message on the screen indicating I should inquire at the counter. I paid a dollar and received a ticket with a code on the back that entitled me to fifteen minutes.

SF Net had the usual PC-based access, but decided to add bullet-proofed terminals in places like La Bohème and the Brain Wash, a combination laundromat, diner, and bar. The terminals had a screen built under a glass table top and the keyboard was covered with plastic.

This was your basic BBS, but with a California twist. After entering the code for time, you were asked for a handle. I chose "Carl." You could then chat with online users, post messages to bulletin boards, send mail, or even buy and sell used CDs.

Aside from the obligatory Love Chat, a digital singles bar, SF Net boasted a large Metaphysics and Astrology area. Messages from people like Spud Muffin and Venus Anemone examined the relative merits of Jupiter and Mars to our daily lives.

Finishing my coffee, I walked through the Mission, past a man piling whole butchered hogs into the back seat of his station wagon, and cut over to 23rd street to Brewster Kahle's gingerbread Victorian house. Brewster was the architect of the CPU of the Thinking Machines' CM2, one of the most innovative computers on the market. He was also a former member of the Artificial Intelligence Laboratory at MIT, home of Marvin Minsky.

After delving into the arcana of message-passing protocols for massively parallel processors, Brewster turned his attention to the much more difficult problem of finding and using information on networks. The result was the Wide Area Information Servers (WAIS).

The living room of Brewster's house was packed full of books on subjects ranging from the works of Goya to those of Marvin Minsky. This was not surprising, since Brewster viewed himself as a publisher and WAIS as the ultimate publishing platform.

WAIS has three pieces. A server has documents and makes them available to the world, perhaps for free and perhaps charging for access. A client gets these documents from one or many servers. Clients and servers communicate using an enhanced version of the Z39.50 protocol, originally developed to search online card catalogs.

Brewster ushered me into his office, where he sat down on a beat-up old easy chair and balanced a keyboard on his lap. The screen and rollerball mouse were conveniently nearby, making this a highly comfortable work or play station.

There was no need to start up his WAIS client since it was already up and running. Deployed for only a few months on the Internet, WAIS was quickly becoming a part of people's routines, and had certainly been integrated into Brewster's daily work.

Brewster typed in a query: "Is there any information about Biology?" The query was sent, in its entirety, to the server of servers that Brewster maintained, quake.think.com. Servers of servers were no different than document servers, they simply kept a list of other servers and a description of the information they maintained.

We got back a list of servers throughout the world that had information on biology, such as a database of 981 metabolic intermediate compounds maintained in the Netherlands. At this point, we refined our query and sent it out to many servers simply by pointing to them on the screen. Servers returned lists of document descriptions; pointing to those documents retrieved the full text.

WAIS makes very few assumptions about servers or clients. In our query, we used natural English. The server has indexed documents by keyword and parsed our query to form the lookup. There is no requirement that a WAIS server handle natural English, it can simply take keywords, SQL queries, and even do fuzzy matches to correct for poor spelling.

The documents stored in the server can also vary. They can be simple ASCII text, as in the case of things like the RFCs. Or, the documents can be in the Macintosh PICT format, PostScript, or might even be some virtual document, dynamically generated from a database at query time.

Likewise, the clients can range from simple to complex. At the most basic, the client used Telnet and VT100 emulation, an interface known as simple WAIS (SWAIS). Clients can be much more intelligent. On a Macintosh or NeXT, complex queries on multiple servers can be monitored in a simple intuitive manner. Queries can be saved and periodically reexecuted, allowing updates to information to be periodically generated.

Most users of WAIS use a Macintosh interface called WAISta-tion, not surprising since Apple worked with Thinking Machines on the initial prototype of the system that was tested at Peat Marwick.

WAIStation uses two metaphors to structure the user interface: storage in folders and searching as a conversation. You started a search by asking a question. You get back document descriptions, and those results are used to refine the query. Eventually, the query returns the information the user wants. The query can then be stored in a folder where it can be pulled up later and reexecuted.

Queries in WAIStation can also be passed by looking for documents "similar to" those already found. The conversation thus consists of asking for documents by a query or by example and pointing to one or more servers. Servers can be remote, or can be local document stores such as the entire hard disk or a folder containing all e-mail ever sent or received by the client.

WAIS, with over 10,000 users in 24 countries by the end of 1991, requires, for decent performance, at least a 9,600 bps connection into the network. A local WAIS environment can easily be put together using Ethernet, either as an alternative or a supplement to the Internet-based servers, useful in places where Internet connectivity had not yet achieved the necessary bandwidth.

When I talked to Brewster, he was working with Apple's Advanced Technology Group on an even fancier interface called Rosebud, named after the sled in *Citizen Kane*. Rosebud would use a newsroom metaphor for the user interface.

Users would give assignments to reporters, a process like the WAIStation query dispatch. Different reporters can specialize in different assignments. The user would then look at the results from a "newspaper" window, which would show the documents recovered by different reporters. Reporters can be instructed to reexecute their tasks on a periodic basis, allowing the newspaper to be dynamic.

Several other client interfaces also exists. NeXT would be shipping one with every workstation. XWAIS uses the X Window System and was similar to the WAIStation. Other interfaces are available for GNU Emacs and DOS platforms.

The number of WAIS servers that had emerged in a few months on the Internet was truly incredible. It started with a couple of databases from Thinking Machines, holding things like manuals and bug reports. Thinking Machines also uses WAIS as a corporate information system and even saved all messages from all mailing lists for future queries.

Other databases that had emerged ranged from CERT advisories to weather maps to archives of USENET bulletin boards to the entire text of the Koran, the Bible, and the Book of Mormon. Three cookbooks, a huge poetry database, Supreme Court opinions, and even the CIA's World Factbook were online.

Between June 1991 and the end of the year, WAIS spread to include over 160 databases in 8 countries, including (of course) Finland, Norway, and Australia. Brewster described WAIS as "uncontrolled and uncontrollable," as any good service should be. For example, Finland had started keeping a server of servers and soon it might be necessary to dispatch queries looking for servers to several different places.

Brewster's goal was to enable anybody with a computer, even a lowly PC, to become a publisher. The first PC-based WAIS server had recently gone online, running in somebody's basement, and Brewster was quite excited by the prospect.

Brewster's interest in publishing was personal as well as professional. His fianceé ran a printing museum and in the basement was an old printing press. For entertainment, friends went downstairs and made calling cards. The only requirement was that they leave one on the wall. Cards from people like John Quarterman and Michael Schwartz adorned the walls of the basement.

After a Salvadorean lunch of pupusas and empanadas, I bid Brewster goodbye and went down to the South Bay to thank Sun Labs for the use of their machines and inform them of the ITU's imminent assassination of Bruno.

Milo Medin is best known in the Internet community as one of the developers of Open Shortest Path First (OSPF), the new and improved dynamic routing protocol. He also runs the NASA Science Internet (NSI), one of the largest operational networks and one of the core backbones for the Internet.

NASA Ames Research Center, where Milo worked, is located at the Moffet Naval Air Station near Mountain View, the site of an impressive collection of wind tunnels that includes one big enough to fit a full-size Boeing 727. Another tunnel can achieve hypersonic speeds of Mach 9. The big tunnel is powered by six 28,000 horsepower engines and takes so much power that it can only be run at night (after first warning the power company).

NSI links all the big NASA laboratories, such as Ames, the Jet Propulsion Laboratory, Goddard in Maryland, and the Kennedy Space Center in Florida. It also links scientists in universities and at research facilities in locations as diverse as the Antarctic, Greenland, and Easter Island.

NSI is both a general-purpose Internet and a mission-oriented operational network. As a mission-oriented network, NSI has some fascinating applications with demanding resource requirements.

For example, a telescope at Owens Valley is connected to NSI, allowing astronomers to reposition the telescope remotely. Another set of applications distribute data from the Upper Atmospheric Research Satellite, moving telemetry data from the satellite to White Sands. From there, the data are moved to Goddard's Consolidated Data Handling Facility, where they are distributed over NSI to remote analysis centers.

Perhaps the most unusual application I saw was a C141 airplane used for infra-red data collection. The plane regularly flies between Ames and Christchurch, New Zealand. The plane has its own Class C network address and is filled with Sparcstations on an Ethernet.

The plane flies its route and collects data along the way. When it lands, a thinwire BNC connection drops out of the back and connects to a cable in the hanger, making the plane a part, once again, of NSI. The movement of the plane from one facility to another is transparent to users. Routing protocols, such as OSPF and EGP, are used to announce the availability of the plane network to the rest of the Internet.

Keeping 70 routers, plus underwater fiber, satellite, and dozens of high-bandwidth terrestrial links up and running is quite a challenge. In many cases, the links not only have to be up but also need to provide adequate performance for the transfer of large images or low latency delivery of operational commands.

The network is managed from within a Network Control Center at Ames. The current status of the network is shown on a wall display, with bad links in red and good ones in green. Operators at workstations monitor these links 24 hours per day.

Given Milo's active IETF involvement, it is not surprising that SNMP is used extensively to monitor network status. SNMP, however, provides in-band network management and does not help very much when the network was down. To supplement SNMP, each of the routers in the NSI network has a modem on the console port, allowing operators at the Network Control Center to dial in and diagnose problems, often while the users on-site sleep.

While TCP/IP is the main protocol suite in NSI, there is also a heavy DECnet contingent. Unlike TCP/IP, DECnet Phase IV has no globally administered address space. The architecture assumes a single network which has up to 63 areas, each area under some management entity.

When a global community starts to interconnect, as in the case of space sciences or physics, you quickly get many more than 63 areas. DEC had a hard time believing that physicists would need more than 63 areas. "Just get organized," they would say.

"Just get expletized," the physicists would respond.

To solve the problem, groups like NSI and HEPnet have been forced to resort to hidden areas. NSI and HEPnet agreed to make areas 1 to 46 globally administered areas, available to the entire physics and space sciences DECnet communities. These areas mean the same thing to all routers in NSI. CERN, for example, used area 22 under DECnet Phase IV and area 23 for Phase V migration.

Areas between 47 and 63 are reusable. A particular DECnet router would know about one of these areas, but another router in the network might use that same area number for a totally different network.

On many links, DECnet and TCP/IP had equal status, being sent across by multiprotocol routers. Occasionally, for political or technical reasons, the underlying link could only transfer TCP/IP traffic. A process known as "tunnelling" encapsulates DECnet traffic inside of IP packets, making two DECnet routers appear to be next to each other.

NSI is both a special-purpose network and a general-purpose Internet. Owning the links means that NSI is able to control them, helping to tune the network for the bandwidth and latency requirements of specific end-to-end requirements. This doesn't mean that the network is isolated, only that NSI planners have a fairly good idea of what is happening on their part of the Internet.

NSI also acts as one of the Internet backbones. Links to New Zealand, Hong Kong, Australia, Hawaii, London, and many other sites come in at NASA Ames, Goddard, or other NSI sites. The data from these sites is routed on through to its final destination, which might well be outside of NSI.

One of the key links into the rest of the Internet, indeed one of the two key hubs in the entire internetwork, is at Ames. This is the Federal Internet Exchange for the West coast, known as FIX West. The other FIX is in College Park, Maryland, and is called Fix East.

FIX West is located in a small squat building in the middle of a sweet potato patch on the edge of Ames. The building is shared by NSI and the NASA Telephone Company, which maintains the underlying bandwidth on which NSI runs.

Inside the windowless building, Pacific Bell has the termination for 12 fiber optic cables. Two other sets of 12 fibers terminate at other locations on site to provide redundancy. The fiber provides 30 to 40 T1 links, but could easily provide as much as a dozen OC-3 links running at 155 Mbps each.

The room is packed with termination equipment, patch panels, and other telesoterica. In a locked wire cage are all the routers for NSI. One 19 inch rack holds routers for the Bay Area Research Network (BARRnet). Another has NSS routers for the NSFnet. Other racks hold equipment for local networks, such as the link to the huge National Aerodynamic Simulation center at Ames. Yet more racks have routers for the Energy Sciences network (ESnet), NSI, and many others.

In a corner is a huge, antique piece of equipment, known as a Butterfly. The Butterfly is made by BBN and is still used by MIL-NET as a "Mailbridge" to the outside world. Prying off the top of this ancient-looking device, Milo showed me the Macintosh hidden inside which is used as the console.

Also located in this building are the electronics for two complete C band satellite earth stations, not to mention videoconferencing equipment, racks for the experimental Terrestrial Wideband network, time servers, and a host of other equipment needed to provide the gateway for the west coast, the Pacific Rim, and much of the rest of the Internet.

Finishing what Milo called the "cheap tour," we drove by the huge hangers of Moffet Field, originally built to house dirigibles and so immense that clouds form inside when the doors are closed. Milo stopped at another hanger, where we saw Harriers, Hornets, U2s, and many other NASA aircraft being worked on. The U2s were used to pinpoint firestorm centers during the Yellowstone fires, helping the firefighters to identify targets.

After a nice lunch of generic Chinese food, I borrowed a terminal to read my mail. Being in the center of the world, I figured my response time ought to be good, and it certainly was.

Heading out, I stopped first at the visitors center. Here you can get all sorts of educational books on atmospheric sciences and scale models of historic aircraft. I headed straight for the astronaut food, where I bought five pouches of freeze-dried, vacuum-packed ice cream, a chalky, marshmallow-like bar that sort of resembles ice cream if you freeze it and squint your eyes.

Tuesday night, New Year's Eve, I boarded the plane for New Zealand. Travelling west on New Year's Eve gives you at least two excuses to celebrate, provided you cross the international date line after midnight. If you cross before, you get no chances unless, of course, you don't tie your celebrations to arbitrary chronometric indicators.

Twenty hours later, I landed in Auckland to await my flight to Wellington. Customs impounded the salami I had bought as an offering for the restaurant critic of *The Bangkok Post* and told me that if I did not reclaim my links within 28 days they would be destroyed. Not wishing to be responsible for the wanton destruction of four innocent salamis, I paid my NZ $5 fee for a sausage hotel at the Ministry of Agriculture and Finance, and assured the officer that I would return as soon as I could.

I must admit that in the course of travelling, I've gotten a bit jaded about waiting lounges, but the Air New Zealand Koru Club in Auckland was a refreshing change. After a breakfast of fresh kiwi salad and coffee, I was offered the use of a shower, razors, and the daily newspaper. Computers, Xerox and fax machines, and other office equipment were warmed up and waiting.

Arriving in Wellington, I was met by Richard Naylor and his two sons, Jeremy and Chris. Richard runs the computer department for the city of Wellington; I had come to learn about City Net.

Even though it was the middle of summer vacation, a "southerly" had blown in and it was cool and windy. Richard dropped me off at the St. George hotel for a nap. Before going to sleep, though, I had to flush the toilet a few times just to watch the water swirl down in the opposite direction from what I was accustomed to. Having empirically narrowed my geographical coordinates to the Southern Hemisphere, I went to sleep.

Two hours later, Richard and the kids picked me up for a tour of New Zealand's capital. We went first to the new NZ $150-million city complex just being finished on the edge of Lambton harbor.

The complex includes not only the city offices, but a hands-on science museum for children, an art gallery, a huge library, and many other facilities for the public.

The Council in Wellington used to own everything from a milk bottling company to the bus service and the power company. Although many of these functions have been privatized, Richard's group still provides computing services to many of them. The collection of computers is known as City Net.

Most of the computing power comes from a large DEC installation, including nine big VAXen and a dozen µVAXen. Over 60 gigabytes of disk space are available, most of it in a VAX Cluster. The cluster provides disk striping, volume shadowing, and dual porting of disks, all facilities that help ensure good performance and reliability. In addition to the DEC equipment, there is an AS400 used to automate the library, as well as 50 PCs, a Honeywell, and an IBM RS 6000.

Since the city used to own the tram service, Richard was able to pull fiber throughout the downtown area, stringing it above the tram lines. Inside the buildings, unshielded twisted pair was used to wire the individual offices. Both voice and data went over this common infrastructure.

With a staff of 55, the computer department is able to deploy an impressive number of applications. A layered mapping database has the entire city of Wellington in it, including everything from sewers to phone lines to all roads and buildings. The mapping system is extensively used by city employees ranging from planners to mechanical engineers, and is even available to the general public through terminals in the library.

What is most interesting about City Net is its open philosophy. An Ultrix machine on the edge of the network is on the Internet and city employees have access to the full range of Internet services. City Net even provides accounts to the general public on the gateway system. Over 500 citizens of Wellington use the machine at no charge.

Wellington has a very active bulletin board community with over 35 boards in a city of only 150,000 people. Many of these boards use the Waffle BBS software, which includes support for the

UUCP protocols, making integration of the bulletin board community into the Internet as simple as dialing up the City Net hub. That night, I watched 9-year old Jeremy composing messages for a pen pal in Pittsburgh on a little Toshiba laptop running the BBS software. The minute Jeremy was done, his older brother grabbed the machine. Periodically, the laptop would be plugged into an RJ11 jack and mail exchanged with the central system.

Everything from a World Wildlife Fund training center to the children's museum to the milk company accessed City Net. Richard even wanted to put a hospitality database on the Internet to allow tourists to Telnet in and plan their vacations.

City Net is one of the best examples of a network as a truly public infrastructure I have seen. Extensive use of e-mail by children as part of Kids Net, the Discovery Museum, or just individual correspondence with pen pals helps to ensure that there will be a new generation of computer-literate children.

Providing a public utility to organizations like the milk company or the general public is done at very little marginal cost to the city. Many of the resources, such as the Internet gateway, are viewed as necessary for the city to do its job. Extending that service to the public or to commercial enterprises helps the city as a whole, as well as the direct users.

Invited for dinner to Richard's house, I brought two packets of Astronaut Ice Cream, which turned out to be the perfect gift. Chris was heavily involved in the local chapter of the Astronautics Association of New Zealand and had heard of this astronomical delicacy only through rumors. Chris wanted more information for his club, so his dad suggested that he Telnet into the NASA public server or send e-mail to some of the online PR hacks. Chris wanted my e-mail address so he could ask me questions later.

After a delicious dinner with a truly computer-literate family, Richard dropped me off back at my hotel. I had a Steinlager beer and watched steer wrestling from Montana in the bar before going up to pack for the next day's trip.

Saturday morning, I gulped down some fresh strawberries and a savory and took the plane down to Dunedin, on the southern tip of the South Island. The plane flew by the Southern Alps, then headed into the white-speckled hills of sheep country. New Zealand has 65 million sheep and 3 million people, and the South Island is the site of huge farms.

In Dunedin, I met Ian Forrester, Chief Scientist of the Ministry of Research, Science, and Technology. A former professor at Otago University in Dunedin, he keeps a house there even though he lives most of the time in Wellington.

The house was an old farm house, honeycombed with gardens and pastures for the horses and sheep. Ian's son, a medical student at Otago, lives there year round and Ian had come down for the summer holidays. We sat in a rose garden and drank Speight's Beer ("Pride of the South" as the label reads, though in much the same sense as Stroh's would be considered the pride of Detroit) while Ian's son cooked up some artichokes from the garden.

Ian started at Otago as a biochemistry professor. He was marginally interested in computers, using tools like Medline to search databases and using an early Apple computer. His main interests, though, were medicine and agriculture. Agriculture is the key industry in New Zealand and Ian was studying problems related to livestock.

Although bats were the only native mammal to the country, deer, elk (brought in by Teddy Roosevelt), and lots and lots of sheep had taken root. Ian's interest was in helping find ways to keep the population of animals genetically healthy. On a Ford Foundation fellowship in Laramie, Wyoming, he looked at topics like how to freeze elk semen to increase the diversity of the genetic pool. Throughout the 1980's, Ian continued this line of research. He spent a few more years at Otago, got interested in biotechnology, and went to Madison, Wisconsin for a few years.

Dunedin

Meanwhile, New Zealand was undergoing a revolution. The 1987 stock market crash had reduced the stock index by one-third and recovery was only marginal. GDP was growing by only a fraction of a percent.

In this dismal economic climate, and with a bloated government bureaucracy, New Zealand initiated a drastic deregulation campaign. Many large government departments became state-owned enterprises and many were then sold off. The telephone company, for example, was sold to Ameritech and Bell Atlantic.

Even traditional government departments began to be run like businesses. Heads of government departments were called chief executives. These executives negotiated contracts with specific output goals with the cabinet ministers for the area. Government employees were put under contracts.

Change was equally drastic in the area of government-sponsored research. New Zealand had long emphasized government laboratories over university efforts for research. The government researchers were spread out in different ministries, such as agriculture and forestry.

A small ministry of 30 people, to which Ian belongs, was formed to advise the cabinet on national research policies. Once the cabinet decided on national policy, money was funneled into a Public Good Science Fund, administered by a foundation. Researchers who wanted money submitted bids and, if they were awarded, signed contracts. Researchers were no longer guaranteed money if their work did not meet the strategic directions set out by the cabinet.

The next step was to remove the research efforts from the operational arms of the government. Ian and others worked as part of a committee which recommended that 10 independent research institutes be established, each headed by a chief executive. This plan was approved in June 1991 and had been implemented so quickly that the institutes were opening their doors a mere one year later.

As Chief Scientist, Ian was both scientific advisor to the government and an advocate for researchers. In going around and talking to people, he quickly saw that getting computers and communications onto the desks of researchers was a way to help the entire scientific community.

Although there was a university network in place, linked to PACCOM, each of the government research groups also had their own networks. The technical level of networking was uneven throughout the country and interconnection was sporadic.

With independent research institutes being formed, it was evident that some form of unified research network was needed. As part of the proposal to form the Crown Research Institutes, a recommendation was inserted to make a national research network a strategic direction. When the cabinet approved the divestiture plan for the institutes, a side benefit was approval for the national net.

Working out the mechanics for institutes and networks kept Ian busy most of the time, but as the first occupant of the post of Chief Scientist, he also had some freedom to help define his job. Looking at a national research network exposed Ian to topics like broadband networks. If this was the wave of the future, was there some way to speed up the future?

This was the genesis for the idea of making New Zealand into a world communications laboratory. Ian started to push the idea that the country could become a testbed for new technologies. Massive deregulation, small size, and an educated workforce would all make New Zealand an attractive place for large corporations to deploy and tune new technologies.

With unemployment at 10 percent and GDP flat, this also might be a way out of New Zealand's economic doldrums. Applications could be deployed to make industry more competitive and the workforce could be trained in high technology. He prepared a paper on the idea for the cabinet which authorized an in-depth study. When the second briefing paper was submitted, the cabinet asked Ian to start working with the private sector to develop a business plan.

In New Zealand's climate of deregulation, the World Communications Laboratory was certainly not going to be a large government project. Instead, Ian was trying to form a coalition, led by government but working with industry.

How could New Zealand get a state-of-the-art telecommunications system, the prerequisite to becoming a world testbed? Ian was hoping to follow the example set by the State of Connecticut. By pooling the purchasing power for telecommunications services and promising a long-term commitment, the state was able to convince Southern New England Bell that it was a sound business decision to invest in a large fiber network.

When I spoke to Ian, many of the details of the World Communications Laboratory were vague; the project was long on vision and short on substance. However, an active campaign was being waged to convince large corporations inside and outside of New Zealand as well as the general population that the project was viable.

The project was publicly unveiled to people in New Zealand in November 1991. To help build a constituency, Ian emphasized the benefits of high technology to traditional industries such as agriculture. He painted a picture of food stores in England using interactive video to decide how they wanted lamb chops cut. The specifications would go straight to the meat packing plant, which would scan the carcasses and make the optimal cuts. Just-in-time inventory management for the meat-packing industry.

At the same time, he was trying to drum up support from large multinational corporations for the project. He held a telephone conference with participants from groups like American Airlines and Citicorp to brief them on his vision.

Ian had adopted the "highways of the future" metaphor of Senator Gore with a vengeance. He saw the ports of the information age being established, and he wanted New Zealand to be one of those ports. The challenge would be building a political consensus and then performing the hard technical work to turn the vision into reality.

Ian Forrestor's World Communications Laboratory might or might not get off the ground, but this high-level policy focus on information technology was an important first step. Even if the only result turned out to be a good national research network, Ian's efforts would have paid off handsomely.

Saturday morning, I flew up to Auckland. With the whole weekend to kill, the largest city in New Zealand seemed to be a likely hunting range. Unfortunately, Auckland in January is kind of like Paris in August. A one-hour walk through town uncovered various flavors of tour groups but no Kiwis.

It was time for guerilla tourism. I reported to my local Hertz dealer and negotiated a rental. Lacking any knowledge of New Zealand, I flipped a coin and headed North. One hour later, I had successfully managed to stay on the left side of the road and hadn't run over any of the locals, so I left the motorway and got onto a sometimes-paved road down the Western shore.

I ended up at Muriwai beach, one of the few nesting sites for the gannet. After watching mama gannets regurgitating fish into their offspring, it felt like dinner time so I headed back into Auckland.

The pretty attendant at the Quality Inn suggested three restaurants for me. At the first, located right on the water, the maitre d' sniffed when I admitted to not having reservations and I was grudgingly shown to a table with a view of the wall next to several screaming infants. I declined.

At the second restaurant, I was summarily dismissed for not being a member of a tour group. At the third, I was told I could have a table, but would have to vacate it within the hour for the next booking.

With visions of being tossed onto the street in mid-potato, I hit the streets to go hunting. Ten minutes later, I spied a hip-looking couple dashing into a nondescript door. I followed them into a funky little place that called itself Four Steps to Heaven.

Four Steps to Heaven had a half-dozen tables and menus written on chalk boards. The grizzled cook in a white chef's hat peered out from behind his counter to see if customers were enjoying themselves. The waiter had a long spiel about the menu prepared and insisted on going through the talk in its entirety (despite the fact that I had heard three other tables receive the identical lecture).

Auckland

The cuisine was absolutely first rate. I started with smoked salmon from the South Islands, served with a mustard sauce dusted with paprika, nestled in a sea shell. My main course was the most impressive rack of lamb I've ever seen served with a piquant mint sauce. My table was so small I kept kicking my laptop in the case at my feet, hoping not to damage my rack of RAM.

Accompanying the lamb was a large platter of vegetables. The cauliflower was steamed and covered with a delicate cheese sauce. The potatoes were gratineed with onions. The piece de resistance, though, was zucchini, doused with ouzo, tomato juice, and hot peppers, and cooked with sesame oil.

The next day, I drove south to the harbors and bays on the eastern coast, cutting through farm land and country homes. Refreshed and ready to work, I dropped my car off and went home to pack for the next day's trip to Australia.

Sitting in the Auckland airport lounge, the power went out. The two ladies next to me immediately blamed the outage on computers and spent the next ten minutes yammering on about how computers had ruined everything and had given rise to a younger generation devoid of any useful skills.

"They can't even add without a calculator," one sighed. I restrained myself from commenting that she probably couldn't program a bubble sort to save her life. The large umbrella she kept in readiness at her side contributed to my reticence.

Arriving in Melbourne amidst a spate of "g'days," I presented my gift salamis at customs for inspection. Despite my pleas, the sausages were impounded and destroyed, leaving me without a food offering for my upcoming visit to Bangkok. Without a food offering, I had no bribe to motivate my friend the restauraunt critic and I had visions of him exacting his revenge by taking me out for Swiss steak and succotash.

I deposited my bags at my hotel and set off to try and read my e-mail. I took a tram towards the city, crossed over the Yarra River and Batman Avenue and headed up the hill to the University of Melbourne. There, I found the location of the Information Technology Center on the map and sat myself down in a large room filled with PCs and Macs. I picked a likely looking 386 and typed "telnet," and sure enough, a few seconds later I was happily deleting messages.

Since I wasn't expected until the next day, I walked back down the hill to find the world famous Royal Botanical Gardens. Both a formal garden and an arboretum, this is the kind of place you find written up in coffee table books and issues of the *National Geographic*.

The gardens certainly deserve their reputation. I walked past a cluster of Hoop pines, past a huge Monterey cypress planted by Prince Leopold in 1910, and through a grove of small but pungent Bhutan cypress. Next to all these evergreens was the Canary Island

Bed, with a rare arrow-wood tree surrounded by cactus-like succulents and asteraceae.

Further down the path was a row of aloe plants ranging from a few inches tall to huge bushes. Spiny agave and Mexican Yucca were mixed in, giving the desert-like setting a sharp contrast to the California air of the evergreens.

Below the beds was an intricate ornamental lake filled with ducks and black swans, edged with English Elms, Irish Strawberry trees, and groves of bamboo and Brazilian Pampas grass. To my disappointment, that evening's showing of *A Midsummer Night's Dream* was sold out, so I set out to find some dinner.

The closest I could find to local food was an Aussie Burger, a nice hamburger topped with the traditional bacon, egg, and beets. I headed instead up to Toorak Road for some Italian food.

Most of the restaurants were BYOs, so I went into the bottle shop and picked up a half bottle of local Cabernet Sauvignon, then went into Molina's Bistro, truly a fortuitous find. The appetizer was a Cervello alla Grenoblaise, lamb brains coated in beer batter and served with a delicate sauce of chives, capers, and lemon wedges, garnished with sprigs of fresh basil and fennel. It was accompanied by fresh, warm bread, dusted with basil and oregano from the herb garden out back.

My main dish was Saltimbocca à la Romano, baby veal in a sauce of sage and white wine, and served with a timbale of potato, onions, mushrooms, and cheese. Dessert was a home-made liqueur ice cream. Stuffed, I walked back to the hotel to get ready for my meetings the next day.

❏

Tuesday morning, I went back up the hill to find Chris Chaundy, Networks Manager for the University of Melbourne. The university network connected 74 buildings with a mix of fiber, unshielded twisted pair, microwave, and leased lines. Originally a massively bridged network, the university was rapidly completing the transition to a network based on routers.

The university is split into Mac and PC camps. The Macs used AppleTalk and 53 Banyan Vines servers take care of the PCs. The backbone network is mainly TCP/IP, although large DECnet and CDCNET applications are still running.

AppleTalk clients access the TCP/IP world using a Webster multiport gateway, a device similar to the Kinetics Fastpath. The multiport gateway was developed on campus before being commercialized by Webster.

All told, the network is your basic professionally-run, production environment. Large machines such as a Cyber 990, an IBM 3090, and a Maspar are all on the net. The library card catalogue, WAIS, X.500, and all the modern information services you would expect are all available.

This is one of those operations that has everything you would want. The information technology center has a regular, frequent schedule of training classes, extensive documentation, a custom programming group, a proactive help desk, spacious labs, and a trouble ticket system.

This is great for the university community, but certainly posed a challenge for the digital tourist. After all, what can you say about a place that does everything right?

After my briefing with Chris, I went across the street to meet the elusive Robert Elz, a long-time inhabitant of the Internet. Robert rarely works, or, for that matter even wakes, during the day, but I was in luck. Cricket matches were on this week and Robert had inverted his chronology to watch the games and post the results into netnews.

Robert's desk was stacked a few feet deep with paper, leaving only enough room for a keyboard and a half-dozen empty Coke cans. Robert had just returned from giving seminars in Thailand and the top of his stack included Thai-language keyboard templates. His wall had a map of all undersea cables in the Pacific region.

After some chitchat with Robert about mutual friends in Bangkok, I had worked a full two hours and then it was tea time. Back at the hotel, sitting in the lobby, I listened to the drivel of a lounge lizard playing a baby grand piano.

Melbourne

After the second drink, I realized that the piano was unmanned. The thing had broken into a jaunty Elton John tune, so I walked over to investigate. Under the piano was a Yamaha Disklavier, a digital version of the old player piano, hooked up with solenoids to activate the keys and provide a very exact replica of the original performance. The Elton John tune was from the album "Don't Shoot Me, I'm Only the Piano [Player]."

Wednesday evening, I flew in over the Sydney opera house and, after checking in, darted across the street for a quick bite of barbecued octopus. With a little time to kill, I strolled through neighboring King's Cross, the home of Sydney's red light district. Sipping a Foster's, I watched the strange melange of prostitutes looking for their first action of the night, world-weary backpackers trying to entertain themselves on a dollar, and a hip-looking hippie driving an antique Jaguar. Several Hare Krishnas trooped by, reminding me that it was time to go to work.

I was soon met by Bob Kummerfeld, chairman of the University of Sydney's Computer Science department. We dodged raindrops from my hotel over to the Hernandez Café, where we sat and talked over a café latte and a cappucino. Bob Kummerfeld was part of the first wave of networking, sparked by the Landweber symposiums. Bob attended his first one in Dublin, and ended up hosting the 1989 symposium in Sydney, the last one before the informal seminars metamorphisized into the much larger INET conferences.

In the late 70s, armed with VAXen and PDPs, Australia, like everyplace else, wanted to connect their computers together. Running an early version of UNIX, the obvious choice would have been to use the UUCP protocols. UUCP had some features that not everyone liked. Its designers had intended UUCP as an interim solution, but, as often happens with prototypes, it rapidly became entrenched.

Kummerfeld and his partner, Piers Lauder, decided that they could do better and set about designing an alternative set of protocols. The result was the Sydney University Network, known as the SUN protocols. The SUN protocol suite started out being used at Sydney, the software was quickly picked up by Robert Elz in Melbourne, and, by 1988, 1,000 sites were on the network. Since the acronym SUN was identified with the Stanford University Network, the collection of computers that used Kummerfeld and Lauder's protocols eventually became known as the Australian Computer Science network (ACSnet).

SUN is a protocol suite optimized for message handling. Unlike TCP/IP, it was not designed for interactive services such as Telnet. Message handling can be much more than e-mail and the SUN protocols supported services such as file transfer and remote printing.

The unit of transfer is the message, which can be infinitely long (although in practice, very long messages are broken up into manageable pieces). While UUCP performs error correction as it transfers the data, SUN uses a streaming protocol to send the entire message, identified as a series of packets. When the message is transmitted, the receiving end sends back a bitmap of corrupted or missing packets and those packets are then retransmitted.

When a connection is established between two hosts, UUCP only supports transfer of a single message in one direction. SUN, by contrast, is multichannel and full duplex. Full duplex means that messages can go in both directions. Multichannel means each direction is divided into four logical channels of different priorities.

Channel 1 is the highest priority and is used for network management messages. An example would be a message to decrease the packet size from the default of 1 kbyte down to the minimum of 32 bytes. On a dirty line, small packets reduces the amount of data to be resent later since an error would affect a smaller chunk of the message. It does so, of course, at the expense of throughput.

The other three channels are used for different kinds of message transfer. E-mail messages would typically travel on channel 2, allowing mail to get through even though a large file might be occupying channel 4. While it might take a longer time to get a large file through a link, it does mean that other applications are not frozen totally off the line.

With multiple channels sending data, a cut in the line can interrupt several different messages. Rather than start sending the message again, SUN allows the session to start up where it left off, something that UUCP does not do.

Use of multiple channels also tends to improve line utilization. When a message is received, the destination node must typically perform some processing. In a single channel application, the line would be idle during that time. With four channels, data transfer can continue.

Riding on top of the message transfer facility are applications. The suite has standard facilities such as file transfer and electronic mail and users can design their own protocols.

The file transfer protocol allows both senders and receivers to initiate transfers. To send a file, for example, the recipient's username and host are specified. The file would be spooled onto the target machine and e-mail sent to the recipient. The recipient could then chose whether or not to accept the file, moving it into personal disk space.

E-mail supported standard Internet-style mail based on RFC 822, making a gateway to the TCP/IP mail system almost a trivial task. E-mail with the SUN protocol suite allows the transfer of arbitrary binary images, a feature that has been only recently added into SMTP and RFC 822.

The architecture of messages and packets used in SUN allows a wide variety of different substrates to be used. Direct lines, modems, and X.25 are all used and the protocols can run on top of IP. Bob even claimed that the protocol could run successfully on telegraph lines, although nobody had yet had a pressing desire to run applications at 50 bps.

While Bob went on and described features ranging from dynamic routing protocols to broadcast and multicast support, I began to wonder why I was using UUCP on my home systems. The answer was fairly simple: UUCP was free and SUN wasn't.

Kummerfeld and his partner had formed a company called Message Handling Systems to market the software. The University of Sydney had a one-third stake in the company and the software was being pedaled as MHSnet. Formed in 1988, the company was still in its early stages, but Bob told me about a few recent successes. One was a large insurance network that links brokers together. The other was the Australian diplomatic corps, which would use MHSnet to link their worldwide operations.

Both groups were attracted to MHSnet by its ability to run over a wide variety of different transports, ranging from telegraph to IP. The message-based paradigm is quite appropriate for environments with only sporadic connectivity. The software is small and efficient, taking less than 100,000 lines of code.

Selling MHSnet to the government brought up the spectre of GOSIP.

"Didn't you have problems with OSI bigots?" I asked.

OSI was certainly an issue, he explained, but eventually it came down to practical issues such as whether software existed that could do the job. OSI as a general architecture certainly had appeal to many, but a lean and mean OSI that could run on low-quality, low-speed lines was not readily available. Indeed, one could argue that searching for such a beast was akin to looking for a hippopotamus capable of doing the limbo.

To Bob and many others in the research community, OSI has actually had a negative effect. If he proposed to do research on message handling, for example, somebody would invariably suggest that X.400 had already solved the issue and further research was superfluous.

Bob's theory was that the OSI wave had finally crested and people were settling on an environment characterized by IP over Foo and Foo over IP. OSI had promise, but while large groups had large meetings in a large number of locations, the IP community had mounted an equally ambitious but much more successful standards effort.

The IP process was organized to suit the needs of the technical people, not the desire to reach a political consensus among marketing representatives. The crucial difference between the two groups was that implementation and testing was the cardinal rule for the engineers. Bob cited the recent extensions to SMTP and RFC 822 to handle different kinds of data as an example. By the time the implementations reached standards status, a half-dozen implementations would already exist and be deployed.

The success of the Internet community didn't necessarily mean that there was no role for the more formal (i.e., slower) procedures like those used at the ITU. Bob pointed to a low-level substrate, such as the definition of a digital hierarchy of line speeds, as an issue that needed to be codified, ratified, and digested by a hierarchy of committees.

Of course, if low-level issues are the province of the public standards cartel in Geneva, that kind of leaves OSI out in the cold. After all, OSI starts work at about the same level as TCP/IP does. Since the OSI standards potatoes insist on defining theory first and leaving the implementations to "the market," they have little to contribute to the upper layers of the network, where implementation and testing are crucial.

I bid Bob Kummerfeld goodbye and went to my room to watch *Dallas*. It struck me that the politics of the Geneva standards cartel had an overwhelming resemblance to the goings-on at the Ewing Ranch. Perhaps I could write a nighttime soap called "ISO," complete with a season finale of "Who Killed FTAM?"

Canberra became the capital of Australia for the same reason Washington, D.C. became the capital of the U.S. In Australia's case, Canberra was chosen because it wasn't Melbourne and it wasn't Sydney and because it was somewhere between the two.

Canberra is also the capital of the Australian Academic Research Network (AARNet), a network managed by Geoff Huston. The network came into being after ACSnet began to feel the strain of, as Geoff puts it, "networking on two bob." ACSnet was strictly a volunteer effort between the computer science departments, with no management and no funding.

DEC's educational group had been providing international access, but after somebody took over the pipe for two days for a massive file transfer, they pulled the plug. Robert Elz, who had been handling most of the international liaison work, arranged an X.25 connection to UUnet in Virginia.

X.25 costs money, so Elz wrote software to provide accounting and chargeback to the users. Then, the first leased line, operating at 2,400 bps, was installed between Melbourne and Sydney. Networking was starting to cost money and it was evident that a more coordinated effort was needed.

About this same time, the central computer departments decided that networking shouldn't be left to computer science. The computer departments put together a proposal for a national research network based on X.25 and the U.K. Coloured Book standards.

This group went to the federal government, but the feds had no interest in funding a national network. Next, they approached the committee of Vice-Chancellors, a group of the heads of all 38 universities formed to lobby for the interests of higher education against other groups competing for a slice of the federal pie.

The Vice-Chancellors were interested, but weren't about to just hand the computer centers carte blanche. They initiated their own feasibility study. With the feasibility study, they decided the idea was worth pursuing and, in January 1989, formed two groups to develop the idea.

The first, the technical group, met for the first and last time that same month. "It was bloody obvious what needed to be done," Geoff said. The network would simply be multiprotocol routers and leased lines. No code to write, no research issues to investigate. You simply took out the price books and tariff charts and figured out what you could afford.

The policy and steering group only met three times. The Vice-Chancellor who chaired that group made it clear that they were there to build a network, "so let's get on with it." Geoff Huston is credited by many in Australia for helping to make sure that the process moved smoothly in both the policy and technical groups.

By November 1989, everything was done. Geoff placed orders for leased lines and Cisco routers, telling both vendors he wanted a delivery date of April. He told Cisco how he wanted the routers pre-configured. With that much lead time, there was no excuse for delivery problems and none occurred.

In the last week of April, all the boxes were in their locations and the 48 kbps lines were up and running. For the next three weeks, Geoff and his one other staff member toured the country turning on the boxes and connecting them to the campus Ethernet and the leased lines. In a total of three weeks, the entire network was up and running.

The network continued to be run with only two people, even though it had expanded to 2 Mbps lines on key routes and had a huge growth in traffic. By January 1991, over 40 Gbytes per week were being transferred on the network. One year later, 77 Gbytes per week went through, and peaks of 120 Gbytes per week were not uncommon.

The lack of religious battles over the network and the clockwork installation are widely credited to Geoff Huston's deft leadership. He defused any attempts to make the network overly complicated and insisted on a multiprotocol backbone so that any traffic the customer wanted to transfer could be transferred. He showed that installing a national network can truly be no fuss, no bother.

While hooking up the network internally was straightforward, there still remained issues in the Internet as a whole that were having a real effect on the operation of AARNet. Geoff gave me a dramatic example of one of these issues.

He started a traceroute to Barry Shein of Software Tool and Die, a well-known member of the Internet community. The traceroute went out from Canberra to the AARNet routers, reached NASA Ames and then failed. Barry is connected to the Internet via one of the Commercial Internet Exchange (CIX) members and AARNet connects to the Fix West. Since the NSFNET had refused to allow its routers to announce the presence of networks that had not signed the Appropriate Use Policy (AUP), the result was a fragmented Internet.

Software Tool and Die was a classic example of commercialization of the network. Barry Shein started the operation as a commercial IP service provider, giving over 1,000 people access to the Internet for an hourly fee, exactly the kind of thing the AUP warned against. Software Tool and Die could have waffled the issue, signing the policy and issuing severe warnings to its users, but that seemed kind of silly.

Since Software Tool and Die was an AlterNet hub, Barry Shein estimated that they had access to over 80 percent of the Internet. AlterNet was on the CIX, and most regionals had set up back door paths to one or the other of the commercial networks. Several commercial links to Europe existed, making international access to the EBONE and its regionals straightforward. In the U.S., only a few regionals in the Midwest had a single connection to NSFNET and were unreachable by Software Tool and Die customers. Most of the Pacific Rim, however, squeezed through the single Fix West link, and was cut off.

Geoff Huston was quite adamant that the Internet was facing many serious issues, fragmentation being one of the more visible. The address space was quickly filling up, there were so many networks that routing protocols were thrashing, and a host of other problems were surfacing.

These problems were not inevitable in Geoff's eyes. The Internet began as a single global community with ad hoc regulation of the network for the common good. Over time, under the pressures of massive growth and commercialization, the common view splintered into many camps. Global connectivity is a key issue for the Australian community. At the end of a long, skinny pipe, much of their traffic is communication with other parts of the world.

There is no group that worries about global connectivity, or even provides much in the way of a global regulatory framework and places like Australia, on the frontier of the Internet, feel the impact of this lawlessness first. The IAB had long been charged with looking out for the Internet, but Geoff pointed out that the heavy American bias of the IAB doomed it, particularly in Europe. Many Europeans continue to refer to the TCP/IP protocol suite as "DoD IP" to emphasize the American military origins of the Internet.

While the IAB had failed to provide a global framework for connectivity, the engineering arm, the IETF, had not always provided solutions to the problems that needed solving. Geoff emphasized that the IETF was a "tremendous asset" but also cited Marshall T. Rose's comment that "adult supervision" was needed.

The problem he saw was the lack of direction given to the IETF. The IAB and the IETF Steering Group (IESG) failed at times to provide a solid agenda and timetables of engineering problems that needed solutions. Problems such as the address space exhaustion were studied in a fairly ad hoc fashion, even as the problems became more and more pressing.

The IETF also suffered from an influx of goers and an increasing tendency by many to treat the occasion as a social forum rather than a working environment.

So what forum should guide the evolution of the Internet? Geoff placed some hope in bodies like the Internet Society, but also wanted to see an operational solution to the problem of global connectivity.

To participate in the global telephone network, you have to agree to certain sets of regulations in order to plug in. Geoff wanted to see some baseline regulations defining how one cooperates in the global network and, most importantly, a place to plug in to a global, neutral backbone.

Tony Rutkowski at the ITU

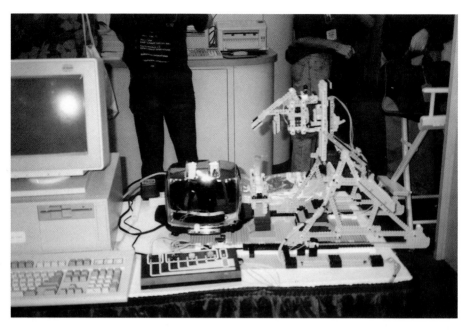

The Powerful Internet Toaster

INTEROP Before Midnight

Author Conducting Research in Honolulu

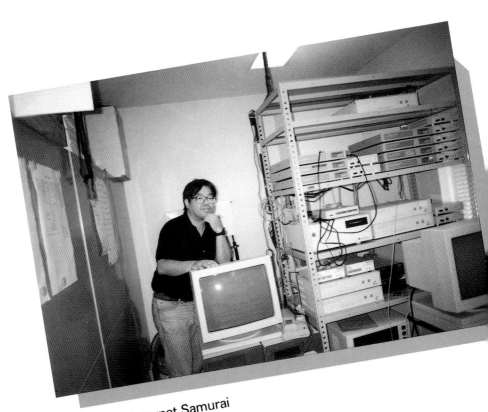

Jun Murai, Internet Samurai

The Akihabara 'With Me' Girls

An ISDN Pay Phone

Hong Kong's Infamous Golden Shopping Center

Motherboard Sale

Dennis Jennings, Uncle of the NSFnet

Vesa Parkkari in His Castle

Juha Heinänen in His Castle

Tom Grundner and his Skeleton Staff

Brewster Khale and his Printing Press

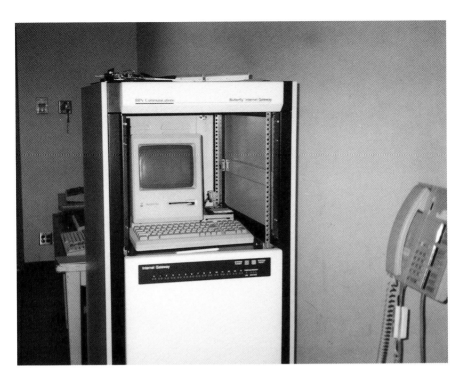

The Hidden Console in the Butterfly

Milo Medin and the Class C Airplane

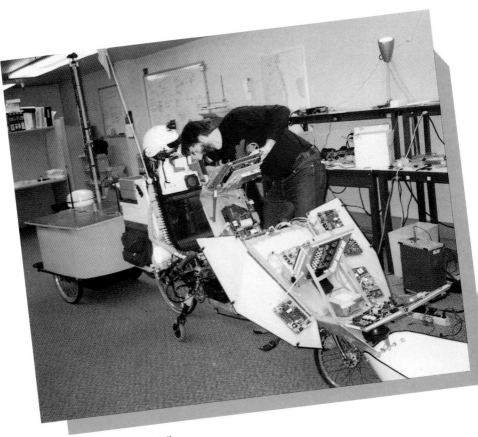
The Guy with the Bike

The Author Gets Grilled by his Translators

Bob Braden Works on the Paperless Office

The Royal Hong Kong Jockey Club

Dr. S. Ramani in Bombay

The NSFNET is an American backbone that also doubles as a global backbone, provided you play by NSF rules. Geoff wanted to see some higher tier, say some FDDI-like point of interconnection. This ring would have no policies prohibiting certain classes of traffic. If you pay your share of the ring infrastructure, and abide by certain technical rules, you can join.

Once on the ring, it is up to each individual member to decide whether or not to accept traffic from other ring members. This bilateral decision would allow the NSFNET to decline to accept commercial traffic without at the same time fragmenting the connectivity of the entire Pacific region.

That night, over dinner and drinks at Geoff's house, I brought up the question of international bodies again. He had high hopes for the Internet Society and I was curious whether he shared the opinion of Bob Kummerfeld in Sydney that the OSI process was a negative influence.

Geoff felt that OSI was a good thing. It had kept all the goers busy, preventing them from turning their attention to forums where real work was being done. Had OSI not existed, all these people would have looked around for something to do and found things like IETF meetings.

Under the Huston theory of standards development (and like any good theory, it helped predict and explain many phenomena of the standards world), one of the best things that could be done for the Internet community would be to initiate a movement for OSI++, keeping the standards potatoes fully occupied for another ten years.

Friday morning, I was up at an obscenely early hour to catch my flight to Adelaide. It was the end of a hectic week in Australia and I was off to meet Simon Hackett.

Simon took me to Internode Systems, his startup company of three people with a suite of offices located behind an Adelaide realty company. While Simon handled the usual run of emergencies caused by being away for an hour, I examined a disemboweled Sun 2 in the corner, an ancient machine based on a Motorola 68010. The huge 100 amp power supply had died, which was just as well because, as Simon pointed out, the thing drew enough power to drive a welder. Instead, a power supply from a little PC had been put into place and the Sun was up and running.

Simon is best known for putting funny things on the Internet. At INTEROP 90, with the help of TGV, he showed off his Internet CD player. The Internet CD player was a stereo system controllable over the network. Connectivity to the net was provided by a "magic box," consisting of a Motorola 68000 CPU, some memory, and a couple of RS-232 ports.

The box was connected to the INTEROP show network using a SLIP link off one of the RS-232 ports. Portable TCP/IP software from TGV and portable SNMP code from Epilogue Technology were put into the magic box.

The stereo system was a Pioneer tuner/amplifier, a Pioneer PD-M910 six-disc CD player, and two Klipsch speakers. The CD player has a "remote control in" jack, allowing control of both the tuner and the CD player. The output signal from the CD player has a mix of digital audio samples and status information.

An SNMP MIB was defined and some X Window System software was written to interact with the SNMP module on the magic box. Of course, any SNMP network management station could have been used, but the X software had a nice visual representation of the stereo system. When the network management station changed a

MIB variable, that information was used by Simon's code on the magic box to control the CD player.

The problem with doing something cute like the Internet CD player is that everybody expects you to top yourself the next year. At INTEROP 91 Fall, Simon separated the speakers from the CD player, using the Internet to distribute sound. The result was the NetPhone.

The NetPhone is basically just a protocol for encoding sound (or any other data) on the network. This protocol, the MultiMedia Data Switch (MMDS), is built on top of UDP. MMDS takes a sample of data, and puts it into a UDP packet along with information such as the sampling rate and encoding format. The protocol can handle most isochronous data such as video or audio.

The user input to the NetPhone is simply an audio board, such as those that are commonly found on Sun, NeXT, PC, or Macintosh computers. A telephone, speakers, or a microphone can all be connected to these boards.

To provide connections between two NetPhones, a switchboard was implemented on a VAX. A phone makes its presence known by registering itself with this central switchboard. To place a call, a user issues a request to the switchboard, which then contacts the destination. If the two devices are available and have compatible sampling rates, a connection is established.

If only two nodes want to talk, it doesn't make sense to have the switchboard in the middle. In that case, the switchboard issues redirect commands allowing the two nodes to send data packets directly to each other. In the case of multiport calls, data goes to the switchboard which replicates the packets and resends them.

MMDS is thus more than just a phone protocol, it is a way of moving sound and video around a wide-area network. At INTEROP 91 Fall, there were NetPhones on various computers, allowing people to talk to each other. People could place calls to the CD player in the TGV booth and listen to music. There were also two tuners, one in Melbourne and the other in Santa Cruz, allowing people to listen to radio broadcasts from either of the two cities.

NetPhones are one paradigm of moving sound over the network, and similar efforts are underway in several places, including

Xerox and ISI, to develop ways to use this technology. Another effort to incorporate sound into the network is multimedia electronic mail.

Were the two paradigms complementary or would one win? Simon felt that not only did we need both message-based and real-time voice transfer, the two technologies should be aligned, so a voice message could be redirected to a NetPhone, or so that a NetPhone might act as an answering machine, recording messages and then mailing them to the user.

Messaging is an important way to interact with people and certainly works on a one-to-one basis. However, the NetPhone also supports broadcast technologies, as in the case of allowing people all over the world to tune in to Melbourne radio and catch the cricket matches.

Simon was continuing to work on the question of moving voice around the network. He was looking at ways that the switchboard could be taken out of the loop and various other enhancements to the MMDS protocol.

His real interest, however, was the ability of the magic boxes to put arbitrary devices on a network. In that vein, he was working with Epilogue Technology to develop portable networking code that could be put on small, cheap boxes. That code includes TCP/IP, SNMP, and even higher level services such as NFS or the lpr protocol for line printing. The code runs on a box as stand-alone software, alleviating the overhead of a full operating system.

The possibilities for such a box are very intriguing. Think about being able to put an NFS server on the network by packaging a few disk drives into a small box. Or, put a tape drive in with a box and use that as a remote backup device on the network. The number of devices one could put on the network with a cheap interface are endless. How about a machine room temperature monitor? Or a toaster?

After we were done playing with the NetPhone and I had read my mail, we went to Simon's house where I met his partner in Internode Systems, Robyn Hill. Robyn is also a naturalist and conducts tours of the Great Barrier Reef, the outback, and other scenic attractions in Australia.

Adelaide

The next day, Robyn, Simon, and I went for a tour of the Barossa Valley, one of Australia's premier wine making regions. As we did the Barossa crawl, I was able to sample wines ranging from the typical mixes of Cabernet Sauvignon and Shiraz to more unusual varieties such as a fruity Alicante.

I was also able to replace the salami that was destroyed at customs with an appropriate offering of food for my friend in Bangkok. Each vinyard sold a variety of condiments, and I stocked up on pickled prunes and kiwi jams.

That night, we went to dinner at the Magic Flute, a posh restaurant in trendy North Adelaide. I started with a truffled boned quail, stuffed with a rich pheasant pate and glazed with aspic. My main course was an exquisitely prepared pigeon served over wild rice and finished with a Madeira glaze. Simon had the peppered kangaroo filet in a port gravy, garnished with the omnipresent beets, and Robyn chose rare mignons of venison.

Over dinner, we discussed the bizarre bribery trial of Joh Bjelke-Petersen, for decades the Premier of Queensland. It was alleged that Bjelke-Petersen wanted money from Alan Bond, one of the more prominent rat-pack Aussie businessmen. Instead of just handing over money in a brown paper bag, however, it is alleged that the bribe had an ingen ious twist. Allegedly as a prearranged pretext, Bond's national television network publicly insulted the prime minister. Bjelke-Petersen turned around and sued for libel and the case was settled out of court for cash.

While our dinner was good, dessert was absolutely spectacular. Robyn insisted we all get different things so she could taste them all. She ordered a gratin of raspberries and blueberries, cooked in a lemon custard and blowtorched on top to caramelize the sugar, then finished with an orange butter sauce. Simon had the hazelnut cake on a coulis of fresh coffee beans, and I had an ice cream confection of raspberry, mango, and passionfruit, separated by thin layers of chocolate licorice ice cream. Many fine lunches and dinners, indeed.

We headed back and I slept in their spare room, along with three very fat tree frogs that Robyn keeps, and a mountain of old disk drives that Simon keeps.

Monday morning, I headed down Singapore's spotless streets and, for Asia, an eerie lack of chaos, up to the National Computer Board to meet with Lew Yii Der, an engineer with Singapore's Public Works Department. On my last visit, I was told that a contract had been awarded for an electronic road pricing system, and I was eager to learn more details.

Since 1975, Singapore has attempted to reduce congestion in the central business district by charging a fee to enter the area during morning and evening rush hours. There are 26 entry points to the central area, known as the Restricted Zone.

Before entering the Restricted Zone, a motorist pays SG $3 (U.S. $1.76) for a license and, when passing the entry point, ensures that the large pass is prominently visible on the left side of the windshield. Failure to prominently display results in your license number being noted by the police patiently waiting by the side of the road and a ticket being mailed to your home.

On a typical day, 300,000 vehicles enter the Restricted Zone, of which 74,000 enter during the controlled periods. While the system has certainly reduced congestion by keeping those without the will or the resources away during rush hour, it has some drawbacks.

The biggest problem is the manual nature of the system. Cars must stop to buy a license and then slow down to wave it around. Fifty-two officers must be present at the 26 entry points to enforce the system.

Many cities throughout the world are investigating ways to reduce congestion in central business districts. Lew Yii Der explained the two classes of solutions: passive and active. In a passive system, people maintain accounts with the government. When you enter a restricted area, a charge is made to a person's account. Passive systems thus require central billing, are difficult to maintain, and, even for Singapore, are considered too intrusive. An active system uses a stored value card. Buying a card for a subway and then running it through a reader to activate the turnstile is an example of an active system.

While I had understood, perhaps wrongly, on my previous visit that a contract for an active system had already been awarded, a bit of further discussion turned up the information that not only had the contract not been awarded, but the RFP was not yet out. An RFP had been issued previously, but it was worded so vaguely that vendors were not sure what to bid.

Lew Yii Der gave me an outline of what the new RFP would specify. Smart cards would be mounted on all car windshields. Value for the cards would be added at sales outlets, where the motorist could also review the transaction log stored inside the card.

When a motorist entered the Restricted Zone, the car would pass under a microwave beam, which would debit the appropriate amount from the card. If the card didn't have enough money on it, a camera would be activated to take a picture of the rear license plate.

Since the system didn't exist, it was a bit hard to get more technical details, so I spent the rest of my allotted hour trying to learn more about other traffic control systems.

Like most big cities, Singapore has computerized its traffic lights in the busy parts of the city. The original system, installed in 1983, was a fixed system, meaning that the lights changed on some pre-arranged timetable. Each light had a phone line to a PDP computer which controlled the lights and attempted to form "green waves" so motorists could drive without stopping.

In 1987, Singapore installed an Australian dynamic traffic management system called SCATS. In addition to the traffic light, each intersection in this system has magnetic detector loops under the pavement, used to measure the flow of cars. A local controller at an intersection can use the absence or presence of cars to change lights. The data from the detector goes to the regional PDP computers, which use the traffic data to adjust light patterns while trying to establish green waves. Data from regional computers goes to a VAX 11/750, which is used by headquarters staff to monitor traffic status.

The traffic subsystem is also tied into the emergency fire system. Every major building in Singapore has a fire detection system tied into the fire stations. When there is a fire, trucks are automatically dispatched from fire stations to the fire location and the traffic system is used to provide a green wave for the trucks.

Between the parking control, the Restricted Zone, the traffic light management, the incredibly clean streets, and the gum-free subway system, it was certainly clear that Singapore was able to control the flow of people and vehicles in the city. I had to ask myself, however, if there wasn't some tradeoff between efficiency on the one hand and, on the other, an atmosphere that promotes a vibrant, creative, and (yes) fun place to live.

□

On my previous visit, I had learned about Tradenet, an EDI application for clearing customs paperwork. I had heard that not only was the customs work computerized, but that the Port of Singapore Authority (PSA) also had extensive systems. As with all things computer related, the National Computer Board was the place to start.

Singapore is one of the world's busiest ports. Since the opening of the Suez Canal in 1869, the island has been a major entrepôt port, serving as a clearinghouse between destinations in Europe and Asia.

That afternoon, Chew Keng Wah of NCB brought me down to the Tanjong Pagar terminal where container ships are loaded and unloaded. We met with Ang Chong Hoat, an MIS manager for the port.

Running a terminal as large as Tanjong Pagar is a highly complex scheduling problem. When a ship arrives, containers have to be unloaded and other containers loaded. Cranes mounted on rails are moved up and down the length of the wharf and are used to move containers on and off ships.

Incoming containers are then placed on trucks and run over to an adjacent storage yard. There, containers are picked up by an even bigger crane, a transtainer, a device that constructs huge piles. When the ship arrives that is to carry the container to its destination, the container makes the reverse journey back onto a ship.

The trick is to pile the containers so they are readily available when needed. You hope that the container you need at a given time is not buried under a pile of other containers that are not needed until later. It also makes sense to keep containers for similar destinations in the same area so the transtainer does not have to be moved around.

The goal of all this is to minimize the amount of time a ship stays berthed at the terminal, thus making more effective use of scarce resources. This minimization is done in an environment of scarcity, where cranes, ships, transtainers, and berths are all finite resources.

Planning the loading and unloading of ships and the subsequent placement of containers in the yard was once the province of a few highly skilled experts churning out plans by hand. A plan for a single ship could take many hours to work out. To automate the process, the Port Authority and the NCB developed an expert system to assist in the process, cutting the amount of time to develop a plan for a ship in half. The expert system was developed on Sun Workstations in Objective C and Lisp and took over 20 person-years.

The ship planning system is the first of six that the PSA will eventually deploy. Other systems will try to place ships in berths adjacent to the correct yards, or try to take ships in a yard and place them in a correct berth, or make available the proper number of resources for the unloading and loading of a ship.

The planning system thus tries to solve a complex optimization problem a level at a time. The results from one planning exercise, such as putting ships in the correct yards, is moved into a Sybase database. The next planning process takes that data out of Sybase and uses it as input for the next level of decision making.

Since a yard has many simultaneous ships, it is still possible for one ship-unloading plan to interfere with another ship-unloading plan. The last planning module is a terminal operations simulator, used to take all the separately developed plans and see if they conflict. If so, adjustments are made back up the chain.

The planning network at Tanjong Pagar terminal consists of two mirrored Sun servers with approximately 5 Gbytes of disk space.

Planners use 13 workstations and various plotters and printers. Some of the modules, such as the ship planning system, were already deployed. Others were just going online.

Planning is one of three major clusters of computer applications in use at the terminal. A large mainframe is used for documentation and a third cluster of applications runs on a Stratus computer for fault-tolerant control of yard operations.

The documentation system contains the raw data, such as when a ship is expected to arrive and the contents of that ship. This information is used to feed the planning process and also is used as input for back-office functions such as billing.

Data for the documentation system is fed in electronically by shipping agents. Small companies emulate a 3270 terminal and dial in to fill out forms. Larger organizations use an APPC-based program to transfer data. Documentation data resides in an Adabase/Natural application and an APPC-based program running on a SunLink gateway transfers data over to the Sybase server for planning.

The output from the planning process is used to feed the yard operations system. This system, which was preparing to go online when I visited, run on a Stratus platform. The Stratus is linked to the IBM using SNA APPC programs and to the Sun workstations using TCP/IP.

The output of the planning process is a series of loading and unloading sequences, specifying container ID numbers, yard locations, ship berth locations, and other identifying data. This information is translated into a series of micro instructions, such as a command to a transtainer to go to a certain location and expect to load a container with a certain label. Another command might give a truck instructions to move to a certain berth.

All this is computerized, with custom PC-based systems on cranes and transtainers. PSA trucks get transponders to track their location and simple display terminals give truckers instructions. Trucks entering the terminal from local shipping companies are given a window during which they are allowed to enter the yard, and at the gate the truck is fitted with a transponder.

Singapore

As we were driving back from the port, Chew Keng Wah told me that yard operations were only half of the port automation program. The other half was a marine-based control system that would automate the deployment of tugs, pilot allocation, and utilization of deep sea channels in and out of the terminals.

Having finished my whirlwind tour of Singapore, I went back to my hotel to meet a friend for a drink. Bob Cook (not his real name) is a salesman for a large computer company. Salesmen for this company are assigned territories by country. One will work in Thailand, another in Singapore. Bob gets whatever is left. His beat includes places like Brunei and Bangladesh.

I had brought Bob a copy of Stacker for his laptop PC. In many places, including Singapore, the only way to obtain legitimate software locally is to pay three times (or more) the U.S. list price. Even then, many U.S. companies refuse to provide technical support or updates.

Lack of legitimate software drives many otherwise honest users into the arms of the software pirates. Bob always gave me a list of software he needed to purchase and I brought it over for him on my trips. Updates and other luxuries he had to get for himself from the pirates.

After taking his software, Bob looked around the bar furtively. Everybody was watching the lounge lizards doing an Elton John tune. The audience was captivated, although the fact that the performers were clearly out of the Barry Manilow school just made me thirsty.

The coast clear, Bob told me he had something for me, giving me a conspiratorial wink and pulling out a package of Big Red chewing gum. Singapore had just banned all chewing gum on the island, a reaction to the fact that somebody had discarded their gum in a couple of subway doors, jamming them. The fine for importing this vile substance with intent to deal had been set at SG $10,000 and a year in jail. The government had just arrested four gum dealers and was threatening swift retaliatory action to any others fool enough to chew and talk about it. A government official was quick to point out, however, that only the importation and sale of the substance was banned, not its chewing.

Bob's frequent travels to free trade meccas like Bangladesh had given him plenty of opportunities, and he had become a key gum trafficker, supplying his teenage daughter and even occasionally offering a stick to friends.

After an interminable wait for my luggage in front of a sign reading "baggage claim," which had spent the time circling a belt in an adjacent unlabeled room, I cleared customs. Nobody was around as I emerged from customs at some obscure side door. Seeing nobody around an exit door in an Asian airport gives one an extremely eerie feeling, as these places usually pack several hundred expectant families into a mob around the exit, making the walk to the taxi stand challenging.

I looked around and saw that the mob was clustered around the other exit. I worked my way through the crowd into the middle, then turned around and walked back out. Sure enough, I soon saw a sign with my name on it and introduced myself to Rafee Yusoff from the Malaysian Institute of Microelectronic Systems (MIMOS).

Rafee spoke perfect English, not surprising since he went to school in Iowa. We drove past palms and the heavy vegetation that grows in this steaming jungle climate. The traffic was a far cry from Singapore. Cars here easily turned three lanes into 4 or 5 as they darted in and out in increasingly complex geometric progressions.

Malaysia is the world's top exporter of integrated circuits, the result of an aggressive government policy of free trade zones, cheap labor, and a strong work force. Malaysia had hoped that the huge manufacturing operations of companies like Motorola, Texas Instruments, and Sony would lead to technology transfer and increased value added by the Malaysian work force.

This didn't happen. The Malaysian computer industry continues to be devoted primarily to chip manufacture and assembly of components. MIMOS was created to help increase the Malaysian R&D effort and thus increase the technology transfer into the local community.

Rafee deposited me in a waiting area and soon ushered me into a large conference room with a very, very large conference table, capable of seating groups of 40 or 50 people at a time.

Two women in chadors came in, followed by Chandron Elam-vazuthi, a bearded UNIX guru. Finally, the head of the MIMOS computer systems division, Dr. Mohamed B. Awang-Lah came in with a very large pile of transparencies.

The purpose of my visit was a bit unclear, an understandable confusion since I was researching the Internet and Malaysia was not on said Internet. Dr. Mohamed gave a nice little speech, welcoming me to Malaysia and MIMOS for whatever reason it was that I had come. I then gave a nice little speech thanking MIMOS for their hospitality and thanking them in advance for whatever program they might have set up.

After the introductory formalities, Dr. Mohamed started pulling out transparencies and sliding them across the table so I could see them. Soon a large stack had been fanned out in front of me, explaining the purposes behind MIMOS and the various projects of the computer systems division.

One project that MIMOS had worked on was to help the Ministry of Education design the specifications for a PC to use in the school. Why not just buy some system that already existed? Chandran excused himself and ran upstairs to get a prototype of the Atom-1 computer for me to see.

The entire PC had been built into a wedge which fit under the keyboard, and included a 3.5-inch floppy drive, serial and printer ports, and even a network interface. When you set the computer on the table, the keyboard tilted up a few inches and used much less real estate than any normal desktop. You still needed room, though, for a display on the desk (or hanging someplace nearby).

After developing the prototypes, the Ministry of Education had then issued a Request for Proposal (RFP) and a private company took over the manufacture and delivered units for a fairly low cost. Sixty schools were in the process of putting in 20 PCs each and the Ministry had plans to computerize all 1,300 secondary schools.

At this point, we paused while cups of Nescafé were poured for all of us, accompanied by sticky green sweets and some spicy meat pastries. While sipping my coffee, I looked around the room and noticed that everybody had notebooks and everyone seemed to be taking lots of notes.

Between bites of pastries, we examined some more transparencies describing JARING, the proposed national research network for Malaysia. JARING means net in Malaysian, but I also learned that in English it had a much longer meaning, spelled out in a little poem at the beginning of a brochure I was given:

Joint Development IT Infra-structure Built Upon
Advanced Technology; Supports Multidisciplinary Collaborative
Research, Development, and Educational Activities; Reflects
Integrated Development Strategy Through Computer
Networking; and has Worldwide Connectivity for
Global Communication and Information Exchange.

Wow! I wasn't quite able to discern from the poem, however, what the network might look like. There were plans to link all the major universities and cities, and JARING was waiting until Telekom Malaysia would be able to deliver a 64 kbps line, a process that would take some time.

In Kuala Lumpur, several institutions were connected together using X.25 with UUCP and X.28/X.29 protocols. An international X.25 connection provided the link to UUnet. TCP/IP links within Kuala Lumpur were running, but I was unsure of exactly where and what they were used for.

MIMOS was planning on making the network some mix of X.25 and TCP/IP. Apparently, they needed a solution that would allow some fairly ancient IBM computers in government ministries to participate in the network without requiring those ministries to spend any money, and straight X.25 solutions were old enough to work on all of these machines.

We broke for a fine lunch of curried chicken, shrimp sambal with chilies, and a delicious omelette stuffed with sweet and spicy vegetables. With some time to kill before the afternoon meeting MIMOS had set up, I was left in the MIMOS library. Perusing the shelves, I spotted a copy of the Internet Managers Guide right next to a copy of the Concise Encyclopedia of Islam.

❏

My MIMOS experience was a bit different from my usual site visit. Normally, I asked people for help in a new country and got back a list of e-mail addresses, which I used to set up a series of appointments. Some appointments were time definite, others were vague promises of intent.

Rather than giving me pointers, MIMOS had set up my entire itinerary. In fact, they would be accompanying me to all meetings. Dr. Mohamed made it clear that the MIMOS name had been advanced on my behalf and it was understood that I should behave accordingly. Rafee continually probed to find out what the nature of my writing would be, perhaps hoping to avert a potentially embarrassing piece.

That afternoon, Chandran and one of the women in chadors, accompanied by a MIMOS driver, were my escorts to go visit the headquarters of Plus, a private toll road that would span the Malay peninsula from the northern border with Thailand down to Singapore.

I had heard that Malaysia was laying fiber optic cable when they built roads and it turned out that the rumors I had been hearing about for two years had to do with the Plus project. While the toll road was being installed, the corporation had planted a bundle of 36 fiber cores, each capable of operating at anywhere from 34 Mbps up to 140 Mbps. The business case for the fiber had been made for internal operation of the toll road, but it was evident that quite a bit of spare capacity had been installed.

I met with a team of five Plus MIS employees, headed by Rosli Md Tan. They joined our MIMOS delegation to form a fairly large party sitting around a large conference table.

The MIS staff estimated that they would take roughly 8 Mbps of the fiber capacity for their internal network. They would also use fiber for the toll plaza voice network. The 8 Mbps data bandwidth was being set up as a large extended Ethernet spanning the entire Malay peninsula.

The lowest unit of operation in a toll road is the lane in a toll plaza. Each lane in Plus would get a lane controller unit, a customized PC that connected to the cash register, the light on top of the booth to signal that the lane is open, and various other toll collection accoutrements.

Up to 17 lanes in a plaza would then be connected by 9,600 bps serial lines into a PC that would act as a data collection unit. An 18th virtual lane controller would be available inside the toll plaza headquarters to be used for collection of cash for things like monthly passes.

The PC concentrator would in turn connect to a μVAX, which would act as the central computing resource for the toll plaza. The μVAX would also support management terminals as well as a point-of-sale terminal.

The toll plaza μVAX would use the fiber infrastructure to periodically upload data to regional headquarters, which are equipped with a VAX Cluster.

Inbetween the region and the toll plaza is an intermediate unit of management, the section. Section headquarters don't have VAXen and must therefore go to regional headquarters for their data. Each section would have a set of terminals connected into the fiber patch panel, just as a voice phone would connect. At regional, a terminal server would take the incoming lines, thus connecting the terminal to the VAX cluster using the DEC LAT protocols.

One interesting aspect of the toll road is that it must break in Kuala Lumpur, since Plus does not have permission to cross the city. To connect the northern and southern segments, Plus had leased an 8 Mbps line from Telekom Malaysia. One more 8 Mbps leased segment linked the northern segment to a VAX 6100 located at Plus headquarters, a building located, for some reason I could not understand, away from the toll road.

Plus hoped to have the first segment, going 100 kilometers northward from Kuala Lumpur, up by August 1992. The entire road, and thus the management network, would be completed by 1994.

How would the spare bandwidth be allocated? Plus was owned by a holding company called the Renang Group, which also owned an electromechanical consulting organization known as Time Engineering.

Time Engineering had applied for a license and was about to become Malaysia's second telephone company, providing at least long-haul data communications and possibly other services such as voice. The fact that Time Engineering had applied for a license was somewhat of a formality as the Renang Group was owned by Malaysia's ruling party, a group that had been in power since 1957. As one embassy official sardonically put it, approval seemed "likely."

□

The next morning, I passed up the opportunity provided by my hotel for a "western breakfast buffet" featuring such delicacies as beef bacon, stale toasted white bread, and a tray of what was labeled "exotic tropical fruits" but contained instead grapes and honeydew melon.

Maybe honeydew was exotic in Malaysia, but I opted instead for a dish one-third the price of the buffet (but still an order of magnitude more than I would have paid on the street) of teocheow, a rice porridge accompanied by small portions of chicken sambal, dried anchovies mixed with peanuts, a pungent fish with black beans, and half a salted egg.

Later, Rafee picked me up to bring me to Telekom Malaysia, the recently privatized government PTT. I was interested to see the status of their fiber infrastructure given the bold moves by Plus and Time Engineering.

I noticed that everywhere we went, people always spoke to Rafee in English, even though I stood in the background. Even parking lot attendants would break into English, asking Rafee how long he intended to stay, as if he had turned into a foreigner by being with me.

We reported to the 21st floor of the Wisma building only to find that the head of the Network Technical Services Division, whom we were supposed to meet, was not in that day. Suddenly, the conversation switched into rapid Malay. After a few minutes, a deputy division head was produced and we were ushered into the division director's office to meet with Ahmad Tarmidi.

Rafee made a nice speech thanking Mr. Tarmidi for seeing us and introducing MIMOS. I introduced myself as a reporter for *Communications Week* and explained that I was interested in the status of the fiber infrastructure.

Ahmad Tarmidi then made a short, indefinite speech explaining that fiber played an important role in Malaysia's future, as did technologies like ISDN. The PTT was pulling fiber down the major north-south roads (with the obvious exception of Plus) and hoped to have coverage of the Peninsula by 1995.

As to the specific services or the specific infrastructure, the conversation was more than a bit vague. Yet, on the way outside, Mr. Tarmadi called Rafee back for a hurried conversation. Rafee explained that the fact that I was a reporter had hit home and Tarmadi was worried I would give away sensitive business plans. I assured everybody that no strategic business advantage would be lost as a result of our little chat.

❐

After a nice lunch in the MIMOS cafeteria, where I decided to skip the fish head curry in favor of less exotic fare, we headed off to visit Tenaga Nasional Berhad, the national electric company and another group that was laying a fiber infrastructure.

At Tenaga, a group of only four people met us, still outnumbering our own delegation of three. The assistant general manager for information systems, Abdul Rahman Bin Shafi, welcomed us and gave us all, including his own staff, a document describing the Distributed Source Data Generation Project.

I flipped through the four-page document, scanning it for information. Abdul called the meeting to order and asked us all to turn to page 1, where he commenced to read the entire text aloud.

Tenaga was proud to have what it called the largest distributed systems project in ASEAN. Implemented over a 36-month period at a cost of 18 million ringgit (U.S. $7.2 million), the project had connected 135 district offices and power stations of the electric utility system.

Processing oomph for the system was provided by a pair of fault-tolerant IBM 4300s. Distributed processing was the realm of Nixdorf computers, the prime contractor on the project. Telekom Malaysia's X.25 network, Maypac, was used to connect district offices to headquarters at speeds ranging from 2,400 to 4,800 bps and occasionally at 9,600 bps.

Applications consisted of various ways to input paper records, such as allowing the fact that a bill was paid and money collected to be transmitted to headquarters. Previously, the data had been input at headquarters, meaning that errors in entry codes and the like had not been caught until the data was well downstream.

After the briefing paper was read, a huge TV was wheeled in. While it was being set up, Rafee made polite chitchat about the recent renovation of the MIS office space. We all commented on how well-lit the offices were, certainly an appropriate attribute for the offices of a monopoly electric utility.

The video was then displayed. Ten minutes and forty-eight seconds long, the in-house video explained the success of ASEAN's largest distributed project, accompanied throughout by a driving disco beat. Near the end, the disco turned into an anthem (though still accompanied by the disco drums), the hyperbole flew thick and fast and then finally the lights went back up to monopoly brightness.

I looked around the table and saw that everybody in the meeting had a briefing packet, consisting of my resume, a Xerox of the cover of STACKS, a letter from MIMOS, and an internal Tenaga memo with a very long routing slip on it.

Next on the agenda was a description of a home-grown communications system, used to control the power substations. Substations could be located in very remote areas, so it was not possible to count on the telephone company to provide even voice service.

The system consisted of twisted pair lines running along with the power lines and providing data transmission at 100 and 600 bps. One function of this communications system was to allow central headquarters to activate an emergency cutoff switch at a substation to prevent damage to the larger network.

Kuala Lumpur

Tenaga was in the process of replacing the control system with a fiber optic network running along the power lines. The fiber would support cascaded, automated remote power substations and would even allow transmission of video images for monitoring and security. Tenaga was laying cables of 10 fibers, giving it a huge capacity for future expansion (or sale to a telephone company).

We finished our meeting just before 4:00 P.M., allowing Rafee to drop me at a taxi stand a few minutes after four. Government employees are released at precisely 4:15, and a 20-minute ride immediately turns into a 90-minute ordeal. I caught my taxi at 4:08, hitting the airport just ahead of the wave.

Kuala Lumpur, like many airports in developing countries, has an acute shortage of terminal space, meaning that you cannot check in until two hours before a flight. It was a hot, humid jungle afternoon and I had several hours to kill before I could check in.

I found a cart with a broken wheel and piled my garment bag and computer case into it and took off my jacket and rolled up my sleeves. I jumped my cart over the high curb, played chicken with a taxi (he won), and went across the street to find a bar.

The airport hotel had a choice of stairs and an elevator. The stairs had a big picture of a durian, with the circle and the slash around it spelling out in terms suitable for international tourists that this hotel was a "No Durian" area. The elevator, used by westerners to get into the main lobby, had no need for such a sign. The picture of the durian reminded me that I was soon going to be in Bangkok, where I would be able to get my fill of this strange, odoriferous fruit.

After a snack in the restauraunt of baby octopi on a bed of shredded jellyfish, I went to find the bar. Sitting in the small crowded bar, I watched a TV special on the wonders of Malaysian industry, focusing in this episode on the life of a pineapple.

At 7:23, the screen went blank and was replaced with a picture of a big clock. How handy, I thought, a time service that randomly appears. The clock was soon replaced by pictures of Mecca and the sound of the call to prayer. Arabic and Malay subtitles started filling the screen and rolling off, accompanied by an upbeat, yet inspirational soundtrack. Around me, the bartenders continued

217

preparing drinks. Prayers finished, the screen did another context switch back to the marvelous Malay miracle, now in the middle of a scene of pineapples getting lobotomies, interspersed with shots that featured happy foreign tourists on idyllic beaches eating pineapple.

I left to stand in line and check in, cleared immigration, and walked past the endless row of duty-free shops, including one selling bags of dried mangoes and prunes, items that I couldn't recall falling under the duty-free exemption in too many countries.

With great relief, I found the doors of the CIP lounge, a cool plush oasis for Commercially Important Persons. Making a living as a writer is kind of the antithesis of the CIP, and I take great delight in making myself at home in such facilities whenever I can fool the authorities into letting me in.

As you travel up the peninsula from Singapore, things get more chaotic, more exotic, more Asian. For sheer density of activity, Hong Kong represents the peak, with things getting a bit more orderly as you head north towards Korea and Japan. Orderly is, of course, relative by Asian standards; the chaos level of any of these places is several orders of magnitude over any U.S. city.

For mystery, though, you find your peak load in Bangkok. This was my tenth visit to Bangkok and I still had only a vague inkling of how the place worked. The chaos is there, but unlike Hong Kong, you can't get a handle on it. Things are happening, but you don't know what, and nobody stops to tell you.

With the temperature a balmy 85° F and the Thais all wearing sweaters to ward off the cold, I set out on foot down Ploenchit Road to find the stock exchange. Dozens of large construction projects were all packed in together, part of Bangkok's expansion as the only real city in a country with the fastest growing economy in the world. For years, the growth in GNP had been averaging over 7 percent per year and from 1987 to 1990, GNP grew at an amazing 11 percent per year.

Each construction site was packed with a hundred or more laborers from the Isan northeast of Thailand, near the Laotian and Cambodian borders. Teenage boys and girls worked alongside a few older workers in their 20s or 30s. They would stay at the same site for weeks or even months, living in the building as it shot up. A dozen or so food stalls clustered around each site, with old ladies and young girls making Isan food such as the fiery som tam, a papaya and chili salad made with lime juice and fish sauce (and, in the more authentic versions of the dish, served with crickets or land crabs for that extra crunch). Other stalls had dried fish, sticky rice, or grilled chicken, with construction workers ambling from one to the other, poking at the food and trying to decide what to eat.

The morning rush hour was in full swing and I waited at the intersection with Wittayu Road, watching the police in their traffic booth act as DJs, interspersing jaunty music with inspirational speeches intended to motivate motorists and pedestrians to conduct their business with dispatch. Of course, everybody went their own way. This particular section of Ploenchit road had once been designated by the police chief as a "traffic law observance zone," a title that did more to underscore the status of laws as suggestions than it did to convince anybody to change their driving habits.

Wittayu road is a wide, shaded boulevard, lined with embassies and a few fancy hotels. I walked past the Imperial Hotel, site of the annual Fourth of July festival that offers free vasectomies and hot dogs. This event is sponsored by a Thai non-profit family planning and rural development group I had worked with.

My appointment was at the Stock Exchange of Thailand (SET) with Dr. Surat Palalikit, a senior vice-president in charge of the MIS operation. I presented my business card to the security guard, announcing myself in Thai. He nodded and picked up the phone.

"A farang is here for Dr. Surat," he said. Except for a few close friends, Thais always refer to me as "farang," a foreigner, rather than by name. I occasionally bridled at being called "Mr. Foreigner," but realized that my name was virtually unpronounceable in Thai. The closest people usually got was "Mah-Lah-Moo" which translates into Thai as "come hunt the pig."

Dr. Surat was an energetic man, full of charm and speaking perfect English. Trained as a molecular chemist, he had been a professor at both Mahidon and Chulalongkorn Universities, two of the top Thai schools.

A lack of computers made it challenging to do much research in molecular chemistry, so Dr. Surat decided to moonlight. A friend of his ran Chase Manhattan's computers in Thailand and asked Dr. Surat to supervise the creation of a general ledger system.

The system went in and worked. His friend was promoted to Hong Kong and Dr. Surat was given the job as EDP manager. After a couple of years doing that, he supervised the creation of an ATM network linking seven large banks. It was evident that, by now, molecular chemistry was a hobby and he had found his calling in the financial markets.

Bangkok

At that time, the Stock Exchange of Thailand was running a few PCs on a local area network. A committee was formed to go up to Taiwan and investigate their EDP system and Dr. Surat was invited along. The Taiwanese exchange was working well and it was evident that Thailand needed to engage in some form of expansion to support a rapidly growing stock market.

The choice was whether to make or buy a system. Dr. Surat presented the case for buying as much as possible, so strongly that they made him the EDP manager. That's when Dr. Surat met Mary Jo Moccia, the person who had built the Midwest Stock Exchange system from the ground up and was porting her solution to stock exchanges all over the world.

I had met Mary Jo on my trip to Thailand the previous year. We had sat next to each other for six hours on a plane and spent the time talking about everything from DECnet bugs to the differences in CPU architectures and their implication for efficient database engines to the long-term financial viability of DEC.

Gruff, chain smoking, highly technical, everybody who worked with Mary Jo described her as one of the best MIS managers they had ever met. We had both been staying at the Regent Hotel, and all week I kept bumping into her. My consulting was done at the end of the week, and we had made tentative plans to get together Saturday morning for breakfast.

Saturday morning, I picked up the phone and asked the operator to connect me to Mary Jo's room.

"I'm sorry, but she has passed away," was the reply. Thinking this was some kind of bizarre translation problem, I went downstairs to investigate.

While I was trying to get a manager at the desk, one of her staff passed by and overheard my conversation. I found out that Mary Jo had gone to bed after her weekly get-together with her staff and died during the night.

Four very young, very shocked staff members stood around not knowing what to do. A U.S. embassy official took care of the details and got them booked on the next flight home, coincidentally the same flight I took.

I tried briefly to cheer them up, but there is really nothing you can say or do that will help in such a situation. I wrote an obituary for *Computerworld*, but the gesture felt empty and meaningless in the face of such a sudden and tragic loss.

Dr. Surat and I talked about Mary Jo Moccia and it was evident that in the year that had passed since her death the project had gotten back on track, but the loss still hurt.

SET had resisted the temptation to run their operation on a large IBM or a fault-tolerant platform like Stratus or Tandem. Instead, their system was based on distributed minicomputers and workstations, centered around a fairly small VAX Cluster.

The back-end matching system, which takes care of the mechanics of buying and selling, is a cluster of two VAX 6510s. Three VAX 3800 systems provide front-end processing to the network of 40 brokers. Each broker has a choice of an IBM AS 400, a Stratus, or DEC equipment.

All the SET VAXen share an Ethernet segment. The brokers connect to the front end VAXen using simple leased lines. Since no modems are involved (and leased lines are hard to hack), security is fairly straightforward.

In case the computer-to-computer links between the front-end systems and the brokers fail, each broker also has a terminal connecting to a terminal server on the SET Ethernet. The terminals function as a backup in case the fancier front-end system goes down.

The day before I visited, the SET had reached an all-time high volume of 8.585 billion baht (U.S. $343 million). The day I was there, as the *Bangkok Post* screamed out the next day, "the bull turned bionic," reaching a total volume of 12.341 billion baht. The business section of the *Post* also went bionic, raving on about the "Super Bull" and the "Galloping Bull," and generally carrying this metaphor so far that I felt like reaching for a shovel.

Despite the metaphors, things were pretty calm at the exchange offices. People drifted in and out of Dr. Surat's office, sat and listened to our conversation for a while, and occasionally he would step out and talk with them for a few minutes.

The system seemed to work fine. One broker switched to the terminal server backup and a meeting was called with the MIS staff and the brokers just to make sure things were under control. Even the broker's offices, in a frenzy by Thai standards, seemed fairly calm to me.

While the bull was going bionic, Dr. Surat and I sipped our coffees and chatted about the other two pieces of his MIS operation. One was the price reporting system, designed to feed out status information to the ultra-modern, wall-sized displays on the walls of most brokerages, as well as VT terminals and PCs all over town.

The other big component was called the SET Information Management System. Under development, this system consisted of an IBM RISC processor running AIX and Ingres. Brokers and companies would use this system to enter and retrieve information such as financial statements, profiles, and other fairly static information about stocks traded on the exchange.

I asked how he planned to support generalized dial-in in an environment where security was an issue. We tossed around the idea of a PC with modems, isolated from the net. The PC would accept uploads from people. At the end of the day, simple virus checks and authentication would be run. Then, the modems would be turned off and a switch flipped to connect the PC to the AIX system. The semi-validated data would be loaded into the Ingres database, presumably with more stringent data checking.

Letting the public retrieve information without giving them access to the Ingres engine could be done in a similar fashion, caching standard reports to a PC and then disconnecting it from the net. The database engine could still be available to the brokers over the network, allowing them to retrieve more sophisticated reports.

Like a good consultant, I threw this scheme on the table, then left before the dangers of reality exposed any flaws. Having worked my two hours for the day, I headed up Sarasin road, passed a pushcart selling crab mousse in banana leaf, and stopped in front of the black chicken joint.

This shop specializes in chickens that have been bred to be black all the way through to the bone. The chicken is steeped in medicinal herbs and is considered to be good for all sorts of things like prosperity and virility (although I must admit, it tastes quite similar to your basic New England boiled chicken). I once brought a farang acquaintance in there and, needing one more dish to round out the meal, ordered "chicken leg in garlic sauce." We were presented with a platter of steamed chicken feet in a sticky gel of garlic and agar.

I turned down Ratjadamri road and walked past the Lumpini Park, one of the few large parks in a city of 8 million people, and headed towards the *Bangkok Post*. I wrote myself into the visitor log and then reached over the receptionist's desk and into the top drawer and grabbed a badge. If you execute this maneuver with enough confidence, you walk right in. Show the slightest hesitation, however, and the bored receptionist will confine you to a plastic couch to await an escort.

In the news room, I walked past desks all jammed together, several feet deep in old newspapers, press releases, books, and posters, and sat down at the empty desk of my friend Bob Halliday. Bob is officially a sub-editor, charged with turning copy for the Outlook section into a semblance of English.

He is better known, however, for his book and music reviews. He approaches legendary status in Bangkok for his restaurant reviews, written under a pen name which means *Sea Toad* in Thai.

Bob and I have an understanding. I bring him offerings of food and he introduces me to some of the best restaurants I've ever been to. I call him periodically from the States and he briefs me in great detail on the latest saffron chicken joint or some obscure noodle pushcart that has a line of Mercedes a mile long waiting for food.

I dug into my dignified-looking black leather briefcase and pulled out a jar of pickled prunes and the last remaining packet of Astronaut Ice Cream. I also told him about the grisly fate of his salami, destroyed by the Australian meat police, a story so sad that it prompted Bob to wax poetic about a previous batch of sausages I brought over.

After a brief period of contemplation over the salami (Bob was sure that customs in Australia was at that moment gorging themselves on the links that were rightfully his), he began eyeing the ice cream. I insisted that this chalky, freeze-dried substance would have much better ice cream-like qualities if served cold, but I could tell that my arguments were having little weight.

While Bob struggled with this dilemma, I went over to the offices of United Press International to meet a friend who rents space in the back. Peter Jansen is a long-time Asia resident who now writes a report about doing business in Vietnam. Writing about doing business in Vietnam is kind of like writing artificial intelligence programs in Cobol, so I always make a point of looking Peter up to see how he is getting along.

Peter and I walked over to the Dusit Thani hotel and took the elevator up to the top floor. Instead of heading into the penthouse bar, we took a set of stairs marked only with a sign reading "members only" to the Foreign Correspondents Club of Thailand. Sitting in this quiet bar, surrounded by pictures of wars and riots in Laos, Burma, Vietnam, Cambodia, and Thailand, we drank a long string of Kloster beers. Most expatriate residents of Thailand prefer Kloster over the better-known Singha, Singha being rumored (probably unjustly) to contain formaldehyde as a preservative against heat.

That night, Bob had a column to write, so we met up with two other friends to do research. Peter Skilling is a noted scholar of Tibetan literature and Norman Bottorff spent years helping to coordinate ABC News coverage for Southeast Asia, including extended stints coordinating the coverage of hot spots like Tianamen Square and the Iran-Iraq war.

The four of us piled into a taxi and headed out to Soi Nana. Our taxi went skidding into a major road and we all groaned as we saw that it was backed up for at least an hour. We piled back out and walked over to Nasir Al-Masri, an Egyptian restaurant that, before the Kuwait war, would have been crawling with Arabs and prostitutes eyeing each other hungrily.

The war had drastically reduced the Arab tourist trade and the restaurant was filled instead with the world traveller set, sitting in pairs looking sophisticated (and bored). We sat down, making lots of noise, and Bob and Peter entered a long, complicated negotiation in Thai with the waiter. Norman and I flagged down another waiter and ordered beer.

First to arrive on our table was a wonderful dish of hummus, labeled on the menu as "creamy stuff of crains Conianing Sesame Paste." We instantly devoured the first plate and sent the waiter back for more.

Soon, more and more plates arrived, filled with roast lamb, a fava bean salad soaked in garlic, stuffed vegetables, and more. Around us, the world travellers stopped eating and watched the parade of food to our table with growing awe. Mountains of bread disappeared in a flurry as we dipped into plates, stopping only to order yet more food or to hand empty plates to waiters as they passed by.

After 18 plates of food, I could see that we had made the diary of the backpacker sitting next to us. She was so impressed she forgot totally about her own dinner, her mouth opening wider and wider as we went for the world hummus-eating record.

We finished the last of the grilled pigeon and ordered Turkish coffee, served in thimble sized glasses and having the consistency of 40 weight motor oil. Our research done, we paid the bill of 1,500 baht (U.S. $60), quite high by Thai standards, and left.

❏

Friday morning, I walked a block from my hotel to Chitlom Towers to meet Narong Intante, president of the Value Group. Like many Thai companies, this one seemed to have a million names. The lobby listing sent me to the Value Systems Co., Ltd. On the seventh floor, the signs read Value Component Co., and Value Data Co, Ltd.

I sat in the lobby of Value* and sipped my cup of freshly brewed Nescafé. The office was chilled to a level that signified a prosperous company and all the office girls wore heavy coats to ward off the cold.

I was ushered into Khun Narong's office while he finished up a deal for a whole bunch of workstations to some multinational. The Value Group was the official distributor for Microsoft and I had come to discuss the issue of intellectual property protection. Khun Narong had started the company four years ago as a distributor and it had grown to over 120 people.

I wanted to know more about how you make a killing selling legal software in a country where piracy is not only rampant but almost legal. For 1,000 baht (U.S. $40) a pirate shop will sell you a complete Microsoft Windows, including disks and a photcopy of the manual. For 5,700 baht, you can buy a legitimate copy from Khun Narong.

Value Systems had recently introduced a version of Windows, localized with Thai fonts and a Thai manual for 4,700 baht. To protect their investment, Value was using a hard lock, a piece of hardware that must be present (usually on a serial port) for the software to run.

Selling the simple English version, Narong estimated he had provided only 2 percent of the copies on the market. With the Thai version, however, he was hoping that legal copies would make up 20 percent, or maybe even 30 percent, of the market share.

With no real copyright protection, Narong had to rely on things like support and service to lure in corporations. A few large Thai corporations were beginning to be concerned about image and would buy at least a couple of legal copies to put into their machine rooms. A few even decided that legal copies reduced the amount of internal support needed and were a sound business decision.

Increasingly though, it was a proliferation of viruses that was driving customers into Narong's hands. Many large corporations had relied exclusively on pirate copies and some were paying the price. I heard from several sources, for example, that one of Thailand's largest banks had used pirated software not only for PCs but for larger systems as well. My sources informed me that the bank had been hard hit by a particularly virulent strain of virus and had only just recovered.

Did the high price of software in Thailand have anything to do with piracy? One of the more persuasive arguments in favor of software piracy was that legal software was quite expensive, selling for several times the U.S. list price in a country with a much lower standard of living.

Narong saw this as a chicken-and-egg problem. As long as software had no protection, there was no incentive to localize for the

Thai market. Lack of Thai language support kept the market low and the prices high.

This argument seemed to confirm an impression I had that most of the piracy was destined for the Thai market. Although I had certainly seen foreigners in the Patpong red light district bring in a laptop and say "fill 'er up," the vast majority of the copies made in Thailand were made as an incentive to sell hardware.

I left Narong's office and went out to the head of the road where a half-dozen teenagers sat passing the time playing checkers with bottle caps on a board marked on the sidewalk in chalk. Every street had one of these groups, serving as a motorcycle ferry to houses located deep within the complex maze of side streets that spread out from each road. Every morning and evening, you could see office girls being shuttled on these bikes, riding sidesaddle in tight skirts and high heels, hanging on nonchalantly with one hand as their chauffeurs went scuttling between lanes and over sidewalks.

That afternoon, I was briefed by a gentleman who insisted that I identify him only as a "diplomat" from a "western embassy." I reported to the guard post of the Western Embassy, went past two sets of metal detectors and incredible numbers of security guards, and entered the inner sanctum of foreign soil.

There, I learned some of the background on the intellectual property dispute between the U.S. and Thailand. The heart of the problem was the patent law, which had explicitly disallowed protection for pharmaceuticals, leading to a huge market in clones. Drugs can be a touchy trade negotiation issue, especially when a huge American multinational is pitted against a poor, sick Thai child.

With the coup on February 23, 1991, a relatively honest government had been put into power, surprising the hell out of the military junta that had installed them to act as puppets. This new government had been diligently at work passing laws, and one that had almost gone into effect was a new patent law.

Likewise, trademark protection was finally going into place. While trademarks had been nominally protected, penalties were so lax that products ranging from perfume to watches to clothing were regularly manufactured and sold both internally and to a huge tourist market. Of course, the pirates don't always get their copies exact—I remember one Gucci watch knockoff with a picture of Snoopy on the dial.

Copyright is a particularly sensitive issue in Thai politics. There was a 1979 law on the books, but the problem was that the Thai judiciary refused to enforce it, throwing cases out on technicalities. Software was not mentioned in the law at all and no cases had gone to court, so pirates had a virtual carte blanche to operate.

The government of General Prem, the first democratically elected government in Thailand, introduced a new copyright law. The legislation was perceived as a bow to foreign pressure in a country that prides itself on its independence. General Prem's goverment fell over the issue.

Prem was followed by General Chatchai who had the honor of presiding over one of the most corrupt Thai governments ever. I remember sitting in Bahn Pitsanulok, the opulent former official state guest house and the offices of the Prime Minister's personal staff. I was talking with one of the most senior members of the Prime Minster's staff in an on-the-record interview and asked him what the current rate for bribes was on large government projects. He promptly let me know that the usual rate was 10 percent, but that this was, of course, negotiable. This same senior advisor cheerfully admitted that almost all the software in the offices was pirated.

This government was so venal that they were actually hurting business, an unpardonable sin. The military, itself a huge business, stepped in to protect their interests. Later, it came to light that several government ministers had managed to save so much on their meager salaries that in one case a minister increased his net worth by U.S. $50 million during only a few years in office.

The government of the Anand administration was run by a half-dozen technocrats who were busily trying to straighten out the mess of the previous few years. (He was later replaced by Suchinda, the junta leader.) Things were simmering on the diplomatic front and negotiations had gone from the noise and publicity of 301 actions to the back room workings of the diplomatic process. Progress was being made, but no firm results had been achieved.

❏

Exploring the Internet

Back at the hotel, I walked down the deserted hall of the hotel's shopping arcade, each shop holding one or two very bored-looking attendants, shivering in the cold of the air conditioning. My room was located in a remote wing, absolutely deserted except for the elevator button pusher. This poor kid stood for twelve hours every day in an uncomfortable uniform, his only job being to push the up button if he saw somebody coming to save them any unnecessary wait.

In my room, I needed to recharge my notebook and I noticed that, while I had packed an appropriate two prong adaptor, I didn't have an adaptor for the three-prong, grounded plugs. I called housekeeping and a uniformed engineer was sent up. I explained the problem and he nodded and smiled, clearly understanding my dilemna. He reached over and grabbed the ground plug and started to snap it off. I recoiled in horror.

"No, not good," I protested, grabbing back all three of my prongs and moving to the other side of the room.

"Cut! Cut!" he repeated over and over, chasing after me. The music wafting in from the hall speakers was playing "Somewhere Over the Rainbow."

❐

Saturday morning, I went out to the Pratunam area, where textile vendors crowd the sidewalks with bolts of cloth and silk, piled onto tables covered with umbrellas to provide some shade from the overpowering heat. Occasionally, an overloaded motorcycle would dart out of a shophouse and onto the sidewalk, somehow missing the milling crowds, and jump onto the street to go make a delivery.

At the edge of Pratunam is Pantip Plaza, a shopping center with a large number of computer dealers. My favorite copy shop, a little shophouse jammed with 6 PC ATs and 6 young women sitting in front of them keeping the floppies humming, had been torn down. These low-rent retail operations were getting harder to find in Bangkok and most of the businesses had moved into the big shopping centers favored by the Thais, huge air-conditioned atriums with three or four stories of balconies.

Pantip Plaza had its share of computer dealers, and even one or two copy shops, but this was pretty tame stuff compared to the Golden Shopping Center in Hong Kong. At Pantip, there were 20 or 30 shops, and a few had some halfhearted employees sitting around playing games. A few customers drifted by, but most had the slow, purposeless amble of the window shopper.

I snapped a few pictures of pirates in action, then gave up and went down to the S&P Bakery for a dish of rice cooked with shrimp roe and chilies. Roe, of course, being a Thai euphemism on English-language menus for the orange fat in the shrimp's head.

Dinner that night was at an unassuming little restaurant, a brightly lit room with a few movie posters on the wall and lots of big, round tables, around which were seated large families, each with several generations present. Bottles of Mekong Whisky and soda water and buckets of ice were piled up on little carts next to each table.

We started with grilled pork, doused in a fiery salsa of lime juice, garlic, and chilies and a big bowl of sour soup. The specialty of the house was oysters and mussels, served half-cooked with egg and vegetables, and we consumed a half-dozen plates of this delicious seafood. Dessert was fried taro root, dusted in pistachio and sugar, leaving even Bob so full that we omitted our traditional post-dinner search for the ultimate durian ice cream.

❑

Sunday morning, I left the hotel for my usual breakfast of a bowl of noodles from a street stand. Returning to the hotel, I gathered a pile of notebooks, business cards, and photos and walked down to the business center. Two young attendants were seated at the desk, waiting for business.

"I'd like to send these papers by Federal Express," I said.

"One hour," an attendant replied.

"Federal Express?" I repeated, with a puzzled look.

"One hour, must go to shop," the other attendant insisted, reaching for my stack of papers.

After repeating this little routine a few times I realized that they were referring to Photo Express, which, of course, didn't really explain why they thought I wanted to have notebooks developed.

My flight wasn't until evening, so I had time to have lunch with Bob. We went to an old hangout, the Italian restaurant Pan Pan. Normally, I try to stick to Asian food while in Asia, but Pan Pan is an exception. The Italian food is good and, more importantly, they have excellent durian ice cream.

Durian is one of those mysteries of the East. On the outside, it's about twice the size of a pineapple, with very sharp spikes about a half-inch tall sticking out all over, making it advisable not to fall asleep under a durian tree at harvest time. Inside, there are a half dozen segments of creamy, pale flesh that looks sort of like a banana. The durian's most famous feature, however, is its powerful, distinctive smell.

The taste is great, but the smell does tend to dissuade many westerners from taking an immediate liking to the "king of fruits." I describe it as tasting something like a cross between a mushy banana and brie, but one Englishman I know refers to it as "a bit like eating strawberries and cream in a public lavatory."

Well, I took an immediate liking to it. The first time I came to Bangkok, a mutual friend of ours, a freelancer who specialized in travel writing and auto magazines, had arranged for Bob to meet me at the airport.

We went straight to a night market where prostitutes, pimps, and the like grab their midnight lunch. I was introduced to a wide variety of tropical fruits, including mangosteens, rambutans, and durians.

On a subsequent trip to Bangkok, I achieved a very modest degree of fame by inventing the durian cheesecake. The creamy durian mixed perfectly with the eggs and cream cheese, and a coconut biscuit crust gave the cake a nice Asian twist. Of course, the cake did still smell like a durian, but for many people that was considered a feature and not a bug. The recipe was an immediate hit at the *Post* and Bob published it in his column the following week.

Amsterdam was 0° C, certainly a change from Bangkok. I made a mad dash to the taxi stand and got to my hotel with plenty of time for a one-hour nap after my all-night flight.

At 1 P.M., I took a tram to Muiderpoort station, then got in a minibus that shot over a narrow little path running next to a canal and dropped me off at the complex of buildings holding Dutch research laboratories including the Centrum voor Wiskunde en Informatica (CWI), the computer science and mathematics institute, and the Nationaal Instituut voor Kernfysica en Hoge-Energiefysica (NIK-HEF), the Dutch institute for atomic high energy physics.

NIKHEF and CWI have both been prominent centers of networking in Europe for many years. NIKHEF was the Dutch HEPnet site, CWI had given an early home to EUnet, and this complex of buildings on Kruislaan road kept popping up in one context or another. It housed the RARE secretariat, it hosted a gateway to IXI, and the president of RIPE was Rob Blokzijl, a NIKHEF employee.

It was to get to the bottom of all these projects and acronyms that I had come to Amsterdam. I had heard more and more about the maze of conflicting institutions, consortiums, organizations, and associations that made up the confused politics of European networking.

I was just in time for the eleventh meeting of Réseaux IP Européens (RIPE), an informal consortium of the TCP/IP research networks of Europe. I figured that RIPE must be something like the IETF, and thus a good place to gather information.

The meeting was about to start, so I gathered my badge and one each of the dozens of handouts and went into a university-style lecture hall. Down at the bottom of the hall sat three serious-looking RIPE officials facing a room of 50 or so equally serious-looking engineers.

Rob Blokzijl was going through a long agenda, reviewing action items from the previous meeting and making announcements. I propped my jet-lagged eyes open with toothpicks and started leafing through the materials I had picked up.

RIPE was formed as a sort of anti-organization, a reaction to the total ineffectiveness of other groups in setting up a pan-European Internet. At the time RIPE was formed, there had been several years of thrashing while people tried to figure out how to make OSI into something real.

Meanwhile, several organizations with work to accomplish had been putting together TCP/IP networks. An Internet was being formed, but on an ad hoc basis. Networks were touching and accidents were starting to happen.

"What kinds of accidents were happening?" I naively asked Rob the next day while we were hiding in his office during a slack time in the working group sessions.

"Routing loops, black holes, the usual," Rob said. To try and solve the problems, Rob had convened a group of six people from the real networks in Europe. Nuclear physics was the lead player, so in addition to Rob there were representatives from CERN in Geneva and the Italian physics community. The Italians were operating the only 2 Mbps international link in Europe at the time. To supplement the physicists, representatives from NORDUnet and EUnet also came.

At first, the six tried to work through the Réseaux Associés pour la Recherche Européenne (RARE), the association of research networking groups in Europe. RARE wouldn't touch this issue, though. The six researchers were operating TCP/IP networks and RARE was exclusively and officially an OSI group.

Borrowing a phrase from Daniel Karrenberg of CWI that the "time was ripe for networking in Europe," an extremely lightweight organization was founded in September 1990 with the mission of helping to ensure cooperation among European IP networks. Rob Blokzijl formally announced the formation of the group in RFC 1181, a very carefully worded one-page document.

In Europe, careful wording is crucial and I've seen more than one group spend several hours wordsmithing seemingly innocuous phrases. Rob proudly pointed out the triumphs in the RFC, such as the sentence that "RIPE serves as a focal point for other common activities of the participants related to IP networking."

Apparently meaningless to the untrained eye, this sentence is rife with subtleties meant to steer a course through the shoals of politics. RIPE is a focal point, not an operational unit. It worries about only its own voluntary participants and is not trying to impose solutions on others. It deals only with IP networking and is thus not advocating against OSI but merely serves as a forum for those who have already chosen.

By the time of the eleventh meeting, RIPE had grown to nearly 30 organizations and was meeting quarterly. NIKHEF hosted many of the meetings and acted as the organization's secretariat. In terms of developing new standards, RIPE was a pretty sleepy forum. Those wanting a marathon of 50 working groups producing mountains of paper were directed instead to the IETF. RIPE was much more collegial and informal.

The week before the meeting, two days had been set aside for informal tutorials to bring new participants in TCP/IP up to speed. At the same time, a bake-off had been held featuring equipment from various vendors and even including an ISDN switch. People worked together to form different network topologies and see what types of problems arose.

The meeting itself was a one-day plenary, followed by a day of working groups, followed by another day of plenary meetings. There were only a few working groups, devoted to issues like routing and European connectivity.

In addition to representatives from most of the central European countries, there was a heavy contingent of East Europeans, including delegations from Czechoslovakia, Poland, Hungary, and Yugoslavia. Most of the representatives from Eastern Europe migrated to the working group session on connectivity. After a brief review of who was coming on line, the conversation turned to problems of mutual interest.

One of the biggest issues was simply getting equipment. All the countries were on the U.S. export restrictions list and the Poles told how it had taken them a year just to get a Cisco router. Various suggestions were bandied about on just exactly how the U.S.

wanted the myriad forms filled out, but it was obvious that the rules the U.S. imposed remained mysterious and arbitrary.

Another working group was devoted to the issue of routing co-ordination. Routing was the single biggest technical issue at the meeting, and it is in this area that RIPE made its biggest contribution. In the U.S., there was a single backbone which used the EGP protocol to announce available routes to the second-tier regional networks. The backbone was centrally managed, so all the regionals got fairly consistent information. In Europe, there was no backbone, so it was pretty much guaranteed that conflicting routing information would be propagated, leading to routing loops and black holes. RIPE took a look at the map of Europe and it became clear that four sites acted as the main hubs.

These four sites, in Stockholm, Amsterdam, CERN, and Bologna, served as the centers for large numbers of secondary networks. Stockholm was the center of NORDUnet and Bologna was the center of the Italian network. Amsterdam and CERN had huge numbers of links going out to different countries.

The four sites agreed to take the lines running from Stockholm to Amsterdam to CERN to Bologna and turn them into a de facto European backbone. The routers at the four sites were combined into a single routing domain, thus presenting a consistent view of the world. To make the backbone a reality, all four sites agreed that transit traffic could traverse their links.

This was certainly not a centrally managed, fault resilient, highly designed backbone, but it did the job of connecting the European Internet. Since the four main sites also had links to the U.S., the European Internet was well connected to NSFNET and the rest of the world.

In a centrally managed backbone environment like NSFNET, low-level networks that wish to make their availability known to the world (and thus enable communications with said world) simply have to inform the NIC or NOC running the backbone. If the low-level network doesn't fill out the appropriate forms or jump through the appropriate hoops, the network is simply not announced and thus is effectively isolated. It would be as if a road existed into a country but there was no indication of the road on any map.

In Europe, maintaining the name space was a trickier situation. RIPE came up with a novel plan to keep information up to date. A European WHOIS service was put into place containing network names, domain names, IP addresses, and the like.

The incentive to keep this information up to date was quite simple. The four backbone sites used the WHOIS database to load their routers. Sites that didn't keep information up to date were simply not announced over the de facto backbone.

RIPE was a simple, effective tool for coordination and instruction, all done on a shoestring. The informal nature of the group and the advocacy of the heretical TCP/IP was too much for the networking establishment and RIPE came under heavy attack at first from officially sponsored groups like RARE.

To understand why RARE would object, one has only to remember that TCP/IP continues to be referred to by many as "DoD IP." In contrast, OSI, developed with very heavy participation from European academics and PTTs, was the open way to do networking.

While RIPE was under attack, it was also clear that IP networking was gaining a strong hold in Europe. In one of those bizarre twists of European politics, RIPE became an official RARE "activity." Not an official working group, mind you, with the connotations of European Commission financial support, official voting by one participant per country, and a chairman appointed by the RARE Council of Administration. Simply an activity.

Under the merger and acquisition agreement, RIPE would continue as an independent group and would elect its own chairman. RARE got to bring the renegades under its umbrella and unity once again reigned, at least on the surface.

To tell the truth, I wasn't exactly sure why the merger took place, but I did get a glimpse when Rob told me about the new RIPE NCC being formed. The informal RIPE backbone had been working well, but members decided they needed a more professional Network Control Center. Not a mere NIC, several people cautioned me (but certainly less than a NOC), this NCC would serve a coordination and troubleshooting function.

The NCC would be funded by voluntary contributions. Since RIPE was not a legal entity, the money would be funneled through

RARE. RIPE/RARE had already put out an RFP for ECU 250,000 (U.S. $307,500), enough they hoped for a manager, two staff, some equipment, a travel budget, and some office space. Obviously, it was hoped that a group like NIKHEF or NORDUnet would respond with an offer within the budget, and would donate resources on top of the ECU 250,000.

A committee had been formed to evaluate the responses to the RFP, consisting of two RIPE officers and two RARE officers. This group, upon making its decision, would forward it to the RARE Executive, which in turn would make its recommendation and send it on up to the RARE Council of Administration. RARE would then officially hire (and fire) the manager.

❏

Following this discussion, I must admit I was still a bit confused as to what was going on. While I wasn't clear on the organizational ins and outs, it was certainly clear that RIPE was performing a valuable coordinating function, allowing the technical people to gather in one room and work out solutions to problems.

Sometimes the issues on the table were highly complex, such as how to do policy routing in an environment characterized by too many policies. Often, though, the issues were painfully simple.

Take the issue of country codes, the two letter abbreviations by which you send a letter or provide the root portion of a DNS name. The list of such codes used to be fairly static, but with the disintegration of the Soviet Union there were a bunch of new roots to the name tree.

Managing that root was a sign of power, and in more than one case, fights had broken out within a country between groups who felt they were the rightful namespace administrators. The right to control the top of the tree was a touchy issue in a place like Yugoslavia. Imagine a Serb administration of the Croatian subdomain, for example.

RIPE served as a place where these types of issues could be ironed out. Not everything can be solved on an informal, technical level, of course, but it is amazing how many problems can be worked out this way.

One exchange in the RIPE plenary that I found interesting was the issue of where to find the current country codes. Officially, these codes are listed in an ISO standard and, in response to a query from the audience, a bureaucrat got up and explained that one obtained ISO standards from one's own national standards body.

Not a very useful solution to a simple problem, so somebody else got up and suggested that the information be obtained from the back of a Sun manual. The representative from Israel suggested that Larry Landweber maintained this information as part of his list of connectivity.

Finally, somebody wanted to know if this information wasn't online. He had heard about some standards server "someplace in the U.S.," but when he tried to obtain standards there he had received an error message.

I had the dubious honor of trying to explain why the ITU had withdrawn their permission for posting standards since the server wasn't helping "the right sort of people." Many of the Eastern Europeans were furious about the decision since it had been their only access to the vital documents. Would ISO be posting their standards, somebody wanted to know?

I explained the concept of a standards haven in some friendly location like Budapest. Everybody laughed and the plenary broke up.

◻

That afternoon, I managed to drag Glenn Kowack away from the center of the vortex he creates to find out about EUnet. Glenn had just finished his first year as the CEO of EUnet. EUnet was sort of the analog of the U.S. USENET, but had evolved into a much more structured network.

In the U.S., the UUCP protocols had long been used to allow people to form a very loose confederation of systems, a sort of network anarchy. A new system would join USENET by setting up an arrangement with some existing system for the transfer of mail and news, usually using dial-up links. The only real rule was the unwritten tradition that if somebody was nice enough to let you join, you ought to do the same for somebody else. In this way, a loose web formed across the U.S. and a de facto network came into being.

The informal nature of USENET meant no acceptable use policies or votes to allow a new member in. Lack of formal structure, together with the low cost, meant that USENET (and the underlying UUCP protocols) spread quickly among small startup companies.

Much of USENET ended up falling under the umbrella of USENIX, the U.S. UNIX users group. In Europe, simple networks were also forming in the context of UNIX user groups and the UUCP protocols. In Europe, though, there wasn't quite the luxury for anarchy that the U.S. had.

For one thing, calls across national borders were expensive enough that it made sense to concentrate traffic through a star configuration of national nodes and a central switch. The central switch was the famous mcvax (now mcsun), housed at CWI in Amsterdam. Since an international call to one point in Europe costs pretty much the same as to any other point, there was no need for a fancy mesh topology, and the star stayed in place.

Because calls cost so much, users started paying their share of line charges from the very beginning. Administration and management was totally volunteer and fell under the umbrella of the European UNIX Users Group (EUUG), and the net came to be known as EUnet.

By the time Glenn joined EUnet in January 1990, it had grown to be a TCP/IP and UUCP network with over 1,600 sites. Over the next year, it was to grow to well over 2,500 UUCP sites, 100 IP sites, and 750 news sites. All this traffic was going from local networks, run by a local UNIX user's group, into a national node, and then over to Amsterdam.

EUnet, with all these users, began playing a major role in European networking, pooling its money with other groups like NORDUnet so that bigger pipes could be leased. Many of these shared lines formed the de facto European backbone of RIPE, and then later of EBONE.

Amsterdam

One of the interesting aspects of EUnet is that it is often the very first network in a country. By January 1992, EUnet already had 22 national members, each representing a national UNIX user's group, running a national node, and paying for their own line to mcsun. The cost of international links, the Amsterdam equipment, and miscellaneous overhead like Glenn were also apportioned among the members.

With the craze towards open systems at a peak, EEUG changed its name to EurOpen to signify openness, truth, and beauty. Thankfully, EUnet did not become OpenNet.

Both parts of the EurOpen name are applied in a fairly loose fashion. Open included things like UNIX and TCP/IP instead of being a code-word for only OSI. European is also interpreted kind of loosely. Iceland, Tunisia, and Moscow are members of EUnet, stretching the word far beyond the confines of the European Community, the European Free Trade Association, and even the European continental boundaries. Egypt and Algeria were coming on line soon and Glenn didn't really seem to care who joined as long as he could provide service and spread networking into new countries.

In fact, it was the desire to spread networking to those who could use it that got Glenn his job with EUnet, in a very indirect fashion. In the 70s and 80s, Glenn led a reasonably normal life, taking jobs like that of an R&D manager for Gould in Champaign-Urbana, Illinois. Of course, he did take a few years out to help found and run a community radio station, a job that many engineers don't sport on their resumes.

At the tail end of his stint with Gould, Glenn ended up as the first employee of the newly formed UNIX International. He enjoyed the job so much that, after the organization was off the ground, he quit and took three months off to go look at computers in Asia, visiting places like Hong Kong and Singapore.

He came back from his sabbatical and set up shop again in Shampoo-Banana, this time hanging out his shingle as a freelance consultant. He was doing various consulting jobs when Eastern Europe collapsed.

Glenn bought a Zenith laptop, packed his backpack, and took off. By the time he looked up, he found himself in Warsaw chairing the first meeting of the Polish UNIX Users Group, an event made all the more challenging by his lack of any knowledge of Polish.

In his travels, he made enough visits through Holland that he got to know the Amsterdam crowd well. EUnet decided to hire a real manager, and Glenn certainly seemed not only highly qualified but highly available. He took the job.

EUnet is proof that networks can be set up with minimal outlays of funds. With a headquarters budget of ECU 600,000 (U.S. $738,000) and a total pan-European outlay of well under ECU 10 million per year, EUnet has become one of the key European networks, acting as the lead player in bringing new countries into the world Internet.

EUnet has also played a key role in helping to form the EBONE consortium. EUnet's historical role in working with other organizations on line sharing has meant that lines to the U.S. and across Europe have been possible even when groups like RARE were unable to act.

One would think that a low-budget, technically astute, extremely effective network would win plaudits from all over, but EUnet has its detractors. OSI-only groups view EUnet and its informality as a definite threat. In some cases, active efforts are underway to try and prevent EUnet from operating.

A recent example was brought to light at the RIPE meeting. SWITCH, the national research network in Switzerland, had barred EUnet traffic from its network. Not only had the traffic been barred, it was cut off without any advance notice to EUnet, causing several days of confusion as people all over Europe tried to figure out their sudden loss of connectivity.

At the RIPE plenary, Michael Nowlan, the Irish chairman of EurOpen, read a prepared statement protesting the lack of notice. What had really happened illustrated the type of politics that EUnet encountered.

In each country, it is up to the national UNIX users group to figure out how to move traffic from the national node out to the rest of the country. In some countries, a simple dial-up star configuration is sufficient. In others, there is enough traffic that a backbone linking regional hubs makes sense.

How to provide that backbone is up to each group. In some cases, the group will simply lease lines and set up a backbone. In other cases, line-sharing agreements with a national research network might be established. In other cases, a contract can be set up with some other entity to provide the backbone.

In Switzerland, the Swiss UNIX group (CHUUG) had been using SWITCH, the national research network, as a backbone. CHUUG and SWITCH got into a squabble over various matters and CHUUG decided to set up its own backbone. SWITCH set up their routers to filter out EUnet IP traffic, thus cutting off connectivity from the 22 EUnet countries to anybody on SWITCH or with a tail link off of SWITCH.

Fortunately, these childish games are the exception rather than the rule. In most countries, EUnet happily coexists with the national research networks. The national nets handle the universities and the UNIX group handles low-volume UUCP clients, IP links to small companies, and anybody else who falls outside the official domain of "research" as defined in that country.

◻

With my work for the day done, I went out for a couple of beers with Scott Williamson, the manager of the new Network Information Center (NIC) in the U.S. The NIC had been recently transferred from SRI to GSI, a subsidiary of Infonet. GSI and Scott had a rough few months as things got going and Scott was now making the tour of conferences like RIPE and the IETF to convince the community that things were back in control.

Running the NIC is no easy task, I learned. Just maintaining the WHOIS database requires an 800 Mbyte database running Ingres, a condition specified by the Defense Communications Agency, the official funding agency for the NIC. Even though a great part of the traffic into the NIC comes from the NSFNET, not the MILNET, the NSF had yet to set up its own similar facility, making Scott responsible for both networks.

One of the big problems was that the NIC had inherited its communications facilities as part of the DCA contract, which specified a

64 kbps link to the Internet. A pipe of that size is not enough for an organization that is at the center of the Internet and the link was quickly flooded. Only after the NASA Science Internet stepped in with a T1 line did things start to get better.

Over beers, I learned that Scott is ideally suited for his job. His background was managing a team of UNIX programmers for various Washington tasks, such as a job for the Federal Emergency Management Agency (FEMA) simulating telephone disasters. More to the point, though, he is a second-degree black belt in a Korean martial art and spent three years in the Australian outback. Both experiences breed qualities that are useful when dealing with Washington bureaucrats.

That night, RIPE had set up a group dinner at a local Indonesian restaurant. Indonesia was a former Dutch colony and an Indonesian dinner provided excellent food, at a price that was affordable on all manner of budgets, an important consideration given the wide geographical representation at the meeting.

Over salads in gloppy peanut sauce, preserved eggs in sweet chili and lemon grass, and fiery beef curries, the conversation drifted in and out of shop talk. I was too jet lagged and burnt out to think about networks, so I concentrated on the food.

Wednesday morning, I brought my bags down to the train station and joined a stream of Dutch commuters. It is not unusual for people in Holland to live at one end of the country and work at the other. I was going half-way across the country to Utrecht, a half-hour away.

The train ran parallel to one of the main Amsterdam canals, lined with houseboats and barges, then past warehouses and windmills. Passing the suburb of Amstel and the sprawling IBM complex, we started picking up speed. Suddenly, we were in the countryside, an elaborate system of canals crisscrossing the fields and forming a series of little islands, connected by bridges and sluices.

It was market day in Utrecht and, since I didn't have a hotel reservation, I headed right into the middle of the town square to look around for a place to stay. Spotting one, I avoided the temptation to stop at stands full of cheeses, herring, and baked goods and got a room.

With a few hours to kill, I brought my laptop into a little café by a canal, one of a half-dozen places crowded with tables of high-school and college kids sipping coffees and beers. At 2 P.M., I gathered my things and went into the shopping center complex surrounding the train station to find Kees Neggers, co-managing director of SURFnet, the Dutch academic and research network.

After seeing so many networks like EUnet in Amsterdam and AARNet in Australia run with a couple of guys and a Sun, it was certainly a change to see SURFnet occupying a whole floor of plush offices. When I asked Kees how many people worked there, he said only 20, but many of them were responsible for supervising subcontractors.

SURFnet is a company that is owned 49 percent by the Dutch PTT and 51 percent by the SURF Foundation, a group started initially by the universities, but which has grown to include research institutes, the research arms of corporations, and other institutions of higher education such as teaching hospitals and vocational schools.

To explain SURFnet, SURF, and the PTT, Kees went to the white board and carefully drew the organizational structure, drawing my attention to the legal status of all the parties and pointing out the differences in Dutch law between the limited liability partnership, the foundation, and the association.

As Kees continued his chalk talk, it occurred to me that he had not said one word about the network itself. I knew that SURFnet was born as a project of SURF in 1986, had become a real company in 1989, and I even knew about things like the fact that it had a capitalization of 3 million guilders (U.S. $1.6 million), and expenditures of NG 14 million per year, of which NG 10 million were cost recovery services from users and 4 million was development paid for by the government. What I didn't know was what the network did.

Well, it turned out that SURFnet started by using the X.25 data service from the PTT. After some long thinking and a big RFP, Northern Telecom got the contract to install and manage a private X.25 network based on 64 kbps links. This net was based on three major hubs, with each leg of the triangle having two or three 64 kbps links. Another 16 sites were equipped with switches, each of these having at least two lines into the network. Altogether, 413 sites had connections.

The network appeared to be your basic FOO over X.25 net. Most of the services had SURF* names. SURFmail, for example, was described in the annual report as "using the RFC-822 addressing mode as an intermediate step towards the international X.400 standard."

Recently, the network had begun the process towards a 2 Mbps backbone. To quell any political problems, five sites were given 2 Mbps links and a "pilot" was run. Some lines ran straight IP, others ran straight X.25, and some ran a multiplexed mess of the two. Needless to say, the results of the pilot showed that running IP on a line was more efficient than running IP on top of X.25. However, with X.25 identified in many European countries as the "pathway to OSI" it was important to conduct the pilot.

All this technical information I learned in a few minutes from Kees and by leafing through the annual report. Very quickly, though, we were back on the subjects of organizational charts, examining how his network management staff served as contract supervisors to monitor the subcontractors that were doing network management.

We moved on from SURFnet to pan-European politics, an area in which Kees is an extremely active player. His first foray was as the EARN representative for his country. When RARE was formed, SURF was named as the Dutch national member, and Kees was named SURF's representation to the RARE Council of Administration (CoA).

RARE, the Réseaux Associés pour la Recherche Européenne, was started in 1986 to promote the use of networks based on open systems solutions, read "OSI." This was to be sharply contrasted to EARN, IBM's proprietary protocol, association, and network, foisted upon unknowing European countries as part of an alleged plot to dominate the market. Well, maybe not quite that sharply contrasted, but it would not do to underestimate the fury of this particular religious war.

At that time, only the U.K. really had a national network. Many people assumed that OSI would be the basis for networking and that the PTTs would provide the infrastructure on which OSI would run. That infrastructure would be a commercial offering, universally available, and available soon.

The focus on the PTT as the service provider led to the assumption of a single national network, and thus RARE is made up of one member per country. There are also various associate members, international members, and liaison organizations, but the basic governance of the organization is by the Council of Administration which has one seat per country.

There is another element of RARE that is worth noting. It gets money from two sources: contributions from member countries and from the European Commission. The European Commission component is strong enough that they wield considerable clout on RARE decisions.

Most of the linkage between RARE and the Commission has been through the COSINE project. (Every acronym must be pronounceable and preferably have a double meaning of some sort, however inane. In the case of COSINE, the expansion yields Cooperation for OSI Networking in Europe.)

COSINE was started in 1986 by another group called Eureka, a research fund subscribed to by a group of countries roughly equivalent to the RARE membership or the European Free Trade Association. The COSINE project of Eureka was handed over to the European Commission to act as project coordinator and they, in turn, picked RARE as the secretariat.

What all this meant was that Eureka kicked in some money, the Commission kicked in some more, and a fraction of that money flowed downhill to RARE. Eventually, so the theory went, money would flow down even further into a series of market-pull activities that would prepare and stimulate OSI in Europe.

Much of the research funded by the Commission was in the area of "pre-standardization research." Pre-standardization was the process of preparing a bunch of documents that are then used as input to the standards process. In the case of COSINE, this meant establishing the subset of OSI that would best fit the special needs of Europe.

The functional profiles of OSI were prepared by a series of working groups. Every country got a member. The chair could invite four "experts," sort of a standards patronage position. The EC paid for the travel expenses of each delegate, kicked in for the cost of donuts at the meetings, and took care of the RARE secretariat.

Paying people to go to meetings in fine places has the sure result of generating a large demand for meetings. The specification process dragged on as people tried to define which portions of OSI would be used in Europe. The assumption was that when those profiles were developed, the lure of the common European market would be enough to attract vendors like flies to a water buffalo.

Vendors and researchers took one of two approaches. A few went ahead and just implemented the portions of OSI that made sense in a product. ISODE was a perfect example of this. Most just went ahead and sold TCP/IP products.

After a couple of years of this process, a set of 10 very thick, very blue volumes of COSINE specifications were issued. These 10 blue books were summarized in a red book, which in turn was summarized in an orange executive overview. I suspect quite a few corporations took that orange distillation and concentrated it yet further until senior management was hearing summaries such as "this stuff is great, trust us."

Once the specifications were complete, RARE developed a CO-SINE implementation plan. In January 1990, this implementation plan was signed as a contract between the Commission and RARE. The RARE COSINE Project Management Unit (PMU) became a reality.

COSINE was designed as a three-year plan with a budget of ECU 30 million (U.S. $36.9 million). Most of that money, over ECU 12 million, went into IXI, the International X.25 Infrastructure (IXI). A large chunk, ECU 6 million, went into the PMU.

IXI is an international X.25 network for researchers. Countries like Greece, Yugoslavia, Ireland, and Portugal all use IXI as their main path into the European mainland. Even the U.K., for some strange reason, links itself into the continent with IXI.

The network is simply a star configuration of a set of 64 kbps lines that link national X.25 networks. Typically, a private, virtual X.25 network is built on top of the PTT's own offering. There are actually two stars, one in Amsterdam and one in Bern. Two 64 kbps links connect the stars, and each country gets one 64 kbps link into one of the hubs.

Except for the U.K., that is. The U.K. is big enough that it really needs two 64 kbps links into Amsterdam. Of course, that means that you're pumping 128 kbps of data into a 64 kbps network, but that's another story.

In a classic example of how networks will grab whatever resources they can, much of the IXI traffic consists of setting up a virtual circuit to NIKHEF, which operates a gateway from IXI into the Internet. While running TCP/IP on top of X.25 is not the most efficient implementation in the world, when that's your only choice, it works fine.

The theory behind IXI, and all COSINE projects, was to stimulate the market with the initial implementation. At the end of the three-year trial, some commercial entity would see the inherent profitability of the enterprise and step forward boldly with an aggressive bid to take the project over as a going concern.

At the end of 1992, IXI would terminate, and there had not yet been a clamor for rights to run the service commercially. Unless, of course, there might be some Commission money in it. This had occurred to a few people, and RARE was about to start lobbying for an Operational Unit.

Meanwhile, a second force reared its ugly head: people needed networks to do their jobs. Most of those national networks had started carrying large amounts of TCP/IP traffic, and many RARE members had to weigh the relative merits of keeping a network running against the desire to attract Commission money.

RIPE, of course, was the answer at first. RARE got in the act with the EBONE proposal, in which Kees took a leading role, along with groups like EUnet and NORDUnet. EBONE took the informal cooperation from 1991 and turned it into a more structured consortium for 1992.

Since the meeting I had attended in November at the Amsterdam Zoo, the EBONE proposal had taken shape. Two key groups, CERN and IBM, had decided not to sign the formal memorandum of understanding, but would still cooperate in the project.

Once the decisions to join (and how much to contribute) were made, the resources were turned over to an EBONE Action Team (EAT) to turn money, routers, people, and lines into a reasonable network.

A 512 kbps backbone had been decided upon between Stockholm, London, Amsterdam, Hamburg, and CERN. Three links to the U.S. were available, with two operating at 512 kbps and a T1 line from CERN (the EASInet IBM line). In some cases, money had been used to upgrade existing facilities. In others, existing resources were simply put into the EBONE pool.

The distinction was important because at the end of 1992, according to the Memorandum of Understanding that chartered EBONE, the group would disband and all resources would revert to owners (except for the money of course, which is kind of hard to give back once you've spent it). No formal company existed and there was no dedicated EBONE manager.

At the end of 1992, the official plan was to have RARE start an Operational Unit. The Operational Unit would provide a home for things like EBONE and maybe even projects like IXI. The Operational Unit would be set up with capital from RARE members (and presumably some nice research grants from the Commission to keep it going). Officially, the Unit would operate as a separate organization, but with RARE members contributing the capital, RARE members would get the shares, and presumably, RARE would have some influence in how those shares got used.

Setting up the Operational Unit and operating it as a more formal replacement for EBONE could be looked at one of two ways. On the one hand, it could be the badly-needed professional operation that would run the long-heralded pan-European infrastructure. A few cynics looked at the Operational Unit in another way, seeing a power grab that could hurt existing operations such as EUnet.

The official raison d'être for the Operational Unit was contained in a report Kees handed me entitled "Final Report of the RARE Task Force on the Establishment of the Operational Unit for the Supply of Network and Information Services to the R&D Community" with a bright yellow cover and attractive GBC binding.

This report was a marvel of detail, containing a complete business plan for the Operational Unit with a cash flow analysis through 1996, job descriptions for OpUnit officers, and an annex of commonly asked questions and answers, my favorite being "Why are data networks important for Europe?"

This report explained how a professionally managed backbone was key for Europe. In fact, it was assumed that you needed to provide this capability through a single organization, sort of the way that the NSFNET had provided a single backbone service in the U.S.

The flaw in this analogy was that the NSFNET had not provided the single backbone service in the United States or for the Internet. The backbone was, as soon as multiple networks came into being, a combination of resources.

The NSFNET, for example, had to cooperate with the MILNET, the replacement for the ARPANET. NASA already had NSI, Energy had ESnet, and corporations had their own networks. A single backbone provider was certainly not the only way to structure European networking.

As I was looking through the business plan for the OpUnit, Kees handed me another document, a report from the European Engineering Planning Group, which in turn had been set up by the RARE Council of Administration.

The EEPG document had a grand plan for networking in Europe. Kees was a key member of the EEPG. The EEPG outlined a scheme in which research networking in Europe would need, to be a success, four bodies. An Operational Unit was one of them. A networking association (RARE), a policy body (people with money), and a "consultative networking forum" were the other three bodies.

Of course, there were other networking associations in Europe, but RARE had been doing a pretty good job of setting up agreements. RIPE had become a RARE activity, a status certainly placing it lower in the hierarchy than an association.

That left EARN. RARE had been engineering an acquisition and merger of EARN, proposing that the two groups form as a way of increasing their mutual power. Like a giant game of RISK, with Europe under control, RARE was taking an active role in the international scene, participating in places like the Co-ordinating Committee for Intercontinental Research Networking (CCIRN) and co-founding the Internet Society.

This wasn't everything, either. I learned that RARE had helped form the European Workshop on Open Systems (EWOS) which would help set up European OSI profiles. RARE was also part of the European Telecommunications Standard Institute (ETSI), the official pan-European telecommunications standards body which was worrying about issues like ISDN or 2 Mbps X.25 networks and had joined the European Council of Telecommunications User Associations (ECTUA).

I left Kees' office with my head swimming. He had let me know that he had to leave by 4:06. I had thought the departure time was a bit odd, but it occurred to me that Kees was in the shopping center of which the train station was a part and that he had probably timed the walk down to the trains. Just in case he felt like getting a jump on things, I left at 4:03.

Walking back to town, to keep warm, I went through all the new acronyms I had learned, hoping that repeating them would generate enough hot air to counteract the chill. Needing a cup of coffee and a blank piece of paper to sort everything out, I ducked in out of the cold into a little corner coffee shop with windows all fogged up a definitely counterculture clientele.

Rubbing my hands to warm up, I stepped up to the counter to order.

"Do you have a menu?" I asked the attendant who ambled over from a table where he was playing chess.

He pointed down on the glass. I quickly realized that I was at the wrong counter. This menu specialized in regional specialties. The left hand side featured different kinds of hashish, ranging from your basic Lebanese to your more exotic Nepalese. The 10 and 25 guilder columns contained how many grams (or portions of grams) you got for your money. The right hand side of the menu was devoted to fine marijuanas, featuring orange bud, sinsemilla, and the like.

Not needing to confuse myself even further, I went down the steep spiral stairs to the coffee bar in the basement. There, amidst the kids rolling joints, the din of pinball, and the very loud music, I read through the stack of documents I had collected that day.

Thursday morning, I sat on the track at the Utrecht station waiting for my train to Bonn. If you're a few minutes early, its fun to go up to the tracks and watch the other trains leave. The 9:23 local was leaving on my track and I watched the clock turn to 9:23. Exactly two seconds later, the train was on its way.

One of the questions that always puzzles me is what conditions lead to a successful infrastructure. The European networking infrastructure was certainly not as developed as it could be. Likewise, the telephone infrastructure had always been expensive and not always on the forefront of technological change.

Yet, the European passenger train system, developed in a highly fragmented period of highly sovereign governments, was a miracle. The trains go to every town of consequence and many of none. Even more remote places are connected to the transportation web by a series of bus systems, coordinated with the train schedules, of course.

Staring at the track, hoping for a flash of insight, I realized that my train was about to leave. A few hours later I arrived at the Hauptbahnhof in Bonn and pulled out my itinerary of travel reservations. To my horror, I discovered that I was booked in a suburb of Bonn, Königswinter.

My instructions to my travel agent had been simple. "No Holiday Inns, no suburbs." Bonn, like Prague, is one of those cities that never has enough hotels and I was lucky I wasn't as far away as Cologne, the provisional capital.

I wandered around the train station for a while trying to figure out how to get to Königswinter. I spied a sign for the tram system with the magic word on it and caught the first one leaving. The tram was labled Bad Honef and I crossed my fingers that the track didn't serve multiple locations.

When I got on, I realized that I didn't have a ticket. All over, colorful signs in multiple languages indicated that tickets must be immediately validated or I would face a DM 60 (U.S. $36) fine.

Having no idea how to get a ticket, or where I was going, I alternated between peering out the window looking for some appropriate sign and looking nervously around for some sign of the ticket police.

Königswinter turned out to be a resort on the Rhine river. My hotel had a view of four castles up in the hills, was right across the town square from the church belltower, and my room was right on the river, looking out at barges and ferries, the tram, a boardwalk, and people out strolling in the cold air.

I went down to the sun room to work. Old men, couples, and mothers with children came in periodically to get a cup of coffee, a beer, or some ice cream. I ordered a cup of coffee, with the waitress checking to make sure I just wanted one cup.

The next morning, at breakfast, the waitress wanted to know if I wanted my coffee in a "can or a cup?" Outside it was still dark and I could make out the fog banks in the hills. Suddenly, the fog started to glow and I could see the black silhouettes of the castles. Then it was daylight and time to try to make my way into Bonn.

I took the tram back into the main train station and went in search of an information booth. I waved a business card in their face and they sent me to track 2. As I was trying to decipher the map of the extensive tram system, one pulled in. I suddenly realized that I had been sent to the wrong track, narrowly missing getting on one going the wrong way.

Armed with a valid ticket, I arrived at the stop in front of the monolithic police station headquarters, walked a few blocks over to the offices housing GMD, and found Klaus Birkenbihl.

Klaus is the manager of the Netzzentrum fuer die Wissenschaft, the science networks center in the Institut für Anwendungsorientierte Software- und Systemtechnik at the Gesellschaft für Mathematik und Datenverarbeitung mit beschränkter Haftung. In the interests of saving space, it is hoped the reader will excuse the informality of referring to the organization as simply GMD.

GMD is a government-owned research institute specializing in mathematics and computer science. Like INRIA, the French institute, the institute gets 60 to 70 percent of its funds from the government, raising the rest through contracts with industry. GMD has 1,200 staff, of which 700 are scientists.

I had come to see Klaus to find out about one more network, the IBM-sponsored EASInet. I had always assumed that BITNET, and its European cousin, EARN, were IBM's contribution to networks. I heard periodically about EASInet, but did not know anything about the network nor why IBM should start yet another network. EARN had started in 1984, originally with six countries but, after Dennis Jennings heard about it, six countries plus Ireland. The IBM model was to fund the program for three years, after which it would become self-sustaining. EARN added many countries and did, in fact, become self-sustaining.

Not only did EARN become independent, but you might even say the board got a touch hostile, planning a transition to OSI and cozying up to DEC. The OSI focus was actually a political necessity, part of a compromise with the PTTs who agreed to loosen some of their restrictions on clients sharing leased lines in return for a promise by EARN to migrate to OSI as soon as the protocols became technically and financially viable. This all happened in 1984 and the OSI migration took a bit longer than anyone expected. By the time I got there, most EARN sites were migrating to the BITNET 2 protocols, more commonly known as TCP/IP.

The upshot of the OSI (and later TCP) focus was that it was quite obvious that EARN was no longer an IBM animal. Creating a network that was self-sustaining after three years was a great public service, but didn't really serve the other goals of maintaining the IBM presence in Europe and, in the long run, selling more iron.

IBM developed a new proposal as a way of providing an incentive to the big mainframe market in the research community known as the European Academic Supercomputer Initiative (EASI). Under the program, IBM plunked down large amounts of heavy metal in selected research institutions and paid for the cost of 64 kbps links between participants, the collection of those links forming a fairly hefty donation of bandwidth. In addition, IBM paid for the cost of a T1 line from CERN to NSFNET and hired GMD to manage the network.

EASInet consisted of 18 sites by the beginning of 1992, with locations from Spain and Italy in the south, to Stockholm, Amsterdam, and Hamburg further north. Most of these sites were not exclusively "EASInet" sites, but were on a variety of networks. CERN, for example, an EASInet site was sometimes referred to as the Center for European Research Networking.

In a few cases, the EASInet link was in fact a dedicated 64 kbps line between two sites. In most cases, however, the IBM money had been thrown together with other sources. For example, a 256 kbps line between Amsterdam and CERN was split between HEPnet, EUnet, and SURFnet. The line sharing arrangements that EASInet started were an important early example of the model later used in EBONE.

To handle multiple protocols, many of the EASInet lines used NET's IDNX time division multiplexers, with most of the bandwidth given over to TCP/IP and SNA and other, smaller, circuits applied to X.25 and DECnet. EASInet was really bandwidth. In some cases, GMD actually took care of the lines, in others the job was split with other organizations. Some of the data flows were point-to-point sessions, others were part of broader networks such as HEPnet or the European Internet.

When IBM had agreed to cooperate with EBONE, what they meant was that the T1 line to NSFNET would become a pathway to the U.S., and thus to Asia. Even though IBM had not signed the EBONE document, the link would be available to transit traffic.

◻

Helping coordinate EASInet was only one of GMD's projects. The site also acted as a key gateway between Germany and the rest of the Internet. Germany had long been one of the most ardent OSI advocates. In 1984, the ministry of research and technology started up a membership organization, the Deutsches Forschungsnetz (DFN), the German research network intended to give the German scientific community the full benefits of OSI.

GMD, part of the federal research establishment, ended up with a sort of schizophrenic role. On the one hand, they took part in the fervent OSI cult built around the leadership of their funding agency, helping DFN on conceptual work and software development.

On the other hand, GMD had work to do and actively helped build EARN, running the German national node since 1987. At the same time, GMD started building a private X.25 network to link German national research laboratories together.

This private network, AGFnet, was not OSI (in fact it was SNA), but at least it contained X.25, the "pathway to OSI," to make it politically palatable to the bureaucracy. What AGFnet did do was prod DFN into action, which resulted in a national X.25 network called Wissenschaftsnetz (WIN or "science network").

DFN had a notable success in building WIN: they made it affordable. With the fairly strong backing of the federal government, DFN was able to convince the German PTT to give it preferential rates and, most importantly, to avoid imposing volume-based charges. The result was a rate of DM 5,000 per month for a 64 kbps line. By 1991, WIN had spread throughout Germany and much of the research community was on the network, including commercial researchers such as Daimler Benz.

After what Klaus wryly termed "a period of difficulty," DFN accepted the premise of multiprotocol networks. In fact, with users paying for their own usage, it turned out that the vast majority of sites chose to use TCP/IP or EARN protocols.

There was still some OSI work on the network, particularly since the federal government was willing to finance such research. X.400 usage, in particular, had significant usage and was growing quickly. GMD operated application gateways to the Internet and EARN worlds to keep connectivity.

Hanging in Klaus' office, high up near the ceiling, was an abacus with a little mouse perched on top. This odd little arrangement was the Birkenbihl massively parallel supercomputer, given to Klaus by his daughter. "Look," he said, pointing to the blue and red beads, "it even has a color graphics display."

I went back to Königswinter, hoping to warm up with a nice, hearty German meal, but it was the off-season and all the interesting places were boarded up. A half-dozen Greek restaurants appeared to be Gyros-only joints, with nary a drop of taramasalata in sight, so

I settled on an Italian restaurant. There I was served limp, over-cooked noodles in a heavy, congealed green sauce.

"That was the worst pesto I've ever had," I told the waiter as I paid up.

"Thank you very much," he said with a proud smile.

I finally found a sausage shop open and filled up on a couple mugs of König-Pilsner and a Riesenbackwurst, a greasy sausage served on a slab of cardboard with a puddle of mustard. Much better than the lime-green pesto.

The next morning, checking out of the hotel, I watched the clerk punch my room number into the computer and we stood staring at each other with forced smiles while the dot matrix printer chugged away. The clerk retrieved the printout, then walked over to an ancient cash register and punched in the room charges, one by one. He then picked up a thick sheaf of bar bills and added them in, one by one.

He took that printout over to a calculator, where he added in my minibar charges. By then, I was not in the least surprised when he took that slip over to his desk and figured out the tax, adding it in by hand.

"Not very modern," he said with a shrug.

I had to agree.

I took the early morning Schnellzug to Cologne. With over an hour to kill, I put my bags into a locker and checked out the bar and café.

It was 8:00 A.M., but the bar was standing room only—there were no chairs but lots of men standing around drinking their pre-train beers. In the café, there were eight of us and five had cigarettes going, all crammed into a space smaller than a Manhattan studio apartment. I went back to the bar.

Two minutes before departure, I went up to the track just as the train to Brussels pulled in. I boarded and spent a dreamy two hours staring at sleepy villages and isolated farm houses, built of stone and sitting precariously on hills in the middle of black fields.

We entered Brussels, the center of the densest train network in Europe. Our track joined others and soon we were picking our way through a yard dozens of tracks wide. Then, suddenly, we were inside the cavernous central train station.

I spent the weekend catching up on my reading and looking for open restaurants in a city where it seemed like even the red light district closed on weekends. Brussels prides itself on being at the geographic center of Europe, and thinks of itself as the logical capital of the European Community, home to the Commission. I think of it more as the Indianapolis of Europe.

After the sleepy calm of the weekend, I figured my two days trying to find out about the infamous Directorate Generale 13 (DG XIII) would be relatively simple and might even yield useful information.

This optimistic mood was soon to change. The weather got even colder, the food got toxic, the taxi drivers started getting into accidents, and, worst of all, I entered the bureaucratic swamp of the European Commission.

❐

260

Brussels

Monday morning, I walked over to the European parliament building and up the Rue du Loi, past huge monoliths filled with functionaries, to the Rue de Trèvres, home to a portion of DG XIII. The European Commission security system requires visitors to leave their passports as identification, but since I had a fax from a DG XIII PR officer I was allowed through. Security didn't even look at the fax to make sure that the letter wasn't a request to have me permanently barred from Europe.

On the second floor, I was ushered into the office of Peter Johnston, an official of the F Directorate of the 13th Directorate-General of the Commission of the European Communities. We were soon joined by another official, also named Peter. There was one seat free on my side of the little conference table, but Peter 2 took great pains to clear off a chair and align himself with Peter 1 on the other side.

With both Peters in place, they began an interchangeable litany of platitudes, trying to explain everything the Commission was doing from promoting networking to ensuring the future of international trade. I had heard about things like COSINE, RACE, PACE, RISE, and the European Nervous System and naively asked if perhaps one of the Peters could explain these pieces, perhaps starting with the RACE project.

There was my first mistake. You see, RACE is a program, not a project.

"No, no, no," Peter 1 chided me, explaining how, in the context of the third framework there were a series of programs such as RACE, each of which was made up of dozens and dozens of projects. RACE was no mere project, thank you.

I learned little of substance in my briefings, but later, digging through over 20 pounds of documents I had amassed, I was able to put together a cursory picture of the programs and projects and themes and frameworks that the Peters were so unable to articulate.

DG XIII is the portion of the bureaucracy of the Commission charged with looking after the areas of telecommunications, information technology, and innovation. DG XIII has taken an active role in industrial policy, funding a great deal of research and development, and also handling some regulation.

The reason for DG XIII is that Europe has traditionally been a stronghold of the PTTs, monopoly service providers of postal services, telecommunications, telegraph, and even, in many cases, banking and other sundry services. Although the size of the European economy is about the same as the U.S., fragmentation of telecommunications has led to conflicting standards, closed markets, and inefficient service providers.

The Commission was taking a variety of steps as a regulatory body to try and open up telecommunications, including requiring PTTs to relax their procurement policies so all European suppliers could compete. Other regulatory steps included requiring a single 112 emergency phone number for all of Europe and a single standard for mobile radiotelephony, replacing the 6 different standards that had sprung up in the 12 EC member states.

In all this regulation, DG XIII worked with the existing PTTs, trying to get them to change their practices. The Commission was less than enthusiastic about taking steps that might lead to the PTTs' demise. In fact, the second prong of the Commission's strategy was to couple regulation with a very strong industrial policy, trying to keep the industry competitive.

This was no minor research program, either. In the fields of information technology and communications, the Commission was funding R&D to the tune of ECU 2.221 billion from the period 1990 to 1994. (The ECU was worth roughly U.S. $1.25 in 1992).

To understand the Commission, it is best to defer the natural inclination to ask where the money was spent and what resulted and instead focus on the process.

The quintessential model for an EC program was Esprit. Started in February 1984, DG XIII bills Esprit as "the key to reviving European technology." The premise behind Esprit was matching funds. The Commission would put up half the money for a research project, the participants would put up the other half.

Rather than have researchers suggest some interesting research, the Commission would issue a call for proposals. To respond, a group had to have at least two industrial partners from at least two EC countries. Typically, a successful group would have up to a half-dozen members, including research institutions, consulting firms, telecommunications companies, and computer companies.

Esprit shelled out ECU 1.5 billion and involved 3,000 researchers in the first phase from 1984 to 1988. From 1988 to 1992, Esprit shelled out another ECU 3.2 billion, involving almost 6,000 researchers.

Probably the best known result of Esprit is the transputer, an example of which is the T800 chip, a 10-MIP, 32-bit, RISC processor useful as a building block for parallel computers or signal processing units. Of course, there are several other chips that the transputer must compete against, such as those from Motorola, Intel, and the Sparc consortium.

Other projects helped train engineers in VLSI design or developed opto-electrical equipment for video reception at medium distances without amplification. Esprit officials categorize these as "major results" and point to "over 500 major results" in the Esprit program.

I examined the list of major results through the end of 1989. There were 343 major results, and it is interesting that 43 of these were in the category of having made a "substantial contribution to the preparation of international standards." If prestandardization activities got their own category and were counted as major results, it was obvious that all this money was certainly not going to develop new technology or to conduct real research.

Though the bulk of Esprit money went to things like high-definition TV standards, a substantial sum was devoted to an area of research projects known as the "Information Exchange System." Best known of these projects was COSINE and its IXI backbone. IXI, connecting 20 different X.25 networks in 17 countries, was listed as the key infrastructure for Information Exchange.

A COSINE brochure proudly stated that IXI was transferring 25 Gbytes of data per month by the Spring of 1991. The fact that IXI was several years late in coming was not mentioned, nor was the fact that 25 Gbytes per month is not a tremendous amount of data. The German DFN X.25 network, for example, was transferring over 70 Gbytes per month of TCP/IP data over X.25, not to mention substantial traffic from other protocols such as SNA.

There were several other information exchange projects proudly trumpeted in the COSINE literature, but my favorite was ROSE, Research Open Systems for Europe. The project started in 1983 and ran for 60 months, involving five European vendors such as Bull, ICL, and Olivetti. ROSE had the novel goal to promote OSI and "reinforce standardization work by implementing the standards and demonstrating them." At a gala demonstration at the Esprit 88 conference, the vendors all demonstrated OSI prototypes that included FTAM, X.400, and the X.28/X.29 PAD services.

With Esprit such a shining success, DG XIII used it as a model for other industrial policy programs. The STAR program, for example, was started to try and get the less developed portions of the telephone infrastructure jumpstarted. From 1986-91, the Commission pumped ECU 780 million into places like Northern Ireland, Portugal, and Greece, with matching funds coming from the member states.

These types of government intervention can be quite useful if the money is put into the right places. The program that really caught my attention was RACE, Research and Development in Advanced Communications Technologies for Europe. RACE was supposed to get a broadband ISDN network into Europe and if there was any place a massive infusion of help was needed, it was the European telephone system.

As the two Peters explained to me, RACE was focused on the area of integrated broadband communications (IBC) and was meant to avoid the problems that ISDN had encountered on its way to market.

According to Peter 1, ISDN had run into a few setbacks because the standards were too vague, leading to incompatible implementations. While the ISDN generation of technology was getting on its feet, it had taken a bit longer than anyone had planned.

In other words, ISDN was a fiasco, consumed huge amounts of resources, and produced few results (but did so consistently over a long period of time). RACE would make sure the next generation of technology had a smoother roll-out.

If the problem with ISDN had been vague standards, then RACE would make sure that all the downstream activities from stand-

264

ards—the implementation profiles, conformance specifications, feature subsets, and the like—were formulated in great detail, thus avoiding incompatibility.

DG XIII had set itself the highly ambitious goal of a B-ISDN network by 1995 and was investing heavily. Between mid-87 and mid-92, RACE would involve 294 organizations in 92 projects for a total outlay of ECU 1.2 billion (U.S. $1.47 billion), of which the Commission was pitching in ECU 550 million.

The RACE literature explained that by bringing all the European players together in one project, the risk of failure was reduced. Everybody would work together for a common goal. Putting all your assets into one investment was a strategy I had not learned in my class on portfolio analysis, but I was willing to hear the argument out.

RACE hoped to somehow speed up the standardization process, a "well-known bottleneck in the exploitation of high technology." Rather than reduce the bottleneck by reducing the size of the stack of paper and focusing on implementation experience, RACE was going to try and increase the volume of paper produced.

The result would be the integrated broadband communications architecture, a pile of documents that would specify everything necessary for the network. This suite of documents would, of course, be adopted by the rest of the world, opening up the vast external market for European suppliers to exploit.

RACE, one of my glossy brochures exultantly proclaimed, was "the current focus of attention of all the intellectual and industrial work on advanced telecommunications in Europe."

When you talked to the Peters, though, you got the idea that the real purpose of RACE was to reinforce the dominant position of the PTTs. ATM cell switching, the technology that forms the basis for most of RACE and B-ISDN, was to Peter 1 simply a means to eliminate "rate arbitrage."

Rate arbitrage is one of those code words that summarizes all that is evil about those who insist on setting up their own networks. By this philosophy, the only reason that a value added network (i.e., anybody but the PTT) can exist is because entrepreneurs take advantage of differential tariffs for different speeds.

If the tariffs did not vary, the philosophy goes, everybody would buy their services from the underlying network provider, the PTT. The evil of the Valued-Added Network (VAN) is that these greedy businessmen skim the cream off the top, diverting funds away from the PTT that is trying to provide service to everybody. If the profitable business accounts go to the VAN, who takes care of the poor widow in the village?

This line of argument makes a lot of sense unless you ask a more fundamental question. Do the PTTs have the capability to do the work in the first place? If not, the cream-skimming argument breaks down at that first assumption. Stopping others from doing important work is not an effective strategy for building an infrastructure.

While I was mulling over the proper way to get high-speed fiber and ATM switches into place, the two Peters had left the now-boring details of the RACE program for their newest toy, a program so new it didn't even have an acronym.

This new program was in the area of telematics, bureau-speak for applications that use networks. To the tune of ECU 376 million from 1990 to 94, the Commission was funding half of the projects in seven telematic areas, including transportation, health care, libraries, and government.

I had been wondering what the purpose of Peter 2 was, and I soon learned that he was heavily involved with the transportation portion of the telematics program. Peter 1 ceded the floor and Peter 2 began his presentation.

He talked for 10 minutes, at which point I started leafing back through my notes. During those 10 minutes, Peter 2 had not uttered one sentence that was evenly vaguely comprehensible. I understood the words, but was unable to parse any of the sentences, let alone extract any semantic content.

Evidently, there had been a separate program of research on intelligent road systems, known as Drive. Drive successfully completed a total of 71 projects in 1991, presumably with many major results and at a cost of ECU 60 million. Of course, overhead took 10 percent away, but this was still real money.

Peter 2 kept referring to the "road transport informatics in the context of the Drive 2 programme," but I had a tough time understanding what that actually meant. Luckily, Peter 1 realized the problem and cut in.

"I must insist," he said, arching his eyebrows, "there is no Drive 2 programme." Rather, it was more appropriate to refer to the transportation "theme" within the larger context of the telematics program.

I still didn't know what this theme/program/project cluster was actually doing, so I asked Peter 2 to give me an example of one of the pilot projects or some technology that was actually being used.

He couldn't. He mumbled on about harmonization of standards and finally explained, as if talking to a small child, that it was "hard to pick out a particular report from Drive and say this was used here," pointing to the table in front of him.

It was clear to them that I didn't realize that I was in a room with policy makers, not some mundane road technician or highway analyst. Peter 1 gave me a lecture about the vast scope of DG XIII. It was as if I had asked the Chairman of the Board of EXXON to tell me how many gas stations he had in Lexington, Kentucky. (Of course, if you asked the Chairman of EXXON to name any one city in which he had a station, chances are he might be able to answer that question.)

I decided to try another tack. The Peters and 40 of their colleagues seemed to spend most of their time issuing contracts under various themes. Was the process computerized?

Peter 1 was insulted. Peter 2 sniffed.

"Of course we're computerized," Peter 1 said, waving vaguely in the direction of his desk, which bore an Olivetti PC and a Hewlett-Packard laser printer.

"What kind of network do you use?"

"Uh, Novell," one mumbled uncertainly. The other one looked down and shuffled some papers.

"And what kind of DBMS do you use to manage your contract boilerplate library?" I wanted to know.

A look of panic crossed their faces. Peter 1 gave an exasperated sigh. Peter 2 seemed to think they were using Foxbase. Peter 1 rose and handed me some brochures. Peter 2 excused himself for an important meeting upstairs.

◻

I took the subway out to the isolated suburb of Beaulieu, where DG XIII has office space, to meet Jurgen Rosenbaum, an information officer. We paid our mutual respects and lied about how much help we would be to each other. I collected another 10 pounds of paper, then left to try and find someplace to grab lunch in the hour before my next meeting.

Beaulieu has at least four huge office complexes and dozens more under construction, and is surrounded by modern looking apartment blocks. Yet, with all these people, there was not a single place to eat, or even get a newspaper. This was city planning at its best.

I got back on the subway and went a few stops into town, hurrying to find a lone Spanish restaurant down the street from the station. After a quick lunch of fish soup (preceded by a 25 minute wait), I hustled back to the subway to find my next bureaucrat.

Halfway through our audience on Esprit, I felt myself getting more and more nauseous. I realized with horror that this wasn't caused by platitudes but that I was feeling the all too familiar onset of food poisoning from the fish.

As I rode into town, I felt worse and worse, just making it back to the warmth of my mediocre hotel before collapsing. I spent the entire next day in bed, trying to gather enough strength for Wednesday's train ride to Paris.

I left Brussels puzzled by the European Commission. There is certainly a place for a strong industrial policy, as the Japanese demonstrated with their MITI program and as the U.S. Defense Advanced Research Projects Agency repeatedly showed with TCP/IP, UNIX, and a host of other successes. Yet in the one field I felt qualified to judge, the Commission appeared to have been a total failure. The European Internet was coming into being, but only after fighting active opposition from DG XIII.

On the Euro-City train to Paris, I started to feel a little better. The conductor looked at my Eurail pass and smiled broadly.

"Ah, un American! C'est tres bon!" he exclaimed with a classic Parisian accent. This was about as out of character for a Parisian as it would be to have a New Yorker tell you to "have a nice day." Still, it was a welcome diversion from the dour gloom of Belgium.

As the train passed through St. Quentin and headed up the Oise river, the countryside started getting familiar, the houses looked French, and even the farms had a characteristic look. I arrived at the Gare du Nord and stepped into the car of a virtuoso taxi driver who shot down alleys and back streets, delivering me to the Montparnasse district for the remarkable fare of FF 70. I gave him 100, the amount such a ride would normally cost.

Flipping on CNN in my room, I was just in time for a commercial featuring "beautiful, bountiful, beguiling, Belgium." Popping open a beer from the minibar, I mentally added "bullshit and bureaucrats" to their list.

After watching President Bush's State of the Union address, I bundled up and went up the Boulevard Montparnasse to fetch my 92-year old great-aunt, stopping on the way for a paper sack of roasted chestnuts to warm my hands and popping into Le Chien Qui Fume for a quick drink.

Over a salad of preserved quail on a bed of dandelions, watercress, onions, and gooseberries, I tried to explain to my aunt the concept of a technical travelogue. She listened carefully, frowned a bit perplexedly, and told me that she was very proud of me, whatever it was that I was doing.

Thursday morning, I took the Métro to the edge of the city, then a train out to Versailles. My taxi took a detour around the immense castle that had housed Marie Antoinette and over to the neighboring suburb of Rocquencourt, where INRIA has a facility.

My 10 A.M. appointment wasn't there. He had sent me mail, but when I logged into a borrowed terminal I saw, to my horror, that I had received no new mail messages for over a week. Something was drastically wrong.

The secretary at INRIA told me where I had to go for my meeting. On the way back into town, I tried to figure out what had happened. The problem was no doubt in my home PC (or, more likely, in the way I had configured it).

The domain of Malamud.COM is a registered domain. When somebody starts to send mail to any of the millions of possible addresses in the Malamud.COM domain, a record in the Domain Name System points to my commercial service provider, Colorado SuperNet.

Colorado SuperNet takes all incoming mail and spools it on a special UUCP-only account I maintain on their machine. A few times a day, my PC calls up that account and retrieves all incoming mail messages. Those messages are sorted, combined with my MCI Mail, any fax notifications I can grep out of my fax log, and some miscellaneous status messages, and the whole lot is sent right back up to the interactive account on Colorado SuperNet that I use while on the road.

In desperation, I stopped at the train station and gave a call to my fax number. Since the fax is answered by a fax board in a PC, it stands to reason that a high pitched tone on the other end would tell me that my PC was still up and running, and, by logical conclusion, that my house was not a charred, smoking wreck.

Having successfully pinged my house (but not solved the mail problem), I continued on to La Défense, a complex of convention centers, shopping centers, exhibit halls, and other public spaces, all surrounding a futuristic looking arch, kind of a 21st-century rendition of the Arc de Triomphe. There, next to the World Trade Center, is the InfoMart, a three story high set of exhibit spaces for computer vendors.

Most of the vendors are your typical IBM, Bull, and Microsoft variety, but there are a couple of odd ducks. One is a "house of the future" exhibit, built to the new European home automation standards. This house-like display, full of spas, jacuzzis, exercise bikes, and other things I would never allow in my own house, was a coop-

erative venture of a dozen vendors, all trumpeting the future of do-
motics.

The other shop that doesn't really fit in is one rented by four
research agencies, including INRIA. There, I met with Milan Sterba,
a young Czech with joint appointments at INRIA and the Prague
School of Economics.

Though officially he had been in the business school in Prague,
Milan had spent most of his time on the large Czechoslovakian project to develop an MVS-like operating system to run on the reverse-
engineered System 370 clones manufactured in Bulgaria and Russia.
Milan had spent several years working in his chosen specialty, telecommunications, developing a VTAM-like telecommunications access method.

At INRIA, in addition to real work like reconfiguring Sun workstations, Milan had an informal role as one of the focal points for
East European countries trying to get on the Internet. He maintained a document detailing current connectivity, chaired sessions at
RIPE meetings, and otherwise helped to spread information around
where it was needed.

The rapid progress in the former Eastern Bloc and Soviet Union
had been truly amazing. As fast as the countries could persuade the
U.S. to process the paperwork for Cisco routers, countries were
plopping in TCP/IP nodes, enhancing EARN connections, and using UUCP and EUnet to spread connectivity into new places.

Bulgaria, for example, was using a dial-up UUCP link to Amsterdam for connectivity. Dial-up was then being used to send messages and files to the 10 Bulgarian EUnet sites. Dial-up UUCP was
a common first step for many countries, a fact worth keeping in
mind before sending long messages to people on the other end of
slow (and expensive) lines.

Poland was typical of countries with higher levels of connectivity. Poland had a 9,600 bps leased line between Warsaw and Copenhagen and used statistical multiplexors to combine TCP/IP with the
EARN NJE/BSC protocols. Another 9,600 bps leased line between
Krakow and CERN used DECnet protocols as part of HEPnet, but
was converted to IP as soon as an export license for a Cisco router
was approved. A 64 kbps leased line between Warsaw and NOR-

DUnet in Stockholm was going operational in 1992 and would greatly enhance TCP/IP connectivity to the country.

Milan and I talked about the effect that posting standards had had in Czechoslovakia. Milan told me that, to his knowledge, only one copy of the ITU Blue Book existed and people spent considerable time going to a central facility to consult standards documents.

The ITU and others in the standards cartel had always insisted that the standards were reasonably priced for those "serious" about doing work. Milan confirmed that this position was nonsense and that many countries in Eastern Europe had particularly welcomed the ability to access documents they needed for their work.

I found it particularly distressing that the ITU policies were having the effect of preventing people in developing countries from accessing technical standards. After all, one of the purposes of the United Nations, of which the ITU is a key part, is to promote a world community. Keeping key documents hidden from those without money, indeed keeping documents hidden from entire countries without money, is certainly a convoluted perversion of the UN mission.

That night, I had dinner in a Venetian restaurant, a classic place with a dozen tables and the owner acting as the head (and only) waiter. In his 50s, stout, distinguished looking and impeccably dressed, the owner showed people to their tables, practicing the art of being apparently servile while in reality insulting everyone he could. While ignoring my waiter and eating a mediocre mezzaluna funghi, I read *Don Fernando*, Somerset Maugham's classic essay on Spain. Maugham was writing about the playwright Lope De Vega, author of 2,200 plays.

Many had proudly pointed to the size of this document base, equating De Vega's proclivity for producing paper with greatness. De Vega himself had not taken this seriously, remarking that "if anyone should cavil at my plays and think that I wrote them for fame, undeceive him and tell that I wrote them for money."

When you reward people for producing paper, they will do so. When the European Commission and RARE paid people's expenses to go to meetings and make specifications, it is not surprising that they took so long to make them, nor that they were so voluminous.

Likewise, when you take a stack of OSI documents and put them next to the RFC series, you can tell pretty quickly which ones were produced by standards professionals and which ones were written by engineers who had software to write and networks to run.

◻

Friday morning, I met Jean-Paul Le Guigner of the Comité Réseau des Universités, a committee of French universities formed to set up a national research network, much like EDUCOM in the U.S. and the vice-chancellors committee in Australia.

We took the subway to Jussieu, changing trains and walking through the long, intricate tunnels connecting Paris Métro lines, ending up at the Université Pierre et Marie Curie. Widely acknowledged as one of the uglier campuses ever built, the university was constructed during the period in the 1960s and 1970s when slabs of unfinished concrete were considered "modern."

At the university, we found the office of Christian Michau of the Unité Réseaux du CNRS, Jean-Paul's equivalent in the research world. CNRS, the Centre National de la Recherche Scientifique, acted as a coordinating body for French research institutions like INRIA and ORSTOM.

The two groups, the universities and the researchers, had banded together to form Renater, the Réseau National de Télécommunications de la Recherche. Funded to the tune of FF 50 to 60 million (around U.S. $10 million) per year, this network would form a national backbone of 2 Mbps in 1992 with the core expanding to 34 Mbps in early 1993.

Renater, like the NSFNET in the U.S., was set up as a network of networks, linking regionals together and France to the rest of the world. Unlike NSFNET, the interface to the network would be provided by the telephone company, in this case France Telecom.

France Telecom, under contract to Renater, would offer a point of presence to which regionals could connect. The regionals, like the R3T2 network I had seen in Sophia-Antipolis, were locally funded. In the case of R3T2, for example, local and regional networks had started the network as a way of attracting industry and promoting education.

After checking to see if my house was spitting up mail yet, Christian, Jean-Paul, and I headed over to Christian Michau's office and sat around a conference table. We were joined by two other gentlemen who were somehow joining Renater and needed a briefing on the project.

It was quickly established that having me speak French was a better strategy than forcing the other four to speak English. Christian suggested I start with a brief description of my project. Somehow, while I was researching this book I found that many of my hosts, though always very hospitable and full of information, never quite understood the concept of a "technical travelogue."

I complied, giving a little speech and feeling quite content that I had remembered enough French to pull this off. Everybody smiled and nodded gravely, each in turn thanking me. Then, one of the observers leaned over to Jean-Paul and suggested that perhaps a good way to proceed would be for somebody to explain exactly what the American gentleman was hoping to accomplish.

Once this was all straightened out, Christian and Jean-Paul proceeded to tell me about Renater. In France, research institutions and universities have a great deal of independence. To make things difficult, any attempt to establish a national research network would cut across three different government ministries.

Through a minor miracle, in February 1991 an interministerial convention was signed which established the authorization for Renater to begin planning. A pilot committee was formed, which spawned a technical committee, which created a project team. By the end of January 1992, a contract with France Telecom was days away from signing and a pilot network was already in place. Remarkably quick, given the number of ministries and bureaucracies involved.

Renater was designed to be a multiprotocol network, but with an interesting twist. The networks in many countries, such as Germany's DFN, ran all protocols over X.25 ("the pathway to OSI"). Running TCP/IP over X.25 was certainly a combination that worked, but for connecting two hosts together a straight leased line made more sense.

Renater was set up in a very pragmatic fashion as two networks, one presenting an IP interface, the other an X.25 interface. At 2 Mbps, the X.25 network would simply layer on top of the Transpac public X.25 network. The IP network, a totally separate system, would be a series of Cisco routers on leased lines.

The network would be quickly upgraded to 34 Mbps in early 1993, at least on core routes. It was hoped that at these higher speeds that ATM-based cell switching would allow the X.25 and IP networks to coexist on the underlying substrate.

Presenting an X.25 interface solved several problems. OSI could run on the network, so all parties in Renater were able to boldly proclaim that theirs was an OSI network which incidently happened to support "immediate needs of existing traffic." The X.25 network also gave a platform on which DECnet and SNA traffic could run.

Michau and LeGuigner were decidedly pragmatic about their work, trying hard to avoid political battles and concentrate instead on getting the network up and running. They strenuously avoided religious decisions they didn't have to make, using mechanisms like study groups to look at questions of SMTP versus X.400.

What I found most interesting was the close working relationship with France Telecom. The telephone company seemed to view Renater as an opportunity instead of a threat, using the research community as a place to test technology and building expertise for future commercial rollouts.

A 5-year contract worth roughly U.S. $10 million per year had been signed with the telephone company, giving them a substantial incentive to provide a working network. In addition, a contract provision was added that any tariff decreases in the future would be used to upgrade the bandwidth of the research network, thus guaranteeing a fixed amount for the telco and at the same time protecting the research community.

How had Renater managed to avoid the need to make OSI their only protocol? Michau had one of the better answers to the question of OSI I had seen.

"Many countries in Europe are beginning to realize that OSI is not X.25," he explained. Instead, he looked to standards like OSI to provide solutions to a range of problems, particularly at the application layer.

If you accept OSI as a set of services instead of some monolithic religion, useful protocols like X.400 and X.500 can be applied immediately instead of waiting for an entire grand design to come into being. In fact, you could, with this view, run X.400 on top of ISODE, which in turn can run on top of TCP/IP, and still provide OSI service.

Defining OSI as a series of applications took Renater out of the debate. After all, Renater was simply providing an infrastructure, a core backbone, and it was up to the users to decide what to run on that backbone.

Running an X.25 interface kept Renater in the OSI game. Even for international links, Renater was willing to use X.25 links. While acknowledging that "some choices are not technically perfect," it was clear that Renater would consider projects like the 2 Mbps IXI extension. After all, the European Commission favored X.25 and the Commission had lots of money. It was clear that the larger European countries like France would quickly catch up to the U.S., putting in high-bandwidth backbones, setting up regional networks, and running multiprotocol environments.

That night, I picked up my great-aunt for a quick dinner. Over glasses of port and a dish of snails soaked in garlic and butter, we talked about her childhood in Russia, her emigration to Montreal and New York in the early part of the century, and her escape from the Nazis in the war, walking over the border to Free France with her 6 year old daughter in the middle of the night. She had been in France for 60 years, even receiving the Legion of Honor for her work at the Pasteur Institute, where she conducted research and later helped numerous visiting scientists get settled. After walking her back to her apartment, I went to my seedy hotel to pack and trade insults with the snooty night manager.

February 1, having visited nine countries in January, I happily landed at Dulles airport, taking my carry-on luggage straight through customs and into my waiting rental car. My hotel was a minor miracle, cheap and comfortable. I went straight down to the bar in the basement and settled in with the *New York Times*, a bacon cheeseburger, and a bottle of Brooklyn Lager, a beer as "vital and diverse as the city itself."

Sunday evening, I met Tony Rutkowski, who had quit his job at the swamp of the ITU and moved back to Washington to work for Sprint International. Although we had exchanged lots of e-mail messages, it was still nice to talk in person. While e-mail is certainly convenient, person-to-person is still a communication medium that has a much higher semantic bandwidth.

Monday, I made an early morning reverse commute out to the suburbs, thumbing my nose at the parking lot heading into the city. In fact, it was so early when I got to Reston that I stopped into the local Sheraton for breakfast.

"We are glad to be able to contribute to the start of your day," the menu proclaimed. "We bid you a wonderful day." Thinking I might have misread my itinerary, I pulled it out to make sure I wasn't in California.

After my power breakfast of a bagel with lox, I wandered over to the headquarters of the Corporation for National Research Initiatives (CNRI), the institutional home of such network luminaries as Drs. Vinton Cerf and Bob Kahn.

My first meeting was with Vint Cerf, the Chairman of the Internet Activities Board (IAB) and an engineer whose involvement with TCP/IP dates back to the very first ARPANET nodes. Vint is famous for his ability, despite a huge stack of lofty responsibilities, for keeping up a detailed knowledge of the protocol suite at all layers.

Vint Cerf is the kind of person who can switch from briefing a congressional aide to an in-depth discussion of dynamic routing protocols, public key cryptography, or the inner details of multi-media messaging. I have never seen him attend a working group meeting at technical forums like the IETF without making at least one substantive contribution.

Technical issues, though still demanding, now have to contend with organizational questions, issues that suck up more and more of his time. The most pressing issue was the future of the IAB and the IETF, two organizations that had been remarkably successful but were institutionally adrift.

The IAB started as a technical advisory committee to the Defense Advanced Research Projects Agency, but when the ARPANET died, the IAB was no longer an official body. Through technical leadership rather than governmental fiat, the IAB continued to guide the development of the TCP/IP protocols in the Internet community.

The IAB had to bear the liabilities of its DoD origins in a changed world. It didn't help, of course, that the IAB remained an all-American group until 1991, when Christian Huitema from France was asked to join. (Not to mention the fact that in 1992, the IAB remains exclusively composed of white, western males.)

Lack of accountability and lack of international representation made it increasingly difficult for the IAB to exercise leadership. The standards-making activities of the IAB and the IETF also raised issues of due process, antitrust liability, copyright, and a host of other issues difficult to resolve without a more formal organization.

Vint Cerf's solution to these problems was to announce the formation of a new professional association, the Internet Society. The IAB and the IETF would become activities of the Internet Society.

The Society managed to attract quite a few other projects as well. The INET conference which evolved from the Larry Landweber seminars would become the annual meeting of the Society. Tony Rutkowski would run the publications board and hoped to produce a newsletter of topical information and a journal of archival material.

Launching an activity of this magnitude is never easy, and by February 1992, Vint Cerf had already spent many months getting the project off the ground. A key activity was selecting the initial trustees and drafting bylaws. Though the Society would be member-run, the first board would appoint itself. Then, in 1993, the first third of the trustees would be up for election. Within three years, the entire 21 person board would have been elected by members.

Self-selection of the first board and the decision to have the first official meeting at INET 92 in Kobe, Japan was causing some grumbling by American engineers, who were used to having IETF meetings in accessible U.S. locations.

One of the key architectural assumptions of the Internet Society is that it must be truly international to succeed in giving legitimacy to the standards-making activities of the IAB. As such, Cerf and many others felt that holding the first meeting out of the U.S. and appointing a truly international board were crucial to its success.

A set of bylaws and other procedures, control by a group of trustees, and other formal structures were also a change from the IETF, which had run its first meetings by shouting out policy at plenary meetings. Even in 1992, the IETF ran as a pretty loose sort of organization.

More elaborate procedures were also crucial if the activities leading to a standard were ever challenged. Standards promote interoperability, but can also be challenged as a potential antitrust violation if it appears that there is collusion to restrain trade.

The big challenge was how to change the process to put in some form of accountability, yet still maintain the effectiveness and flexibility of the IAB and the IETF. Too much process, and the whole thing would degenerate into just another standards body, pumping out paper and enjoying many fine lunches and dinners.

The Internet Society had been simmering in the six months since the announcement of its formation at INET 91 in Copenhagen. Despite the low profile, 800 members had joined. Though this was a small fraction of the 95,000 members of the Association for Computing Machinery (ACM), Cerf was encouraged and saw it as a good start. The board was also falling into place, with members from Japan, Australia, and several European countries joining the American members.

Next to Vint Cerf's office is that of Bob Kahn, the founder and president of CNRI. Kahn was a Senior Scientist at BBN responsible for the design of the ARPANET, then moved over to DARPA as Director of the Information Processing Techniques Office where he initiated the largest computer R&D program ever undertaken by the federal government, a billion dollar Strategic Computing Program. He still plays a crucial role in the Internet, with CNRI coordinating the 5 gigabit testbeds he helped to establish.

A former MIT professor, Kahn is described by most people who have met him as an extremely quick study. Hand him any topic and in a few minutes he will have something intelligent to say about it. A classic long-range thinker, he devotes much of his time to the question of how to build an effective infrastructure.

We talked about the "look and feel" of an infrastructure—what somebody needs to know in order to use it. Cars and roads, for example, require a fairly extensive knowledge base, ranging from how to use the pedals to how to read a street sign. Other infrastructures, ranging from electrical systems to education to banking and insurance, all have their own particular look and feel.

The issue for the Internet was providing a growth path for this infrastructure, which would support a pervasive, global Internet. With 4 to 7 million people already on the Internet, how would it grow to support an order of magnitude more?

It was interesting to look at what types of organizations were getting plugged into the Internet. Small users were rapidly getting on to some portion of the network, even if it meant something as simple as getting an MCI Mail account and learning how to use a modem and address messages.

Likewise, very large (or very high tech) users were getting plugged in, linking their campus networks to regional providers. They had the staff to manage their own networks, extending the Internet out to the users.

What seemed to be missing altogether, though, was a way for medium-sized enterprises without a high tech component to get on the network. Even getting a simple Novell network up and running was causing more stress than necessary.

I continued my day of meetings and greetings, ending up the evening having dinner with one of my editors, Stephanie Faul. Over a dish of crunchy jelly fish salad, we talked about her latest projects in the world of freelance. In addition to her usual stint acting as a ghost editor for the *AAA Magazine*, Stephanie had just landed a corporate writing gig, helping to organize a seminar with the prescient theme "The Future is Tomorrow."

◻

Tuesday was spent hiding from the cold, doing research in the Hawk and Dove, one of a half-dozen Irish bars on Capitol Hill. After paying a call at the Office of Technology Assessment to brief a staff member on the Bruno project, I took the metro under the mall to the offices of the National Science Foundation.

Steve Goldstein, the manager of international programs for the NSFNET, had invited me to his home for dinner and we would join his carpool from the NSF. He had just come back from a WAIS symposium and brought me a set of the conference materials. We both agreed that WAIS could easily prove to be the Lotus 1-2-3 of the Internet, providing users with a simple, intuitive way to get real information.

Steve and his life-partner Isabelle were both members of a gourmet cooking club and my timing was lucky enough to get the leftovers. While we waited for Isabelle to get home, Steve heated up a pork roast stuffed with mushrooms and a dish of fennel bulbs in a delicate cheese sauce while we talked about the NSF and the NSFNET.

The NSF has taken its charter to help U.S. science and engineering as a broad mandate which ranges from hands-on science museums for children all the way to funding research into teraflop computers.

The NSFNET is a perfect example of the broad interpretation NSF takes of its mandate. Instead of dedicated networks for supercomputer centers, the agency built a system of general-purpose regional networks connected by a backbone—a true infrastructure.

Steve Goldstein described the NSF funding philosophy as strategically placed "drops of oil," hoping to leverage comparatively small expenditures to achieve a broad impact. The drops of oil philosophy was necessary because the agency's budget was fairly small. Program directors have to husband their money carefully and overhead is kept down to a paltry four percent.

The international program of NSFNET, for example, makes do with a budget well under a million dollars per year, a minuscule amount when you consider how high telephone tariffs are and what an important role NSF played in building a global Internet.

To spread the money out, NSFNET usually funds half-circuits. Most international circuits are actually operated by the two PTTs involved, each making up the tariff for the outgoing line. Typically, NSF only picks up the cost for the U.S. half-circuit, which are often significantly lower in cost—anywhere from 20 percent to factors of 2, 3, and even 4 times less. In some cases, the international partner will pick up the cost for both half-circuits. NORDUnet, for example, paid for the whole line to the U.S. for some time until the NSF was able to pitch in.

In the case of the "fat pipes," the high bandwidth circuits overseas, there is usually a consortium of agencies that pay. The link to the U.K., for example, has the NSF, DARPA, and NASA sharing the costs in one direction and the Joint Network Team and the Ministry of Defense sharing the other side.

In addition to sharing costs for general-purpose infrastructure, NSF is able to get a lot for its money because of simple competition. Sprint, for example, is the manager of international connection services for NSF, and won that contract because of a very agressive bid response. Sprint didn't do this out of altruism—the experience it gained with NSF was invaluable in capturing other international business.

NSF encourages regional solutions as a more efficient way to connect the world. To Europe, for example, the NSF helps fund the lines to INRIA in France and NORDUnet in Stockholm, both major gateways for their respective regions.

The agency also uses line sharing to buy larger pipes. The NSFNET backbone, for example, does not actually lease telephone lines. Instead, NSFNET contracts for a T3 service which runs on an underlying network owned by ANS. That underlying network carries traffic both for NSF and for ANS commercial customers, with packets from the two sources freely commingling.

Line sharing is applied to international links as well. NSF joined the EBONE consortium as an informal "supporting organization," the same category chosen by CERN and IBM. Supporting in this case meant that NSFNET and EBONE would be connected, but that NSF would not sign the memorandum of understanding.

Line sharing in EBONE meant that traffic from AlterNet and NSFNET might share the same lines. Government regulations prohibited NSF from funding commercial traffic, and this was the root cause of many of the appropriate use restrictions on the Internet. Allowing traffic from commercial services to share a link with NSFNET, provided the commercial service paid its own way, was an important step forward.

Acceptable use policies were set up in the era of the physical networks when NSF leased 56 kbps lines. The idea was that NSF should not be subsidizing traffic generated by those outside the community it meant to serve—the scientific and engineering researchers.

This policy was getting harder and harder to enforce, particularly if the enforcement mechanism was to bar all traffic originating from certain broad groups from traversing key links. With NSFNET simply paying for service, it no longer really mattered if packets fraternized, so long as the educational and research communities got their money's worth.

□

Wednesday morning, I walked a few blocks north to Dupont Circle to the home of Bob Barad, founder and sole employee of Baobab Communications. Bob runs the Baobab bulletin board, a Fidonet node specializing in African development.

His house is full of old maps of Africa, and blankets, baskets, and masks collected during his two years in the Peace Corps in Sierra Leone and on many subsequent visits to the continent. After his two years in swamp rice development in Sierre Leone, he came back for a law degree, then returned to Togo on a Fulbright scholarship.

Following that he spent a couple of years at the World Bank, an experience he diplomatically called "an extension of my education." Bob started spending his spare time dialing into bulletin boards. He got an account on PeaceNet and found he could start talking to people in Africa. He was hooked.

Soon he had hung out his shingle as a freelance development consultant, a business that seems to draw heavily on his Fidonet expertise. He had quickly tired of being a user of other peoples' boards and wanted to set up his own node.

Bob had been corresponding with a digital nomad named Mike Jensen, a man who travels the world with a laptop, setting up Fidonet nodes. Jensen blew into town one day late in 1989, stayed at Bob's house for a day, and Baobab was in business.

Fidonet is a network which can be thought of as the PC equivalent of the UNIX USENET system. It provides mail, file transfer, and news feeds, all managed by an informal volunteer hierarchy of city, regional, and national hubs. The free software and the cheap platforms it runs on have attracted the attention of many human rights, environmental, and other public interest groups.

Being able to set up a network anyplace there was a PC had proved valuable in Bob's business. He had just completed a job putting in nodes between Chad, Mauritania, and a group in Arlington, Virginia. The Virginia group was a subcontractor on a U.S. AID program to provide a famine early warning system.

Satellite images of the weather are periodically broadcast by the European Space Agency. Data would be downloaded and processed, resulting in graphic images of the affected areas that would be placed in files totalling roughly 70 kbytes. These files would be transferred to floppy disks and sent by DHL to Chad and Mauritania for use by regional workers.

This was a situation ripe for automation. By elimination of the weekly DHL runs, the payback from the use of computers could be immediately quantified, a situation very different from those trying to justify the more nebulous benefits such as "increased interaction" resulting from general-purpose e-mail.

The Fidonet software was successfully installed and the first files transferred. The system worked so well that one site immediately requested the previous week's file, which had not yet arrived by DHL.

The transfer of data uses the zmodem protocol on a direct call between the African sites and Arlington. Direct polling to the end destination is not unusual in Fidonet. While it is possible to hand off messages to a local gateway for percolation through the network, high priority data usually cuts through the hierarchy. To send mail to Africa, for example, Bob placed a biweekly call to the London hub, a site only a hop or two away from the African destinations.

The number of bulletin boards like Baobab in operation all over the world is truly incredible. Merely listing the boards in ASCII format makes for a file of 1.44 Mbytes. One of the great challenges of the Internet will be to give those BBS systems an easy way to integrate into the global network, providing better connectivity than just mail delivery, but doing so in a way that is cheap and easy.

I returned to my hotel to check out, only to discover that the window to my car had been broken in the overnight parking garage. I filled out forms for the parking garage, the police, Hertz, and American Express in order to get my keys back and sit on a pile of broken glass, sucking wind on the drive to Dulles Airport.

Having never been to Cleveland, I was firmly convinced that I didn't want to go. To my surprise, my visit was delightful. My hotel was a 1910 mansion, renovated in 1988 to be warm and to support modems and CNN. Dinner was just a stroll down the block to another renovated mansion, where I made short work of fresh rainbow trout, grilled with a pungent caper and garlic sauce. The conversation around me was, not surprising given the proximity to Case Western Reserve University, full of graduate-student angst and plans for monumental careers in the "real world."

Thursday morning, I met Tom Grundner, the founder of the Cleveland Free-Net and an apostle of populist computing. Grundner became a BBS hacker in 1984 when, as an assistant professor of family medicine, he was looking for a way to deliver community health information to the public. His St. Silicon bulletin board was such a success that, as Tom relates it, "it ate my career."

St. Silicon blossomed and by 1986 had become the Cleveland Free-Net, a multi-user service running on a UNIX platform with functionality similar to CompuServe. Users could chat with each other, could go through bulletin boards, and send mail.

There were, however, some big differences from CompuServe. For one thing, the service was free to the user. Grundner draws an analogy to television, where commercial networks fill one niche and the Public Broadcasting System (PBS) fills another. Grundner sees the Free-Net movement as the PBS of videotex.

In Cleveland, the network quickly expanded as more and more volunteers agreed to act as moderators for different topic areas. Lawyers, doctors, librarians, veterinarians, and many other professionals quickly joined. Rollerskating and Sci Fi SIGs came into being, until there were more than 400 different topic areas.

While people were using the system, keeping it going was costing money. It was kind of hard to claim that this was tenure-track research for a professor of family medicine, so Tom looked around for another institutional home.

Cleveland

He struck a deal with Case Western Reserve University's computer group. They were in the process of spending U.S. $10 million for an all-fiber campus network but, according to Tom, "no one gave a thought what to put on it." Cleveland Free-Net became a university project that also served the community, running on five Sun servers maintained by the department.

Tom got a salary, a couple of big offices, and a place in the bureaucracy far away from daily control of the Free-Net. Of course, he still had the ultimate control weapon, the ability to cause a loud fuss if things went too far off track.

So what to do? In 1989, he started the National Public Telecomputing Network (NPTN) and started pushing the Free-Net concept in other cities and countries. It was to the offices of the NPTN that Tom had brought me.

Both rooms were jammed with shelves, tables, postage meters, and ratty old couches, making these offices no different from countless public interest groups all over the country. This was obviously the kind of place where lots of volunteers spent their evenings.

It was morning, though, and the place was deserted. I sat down next to a life-size balloon with a skeleton painted on the front.

"Meet my staff," Tom said wryly, while he flitted around the room checking Macintoshes. He lit a cigarette and sat down in an easy chair to tell me about his populist computing movement.

The model for a Free-Net was based around a local organizing committee. This group of volunteers would organize and run the Free-Net, raising money wherever they could for a multi-user system, a copy of UNIX, and some modems and phone lines. The committee would then get on its collective knees and plead with the nearest college with a router for Internet access.

Software to run the Free-Net comes from Case Western Reserve in Cleveland. Long available for only U.S. $1, the University had gotten stars in its eyes and raised the price to U.S. $850 for non-profits, and much more to corporations.

In addition to the software, Tom's NPTN group provides what he had dubbed "cybercasting services." His first cybercasting success was convincing *USA Today* to allow him to distribute at low cost an online, electronic version of the newspaper. *USA Today* got supplemented with a variety of other news feeds.

When the Supreme Court started its Hermes project to distribute opinions electronically, it selected 12 groups ranging from the Free-Net and UUnet to UPI, Reuters, and Mead Data. Other information on current events ("teledemocracy" in Free-Netese) comes from the Congressional Memory Project. Every week, NPTN takes three Senate bills and three House bills and types in a two- to three-paragraph summary of the bill and how officials voted. The database builds every week, allowing people to start scanning the voting record of incumbents during reelection campaigns.

Cleveland Free-Net has grown over the years to 40,000 registered users, with 1,000 to 1,500 unique logins per day. Other Free-Nets are operational in Cleveland, Cincinnati, Peoria, and Youngstown. There is even a rural Free-Net in Medina County, southwest of Cleveland. An old, donated IBM RT running AIX is maintained at a 100-bed community hospital in the county seat. The local agricultural agent is on the system, as are librarians and other professionals in town.

Medina County is typical of most midwestern rural counties. It is perfectly square and the county seat is in the middle of the square. A call from anyplace in the county to the seat is considered a local call. Farmers, practically all of whom have PCs to run their farms, have a strong incentive to avoid long rides into town. Grundner felt that Medina County could serve as a model for the entire Midwest.

Financing Free-Nets is an interesting proposition. In Cincinnati, Cincinnati Bell sponsors the system. Many of the other sites operate on a shoestring. Grundner offers two financing models to the local organizational committees. On the pay-as-you-go model, the local Free-Net pays for services. A *USA Today* feed, for example, is based on the number of lines and will cost a typical Free-Net U.S. $1,000 to $2,000.

The other model has the Free-Net gather the names and addresses of users and ship them off to Grundner. Grundner, in turn, sends out tear-stained letters pleading for contributions. Of the five existing Free-Nets and the five others about to go into existence, three opted for the pay-as-you-go plan.

Whenever Tom could get a plane ticket abroad, he tried to spread the Free-Net concept to other countries. Often, though, he spreads the Free-Net concept by electronic mail, as in the case with his correspondance to the Helsinki Free-Net or to Richard Naylor in Helsinki.

Grundner was even invited to give a seminar in Singapore, sponsored by the National Computer Board. I found this a bit strange as Singapore's government, and especially the NCB, is pretty much the antithesis of the populist ideas Grundner represents. Interestingly, Grundner was invited back to Singapore, this time not by the NCB but by the Singapore Microcomputer Society.

The aspect of NPTN that was the most fascinating was Academy One, a K-12 computer literacy project based at Cleveland Free-Net that uses the Internet to try and include kids from all over the world.

Academy One sponsors periodic special events, such as the TeleOlympics. Any school with an Apple II (or any other cheap system), a modem, and Telnet prompt could participate in the TeleOlympics.

Four events were picked, including a 50 meter dash, standing and running broadjumps, and a tennis ball throw. The kids went to the school yard and ran the events, then came back in and posted their results.

The day started in New Zealand, then moved on to California, Cleveland, and ended up in Finland. The Free-Net kept a leader board of individual results, class averages, and a running news commentary with late breaking bulletins like "Mrs. Jones and her 4th Grade Class Break into the Lead."

A more sophisticated event was the space shuttle simulation. University School in Shaker Heights had a full scale mockup of the interior of the space shuttle, courtesy of a NASA program, complete with tape loops of the Earth from space running on TVs located behind the portholes.

With children's games, the kid with the toy gets to name the game, so University School acted as mission control, running 24-

hour simulations of a shuttle run. Other schools got to play other roles.

A school in California was selected as the alternate landing site. An alternate landing site has to furnish weather data to mission control, so the kids would go out and gather data on temperature, humidity, and barometric pressure. The data would go to mission control, which would respond with the current shuttle status. Status information was used to plot the current location on a map.

For all the Academy One events (and for Free-Net as a whole), the focus is on accessibility. This means cheap and easy to use. Tom looks with great skepticism at things like gigabit testbeds, preferring instead to convince a librarian to start an online book club.

I dropped off my rental car and went to the airport restaurant for a nondescript meal, spiced up by an article in the *New Yorker* about a group of Tibetan refugees in Scotland. In a strange form of cross-cultural exchange, the Scottish haggis would be used as a base for the traditional Tibetan momo dumplings. Poems by Robert Burns and the Dalai Lama were read at these affairs. One of the Tibetans had tactfully suggested to his countrymen that the momos were even more delicious when doused with liberal quantities of hot sauce.

With great relief I arrived at O'Hare airport, knowing that my next plane ride would bring me home. I drove out the I-88 toll road, past AT&T's Bell Laboratories, to the little town of Warrenville. When I first moved to Warrenville in 1969, the town of a few thousand people was in the middle of farm country.

Robert Wilson, the legendary high energy physicist had gathered many of the best experimental physicists in the world to 6,800 acres of prairie to make the largest accelerator ever built. Over the years, the accelerators they constructed became capable of smashing protons against antiprotons at the incredible energy of 1.8 Trillion Electron Volts (TEV).

Collisions of subatomic particles at high energies help reveal information about quarks and leptons, the fundamental forms of matter. Acting like a giant microscope, the Fermilab accelerator used higher energies to create and discover particles unobservable at lower energies.

In the mid-1970s, the accelerator provided evidence of the existence of the upsilon, a subatomic particle composed of a bottom quark and an anti-bottom quark, a discovery that provided strong support for the Standard Model. In the 1990s, the lab was hot on the trail of the top quark, the last quark yet to be observed experimentally.

When I moved to Warrenville, though, there was nothing but prairie where Fermilab now stands. My father and the other physicists did their work in a suburban office complex until they could start using houses in a subdevelopment on the site that had been purchased under eminent domain. Old farmhouses from the countryside were moved together into a cluster, to house visiting scientists. The subdevelopment was painted bright primary colors, and a chef was brought in to staff the village cafeteria (although the food was lousy, at least there was a chef).

At that time, Fermilab was just beginning to coalesce. While everybody slaved away building the accelerator, Wilson continued to put in those unique features that made the lab such a special place. A herd of buffalo was brought in and a project was started in the middle of the 4-mile circumference main ring to restore it to the original prairie grasses. One of the lab buildings was even constructed as a geodesic dome, with the panels of the dome made out of panes of plastic, sandwiching thousands and thousands of aluminum cans, collected in a recycling program by the neighboring schools.

My visit to Fermilab on Friday had been set up over the past two months via electronic mail. Around Singapore I had received a message from a lab public relations engineer asking if we might make my visit a two-way exchange of information.

Of course, I wrote back, two-way is good. By the time I hit Amsterdam, I had another message from the lab wanting to know if I would be discussing the future of networking on my visit. With another 100 messages to plow through, I dashed a hurried (but puzzled) acknowledgment.

Arriving at the lab, I saw that the little two-way exchange had blossomed into a full-blown public seminar with the title "The Future of Networking." A nice topic, no doubt, but one best left to astrologers and marketing analysts.

I asked around to see if perhaps some physicist had spoken on "The Future of Cosmology" in a recent seminar, and perhaps I was just part of some series. No such luck, so I took advantage of the rule that states the one with the white board gets to set the agenda and changed my topic to a more manageable one.

After my talk, I sat down with some of the Fermilab networking staff, including the managers of the U.S. High Energy Physics network (HEPnet). HEPnet ties physicists in dozens of countries to the major world physics laboratories, such as Fermilab, CERN in Geneva, NIKHEF in Holland, KEK in Japan, and many, many, other sites.

HEPnet started as a physical network, a microwave link between Lawrence Berkeley Laboratory and the Stanford Linear Accelerator Center (SLAC). It was based on DECnet protocols, a natural choice considering the overwhelming use of PDP and VAX computers in the physics community.

The network quickly grew, using the big laboratories as hubs to run tail circuits to regional (and sometimes not so regional) research universities. CERN and Fermilab were two of the more aggressive hubs, bringing some of the first network lines into places like China, South America, and Eastern Europe.

Connecting the hubs together were the lines that made up the HEPnet backbone. While some of the tail sites were strictly DECnet, many of the backbone sites began using multiprotocol routers, letting HEPnet finance a part of the line and having the other user communities fund the rest.

Many of the universities at the ends of the tail circuits began joining the Internet, and the HEPnet lines became one of many possible paths, or often just a virtual network layered on some other service provider.

Gradually, HEPnet grew from a single protocol network to a multiprotocol one, and from a physical network to a shared line use model. The shared line use just made HEPnet a convenient label for the bundle of resources that the high energy physics community was purchasing for its users.

In the U.S., HEPnet was partially swallowed up by a larger network run by the Department of Energy, the Energy Sciences network (ESnet). Rather than lease many lines between labs for individual communities, ESnet would furnish the backbone.

Although HEPnet relinquished the role of backbone, it still furnished quite a few tail sites, particularly medium-speed links to places that ESnet did not serve, such as Brazil, or those sites that need special high-speed dedicated capacities, such as the physics departments of many large universities. In addition to managing the dedicated links, the HEPnet group was trying to move towards providing higher level services, such as running a mail gateway and starting video conferences.

In addition to the HEPnet WAN links, the Fermilab Computer Division had to manage a vast array of internal resources, including what was reputed to be the largest VAX Cluster in the world. Workstations are a dime a dozen, and large Amdahls provide local mainframe support.

The network architecture at Fermilab was originally, as can be expected by the DECophilic physicists, set up as a huge extended Ethernet running protocols like DECnet and LAT. Over time, though, UNIX-based workstations made TCP/IP an important part of the network.

Routers were introduced to segment the traffic into subnetworks. With some of the Local Area VAX Clusters (LAVCs) having as many as 60 workstations as clients, segmenting the network certainly made management easier.

The biggest concern, though, was how to continue migrating to higher and higher bandwidth LANs. Fermilab is the kind of place that will always be using the latest equipment in all sorts of custom configurations. To accommodate FDDI and any future LANs, the laboratory laid bundles of 48 single and multimode fibers around the ring.

All that fiber around the lab meant that in addition to one or more lab backbones, the Computer Division could take a fiber to an experiment or workgroup, thereby creating rings on demand. Like many sites, Fermilab was trying hard to go through the exercise of laying fiber in a large area only once.

❐

After a quick lunch, I went into the building housing the Linear Accelerator (LINAC), the first of the seven accelerators linked together at the laboratory. Behind racks and racks of electronic equipment, I found the office of Peter Lucas, one of the designers of the accelerator control system.

Controlling a series of accelerators involves monitoring and setting a huge number of devices on subsystems ranging from vacuum pumps to refrigeration units to superconducting magnets. In the case of Fermilab, the accelerator control system must handle over 45,000 data points, some of which operate at very high frequencies.

Most devices are managed by CAMAC crates, a venerable backplane architecture that can hold up to 22 cards per crate. CAMAC crates are controlled by serial links, which in turn plug into a computer, usually a PDP 11.

The computer can poll each of the cards on the crate to gather and set data. If a card needs to generate an interrupt, it can set a single "look at me" bit on the crate. The computer then polls each of the cards to find out which ones need attention. The basic control flow on the front end was thus a PDP 11 to a CAMAC crate to a card to the device being controlled (although the PDPs were scheduled to be swapped out at some point for μVAXen).

In the early 1980s, when this system was first being put together, VAXen were just being released. A series of 3 11/785s, later supplemented by an 8650, acted as database servers, keeping track of information on each of the data points, such as which CAMAC and PDP that data point was accessible from.

The last part of the system were μVAXen (originally PDPs) acting as consoles. The basic operation would be for a console to log a request for a certain data element at a certain frequency. The database server would define the elements and the PDP 11s were responsible for delivering the data.

So how to connect all these systems together? In 1986, when the current network was being designed, the great Ethernet versus Token Ring debate was raging. After extensive deliberations, the lab decided the predictable latency of the token ring was needed for the main ring control system.

DEC, of course, was firmly in the Ethernet camp, but lack of product support by the vendor doesn't faze experimental physicists. They turned to their electrical engineers, who built token ring cards for the Unibus used by the PDPs and VAXen.

Running on top of the token ring, the lab put their own Accelerator Control network (ACnet). ACnet allows any console to monitor and manage any device, a capability that makes operators at other accelerator centers stuck with special purpose consoles green with envy.

ACnet is a protocol in which a console logs a single request, which can generate a stream of data. A request might be for a certain data item at 1 hz, which would yield a stream of data spaced one per second. In addition to logged requests, certain events trigger alarms, sending the front-end PDP into the database to decide who should be notified.

The token ring choice worked, but it turned out that there really wasn't that much difference between it and Ethernet. Not only that, DEC kept coming out with new μVAXen, each sporting a newly incompatible variant on the Q-bus. It was evident that Ethernet had to be incorporated into the network somehow.

An Ethernet was added and VAXstations started to pop up around the laboratory as consoles. To link the Ethernet with ACnet, the lab designed and wrote an Ethernet-to-token ring bridge running in software on one or more of the VAXen.

The ACnet was still token ring, but the addition of the bridge meant that authorized users from all over the lab had access to accelerator data. One of the VAXen was even set up with the X Window System, allowing X servers to access the data.

Since X runs just fine on top of the Internet, especially if you are communicating between two core sites, it is even possible to run the accelerator remotely. On one occasion, lab employees at a conference in Japan pulled up the accelerator control panels. To prevent any possibility of accelerator hackers, the lab set up the system so that remote terminals could only read data items.

This architecture proved to be quite flexible, easily expanding to meet the needs of the Tevatron and other newer subsystems. PDPs controlling CAMAC crates could easily be added if new data points needed to be controlled. Over time, CAMAC crates became a bit old-fashioned and newer devices simply had a VME crate directly on the token ring, alleviating the need for the front-end PDP.

Even the token ring decision turned out to have been wisely made. Networking at the lab grew like a prairie fire, with workstations going in as fast as physicists could unpack them. This is not a user community that will wait for official installers to unpack boxes. In fact, if pieces are missing, they are just as liable to manufacture a replacement themselves as they are to call up the shipper and complain.

After walking me through the architecture, Peter Lucas took me over to an X Window System console and showed me some of the 1,000 application packages that had been written for the accelerator.

All the screens were color coded, providing visual clues on which items in a complex form led to other screens and which items could be changed by the user. Clicking on a line item with the ID for a CAMAC crate, for example, would result in a graphic representation of the map, with each card and its ID depicted. Clicking on one of the cards would show the data items kept by the card and its current status.

All these programs were written at first for PDPs, in a day when that level of user interface was real, heavy-duty programming. These were the kind of programmers who battled their way through RSX, FORTRAN 2, and TECO, languages that make me shudder whenever I think of them.

❐

When the superconducting magnets in the main ring generate proton-antiproton collisions at 1.8 TEV, there needs to be a way to collect data describing the event and store it away for further analysis. The detectors used in high energy physics are as complicated as the accelerator itself.

I drove around the main ring to D Zero (DØ), the quadrant of the ring containing a detector that had been under construction for over nine years. The instrument had consumed most of the time of 400 physicists and the U.S. $50 million camera was almost ready to be inserted into the ring.

DØ was a six-story building, just large enough to house the detector. When it was operational, the detector would put out 100,000 data points per collision, and there would be a collision every 3.5 microseconds. With roughly 250 kbytes per collision, this results in a data rate of 75 Gbytes per second.

This is quite a bit of data, especially when you consider the fact that the experiment would run 24 hours per day for six to nine months at a time. One of the great hopes of the DØ detector was that it would provide experimental evidence of the existence of the top quark, the only one not yet empirically observed.

Top quarks are very rare, and it was quite likely that only one (or less) would be found per day. In a day of operation, the data acquisition subsystem on the detector thus had to somehow filter through 6.48 petabytes (6.48 million gigabytes) looking for the interesting 250,000 bytes.

DØ was pandemonium. With the pins being pulled in a few days to roll the detector in, desks were littered with piles of empty styrofoam cups and coke cans, boards were everywhere in various stages of assembly or disassembly. A pager went off every few minutes, directing people to where they weren't.

I found Dean Schaumberger, a professor from State University of New York at Stony Brook who agreed to give me a quick briefing. We walked through the data acquisition system, concentrating on the data and ignoring the physics. To decide which events to keep, an event mask provided the first level of filtering, allowing the physicists to hone in on a few dozen attributes that characterize interesting events. Once the event mask was tripped, boards housed in 79 VME-based front end crates would digitize the data on the detector. The goal of the mask was to reduce the data flow to 200 to 400 events per second.

Since it was possible that two interesting events could occur back to back, the front-end boards were double buffered. After the two buffers were full, though, events that tripped the mask had to be discarded until space became available again.

The 79 front-end crates were distributed among eight data cables, each cable providing a 32-bit wide data path running at 10 Mhz, yielding a data rate of 40 Mbytes per cable. With all eight cables running in parallel, the data flow reached 320 Mbytes per second.

The next level of analysis was provided by a farm of 50 μVAX 4000s, each machine running at the rate of about 12 times a VAX 11/780. Each μVAX had 8 custom boards, one for each of the 8 data cables. The data cables thus came out of the VME Crates and snaked through each of the μVAXen allowing any machine to collect all the data on one event.

The μVAXen, running the ELN real-time operating system, were also connected to a scheduling VAX, a machine that decided where on the farm there were available cycles to process the next event.

With the major pieces in place, Dean walked me through the data path. When the mask got tripped, data would go into the front-end boards. If the data bus was clear, the token generator (another µVAX at the end of the data bus) would issue a token with the current event number.

Each of the eight data cables would get a token. On any one of those cables, if a VME crate saw a token, it was able to capture the token and send as many bursts of data as it needed, releasing the token downstream when it was done to allow the next crate to dump its data. When all eight tokens got back to the token scheduler, the next event could proceed.

When the data reached a µVAX on the farm, it would undergo scrutiny by a variety of programs designed to filter interesting events from the subatomic chaff. The goal at this stage was to winnow down the data rate another 200 to 400 times.

Events that met the second level of filtering would emerge from the µVAX farm and go to a VAX 6000 to be spooled to tape. I saw a rack with 11 Exabyte tape drives on it, and Dean informed me that the experiment had well over 50.

This was not excessive when you consider that one event per second for six months would be close to 4 terabytes of data. Eventually, a physicist would spend up to a half hour with each interesting event, looking for clues. Some events that looked particularly promising were also spooled on the VAX 6000 for immediate analysis during the run.

❏

The next morning, I went with my father to see SciTech, a hands-on science museum for kids he had spent the last two years building. SciTech had managed to obtain a cavernous old post office in the middle of nearby Aurora.

The museum specialized in the very big and the very small, teaching kids about light, sound, astronomy, and even particle physics. Every exhibit was hands-on. To explain quarks, for example, SciTech was modifying slot machines, replacing lemons and cherries with rare quarks and adjusting the probabilities to match. Pulling the lever to create a particularly rare particle would result in a prize.

Exploring the Internet

All around were prisms, tuning forks, echo chambers, computers, and dozens of other devices making up the exhibits. Signs were next to each exhibit and teenage "explainers" would walk around telling people what they were seeing. A group of girl scouts trundled down to the basement to help build a new exhibit. Upstairs, some six-year olds were playing in a science club.

Starting a museum is never easy, and SciTech had managed to surprise everybody with its rapid growth. Still run on a shoestring, the museum was able to get enough grants, admissions, and members to keep expanding the exhibits and start filling up the huge old post office.

I admired the exhibits, then ran to catch my plane. O'Hare was not as bad as usual, so I had a little time to kill. Walking down the moving walkway, I came to a stop behind a little girl and her mother.

"Move over, honey," the mother said, "this is an airport and the nice man has to hurry and catch his plane."

The little girl smiled sweetly and moved over, just in time for me to get off the ramp and head into the nearby cocktail lounge.

On the flight back to Boulder, I struck up a conversation with the prosperous looking yuppie on my left. He worked for Trammel Crow, the quintessential Texas real estate developer. We talked about the current fiscal performance of Compaq, his Vail vacations, and the relative profit potential of commercial and residential development in the greater Houston area.

Over a second drink, I asked this seemingly normal modern businessman what sort of activity brought him to Boulder. A merger, perhaps or an acquisition? Dividing virgin forest into poor imitations of Southern California?

"I've quit my job to open a Great Harvest outlet in Madison, Wisconsin, " he explained, referring to the popular whole wheat and granola bakery located in a Boulder shopping mall.

Back in Boulder, I brought a box of Parisian chocolates over to my neighbor, a freelance wholesale carpet salesman and the proud owner of at least a dozen vehicles. The vehicles gave the place a bit of a hill-country look, but I didn't mind since it made it harder to tell that my house was deserted most of the time.

"Do you ever suffer from writers block?" he wanted to know. "How about jet lag?"

"Um, sort of," I said with a lack of conviction, pretty sure this wasn't just an idle question.

"Here," he said, handing me several packets of powders. "I've added a new line," pointing proudly to the pouches of Wow!™ and Focus!™ ("Nutrients for the Brain"), products of Durk Pearson & Sandy Shaw®, the founders of Omnitrition International and the inventors of Designer Foods™.

Pearson and Shaw have built quite a nice little business taking the hopes we all share for intelligence and vigor and peddling them nationwide in a hierachical sales scheme of life extension that has taken in such world-famous businessmen as Jerry Rubin. I thanked my neighbor and told him I'd be in touch, remembering the advice my mother gave as I left home to never fight with the woman who feeds your cat when you are going away soon.

Soon, in fact, was an understatement. I had less than two weeks to dump the text I had accumulated, sort out my finances, and get back on the plane for my third round-the-world. First on my list was to bring my primitive PC in for a new disk drive, the cause of its failing to function as my mail system for the last few weeks.

Next on the list was responding to a couple of hundred messages from people trying to understand why they couldn't get ITU standards anymore. Bruno was dead and engineers all over the world wanted to know all the grisly details. Most agreed that the situation was ridiculous and couldn't understand why the ITU would reverse such an obviously useful service.

Most touching was a message from a blind engineer in Australia who had hoped that he could work with the ASCII text, piping it out to /dev/audio so he could hear the texts. The message reminded me of Milan Sterba, who told me about the pitiful number of copies of the standards that existed in Czechoslovakia. I forwarded both bits of information to Dr. Tarjanne at the ITU, inquiring if it was truly the policy of a major UN agency to deny access to the physically handicapped and those in developing countries. A cheap shot perhaps, but that's politics.

In the middle of the week, while trying to come up with 12 pithy columns for *Communications Week*, I checked my mail to see an urgent note from Mike Schwartz. David Farber, a grand old man of networking, was giving a lecture in an hour and a half and nobody in Computer Science seemed to have been aware of the event.

When Mike found out from out-of-band sources he promptly broadcast a message to those of us who would realize that this was a worthwhile way to spend an afternoon, and I promptly rearranged my schedule.

David Farber had actually been on my mind that morning. One problem with trying to write a technical travelogue is that you can't possibly see everything. I wasn't going anywhere in Africa, Central America, or South America, for example. I wasn't going to any of the supercomputer centers. I wasn't even going to visit Merit, the network operations center for the NSFNET.

And, I couldn't figure out how to squeeze in visits to try and meet people like Ira Fuchs and David Farber, people instrumental in a host of key projects ranging from ARPANET to CSNET to BITNET to the NSFNET.

It was my luck that Boulder is close to enough ski areas to attract frequent guest lecturers, including David Farber. When I got to the lecture hall, it appeared that the computer science department wasn't as awed as I was. Only Mike Schwartz came from the department, the rest of the professors being unable to climb down from their towers in time.

Farber started by explaining how the gigabit testbeds came to be. People like Farber, Gordon Bell (the father of the VAX) and Bob Kahn from CNRI had spent several years working to get the project funded by NSF and DARPA. The genesis for the testbeds came when researchers started asking what would come after Broadband ISDN and ATM cell switching.

In particular, the researchers wanted to know what applications would run on these testbeds. Visits to places like Bellcore and Bell Labs didn't yield any answers: the telephone companies didn't see a market for gigabit networks and weren't paying attention to them yet.

Even if gigabit networks existed, the researchers saw a fundamental problem: the current technology would not evolve gracefully into gigabit or multi-gigabit speeds.

Switching technology, for example, had progressed up an evolutionary chain from T1 to T3 to the 622 Mbps speeds of Broadband ISDN. These switches had become increasingly complex, and many felt they had reached the edge of the technology. What DARPA called a "paradigm shift" would be needed to move to the next stage.

Government leadership was obviously in order here, and Kahn and Farber made a proposal to NSF for the gigabit testbeds. The proposal had a few unusual features to it. For one, the testbeds would depend extensively on participation from industry, and industry would have to pay its own way.

Money from NSF and DARPA would go to pay for the academics and program overhead, and this leverage would be used to bring in industrial participants. To prove that industry would indeed participate, Farber and Kahn produced letters from IBM, DEC, Xerox, Bell Labs, and Bellcore.

The other unusual twist to the proposal was that although government would start the program, the operation of the project should be left in the hands of what Farber called "an organization with a faster metabolism." Ultimately, this management group ended up being CNRI.

After a series of white papers, proposals, and intensive lobbying, the project was set up with U.S. $15 million in funding. Bob Kahn hit the road and used that seed money to raise another U.S. $100 million in facilities and staff commitments from industry.

All the resources were put into a pot and reorganized into the five gigabit testbed projects. In some cases, additional participants (particular telephone companies to provide fiber) were added to round out a testbed.

Most of the testbeds were set up to look at a combination of the underlying technology and applications. The CASA project in California and New Mexico, for example, would run three test applications over wide-area gigabit channels.

The Aurora project, the testbed that Farber had joined, was a bit different, concentrating on the underlying technology. The chief participants were a group from MIT led by David Clark, Farber's group at the University of Pennsylvania, and teams from Bellcore and IBM. Several telephone companies were also participating to provide up to 2.4 Gbps of wide-area bandwidth.

Typical of the research flavor of Aurora was the work being done in the switching substrate. Bellcore would look at cell-based switching using ATM technology. IBM would run an entirely different datagram substrate based on their PARIS project.

Farber and Clark were looking at the upper levels, the protocols that ran on the fat pipes. Both felt that current protocols, such as the TCP/IP suite, might not work on the next generation of networks.

Most protocols were based on many modules that exchanged messages, with protocols layered on other protocols. While this was architecturally convenient, the result was that software layers would endlessly transform data, copying it from one buffer to another.

The immediate problem was thus not on the network. A gigabit was more than most hosts could handle. The problem was not only in the CPU or the programming model, either. The problem was the network software. Clark was advocating application-layer framing, collapsing the protocol stack and giving the application much better control over network operation. He saw many of the flaws in today's networks as the result of modules making decisions in areas such as flow control that didn't make sense in the context of the upper layer user.

Farber was proposing an equally radical solution, doing away with the message abstraction of current protocols and moving towards a totally different way of looking at the network. Instead of messages, Farber wanted to look at the network as a memory moving mechanism, a backplane.

Programmers on a single host, or even a multiprocessor, deal with memory as the main abstraction. Calling a subroutine by name, for example, is a simple way to refer to a segment of memory. If the network implements that same abstraction, programmers can continue to work within the model they were used to and the network simply becomes an extension of that model.

With its roots in an early research project conducted by Farber and his student Paul Mockapetris, the concept first really took shape in a 1985 Ph.D. thesis by Gary Delp, another one of Farber's students. The system was called Memnet, and consisted of a bunch of PC ATs connected to a modified memory interface and a cache, connected in turn to a 600 Mbps token ring.

The LAN acted as a way for requesting, moving, and writing segments of memory. The caches on other hosts could keep copies of segments, alleviating the need for a network operation on frequently accessed pages.

Memnet demonstrated that a LAN could indeed be a simple extension of memory. It operated within the flat address space of DOS and enforced tight consistency guarantees on pages of memory through mechanisms such as only permitting one writer per segment.

By 1988, the Memnet concept had been moved up to software, running on an Ethernet LAN. A modified version of Sun's UNIX, developed by Ron Minnich, another Farber student, allowed several hosts to share memory. The software was actually put into production use at a supercomputer center, being a useful mechanism to provide parallel processing on certain classes of applications.

It was clear to Farber and his students that Memnet was one example of a general class of networks. To extend Memnet to a wide area environment, some changes would have to be made. A ring topology or a simple bus was not appropriate, and constraints like the flat address space would certainly have to be relaxed. Most importantly, looser consistency guarantees would be needed if the system would successfully scale to become a "national memory backplane."

Farber and his students were actively working on an implementation, called GobNet, that would eventually work on the Aurora testbed. On a gigabit testbed, the software certainly showed promise. The latency of a 3,000-mile gigabit network is roughly equivalent to a local page fault on a machine, meaning that the network could appear to the host as the equivalent of a memory segment that had been paged to disk.

While page faults were natural on a host, they were also something to be avoided. Virtual memory systems would preemptively cache memory segments to try and have the proper segment waiting when it was asked for. This was also going to be the key to good performance on a wide-area Memnet.

The switches in GobNet would have the caches. If a host requested a segment not in the cache, the cache would have to go and find the requested object. In a token ring or Ethernet, finding an object is simple: you ask for it.

In a WAN, though, the topology may be quite complex and finding the correct path is the real challenge. GobNet would use a flooding algorithm, similar to what a bridge would use in trying to decide where a host lay on an extended Ethernet.

For the first request on a segment, the request would be flooded, being sent out every available path on the network. Eventually, one hopes, the page would come back on a certain path. Each of the switches on that path would set up a segment to host binding so that future references to the segment would be easier to find.

Flooding a network to find an object and then setting up a binding for future references turned out to be a strategy that was good for more than just memory segments. Researchers at Bellcore were using the same technique in personal communications systems to find the current location of a portable phone anywhere in the country.

The view of the Internet as a national memory backplane was exciting, but what impressed me the most was the overall scope of the research being conducted in the gigabit testbeds. It was clear that this was money well spent and that we would all benefit from the incredible collection of talent that had been assembled.

After the lecture, with my column deadlines looming, I raced to the Trident, a coffee shop and bookstore, to try and find some pithy sayings to write. Munching a Blueberry Tahini bar, I walked around the bookstore hoping to get inspiration.

I picked up a copy of *The Secret Books of the Egyptian Gnostics* but couldn't find any parallels to my current subject. When *The Aromatherapy Workbook* didn't prove to be any help, I sat down and tried to grind out words of MIS wisdom while around me people layed out tarot cards and discussed the many paths to personal fulfillment.

Round 3

In Search of a Standards Haven

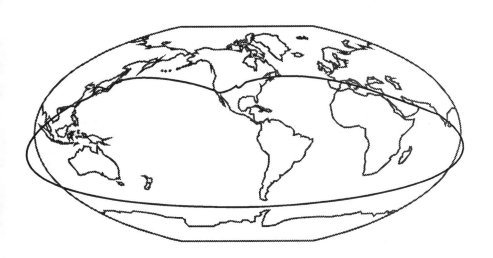

Sitting by the lagoon in Marina del Rey, I sipped a Pilsner Urquell and watched the planes at LAX, two taking off followed by two landing in an infinite repetition. In addition to the world's largest man-made small boat harbor, Marina del Rey is the home of the Information Sciences Institute (ISI), a research group that has played a key role in the development of the Internet.

Monday morning, I got in my car to find ISI. Since the Institute is part of the University of Southern California, I expected to arrive at some ramshackle house on the edge of campus, but instead found myself on the 11th floor of a modern office building, right on the edge of the harbor.

With 200 staff members and most of its funding from the Defense Advanced Projects Research Agency (DARPA) and other government agencies, ISI plays an important catalyst role in several areas. The MOSIS service, for example, is a way for researchers to get small quantities of custom VLSI circuits. MOSIS gangs together designs from many researchers onto one mask, breaking fabrication costs down to manageable levels.

My goal, though, was not to learn about MOSIS but to try and learn more about the many networking projects ISI undertakes. First stop was to find Dr. Jon Postel, Director of ISI's Communications Division. Jon was reading his mail when I came in, a never-ending task when you get over 100 messages per day. He looked up from his two-finger typing and gave me a warm welcome, evidence of his long residence in California.

Postel is one of the best-known figures in networking. The editor of the RFCs titled "Internet Protocol" and "Transmission Control Protocol," he is certainly the person most often cited in the footnotes at the back of research papers. In addition to writing key protocols, Postel is the editor of the Request for Comment (RFC) series, and has thus been responsible for the documentation of the TCP/IP protocol suite.

Jon had set up a demanding schedule which we promptly shot to hell. All the projects were so interesting, I kept dallying to find out more. Even then, I saw only a fraction of what ISI had to offer, not even getting to talk to people like Clifford Neuman, codeveloper of key network services such as Prospero and Kerberos.

We started talking about the networks to which ISI belongs. Several years ago, Postel sent a mail message around proposing that a network, now called Los Nettos, be started. The very same day, Susan Estrada of the San Diego Supercomputer Center proposed the establishment of CERFnet.

Both networks went forward and they illustrate two different, yet complementary approaches to providing network service. Jon describes Los Nettos as a "regional network for Blue Chip clients." Los Nettos connects 9 big players, including UCLA, Caltech, TRW, and the RAND Corporation. The network assumes that the clients are self sufficient and thus has little overhead. As Jon puts it, "we have no letterhead and no comic books."

By contrast, CERFnet is a full-service network provider, one of the most aggressive and best-run mid-level networks. CERFnet has aggressively pursued commercial customers and helped to found the Commercial Internet Exchange (CIX). CERFnet provides a wide range of user services, including comic books, buttons for users, and other introductory materials.

Both models are necessary and the two networks interconnect and work well together. T1 lines from UCLA and Caltech down to the San Diego Supercomputer Center give Los Nettos dual paths into the NSFNET backbone. Having the two types of service providers gives customers a choice of the type of service they need.

ISI is also a member of two other networks, DARTnet and the Terrestrial Wideband (TWB) network, both experimental systems funded by DARPA. TWB is an international network, connecting a variety of defense sites and research institutes, including UCL in London.

TWB is a semi-production network used for video conferences and simulations. The simulations, developed by BBN, consist of activities such as war games with tanks, allowing tank squadrons in simulators across the country to interact with each other so commanders can experiment with different strategies for virtual destruction.

DARTnet, by contrast, is an experimental network used to learn more about things like routing protocols. To learn more about DARTnet, I walked down the hall to find Robert Braden, executive director of the IAB. Braden was buried behind mountains of paper, including a formidable pile of RFCs.

DARTnet connects eight key sites such as BBN, ISI, MIT, and Xerox PARC. Braden described the network as "something researchers can break." Although applications such as video conferencing run on the network, the main purpose is experimentation with lower layer protocols.

Each of the DARTnet sites run Sun computers as routers. Periodically, network researchers, such as the elusive Van Jacobson, modify the code in those routers to experiment with new routing or transport protocols.

One of the key research efforts is supporting different classes of traffic on one network. Video, for example, requires low delay variance in the data stream, a requirement not necessarily compatible with large file transfers.

DARTnet researchers are examining ways that resource reservation can be accommodated in a general-purpose network. Connection-oriented protocols, such as ST, share the underlying infrastructure with the connectionless IP protocol. IP multicasting and other newer innovations are also implemented in the network, allowing bandwidth-intensive video to be sent to several sites without necessarily duplicating the video stream.

The next stop on my tour was a visit with Gregory Finn and Robert Felderman, two of the developers of ATOMIC, an intriguing gigabit LAN under the direction of Danny Cohen. ATOMIC is based on Mosaic, a processor developed at Caltech as the basis for a massively parallel supercomputer.

One of the requirements for a message-based, massively parallel system is a method for passing messages from one processor to another. Mosaic had built this routing function into the processor. ISI decided to use that same chip as the basis for a LAN instead of a supercomputer.

Exploring the Internet

The prototype Gregory and Robert showed me consisted of three Suns connected together with ribbon cables. Each Sun has a VME board with four Mosaic chips and two external cables. It is interesting to note that each Mosaic chip runs at 14 MIPS, making the LAN interface board significantly more powerful than the main processor.

The four channels on the board have a data throughput rate of 640 Mbps. Even on this rudimentary prototype, 1,500-byte packets were being exchanged at a throughput rate of over 1 Gbps. Small packets were being exchanged at the mind-boggling rate of 3.9 million per second.

The system I saw simply had host interface boards connected directly to each other. The same Mosaic chip is being used as the basis for a LAN switch, an architecture that seems to provide a viable alternative to the increasingly complex ATM switches.

The Mosaic-based supercomputer consists of arrays of 64 chips, configured on boards 8 square. The ATOMIC project was going to use those arrays as the basis for a switch, connecting host interfaces (and other grids) to the edge of the array.

Messages coming into the grid would be routed from one Mosaic chip to another, emerging at the edge of the grid to go into a host interface or another grid. Source routing headers on the messages were designed to take advantage of the hardware-based routing support in the processors. In effect, 896 MIPS of processing power on a grid would sit idle while the routing hardware moved messages about.

What was so intriguing about ATOMIC was the simplicity and elegance of the architecture. While ATM switches had become ever more complex in order to support more users or higher speeds, this appeared to be an architecture that could scale evenly.

Even more intriguing was cost. The individual Mosaic chips and the 8 by 8 grids were being made in large quantities for the Caltech supercomputer and costs would descend to very low levels if ATOMIC ever went into production. The tinker-toy approach to connecting grids together meant that a LAN switch could easily grow at small incremental costs.

ATOMIC is implemented as a LAN under the Berkeley sockets interface, allowing TCP/IP to run over the network. There is no reason, however, that ATOMIC couldn't be made to send fixed-length packets of 54 bytes, making the technology well-suited to ATM and B-ISDN, as well as more flexible packet-based architectures.

With only a few researchers, ISI showed that gigabit switches didn't necessarily have to involve huge development teams or complex designs. By piggybacking on the Mosaic effort, the ISI researchers quickly prototyped a novel solution to a difficult problem.

Just down the hall from the laboratory housing the ATOMIC project is the ISI teleconferencing room. Multimedia conferencing has always been a highly visible effort at ISI, and I met with Eve Schooler and Stephen Casner, two key figures in this area, to learn more about it.

Traditional teleconferencing uses commercial codecs (coder-decoders, sort of a video equivalent to a modem) over dedicated lines. ISI, along with BBN, Xerox, and others, has been involved in a long-term effort to use the Internet infrastructure to mix packet audio and video along with other data.

The teleconferencing room at ISI is dominated by a large-screen Mitsubishi TV split into four quadrants. In the upper left, I could see Xerox PARC, in the lower right, the room I was in. In the Xerox quadrant, I could see Stephen Deering, a key developer of IP multicasting, holding a meeting with some colleagues. In the upper right hand quadrant, I could see the frozen image of a face from MIT left over from the previous day.

Working on multimedia networking began as early as 1973 when ARPANET researchers experimented with a single audio channel. To get more people involved, Bob Kahn, then director of DARPA's Information Processing Techniques Office, started a satellite network. In time, this network evolved into the Terrestrial Wideband (TWB) network.

Over the years, the teleconferencing effort settled into a curious mix of production and research. Groups like the IAB and DARPA used the facilities on a regular basis to conduct meetings, with TWB logging over 360 conferences in the past three years.

On the research side, people like Eve Schooler and Steve Casner were experimenting with issues as diverse as the efficient use of underlying networks to high-level tools used by meeting participants.

At the low level, one of the big constraints is raw bandwidth. Video channels can take anywhere from 64 to 384 kbps, depending on the brand of codec and the desired picture quality. Codec researchers are examining strategies to squeeze better pictures out of the pipes, ranging from better compression to clever techniques such as varying the amount of data sent depending on the amount of motion.

Teleconferencing, because of high codec costs, had been based on connecting special, dedicated rooms together. With the cost of codecs coming down and even getting integrated into workstations, the focus is rapidly switching to office-based group applications, allowing people to sit at their desks in front of their multimedia workstations.

While desk-based video was still a ways down the pike, audio was maturing rapidly. ISI has been working with people such as Simon Hackett in Australia to come up with a common protocol for moving audio around the network.

After this whirlwind morning of research projects, Jon Postel took me to lunch and I returned to learn more about the key administrative role ISI plays in the Internet.

First stop was the famous Joyce K. Reynolds, Postel's right arm. In addition to announcing new RFCs to the world, Joyce manages the Internet Assigned Numbers Authority (IANA), the definitive registry of constants like TCP port numbers, SNMP object identifiers, and Telnet options. IANA included all administered numbers except for Internet addresses and autonomous system numbers, an area in which ISI acts as a technical advisor to the NIC.

Although Joyce's job in RFC processing and IANA functions would seem to take all her time, she also manages the IETF User Services area. For several years, she had been pushing the IETF to try and make using the network as important a priority as making it run. Finally, User Services got elevated to a real "area," and Joyce led the effort to publish tutorial documents and introductory guides.

Right next to Joyce's office is that of Ann Cooper, publisher of the Internet Monthly Report containing summaries of X.500 pilots, IAB meetings, IETF and IRTF meetings, gigabit testbeds, and other key activities.

One of Ann Cooper's functions is administrator of the U.S. domain. While most U.S. names are in the commercial (.COM) or educational (.EDU) name trees, the rest of the world uses a country-based scheme. The U.S. domain is an effort to bring the U.S. up to speed with the rest of the world.

My own domain name is Carl@Malamud.COM. While this is nice for me, placing myself this high on the name hierarchy starts to turn the Domain Name System, in the words of Marshall T. Rose, "from a tree into a bush." In fact, Rose, being a good citizen of the network, has registered himself under the mtview.ca.us subdomain.

While most U.S. members of the Internet are still under the older .COM, .GOV, and .EDU trees, the .US domain is beginning to catch on. In fact, enough people want to register that ISI has delegated authority for more active cities to local administrators. Erik Fair, for example, the Apple network administrator, has taken over the task of administering names for San Francisco.

My day at ISI was finished just in time to go sit in traffic. I had proved myself to be a non-native of California by booking my flight in the wrong airport, so I wheeled my car past three Jaguars heading into the Marina and started the 3-hour drive south to San Diego, watching the snow-capped mountains poking their heads over the Los Angeles basin fog.

Tuesday morning, I took the shuttle from my hotel to the airport to await the arrival of the flight from Tokyo so I could meet George Abe, a manager of Infonet, a commercial, global IP network. The driver asked us for our airlines.

"United, Domestic," one person shouted.

"United, International," chimed in a second.

A couple in the back looked at each other in bewilderment. The lady elbowed her husband.

"Uh, United, Hawaii," he said.

I met George in an airport lounge. Incredibly energetic after a 15-hour flight, he bounced in, whipped out his view graphs, and started to tell me all about Infonet.

Infonet was originally started as a time-sharing company owned by Computer Sciences Corporation (CSC), offering application programs on a series of Univac 1180s running their own proprietary operating system. To access the mainframes, by 1971 the company had started offering an X.25-like packet service in competition with companies like Tymnet.

In the mid-1980s, George Abe worked as a member of a 3-man team to upgrade this proprietary network to X.25. Then, CSC decided packet networks were not their cup of tea and decided to divest. Infonet managers were able to convince a large number of PTTs around the world that they needed a way to compete against global giants like IBM and AT&T. The sales pitch worked and Infonet became 100 percent owned by telephone companies, with major shares held by MCI, the German Deutsche Bundespost, and the French Transpac, with smaller stakes help by eight other PTTs.

By the late 1980s, the network had grown and was based on multiplexors located in 34 key locations. Attached to these core nodes were X.25 switches, PBXs, and other interface devices, all connected together by international circuits.

In 1990, Abe spent a week in Finland with Juha Heinänen, and the network soon added Cisco routers along with the X.25 switches, allowing Infonet to provide IP service. Like the Finnish PTT service, the IP service was a way of connecting corporate networks together.

The first question from MIS managers when George described the service invariably was "Are you connected to the Internet?"

At first, George would hem and haw, sheepishly admitting that they weren't connected with the rest of the world.

"Good!" was the usual reply. Large corporate MIS staffs were scared stiff of the security implications of the Internet, imagining hordes of hackers breaking into their systems.

Increasingly, though, users were beginning to demand some form of interconnection, at least mail connectivity if nothing else. Infonet was using PSI as a service provider, although I noticed that George Abe had only an MCI Mail address.

The solution to access to the broader Internet was similar to the one I saw in Finland. Inside of Infonet, a router at the border of the PSI domain has access control lists. If a customer of Infonet pays a fee, traffic for that particular Internet address can make it through the router. Otherwise, even though there is data link level connectivity with PSI, the router acts as a firewall, keeping out IP level traffic for those who don't want it.

What was interesting about Infonet was not the few hundred customers it had signed up by the end of 1991, but the corporate backers. In addition to its shareholder PTTs, Infonet had enlisted most of the other monopoly carriers around the world as sales affiliates. In many countries, therefore, a company that wanted international IP service would have to deal with Infonet.

I wasn't quite sure what to make of this company, but made a mental note that it was certainly worth watching. I left George Abe to run a crucial errand down at Interop.

Ole Jacobsen, publisher of *ConneXions,* had asked me to help settle an Acronym Dispute (AD). Barry Leiner, a former DARPA program manager, had submitted an article which discussed, in part, the International Standards Organization. Ole, with his eagle eye, had tried to explain that ISO really stood for the International Organization for Standardization, but Leiner insisted that a dyslexic acronym could not possibly be correct.

I brought Ole the cover sheet from an ISO standard, a worthless piece of paper that cost me U.S. $10. Sure enough, the International Organization for Standardization had its name proudly embossed on the front. Using the document to silence Barry Leiner was perhaps the first time this particular standard had found a useful application.

Friday morning, after a breakfast of green beans, cocktail franks, and a salad, I met Kenji Naemura, at the time a vice president of Nippon Telegraph and Telephone who has since become a professor at Keio University. We sat in the back of a car with shiny white seat covers and drove 50 km south of Tokyo to NTT's Yokosuka research laboratories.

Naemura began his career in the 1960s in Tokyo using a machine developed by NTT that preserved the Illiac I interface but had a different architecture, possibly the world's first clone. Naemura developed the hardware architecture for NTT switches, then spent two years at Champaign-Urbana working on the Illiac IV.

When he got back to Japan, the focus moved from switch architectures to communications software, and Naemura began playing a central role in the Japanese delegation to ISO. He was involved in the very first OSI meetings where the seven-layer Reference Model was developed. Although the Japanese delegation would not have been unhappy to have been referred to as the seven samurai, Naemura felt that perhaps the archiecture should have a less rigid stratification of the protocol architecture.

Naemura was bringing me to Yokosuka to learn more about NTT's vision of what the telephone network would look like in the next 25 years. Dubbed VI&P, for "Visual, Intelligent, and Personal," the vision had been developed over several years as a broad consensual effort within the corporation. The previous shared vision had been the installation of narrowband ISDN around the country, and with that effort well underway, NTT, the largest corporation in the world, wanted to give its employees a sense of common purpose.

Basically, VI&P outlined a B-ISDN, all-fiber telephone network with 620 Mbps channels into the home and one or more terabits of capacity inside the network. NTT was targeting a 15 year development effort, with large-scale deployment in the early years of the 21st century.

Much of the VI&P effort dovetailed into current products. For example, NTT had recently announced a 230 gram portable telephone. One of the VI&P goals is for a 50-gram personal phone, coupled with an intelligent network to find the phone wherever the person might be.

We started our tour by looking at some of the prototypes, developed for press briefings, management demos, and other shows. Although there were a half-dozen systems, the one that I found the most interesting was called "teleview."

The heart of teleview was image processing software to extract objects from a video feed. The prototype had a camera trained on an NTT office and used ISDN to send the video to a Yokosuka workstation. Based on movement of people and the location of desks, the computer could determine if people were sitting at the desks.

My immediate reaction was that this was highly Orwellian, allowing supervisors to track the length of bathroom breaks. While toilet tracking was certainly one of the possible applications, there were others.

For example, a touch screen on a workstation had a grid, with one square for each employee. If the employee was at the desk, the square was green. Touching the square automatically dialed the telephone. Of course, if a dog were sitting in the employee's chair, the square would also be green, but the phone might not get answered.

We touched a button and a poor harassed employee of NTT ignored it for a while, then finally picked it up.

"Just testing, thanks a lot," my tour guide said. The employee didn't bother turning around and I got the impression that he wasn't as thrilled with teleview as the researchers were.

The marketing video for VI&P showed a couple of other teleview applications. Applied to a parking lot, teleview could direct drivers directly to empty spaces. At an amusement park, the system could count the number of people in line, displaying the expected delay for each ride on monitors.

After a walk through various labs, looking at ATM switches, HDTV systems being fed with 150 Mbps lines, and prototype equipment for distributing fiber from poles to homes, we drove back to Tokyo to NTT's Kasumigaseki showroom to look at ISDN equipment.

Japan has very aggressively deployed narrowband ISDN, providing service in two thousand service areas distributed over all the islands. Both basic rate and primary interfaces are available, and I met several people with basic rate service in their homes.

The showroom was full of slick equipment ranging from G4 digital fax to dedicated floppy disk transfer devices. Videoconferencing stations, ISDN pay phones, and portable video phones were all available. Although the cost for equipment and service is not cheap, NTT had managed to attract over 60,000 basic rate lines by the end of 1991.

Throughout my visit, people kept pointing to picture phones, and it was obvious that they hoped this device would spur personal ISDN use. While picture phones didn't appear to me to be the Lotus 1-2-3 of the ISDN market, I did see one device that had real promise, the ISDN Karaoke Machine.

Using 2 64-kbps B channels, a large database server could send audio down one pipe and a video image with song lyrics and a bouncing ball down the other. The system kept the bouncing ball synchronized with the audio track. Here was a way to turn every room into a karaoke bar.

Dr. Naemura dropped me off at NTT's R&D headquarters where I met the three scientists who were translating *STACKS* into Japanese. Shigeki Goto, Ken-Ichiro Murakami, and Hisao Nojima came walking into the conference room armed with huge stacks of paper. For the next two hours, we went through a long list of what they politely referred to as "questions."

Most of the "questions," of course, were examples of typos, miscalculations, and other errors on my part. Not only had they scrutinized my text on a word-by-word basis, but in most cases had gone back to the original protocol specifications to check all data. It occurred to me that perhaps we should translate the Japanese version back into English for the next edition.

❐

Exploring the Internet

Saturday, Jun Murai had asked me to come to the monthly WIDE meeting. With a few hours to kill before the meeting, I went to the Akihabara "Electric Town" to look at the latest palmtop computers.

An intriguing discovery was the Takeru Club, a vending machine for selling software. In the center of this 4-foot high machine was a touch screen to select software. On the right were receptacles for bills and coins. On the left were floppy drives for three different diskette formats, and even a slot for dispensing laser discs.

Restraining myself from buying software, and tearing myself away from a 14-channel programmable controller, I caught a series of trains down to the Yagami campus of Keio University. I got a can of hot coffee from the vending machine and sat down to wait for Jun.

When we arrived at Keio, we found a room full of 40 volunteers, students, and scientists, hard at work discussing internetworking issues. Research results were presented, the latest routing tables were discussed, and new plans for WIDE were formulated. This group gathered once a month for an all-day Saturday session and had previously met twice a month. Monthly meetings by these volunteers are supplemented every year at two camps, where all 65 WIDE researchers and students collect in the middle of Mt. Fuji, wiring themselves into the network with Ethernets and ISDN.

I gave my lecture, a rambling discourse on resource discovery, then read my mail and went back to Tokyo and wandered around the Ginza entertainment district. In a liquor store, I decided against buying a bottle of Lemon Pie and Cream and went next door to a random sushi joint for a dinner of uni and kazunoko. On the way back to the hotel, I stopped into the Atlantis Blue bar, a fairly new establishment proudly sporting "Since 19XX" on its sign, figuring they deserved my money for using wild cards on their date.

❏

Sunday morning, suffering from newspaper withdrawal, I went in search of the *International Herald Tribune*. In Japanese, one asks for the paper as "the Geraldo," but a search of a half-dozen hotels in my area yielded nothing.

After two hours of walking, I was getting hungry, so I followed the railroad tracks to the next station. Under the tracks was a little sushi restaurant, no bigger than your average closet. A dozen stools were set around a circular counter. In the 2 by 3 foot space in the middle of the counter was the chef. A conveyer belt full of plates circled this island and customers simply grabbed plates as they came by.

Over the belt was another level which held tea glasses, chopsticks, jars of radish, and, in front of each stool, a spout for dispensing hot water, and a bucket of tea bags. If you didn't see what you wanted, you shouted out and the chef would make it and hand it out. After a half-dozen dishes, I forked over 480 yen (U.S. $3.84), amazingly cheap for Tokyo.

Fortified with octopus, I spied a bookstore, found my Geraldo, and went back to the hotel to await my dinner appointment that night at Jun Murai's house.

Jun lives in Seijogakuen, the Japanese Hollywood. I boarded the wrong train and ended up in Sagami Ohno, the equivalent of going across Manhattan by way of New Jersey. The trains were full of commuters, many wearing white surgical-style face masks worn when sick to prevent the spread of disease.

After a few more wrong turns, I finally ended up at Jun's house. The house, on the same plot with his parents, is unusual by Japanese standards. Apart from its large size, it features built-in Ethernet cabling, wiring for 5-channel Dolby stereo, and a truly impressive area of electronics gear. A little table near the entrance held a stack of 12 remote controls for the VCRs, televisions, CD players, and other evidence of many, many trips to Akihabara.

Over a dinner of salsa and margaritas, smoked salmon wrapped in horseradish and California wine, and roast pork with champagne, we talked about—no suprise here—computers. Jun keeps his finger right on the pulse of the latest technology and seemed to already have used most devices that I had only heard about.

Monday morning, I found a Yashinoya shop and had a bowl of fatty beef over rice garnished with a raw egg. Totally enamored by this time with Japanese food and electronics, I pulled out the *Japan Times* to look for a place to live. A three bedroom apartment—"with telephone"—was available for a mere 1 million yen (U.S. $8,000) per month, but the six month deposit would have put a real crimp in my hardware acquisition plans. A nice room of 42.05 square meters was only 200,000 yen, but I wasn't quite sure how I could fit my computers into a space that small, let alone find room for a bed.

At 9 A.M., I met Tomoo Okada from Fujitsu for a trip down to the new Tokyo city hall, at 60 billion yen (U.S. $500 million) reputed to be the most expensive building ever built. We took the train to Shinjuku station, which handles a mind-boggling 3 million passengers per day, and walked out the west gate to the city hall.

The complex consists of two towers, 34 and 48 stories high, and a 7-story city council hall, all clustered around a 5,000-square-meter outdoor Citizen's Plaza. All the buildings are made of a lattice of light and dark granite, which, along with the reflective glass makes the complex look like a huge integrated circuit.

We started on the first floor in the main control room for the large tower. The room is divided into regions, one for each of the major subsystems. Each region has a series of video screens and keyboards. The elevator panel, for example, shows the status of all 20 elevators and has emergency shutoff switches for each one below each screen.

Another set of screens shows the status of all 800 card readers in the complex. All employees have magnetic cards, and these are used to clock in in the morning, to open conference rooms, and even to start up computers. At the far end of the room, a technician was using a mouse to click on the diagram of one of the floors. He selected a room, and with his mouse adjusted the humidity setting from 40 to 50 percent.

We took an elevator, equipped with extra buttons at waist level for handicapped access, up two floors to a public videotex room. Here, citizens can pull up and view or print demographic data, schedules of cultural events, and city council meetings, as well as a wide variety of other types of information. That same floor features a publications sales outlet, a citizen counseling area, and other public services.

On the 13th floor, we entered an office area 108 meters long housing part of the MIS group. This floor, like all the other office floors, has an "OA Room," which houses PCs for secretaries as well as the wiring closet.

The complex features an optical backbone with 7 km of fiber running FDDI. Access to this backbone is through 100 bridges located in office complexes, machine rooms, and other locations. Attached to the bridge is a star coupler which is used to distribute fiber out to the workstations. These local loops run Ethernet and add another 295 km of fiber.

On the 9th floor, we looked down from the viewer's gallery into the 2-story room housing the Disaster Prevention Center. This control room is used in the event of natural disasters, such as earthquakes, typhoons, or large fires.

In the middle of the room are two 200-inch video screens. Video feeds from helicopters and other sources can be displayed on the screens, as well as computer simulations which show the expected spread of fires. On either side of the screens are other displays that show the current weather conditions, the reporting status of civil disaster teams, and other information needed to determine strategy.

Next, we went up to the 10th floor, devoted to seven 3090-class mainframes from Fujitsu, Hitachi, and IBM. Another machine room in the other tower has another five large systems, for a total of 3,000 square meters of machine rooms.

Each machine room has a fault-resilient IBM System 88, featuring dual processors, dual disk drives, and dual buses. The two machines act as hot backups for each other, providing a second level of protection. The System 88s are used for environmental monitoring, using a token ring to control and read information such as power status, humidity, and temperature. In case of an exception condition, the environmental monitoring system could initiate an orderly shutdown, dial telephones for system programmers, and sound alarms.

Each of the machine rooms features a special earthquake-resistant raised floor. In case of large shocks, the steel lattice will absorb and dampen vibrations, rolling the entire machine room in the opposite direction from the building.

Impressive as all these systems were, I was most intrigued by the analog data jack on the ISDN pay phone in the lobby. The next morning, I called up Jun Murai and asked him to set me up a local login, then headed back to Shinjuku.

I set up my office in the lobby, balancing my fax modem and laptop on the counter. Ten minutes later, I was reading my mail in Colorado, using the talk program to bother my systems manager, and even Kermiting my files down to my laptop to work on later.

Periodically, people would sidle over to try and figure out what this crazy Gaijin was up to. Each time I spotted somebody looking over my shoulder, I would point excitedly at the screen and say "America!" This was usually enough to evoke a polite smile and a hasty retreat.

At Narita airport, I set up my laptop in the lounge to work on the files I had downloaded. Sipping a scotch and munching dried squid, I noticed that people kept their distance.

My previous visit to Korea had been a six-hour transit stay just before the Olympics and I had been used as training material for a half-dozen different security teams getting their procedures ready for the onslaught of tourists and athletes. My current visit was considerably less high-strung, although there was still an awfully large number of security personnel in evidence. It was a traffic violation control day and each intersection had one or two cars pulled over for traffic violations and the expressway had police vans every few hundred meters, waiting for potential perpetrators to pass.

Wednesday morning, I took a cab out to the Korea Advanced Institute of Science and Technology (KAIST) to meet Kilnam Chon, a professor in the computer science department. KAIST is the center of one of Korea's R&D networks, the System Development Network (SDN) which, for some reason, is also known as Hana. SDN has hubs at the two major KAIST locations in Seoul and at the Daeduk Science Park.

Fifteen universities and research organizations connect to the two hubs at speeds ranging from 9.6 to 56 kbps. A 56 kbps line to the University of Hawaii links this TCP/IP network into the Internet. SDN supports OSI applications such as FTAM and X.400, but usage was declining rather than increasing. Five years ago, in the middle of a large OSI push, 20 percent of traffic was X.400, but the number faded to insignificance as users switched over to SMTP-based mail handlers.

There are two other TCP/IP networks in Korea. While SDN supports itself by fees from members, the other two are government supported. The Korea Research Environment Open Network (KREOnet) is sponsored by the Ministry of Science and Technology and was originally established to provide an access path to a Cray. KREOnet was linked to SDN in two locations, providing a fairly seamless Internet.

KREOnet also maintained a 56 kbps link to CERFnet in San Diego, but it appeared that most Internet traffic moved across the

PACCOM link to Hawaii. Though the Hawaii link was saturated at times, for some reason the CERFnet link had been relegated to a role as a backup.

The third network was the Korea Research Network (KREN), sponsored by the Ministry of Education. The network linked eleven BITNET sites in Seoul to Japan via a 9,600 bps line. KREN also linked nine universities together with 9,600 bps TCP/IP lines and provided a path into the rest of the Korean Internet.

After a morning briefing on the networks, Professor Chon invited me to choose between hamburgers and "lousy Korean food" in the KAIST dining room. Lousy was an overstatement, but it certainly would not be described as spectacular.

What made the lunch palatable was the conversation. Professor Chon was the chair of the JTC1 Korean Committee, the key committee for OSI work, and was also active in the CCITT standards arena. He had heard that the Bruno project had been killed and grilled me for the reasons.

Professor Chon had been planning on replicating Bruno for Korea and we discussed whether Korea really needed the ITU's permission. As an individual, one could argue that I had in fact needed their permission, assuming you take the copyright assertion at face value.

A country, on the other hand, was in a different situation. After all, the ITU had come into being when countries like Korea had signed the ITU treaty. A key aspect of international law is that any right not explicitly delegated is retained by sovereign states, and one had to wonder if the ITU could prohibit Korea from distributing standard documents to its citizens.

One could even read the ITU treaty as encouraging this behavior. The treaty required that all members take all possible steps to achieve the broadest dissemination of ITU recommendations. Though online distribution of standards was not specifically mentioned, it was certainly not explicitly prohibited.

I explained my concept of a "standards haven," where a country would ensure that standards were available online to its citizens. Not for anonymous FTP, mind you, since that would muddy the issue of sovereignty. Once the standards were online in one country, though, it would be a simple matter of cutting tapes for other countries.

"Let's do it!" Professor Chon said. I cautioned that there might be political fallout, with the ITU possibly objecting to the Foreign Ministry, a common bureaucratic home for the official delegate to the ITU. In Korea, though, the ITU representative happened to be in the Ministry of Telecommunications. To my delight, the Ministry had already gone on record as actively supporting online distribution of standards and had passed the requirement for such a fileserver down to Korea Telecom, the PTT.

Lunch started to taste better and I finished my kim chi. Korea was looking more and more like it might become the world's first standards haven.

The conversation then shifted to other standards documents, particularly OSI. There were two types of OSI documents that interested Professor Chon: working group documents and the final products, the International Standards.

Working group documents constituted enormous piles of study papers, submissions, drafts, technical corrigenda, and other documents in such profusion that simply moving paper around to participants had become the key bottleneck in the standards process.

ISO had formed a working group on working group procedures, but the working group was still bogged down in formulating the procedures under which it would operate. The best that they had come up with had been to use floppy disks to exchange ASCII-based files.

The secretariat for JTC1 was, unfortunately, ANSI. Any attempt to provide a file server for distribution of working documents would require the cooperation of the ANSI secretariat and it was highly unlikely that this notorious group of luddites would want any part of it. ANSI had been the single most vocal critic of the Bruno experiment, sending their objections straight to Pekka Tarjanne.

Online distribution of working documents would certainly improve the ISO process, but I wasn't so sure that I wanted to improve it. It would be much more interesting to get the product from that process available to those mere mortals who didn't have the time or money to fly to exotic locations and stay in expensive hotels. People in developing countries, students, and others without extensive resources should at least be able to read the international standards.

ISO standards, centrally produced and all in a common format, were a prime candidate for scanning and optical character recognition. A single format and high-quality documents means that the OCR software can quickly learn and can produce a fairly accurate rendition of the standards. Modern OCR software can go so far as to save markup information such as the font size or the location, making semi-automatic conversion into a language such as SGML very feasible.

The only hitch was that distribution rights went from ISO to the national standards bodies and ISO appeared to have inserted a minimum selling price for international standards. For draft international standards, though, there was no minimum selling price. In other words, a national standards body could give away a DIS but not an IS.

In most cases (but not all), the draft standard was virtually identical to the final product. The definition of a draft standard is that there are only minor technical corrections to be made. It would certainly be nice to distribute the final product (the idea of giving students an inferior product certainly grated), but this might be a loophole that would force some change.

The goal of setting up standards havens was not to get countries into the standards distribution business. Instead, I was much more interested in getting ISO and ITU to see the light and begin the process of distribution themselves. After all, it would make so much more sense to put a series of FTP (or FTAM) servers around the world and release all documents over the Internet.

Professor Chon set me up to visit Korea Telecom the next day to pitch my idea, and I went back to town to take care of unfinished business. First on the list was a new power cord. The lounge at Narita Airport had only 2-prong straight outlets and, desperate to get some work done, I had finally snapped the ground prong off the cord for my laptop.

Luckily, Korea used the same outlets as the U.S., including the same grounded outlets. Unluckily, however, getting the concierge at the hotel to send me in the right direction was a bit of a challenge. Arranging a visit to the North Korean border would have been a snap, but computer components drew a blank.

I made typing motions until the concierge shrugged her shoulders and wrote the name Se-Woon Sang Ga on a piece of paper. I handed the paper to the cabby who shot me a puzzled look, shrugged his shoulders, and took off. Ten minutes later, he pulled in front of a run-down 5 story concrete building.

Turned out this was where people rebuild old video games. Room after room was filled with old motherboards, technicians squinting at oscilloscopes and old men playing Go. The halls were crowded with rebuilt machines and school children came flooding in to play free games, testing the machines.

I wandered past a store that sold nothing but joy sticks, another that had ribbon cables, several video tube stores, and, inexplicably, a sculptor making plaster busts of the dearly departed. Finally, I found a shop with a few PCs running Tetris. I made jabbing motions at the wall, ran my hands in a snaking motion towards a PC, and reached for the power switch, making flicking motions.

One of the kids, realizing that I probably wouldn't just disappear, got up from his game and I repeated my charade. He nodded and reached up to the top shelf and handed me a power cord. I forked over my 3,000 won (U.S. $4) and went happily back to the hotel.

❏

The next day, I took a cab way out to the outskirts of Seoul to the research laboratories of Korea Telecom. The Umyon Dong building, I found out sitting in Future Hall, was the most intelligent building in Korea.

It certainly looked smart. Everything gleamed, the halls were empty, and there were lots of video screens all over. Ushered up to the second floor, I met Moon-Haeng Huh and Joo-Young Song, two senior officials of Korea Telecom. They showed me around the building, pointing out CATV servers, the FDDI backbone, and even fingerprint recognition equipment for entry to high security areas.

The place didn't even have light switches or temperature controls in the rooms: you used the telephone to call the automated control server, keying in the temperature you wanted for a room.

After some ginseng tea, we discussed the idea of a standards server. The labs, with an IBM 3090, Pyramid superminis, VAXen, Sun servers, and lots of other equipment, certainly had the resources. They also had the mandate. We agreed that this looked like a likely project and I left agreeing to send in a formal proposal. I couldn't wait to get home to get this started, but I had a few more stops to make first.

I handed over TW $1,000 (U.S. $40) to the cab driver and checked into my hotel, asking for a 4:45 A.M. wakeup call. It was 9 P.M.. While waiting for my baked dried squid with chili sauce to come up from room service, I read about SEEDNET, half of the Taiwanese Internet.

As with many countries, the Internet was split among multiple ministries. Education ran TANET for the universities and the commercial SEEDNET was run out of industry. The namespace was split between the two groups.

What was interesting about SEEDNET (but certainly not brought out in the paper I read) was that SEEDNET used a block of 249 Class C addresses. SEEDNET was connected to JVNCnet, which in turn was connected to the NSFNET backbone.

Having a country take 249 separate Class C addresses was an interesting illustration of the problem of the IP address space. Class B addresses were being rationed because of exhaustion of that portion of the address space, but giving out multiple Class C addresses could put an additional strain on the routers, already working hard to keep up with close to 5,000 known network addresses.

At the time of my visit to Taipei, SEEDNET was physically connected to JVNCnet, but the SEEDNET world was not announced over the NSFNET backbone to other regionals. If you attempted to connect to SEEDNET from JVNCnet, the routers would know how to route the packet. If you tried to do so from another regional, packets would disappear.

The SEEDNET problem was certainly just a temporary one, but it showed the strains that were beginning to appear on the routing infrastructure of the Internet. Older networks, such as the MILNET, had even more problems.

The MILNET routers could only handle routing information for 3,750 networks. Since the NSFNET had over 5,000 networks, the MILNET administrators had to decide which routes to accept and which to ignore. The decision had been that all international networks that were not associated with peer military organizations were cut off inside the MILNET. The Australian AARNet, for example, could no longer communicate directly with hosts inside the MILNET.

Cutting off people who probably wouldn't talk to you is certainly a rational response to the problem of saturating the Internet. The problem, however, was that this didn't solve the long-term problem of scaling the Internet. The Internet was doubling every 7 to 10 months and there were projections that the routing table size could easily grow by an order of magnitude if nothing was done.

Address space resolution was a big issue at all the IETF meetings. One solution which was proposed was to do away with the distinction of address classes and instead delegate arbitrary blocks of addresses to the regional networks, which would in turn delegate blocks to their clients.

Using blocks of addresses and delegation on the hierarchy meant that, with suitable changes in the routing protocols, a single network prefix and mask could be used to refer to what otherwise might have been several hundred (or even thousand) entries in a routing table.

I fell asleep trying to figure out why it had to be so hard to put together an integrated global Internet. There was obviously a need for many types of networks: the day of "the" network had long passed. Yet, this diversity meant that the network was starting to fragment and splinter into subsets of connectivity.

The next morning, dozing on the airplane to Hong Kong, I was awakened by the flight attendant who presented me with a large box with the imprint "Name Card Holder" on it. Looking around, I saw all the other business class passengers stuffing their gifts into carry-on bags.

I opened mine to find a handsome slab of wood with a large blue and green ceramic duck mounted on it. Presumably, the business cards would be inserted in the beak. While this functional yet attractive desk accessory would certainly have made an impressive addition to my office decor, I felt that my seatmate might make better use of it. I handed my gift to him and he whisked it into his bag before I could change my mind.

Hong Kong was hell. I got in at 9 in the morning and had 12 hours to kill before my flight to Bombay. My first stop was out to Sha Tin to visit Chinese University. Eric Lo Hing Cheung started me up a visitor account and let me read my mail, telling me about the latest status of Internet access. To nobody's surprise, the system had moved forward at a remarkable rate since my last visit and most of the Hong Kong universities were up and running.

Eric and Dr. Michael Chang were both gracious as always, but I had a problem. My back went out and I could barely move. I travel very light when it comes to clothes and other luxuries, but all the books I insist on bringing with me brings the weight up to the level that is enough to seem light but can strain the back when you take a different plane every day. Sure enough, I felt like lying on the floor at Chinese University, but that would have been less than polite.

I took a cab to the main island to find a place to lie down. The fare card in the taxi had a list of all the surcharges, including HK $4 (U.S. $0.50) for each "piece of luggage, animal, or bird." At the bottom, though was an addendum which said that "wheelchair or crutches, carried by a disabled person free." I tried to think of the legislative history that must have gone into such a clause.

I spent the rest of the day with my friend Harry Rolnick, the writer. Harry is not the kind of person who minds if you spend the afternoon lying on his floor and I hoped that my back would recover.

It was deadline day for Harry, a weekly columnist for the *South China Morning Post*. It being March 6, he decided that the Michelangelo virus would be a likely topic. Harry is not your most technically astute type—this is somebody who still uses Wordstar—but has a great sense of humor.

We spent the next hour trying to dream up new viruses. The civil servant virus was easy enough: it simply dims the screen and does nothing. The Hong Kong waiter virus has possibilities: you can't find the thing, but it will pop up occasionally and snarl at you. And, of course, there is the expatriate manager virus, which won't go off until mid-morning, when it displays "what a night, what a night" on the screen and then goes to lunch.

While Harry finished his column, I laid on the floor and looked up at the walls. The walls were certainly interesting. When he is not reviewing concerts or restaurants, Harry does things like travel to Korea to write feature pieces about kim chi or travel through the mountains of Pakistan to get a little exercise. His walls show the results.

On one wall was a framed copy of the *Pyongyang Times* from North Korea. "Comrade Kim Jong Il Inspects Kwangbok Department Store" blazed the headline. On the other wall was a 1991 calendar from Kampuchea Airlines, certainly a rare item.

To help me pass the time, Harry handed me down a copy of a North Korean-English phrasebook he had acquired on a recent visit. Verb conjugation was illustrated by the following sequence:

"We fight against Yankees"

"We will fight against Yankees"

"We have fought against Yankees"

My favorite section, though, was the one on admirations, pointing out ways to say nice things about people.

"What a wise leadership."

"Fancy abolishing taxation!"

"This is a success for the people indeed."

This phrasebook made me want to spend some time in North Korea. After all, where else can you find such an interesting permutation of the language?

I started to count the number of cities I had been in the past 5 months. Flat on my back, nursing a Mekhong whiskey to ease the pain, I wondered if it was worth it. There had to be an easier way to earn a living.

Then, Harry walked in and showed me some of his clips, including his story on kim chi, the fiery Korean pickled cabbage, made by burying cabbage and peppers for the winter to ferment. Perhaps there was an easier way to earn a living, but sitting in a cubicle hacking UNIX kernels would never expose me to the wonders of kim chi.

I dragged myself downstairs, caught a taxi, and gritted my teeth all the way to the airport, dragged my way through customs, and finally got on the plane. Even the dumpling stuffed with yam ice cream and served with a delicate, blue peanut sauce didn't ease the pain.

At 2 A.M., I crawled off the plane in Bombay feeling miserable. British Airways whisked me through the diplomatic line and carried my luggage out to the curb where I grabbed a shuttle to the closest hotel I could find.

Twelve hours later, after an hour under a hot shower, I finally felt up to a taxi down to Juhu Beach, south of Bombay, where I lay in my hotel room for the next two days recuperating. Lying on the floor, I spent my time reading marriage ads in the *Times of India* and watching Hindi films. Outside, the beach was teeming with people riding horses, watching the horse races, or gathering around acrobats doing flips. Looking down, I could spot a row of Kalaghatta stands advertizing the cold, ink-black drinks known as the "poor man's Coke" and thought to myself that a beer would be nice. Just then, the phone rang.

"Mr. Carl, this is room service. Would you like some tea or something to drink?" The idea of telepathic room service appealed to me. I began to feel much better.

□

Monday morning, Dr. S. Ramani, director of the National Center for Software Training, sent a huge old empty Tata bus to collect me. We rattled our way through the swarming vehicles adorned with "Horn OK Please" bumper stickers, past the shack which specialized in rewinding old fans, to the NCST headquarters.

My day with Ramani was a whirlwind of activity. Fascinated by how to use networks to help his country, Ramani rapidly jumped from ways to help the Indian Antarctic expedition to how to control infectious diseases to railway reservation systems to ways to disseminate Indian news to graduate students overseas.

He would leap to the white board and draw a diagram, then call out for his secretary to get certain staff members, then he would grab first one, then two telephones and start placing calls to officials and corporate executives for more information.

"Ramani, here," he said, calling the managing director of the Press Trust of India, a wire service with over 1,700 employees. "I have some ideas to discuss. Can you have dinner tonight at 9?"

The managing director had just gotten back from a trip to Delhi to meet with the Prime Minister, but dinner was arranged.

Meanwhile, we discussed ERNET, the Indian research network. The backbone was built around hubs in four cities—Bombay, Madras, Bangalore, and Delhi—which were connected to each other by 9,600 bps leased lines running TCP/IP. Other sites all over the country used UUCP into these hubs.

Over 70 sites in ERNET shared a single 9,600 bps satellite link to UUnet for international access. Needless to say, I felt more than a little bit guilty using Telnet to read my mail back in Colorado.

Low bandwidth, both domestic and international, was partly due to India's economic situation and partly to some technical detours towards satellites instead of terrestrial lines. Unlike some other countries I had visited, the underdeveloped Internet infrastructure was certainly not due to the lack of qualified engineers or a demand among users. India has one of the largest cadres of scientists in the world and the computer scientists I met at NCST were highly capable and fully aware of current developments in the Internet.

The economic situation was certainly a prime stumbling block in putting together a real research network (let alone a commercial service offering). The rupee had only just started to become convertible when I visited India and foreign exchange was at a premium. The U.S. half-circuit for the 9,600 bps line had been funded by the United Nations Development Program (UNDP).

Even within India, getting phone lines was no mean feat. Lines cost roughly the same as in the U.S., but average salaries in the U.S. are an order of magnitude higher than in India. The telephone infrastructure in India was notoriously underdeveloped, with electro-mechanical exchanges (i.e., something has to move to complete a circuit) still in operation in many locations. The wait for a residential line could easily take several years. Businesses pay a substantial surcharge to cut the wait to weeks or months.

In rural areas, lines are so unstable that running UUCP over them could lead to endless retries. Even when the lines are operational, overhead of 500 percent is not uncommon. In fact, in some areas the lines were so bad that ERNET used a novel "floppy-based e-mail system." It turned out to be significantly more cost effective when the line got bad enough to simply spool mail to floppies and hire a courier to bring the diskettes down to the nearest hub. One system manager in Kanpur was once observed going through this biweekly ritual, neatly labeling floppies and stacking them into a pile.

"These guys have no other business," he grumbled, "all they do is keep sending mail through the day and night." Ramani showed me the network management utility which showed 30 to 70 messages exchanged per courier run with one of the FloppyNet sites in Kanpur.

Even in Bombay, local lines are not immune to problems. During the summer monsoon, 80 to 100 inches of rain can fall in 80 days of the monsoon season, knocking out service for 7 to 10 days per year. For this reason, the main international gateway had been located 20 km south of NCST in downtown Bombay. This machine, Sangam, was located in the Air India building and was just a kilometer from the telephone company's point of presence, making it fairly immune to disruptions during the monsoon.

'20 kilometers south of NCST, in downtown Bombay'.

A poor telephone infrastructure led Ramani and others in the Indian academic community to look to satellites, particularly the Indian manufactured INSAT series. The satellites gave high bandwidth, used Indian technology, and needed only a dish on the roof instead of depending on local infrastructure.

The original ERNET project plan from 1984 envisioned linking the 8 large academic and research institutions together with 4.5 meter dishes. For 1.5 million dollars, this infrastructure would provide multiple data paths, based on, of course, OSI protocols. By 1988, the project had evolved to specify 64 kbps data paths for the transmission of voice, data, and fax.

The voice requirement would satisfy needs for voice broadcast services for seminars, and would allow network management to have their own voice channels. The data channels would be established using the X.25 protocols and very coarse time slots of 1 second or even more would be provided. The data channels were thus suitable only for file transfer and electronic mail.

Although the project plans developed on schedule, the satellite kept getting delayed. By 1988, though, some Indian students returning from the states started agitating for Telebit modems, capable of running at fairly high speeds over voice-grade lines.

Anil Garg and some other NCST staffers began playing with UUCP dial-up transfers. The first links were in Bombay between NCST and a sister institution, the Indian Institute of Technology (IIT). At the time, the only phone available at the IIT computer science department was located in the office of the chairman.

To transfer mail, Anil would call up the chairman of the department, apologize for the interruption, and ask him to place the phone on the modem. If the phone was needed for voice sessions, then e-mail would have to wait. Eventually, a set time slot on the telephone was allocated and, assuming calls got through, e-mail started to flow regularly.

Over time, the terrestrial network started to grow. By 1991, with a little prodding from Vinton Cerf, an advisor to ERNET, the network was based on leased lines and Cisco routers. In early 1992, Ramani was in the midst of careful negotiations with the Department of Telecommunications to use a 64 kbps chunk of a new 140 Mbps fiber line to Delhi and maybe even to get a piece of the digital microwave links to Bangalore and Madras.

Meanwhile, the satellite project was finally getting off the ground, but its purpose had to be reevaluated. The terrestrial ERNET was obviously much more suitable for interactive applications and with 64 kbps terrestrial lines coming in the foreseeable future, Ramani was searching for a use for the satellites. Ramani was hoping that the satellite WAN could supplement the terrestrial network, perhaps being used by applications with a broadcast focus, such as the distribution of news.

Exploring the Internet

Over a lunch of aloo bhindi and carrot halwa in the NCST canteen—equipped with a PC and custom software, of course—Ramani explained his attempts to automate the infectious disease units of the local hospitals.

Bombay hospitals get several hundred admissions per day for diseases ranging from dysentery to measles, polio, and hepatitis. An estimated 20,000 deaths per year are caused in Bombay by diseases that are preventable by vaccination, boiling drinking water, or other simple means.

When an admission occurs at a hospital, the admissions officer fills out a slip and places it in a pigeonhole for one of Bombay's 23 wards. The slips are picked up and, within 24 hours or so, make their way to public health officers in the wards who take appropriate actions. In the case of measles, for example, the health officer might go to a child's building and look for unvaccinated playmates.

Ramani had been conducting briefings and otherwise pushing people to computerize the process. He was hoping that a small number of computers could easily cut out the 24 hour delay. More importantly, aggregate information could be quickly examined for trends. A cluster of hepatitis cases, when displayed on a map would quickly indicate contaminated drinking water in a neighborhood. The information could be used to make special efforts in those neighborhoods to try and convince people to boil their water, at least for a while.

That afternoon, I FTPed my mail down to a local account to avoid tying up the international link, then went downstairs to give a lecture on the politics of standards. The audience of several dozen people were all active in implementing standards or using them as part of their work. This was certainly a sympathetic audience and everybody laughed when I explained the theory the standards potatoes advanced that anybody "serious" about implementing standards could certainly afford to participate in the process. Somebody came up to me after the lecture and explained how tough it was to get foreign exchange allocated for buying documents, let alone taking trips to conferences and standards meetings.

After the lecture, I went back to my hotel and pressed (having finally reprogrammed myself) the elevator's up button to go down to the coffee shop. The coffee shop was playing a rousing polka over the intercom, but I didn't see any kielbasas on the menu so I ordered some samosas and sweet lime water instead.

That evening, Dr. Ramani picked me up and we went to a local restaurant to meet Gourang Kundapur, managing director of the Press Trust of India (PTI). Over a dinner of brains masala and tandoori cauliflower, we gossiped about Indian politics, a topic even more complex than the politics of standards.

❏

Tuesday morning, my driver took me from Juhu to Bombay to see the railway reservation system at Victoria Terminus, one of the main train stations and a Bombay landmark. Smack in the middle of rush hour, we dodged goats tied to shacks on the side of the road, pushcarts loaded with potatoes, and cows that ambled along content in the knowledge that they alone were safe on the roads.

My driver took what might charitably called a fairly aggressive approach to driving. He clearly felt that the green light was an indication that he should have already cleared the intersection. Even stuck behind several dozen cars, he would keep his hand on the horn. The side mirrors were carefully folded flat against the car, giving at least 3 inches of extra maneuvering room.

Arriving at the Central Reservations building, I entered a very large room filled with an incredibly dense mob waiting for tickets. Fighting my way up to the information counter, I was handed a form before I could even open my mouth, then was promptly swept along with the crowd.

The Indian Railways system is one of the largest in the world, moving 10 million passengers a day in over 6,000 trains. Tickets for these trains come in 7 categories (e.g., express or local), 32 kinds of quotas (e.g., foreigner or defense official), 100 types of discounts (e.g, veteran or handicapped), and 7 classes of reservations (e.g., first class or first class air conditioning).

The old, non-computerized system had, although I had a hard time picturing it, been known for incredibly long lines, which presumably meant that the lobbies must had somehow fit in even more people than I saw. To make a booking, you needed to be in the right line for the particular class of tickets for the particular train you wanted to take.

Demand has always far outstripped supply for Indian trains, so it was not unusual to have 1,000 people clustered around one clerk, while the next counter was empty. An 8-hour wait in line only to find there were no seats left was not unheard of.

Assuming you were able to fight your way up to the top of the line and get the clerk's attention, the process still had no guarantees. Complicated rate calculations, manual ledger books, and a host of paperwork led to lots of errors. When you got to the train, you might easily discover that there were duplicate bookings or that a supposedly sold-out train had dozens of empty seats.

To find out about the new and improved system, I met with officials from CMC, Ltd. the government-backed system integrators that had computerized the reservations process. CMC had set up five separate reservations systems for each of the five main regions of India, centered in Bombay, Delhi, Calcutta, Hyderabad, and Madras.

Four of the five systems were based on VAXen. For some reason, Hyderabad had some small CDC systems. Bombay was typical with two VAX 8650s and a 6310 clustered together. All the code was written in FORTRAN and even the database management functions had been locally developed.

The Bombay system handled 7 different reservation centers. Victoria Terminus was the largest, with 80 terminals, and the nearby Churchgate station had 20 terminals. Muxes and modems linked remote terminals to the cluster. A satellite office in Ahmedabad, 500 km away, linked 45 terminals over a series of eight 4,800 bps lines. All told, around 200 terminals handled 50,000 to 60,000 transactions on a typical day, with peaks up to 90,000 in the busy season.

For customers, the system meant that a reservation for any train in any class could be made in any line. Just as importantly, far fewer errors were made, since fares were automatically calculated and it was much harder to double-book seats.

Oddly enough, there was a downside. On the old system, it was possible to gauge your approximate chances of getting a ticket by the size of the queue and your ability to step over people and get to the front. On the new system, it was much harder to estimate your chances, since you competed with people all over the city. Monitors were posted at the stations indicating how many seats were available on the more popular runs, but the Chief Commercial Superintendent told me he was certainly receiving complaints from people unable to get tickets.

The huge excess demand for tickets made scalping a profitable business. Ticket sales were limited to 4 to 6 per person to prevent scalping and each ticket had imprinted on it the name, age, and sex of the passenger. An ID was not required to ride the train, but conductors attempted to make sure that the holder of the ticket had at least some resemblance to the data on the ticket. The main result was that scalpers had adopted more sophisticated inventory management techniques.

While the seven main reservation centers in the Bombay region were online, smaller stations still used electromechanical teleprinters to communicate with Bombay. The messages would be received on slips of paper, a clerk would key in the data to the computer and send a message back to the station which would issue the ticket. Recently, data from a few teleprinter sites had been fed straight into the VAX. Hooking teleprinters to the VAX allowed properly formatted messages to be automatically answered. Not quite an interactive terminal, but much quicker than the old system.

This same message switch was being used to connect the independent systems for each region. When I visited, each center had a few terminals for each of the other regions, allowing a Bombay passenger to book passage on a train originating in Calcutta. Hooking those lines into a local VAX instead of a terminal would provide a way for one system to be a virtual teleprinter to a remote region.

After my briefing, my hosts insisted on showing me their machine room, which we entered via the washroom. Afterwards, I rode back out to Juhu, passing a line three blocks long waiting to enter the temple of Ganesh, the god with the elephant head.

❐

Exploring the Internet

Wednesday, Ramani sent one of the NCST jeeps to pick me up. The jeep was prominently adorned with "Govt. of India" on the front and back. NCST is not technically a part of the government, but Ramani explained that the labels made parking significantly easier.

I spent the day at the edge of the Ramani cyclone, periodically leaving to check on my FTP jobs, which were downloading source code for utilities that I thought might be useful to NCST. By the end of the day, netfind, perl, traceroute, and WAIS had all made it over the link.

The only thing I really wanted to bring down was the code for Cleveland Free-Net. A Free-Net is typically linked to Cleveland over the Internet and has a local bank of modems for public access. Ramani and I couldn't see how NCST could meet this requirement, but wanted to see if there was some way that the Free-Net concept could be applied in India.

Unfortunately, Free-Net wouldn't let us do that. Public access or nothing. People in India rarely had PCs and modems at home, and adding substantial traffic to an already saturated 9,600 bps link just didn't make any sense.

WAIS had no such arbitrary administrative restrictions, however. While ideally a WAIS client accessed servers all over the world, it was certainly technically feasible to run an isolated WAIS world on an Ethernet, providing a local information environment. Running WAIS with the NCST LAN was useful as a way for building up local expertise and seemed to fit right in with another current project.

NCST was taking the wire service from the Press Trust of India and feeding it into a VAX. There, the news feed was automatically broken up into individual items and fed into a local USENET news group. Every Friday, one day's worth of news was posted globally, providing information on Indian politics, sports, and culture to graduate students and professionals overseas.

Once the news hit the VAX, applications like WAIS might be an interesting method for searching and reading the news. NCST programmers were also developing their own sophisticated applications for sifting through information, such as a stock and news monitor that was built on SCO's Open Desktop.

Bombay

All these fancy user interfaces made me curious how the news got produced. The next day, I went back into Bombay to visit the headquarters of the PTI. We drove past a police officer on a chauffeur-driven scooter and ended up at Flora Fountain in the center of India's banking district.

The Uco Bank building, where PTI was located, was a few blocks away from where my driver left me off. He waved his arms vaguely in the proper direction, and I headed off down the street. Every block or so, I would stop a policeman or a rickshaw-wallah and say "Uco Bank Building" a few times.

I happened to be clutching a few random notes in my hand and every time I stopped to ask for directions, the person would grab the paper out of my hand and scrutinize it for several minutes. The notes had nothing to do with Uco Bank, but after a while the person would look up and wave me on down the street.

This method apparently worked because I soon saw a sign for the Uco Bank Building. I found it interesting that no matter which paper I had in my hand, it would be grabbed and examined. With a chuckle I thought of Cliff Lynch, one of the more active members of the library automation community. Cliff is famous for always clutching a stack several inches thick of business cards and scraps of paper. It would have taken him all day to get directions.

I went up the rickety stairs to the PTI offices and met Gourang Kundapur. Over cups of sweet coffee, he told me the history of PTI. Formed as a cooperative for small and medium newspapers in the early part of the century, the service was taken over by Reuters before the war. When the British left in August 1947, Reuters also pulled out and PTI was formed as a non-profit cooperative.

The news is gathered by over 400 journalists spread in 135 offices throughout the country. Before automation began, stories were typed on a teleprinter and punched to paper tape. The paper tape was fed in and the data went over a 50-baud line to one of four main centers.

In 1980, when Ramani began acting as a consultant to PTI, the entire network of 100,000 km of 50 baud lines was based on manual switching. The data came into a regional center and a tape was punched. A subeditor edited the story, and a new tape was be produced.

The tape then went to the transmission room, where an operator flipped switches to indicate which lines should be active, and the story was sent out. If the story had wide enough distribution, regional centers got the data, punched a tape, and sent it out to their local clients.

The obvious places to computerize were the four regional offices. PDP 11 systems were installed with custom code to terminate the teleprinter lines, acting as a switch and also providing an online editing environment for editors.

Connecting teleprinter lines turned out to be no mean feat. Each line transmitted at a slightly different speed. Custom boxes were developed that adjusted the speed to an exact 50 baud, manually at first and later automatically. The code from the PDP system was later ported to Xenix, with the Xenix system acting as an editing environment and a backup to the message switching function of the PDP.

While the regional offices were fairly well automated, Mr. Kundapur explained that it was not quite as easy to get rid of the teleprinters or even the 50 baud lines. The 50 baud lines were available to the press at 1/6 of the cost of normal lines, and, while it was possible to drive the lines at higher speeds locally, this would not work in remote areas.

People were another consideration. Electromechanical printers were noisy and dirty, but they had been used so long that people knew how they worked. Old-time journalists were not quick to adapt to electronic teleprinters (i.e., a dot matrix printer and a keyboard), although the mechanics tended to love the new systems as they required air conditioning.

For larger sites, teleprinters had been replaced with PCs or Atex systems. A custom device was built by a PTI subsidiary which adjusted the incoming voltage, changed the speed to 300 bps, and converted 5-bit BAUDOT code to ASCII, allowing most computers to easily accept a teleprinter feed.

PTI didn't have the most hi-tech system in the world, but it illustrated how to work in a technically challenging environment and still get work done. The system was continuing to move forward, with the central code being ported to an 80486 running UNIX and TCP/IP to link regional centers being investigated.

I got back to NCST in time for a quick lunch of baingan ka bhartha, a delicious eggplant dish similar to the Middle Eastern baba ganouj, accompanied by flat chapati bread. That afternoon and the next day I spent giving lectures on topics as diverse as WAIS and high speed networking and meeting with NCST students and staff. Saturday, Ramani and I got together to talk about standards.

Ramani was chair of a key committee in the Bureau of Indian Standards (BIS). One of the challenges in India was training large numbers of engineers, both for developing local systems and to stimulate the growing software export industry.

Training engineers meant giving them the information they needed and that meant giving them access to standards. BIS had been grappling for several years on how to distribute information, and online standards was high on their list. Ramani's committee had already decided that dissemination of information was a key priority.

Would Ramani be interested in posting standards for the Indian community? "In a minute," Ramani said without any hesitation at all.

This was the second place that felt that training people was much more important than playing international politics, and it was obvious that many other countries would post standards if the data were available.

It was obvious to me that I should get off the road and get busy preparing data, a task I couldn't do very well from an airplane. Before I could go home, though, I had one more stop to make.

I reported to Bombay's international airport for my 3:30 A.M. flight to London, Chicago, and Madison, Wisconsin. After seven stamps on my boarding pass, three in my passport, a special line and three stamps to clear my computer, a half-dozen luggage checks, and several lines with no apparent purpose, I was on my way.

While killing time in the lounge at Heathrow waiting for my plane to Chicago, a group of three couples sat down next to me and started playing dominoes. Obviously on a tour of some sort, they played their game and babbled on about some market they had visited in Cairo.

A few minutes later, a young lady bearing a name badge with the title "Travel Coordinator" came running up, all out of breath.

"I almost didn't make it," she told them, "I was on the wait list."

"Oh dear!" one of her charges commiserated. "Was your luggage too heavy?"

☐

Monday morning, I felt great despite my 12-hour jet lag and 26-hour trip. This was my last stop, my 56th city since INTEROP 91 Fall, less than 6 months ago, and I was certainly looking forward to terminating this little journey.

I had come to Madison to learn how the Internet had gone from a DoD-centered ARPANET to a collection of autonomous systems in the early 1980s. To learn this ancient lore, I had come to meet Larry Landweber, one of the key figures in the early development of the Internet.

In India, some of us had been sitting around over a beer speculating on the topic of Larry's age. He was a fairly prominent theoretician before his entry into networking, and the consensus was that Lah-Ree (as his name is pronounced in much of the world) must easily be in his 60s and close to retirement.

When I mentioned this little anecdote to Larry, he quickly established that he was well under 50 and had no immediate plans to retire. It's always good to start an interview by putting your subject in a pleasant, relaxed state of mind.

We walked down to the computer room in the Computer Science department for a quick tour. Computer Science at Wisconsin is large, with over 35 faculty, and extremely well equipped. The machine room is huge and includes such sports computers as a Thinking Machines CM5 and a now ancient 32-node HyperCube, each node equipped with a 300 Mbyte disk drive.

As we walked past old VAX 11/750s, kept in place so the university auditors didn't reclaim machine room space, we stumbled across two brand new Silicon Graphics computers. Larry called over the computer room manager, who was busy trying to get some equipment packed and shipped back to the manufacturer.

"Whose SGI machines are those?" Larry asked.

"Those are yours, Larry," the manager said with a patient smile.

At the corporate offices of Me, Inc., the arrival of a new RS-232 cable is enough to stop work for a celebration, so I couldn't imagine having so much equipment you forget about two Silicon Graphics machines.

Outside the machine room, Larry logged onto a little terminal next to a coke machine and typed in his request for a Diet Coke, which soon came slamming out of the slot. I commented on how clever it was to rig up the machine to a host.

Turned out the reason for this automated soda server was fairly practical. The campus administration had passed some sort of rule that would have removed the machine from its convenient location outside the machine room. By hooking it up to the network, a mere soda server became a full-fledged example of computer science research. The machine stayed.

Back upstairs, we sat down for a history lesson. Larry's first exposure to networking came in the summer of 1977 when he was sitting in a bar with a few other theoreticians lamenting the lack of communications among themselves. They dreamed up the idea of TheoryNet for exchanging e-mail and, luckily, an NSF official was sitting with them.

"Give me a proposal," he said.

Next thing he knew, Larry had a grant for U.S. $136,000, which for a theoretician was a lot of money, far surpassing any previous grant he had received. Soon, theoreticians all over the country were happily banging away on their Texas Instruments paper terminals, exchanging missives on NP completeness and computational complexity.

In 1977, Larry became chair of the department and started looking around for ways to improve computing facilities. He began casting covetous glances at the ARPANET, but Wisconsin didn't have nearly enough defense contracts to justify its inclusion in the elite dozen or so nodes.

Wisconsin certainly wasn't the only school not on the ARPANET, and Larry started looking around for ways to get the have-nots on the network. He was primarily interested in Computer Science departments, a logical focus given the level of penetration of networks at the time.

Kent Curtis was director of the Computer Science section of NSF and was quickly sold on the idea of a CSNET. A small group of computer scientists was convened in May 1979 to discuss the idea. First on the agenda was to see if maybe they could just get into the ARPANET. While the ARPANET had plans to grow, it wasn't clear that it would grow so fast that it would include them. Just in case, Kent Curtis encouraged the group to submit a proposal.

In November 1979 the proposal for CSNET was submitted and went out for review. The results were disastrous. Reviewers thought TCP/IP was far too complex for end-users, networking should be left to the ARPANET professionals, and who did these amateurs think they were anyway?

Not exactly a vote of confidence. Kent Curtis looked at the reviews, thought about it, and sent Larry back with U.S. $49,000 to make a study. By June 1981, a second proposal for CSNET was submitted and the reviews were again negative.

Kent Curtis looked at the reviews, and called an advisory panel together. They didn't like the idea, either. Curtis kept on supporting the idea though. What made CSNET possible was the skillful lobbying by Kent Curtis inside the government and the cooperation of DARPA. Vinton Cerf had attended a CSNET planning meeting and indicated that DARPA looked on the project favorably and would be willing to work with CSNET on ways to interconnect. January 1980, after some fairly intense lobbying, NSF awarded U.S. $5 million for five years to the CSNET project.

Armed with money and the blessings of NSF and DARPA, a group of five people was put together to manage the project. A classic exercise in distributed management, CSNET was run by Larry Landweber, Peter Denning, Dave Farber, and Tony Hearn, along with Bill Kern, the NSF project manager. The project began the task of putting together a comparatively low-cost solution that would allow a sharp increase in the size of the Internet.

One of the immediate effects of the NSF award was to get Madison and the other key development sites onto the ARPANET. These sites—Madison, Purdue, RAND, and Delaware—formed the core of CSNET. For the rest of the CSNET world, there were three levels of connectivity: exchanging mail, using a service host, and full TCP/IP connectivity.

For exchanging mail, CSNET used a technique known as Phone-Net. PhoneNet used the MMDF software developed by Dave Crocker and Dave Farber to transfer messages over telephone lines, much in the same way UUCP did.

There was a big difference from UUCP, however. Mail which arrived at the PhoneNet relays at RAND and the University of Delaware could continue on into the ARPANET. DARPA had agreed that the CSNET sites, a group of hosts outside of their direct administrative control, could exchange mail with ARPANET sites. This was thus the first example of two autonomous systems connected together with gateways. Although the initial exchanges were e-mail only, this was soon expanded to IP connectivity.

The agreement between ARPANET and CSNET to allow connection was a carefully worded agreement, prohibiting sites in the CSNET from forwarding data originating from the ARPANET to "non-authorized users." Most importantly, though, the agreement delegated authority to the CSNET to administer its own network, only requiring that the members of CSNET abide by the rules of acceptable use of the network.

The issue of charging was also carefully dealt with, specifying that there would be no charges between the autonomous systems: you accept my traffic and I'll accept yours. Lack of settlement procedures has remained a tradition in the Internet even today. The Commercial Internet Exchange, for example, uses a system of flat fees based on the size of pipes, not on the amount or attributes of the data flowing through those pipes.

PhoneNet allowed message exchange within CSNET and to the ARPANET, but didn't give people access to services like Telnet and FTP. To provide this higher level of connectivity, CSNET provided a service host at Madison.

Users were given individual accounts and used X.25 or dialin to log onto the service host. From there, they had full access to the ARPANET. The service host also held a collection of useful documents and some nameserver software to help users find electronic mail addresses.

PhoneNet and the service host caught on like wildfire. By December 1981, the RAND and Delaware relays were up and running and Purdue, Princeton, and the NSF were PhoneNet clients. By the summer of 1982, 24 sites were on PhoneNet and two years later there were 84 sites. The population of PhoneNet peaked in 1988 at 170 sites.

Getting sites fully integrated into the ARPANET with IP access was a bit tougher. At the time, X.25 was viewed as the way to set up widely dispersed hosts and the common carriers were telling people that in the future, X.25 networks would become cheap and leased lines expensive.

There were two well-known public data networks at the time, Tymnet and Telenet. Tymnet didn't return phone calls from CSNET, so Telenet became the candidate network for interconnecting CSNET hosts at the IP level. (Note the difference between the Telenet X.25 network and the Telnet virtual terminal service.)

All the X.25 networks at the time were optimized for the holy X trinity, X.3, X.28, and X.29. These standards defined how an asynchronous terminal could connect to a Packet Assembler/Disassembler, which in turn set up virtual circuits to hosts on the X.25 network.

Optimizing for terminals made it tough on hosts. Telenet used 128-byte packets and a virtual circuit could only have two packets outstanding. This certainly slowed down potential throughput, but to make matters worse, the data link level of LAP-B enforced a limit of 7 outstanding packets for all virtual circuits sharing a link.

What this meant was that a host with a 9,600 bps link to Telenet could only get 1 to 2 kilobits of throughput on one virtual circuit. This was a best-case scenario, and during peak periods congestion reduced the throughput even further.

Douglas Comer of Purdue took on the daunting task of trying to integrate X.25 and TCP/IP. Comer and his group developed a solution using multiple X.25 circuits, one of the first examples of path splitting. Comer's group also developed the software that set up and tore down virtual circuits in a manner that was transparent to IP.

Comer's group mapped datagrams over virtual circuits. The approach of layering connectionless traffic over connection-oriented circuits was considered controversial at the time. Another group at University College London took a different approach, using protocol translation to turn TCP circuits into X.25 circuits. Comer's group went off and hacked, and came back with a working IP over X.25 demonstration between Madison and Purdue.

Even with this clever software, X.25-based networking never really caught on in the U.S. Not only was performance poor, but the cost for running TCP/IP over X.25 could be astronomical. Remember, these networks charged by the packet and a single character typed for a Telnet session could consume 4 packets (send character, acknowledge, echo character, acknowledge).

Even though the cost was high, a few sites wanted IP access badly enough that they were willing to pay. After Purdue built and tested the software, Rice was the first X.25 customer in the fall of 1984, and was soon joined by DEC's Western Research Laboratory, and BBN. Later, as it became clear that leased lines were more economical, the Purdue group developed a low-cost leased line network called Cypress, which was offered as an alternative access path in CSNET.

BBN also became the site for the new Coordination and Information Center (CIC) and became the support center for CSNET. The service host and MMDF relays were moved, and the CIC maintained the document database and helped new users get started.

Although NSF funded CSNET, they also made sure that a clause was inserted in the project plan that the network should be self sufficient at the end of five years. At the end of five years, it was in fact self sufficient, charging universities U.S. $2,000 to $5,000 per year and industrial sites such as DEC and IBM $30,000 to participate. Self-sufficiency of CSNET was used by the NSF as an important justification for funding future projects such as the NSFNET.

In addition to self-sufficiency, CSNET helped establish a tradition in the U.S. of projects of limited scope. Instead of expanding CSNET to be a backbone, to serve other communities, and to achieve world peace, CSNET remained focused on one problem. Over time, other solutions such as regional networks became more attractive and by 1988 the number of CSNET hosts was beginning to decline. By 1989, CSNET had merged with BITnet and by 1991, PhoneNet was dead.

CSNET was not just limited to the U.S. It formed an important way, along with BITNET, to spread the Internet overseas. The international spread of the Internet was directly linked to an annual series of meetings that came to be known as the Landweber Seminars. I was interested to learn that Larry was not even present at the first Landweber Seminar.

In September 1982, Peter Kirstein of University College London convened a "meeting on U.S.-European Academic Network Collaboration." The meeting was small, but included representatives from a half-dozen countries.

At this meeting, Germany described their DFN project, the Scandinavians described active projects in Norway and Sweden, and the U.K. described the Coloured Book. There was a CSNET presentation, and CERN described the early stages of what would become HEPnet.

In other words, this was a collection of people who were actually doing something about getting together to exchange information. One of the most useful functions of such a meeting was what occurred in the halls and at dinner where synergy between different groups quickly led to new projects.

In 1983, Kirstein and Landweber jointly organized another seminar in Oslo at which Larry announced that CSNET was going to go international. Needless to say, the question of where it would go international first occupied much of the discussions at the breaks.

In February 1984, Israel became the first international member of CSNET. A carefully worded agreement was signed stating that data originating from the ARPANET would not be forwarded. International access, after all, had the potential to become a political issue.

The Israel PhoneNet connection was rapidly followed by Korea, with Professor Kilnam Chon aggressively pursuing connectivity. By September 1986, PhoneNet access had spread to Australia, Canada, France, Germany, and Japan. Israel, Korea, and the Japanese NTT soon got IP access.

The Landweber Seminars became firmly established as a place for people to meet and things like CSNET connectivity, gateways, and other projects to get started. In 1984, the Seminar convened in Paris, followed in subsequent years by Stockholm, Dublin, Princeton, Jerusalem, and Sydney.

Princeton, in 1987, was the breakthrough meeting. The invitation-only seminar had reached 100 people and the attendance list was certainly impressive, including most of the people active in spreading the Internet.

By Sydney, the meeting had grown so big that the seminar format began to outlive its usefulness. It was decided that year that the seminar should metamorphosize into a conference, and the next year INET 91 was held in Copenhagen. At INET 92, in Kobe, Japan, the conference turned into the annual meeting of the Internet Society.

❐

After a nap to shake off jet lag, I drove across town for dinner with Larry and his wife, Jean. Also there was Tony Hearn, one of the CSNET founders, who was driving through on a college inspection tour with his son and had stopped for the night in Madison.

We had a nice dinner of vegetarian lasagna and steaming home-made rye bread, finished by strawberries with a soy powder custard. When the second bottle of wine was cracked, a 1969 Pinot Noir, Tony Hern sniffed his glass appreciatively and smiled mischievously.

"Gee, this would taste great with meat," he teased. "Honey," Larry said, turning to his wife, "do we have any cow left?"

"I think we have a slab in the freezer."

I began to fade from jet lag and went back to my hotel, anxious not to miss my early flight the next morning back to Boulder.

It was Tuesday afternoon, and I was home. I wandered over to the Ideal Market, the kind of place that has a "customer-of-the-month," to get myself a bagel with lox and cream cheese.

"Have a nice day," the bag person said to me as I walked in the front door.

"Have a nice day," the deli person said, handing me my bagel.

"Have a nice day," said Dennis, the chi-chi butcher, as he vacated his table to go back to selling ground buffalo and turkey bratwurst.

That did it. Enough was enough. I went over to the pay phone and called my realtor. Minutes later the formalities were complete and my house was on the market.

Before I could leave Boulder, however, I had to finish this book. Mind you, this was not out of some sense of duty or an overwhelming desire to clean up loose ends. Half of my advance was payable when I turned in a manuscript suitable for publication, and I needed the money to move.

I did what many Boulder residents do during those rare moments when they have to concentrate, and went to the Trident Cafe. Sitting down, I looked around.

At the next table, a man with unfocused eyes was flipping through a book of star charts, trying to find astrologically similar periods in the past to shed light on the future. In a booth nearby, a guy was dealing out Tarot cards, stopping periodically to stare at his destiny and grumble to himself. The table next to him was spread out with materials for advanced Shambhala training, and next to that three people were engaged in some strange form of group massage.

With so many people looking for inner truth and sharing their feelings, I decided to try and list the good qualities of OSI. After thirty minutes of protocol meditation, however, I looked down at my piece of paper. It contained only one item.

"We have to live with it," my list read.

The goals of the OSI effort are certainly laudable. The concept of open systems is about as hard to argue against as any other lofty ideal. But, saying that being against OSI is to be against open systems assumes there is only one road to truth, beauty, and interoperability.

Quite simply, OSI has not achieved anything close to its goals. Too much complexity, lack of hands-on experience, and far too many fine lunches and dinners had hindered the creation of a lean, mean, finite-state architectural machine.

Just because OSI is not ideal, however, doesn't mean that it can be ignored. OSI has been adopted by many governments as a lowest common denominator of connectivity, taking its place as the logical successor to IBM's RJE and Bisynch protocols.

OSI has become one of those challenges that keep system integrators and consultants employed. OSI is just one of those ugly things you have to deal with when putting together a system, no different than COBOL-driven ISAM files, sendmail configurations, or VTAM routing tables. In fact, OSI has become one of those things that made ideal fodder for students taking MIS classes in business schools:

> "Final Exam, Essay Question: Finance has OSI, Accounting has SNA, and Personnel uses Novell. FTAM over LAN Manager has been proposed for an enterprise-wide file system. Discuss. Extra Credit: Write a justification for the proposition that NetWare is actually compliant with OSI."

While OSI has not achieved the goals the committees have set for it, neither was the effort totally wasted. Certainly the careers of hundreds and hundreds of standards potatoes could have been better spent, but there are a few pieces that can be salvaged.

The only way to salvage the work, however, is to get the process out of the hands of those who would build machines in the abstract and back to those who are engaged in the hard, dirty work of building networks. To salvage anything about OSI, the standards have to be known or the work will simply be ignored.

Just because the approach to building networks by committee didn't work doesn't mean that lone wolves can do any better. Rather, a special type of person is needed, one who understands people well enough to mobilize resources and understands the technology well enough to know which resources to mobilize.

In my journey, I met many people who effectively built national networks. Geoff Huston in Australia, Juha Heinänen, in Finland, Jun Murai in Japan, Glenn Kowack from EUnet, and Rick Adams from UUnet are only a few examples of people who successfully built large networks, providing the leadership necessary to turn technology into infrastructure.

While there are many people who succeeded, there are many, many more who spent their time building castles out of air. Efforts like the COSINE project in Europe, for example, kept many people busy making presentations instead of stringing cable.

The ratio of goers to doers in the world of research is just as lopsided. For every Marshall T. Rose, Steve Hardcastle-Kille, or Christian Huitema, there are a hundred people arguing about what to call the TCP/IP protocol suite instead of writing code.

The trick appears to be to provide an environment which allows people to do useful work, and then letting them get on with it. Part of that means providing appropriate resources, but resources alone don't guarantee anything. There are too many multimillion dollar mega-projects that went nowhere to think that throwing money at a problem has any relationship to the final outcome.

In fact, the contrary appears to be the case. There are many projects that started on a shoestring, with a few researchers borrowing a modem and appropriating a phone line. The common denominator in most of these projects was a desire to get work done and a fascination with the technology.

An ad hoc approach to building networks convinced the standards potatoes that the Internet was some kind of academic toy, unsuitable for doing real things. They were wrong and the toy turned out to be the piles of OSI paper.

The Internet is a machine, built by thousands and thousands of engineers to solve real problems. So how can this machine be turned into a truly global infrastructure? How can the spirit of in-

ventiveness that had built the machine in the first place be preserved?

One can think of infrastructure in layers, and it seems that most
of the failed efforts can be traced to a tendency to concentrate on
one layer to the exclusion of others. As they would say in Boulder
(if they thought about it), infrastructure is holistic.

At one layer, you have the real things, the technology that makes
networks. Protocols, hardware, and all the technical details that are
studied in engineering schools are all part of the real layer.

Technology alone doesn't make a network, though. The next
layer is the people layer where technology is applied, deployed, and
networks start being used. The leadership of the NSF, DARPA, and
the IAB are all functions at the people layer.

Don't think that you can do one layer without the other. NSF
provided money and leadership, but the NSFNET also required the
solution of many technical problems before it became a reality.
Likewise, there are many great technologies that remain research
prototypes because nobody takes the time to move them into the
field.

One can think of the people layer as the process of governance,
but that does not imply government. EUnet and the USENET, for
example, are strong evidence that resources can be organized and
deployed without the involvement of official bureaucracies.

Eventually, we reach the paper layer, where things are documented. One hopes, of course, that the paper is actually some form
of data online. Documentation is the key to allowing the activities
in one part to spread to other communities.

Too often, technology remains a black box. By writing down
what is happening, others can learn what goes on inside of that
black box and improve it. This is the crucial mistake that OSI made
when they invented paper, but forgot to show it to anybody.

Paper can mean standards, but it can also mean procedures and
policies. Paper has a big impact on how the network is used and
who can use it. Standards and the other forms of paper, virtual or
real, are the laws and regulations of networks.

These laws have a real effect. Is your routing protocol complex?
You've raised the cost of entry. Do you have an acceptable use pol-

icy? You've limited your population. Have you invented an anonymous FTP mechanism and an RFC series? You've encouraged the spread of the network.

Paper thus reflects something even deeper, the fundamental human values that say what we can do and how. The technology, standards, and networks are all reflections of those values.

Infrastructure, at all levels, reflects how we apply these fundamental human values. Privacy, for example, can be protected or destroyed by a network. There is no inevitable loss of privacy on computer networks, but that is certainly one possible outcome. Likewise, free speech can be encouraged, property can be protected, and we can mold the technology to reflect what we want.

It is the coupling of an awareness of these fundamental values with an understanding of the technology that allows us to build a truly global infrastructure. Technically unsophisticated policy makers make bad laws, just as politically unsophisticated engineers make bad networks.

❒

Educating policy makers and engineers is certainly a nice, long-term goal, but it doesn't provide any concrete steps to be taken today. Putting standards online, though, is a concrete step. The task is technically simple and the benefits were clear.

The Bruno project demonstrated how trivial it is to make information available on computer networks. That this information should, indeed must, be available to all is, to borrow the words of Geoff Huston in Australia, "bloody obvious."

Yet, in pursuing this goal, I ran into a solid wall of resistance. To the people running the process, posting standards leads to the demise of international standards and takes money away from developing countries.

In visiting twenty countries, though, it was obvious to me that the developing countries are the ones most hurt by the policies of the international standards bodies. They are the ones that need most to train engineers, to develop products for export, and to apply cheap, easily-available technology to pressing problems.

Even the developed countries are not helped by policies that restricted participation to a bureaucratic elite. The real networks that I visited were built from the ground up. The most effective networks were built by people with problems to solve. If we want those networks to be interoperable, certainly a goal of the standards process, people building the networks have to be able to get the standards.

The concept of the standards haven is one way around the bureaucracies, but it is not a very productive way to solve the problem. While a few countries probably will post standards for their engineers, nobody had confirmed their intention to do so officially. Indeed, while Korea and India liked the standards haven concept, the idea was caught in the mire of their own bureaucracies. Ultimately, the standards haven concept is a temporary stopgap and a more permanent solution must come directly from the standards cartel. This is a problem crying for global leadership.

Availability of information is one of those fundamental human values that needs to be established as a conscious decision, a fundamental part of the infrastructure. Bruno was a stopgap, and even if a few people working on their own could come up with a new stopgap, what we need is a real solution.

❐

Returning from the coffee shop, it was time to tackle a three-foot-tall pile of mail that had come while I was gone. Having the SnailMAIL to process in a batch let me have a little fun.

As I sorted my mail, I pulled out all the postage-paid cards and put them into a stack, throwing everything else into the recycle bin. I then performed triage on the stack, dividing them up into things I wanted information on (a total of two cards), things I didn't care about, and companies and interest groups I didn't like.

The cards for the bad organizations were left blank and deposited in the nearest post box. Voting with postage-paid cards was a form of economic democracy I learned from my politically-active mother. Over time, individual action can snowball and even the bulkiest bureaucracies will give way.

A

Abe, George, 318-19
Academic Computing Services, 134
Academy One project, 289-90
Acampora, Anthony, 141
Acnet (Accelerator Control network), 295-96
Acorn project, 141-43
 applications, 142-43
 architecture, 142
 basis of, 142
ACSnet, 193
Adams, Rick, 363
Address space resolution, 336
Adelaide, Australia, 198-201
Advanced Network and Services (ANS), 103, 145, 282
AFGnet, 258
Aiso, Dean, 45
Akihabara, 49-50, 55, 324-25
 "Electric Town," 324
AlterNet, 195
Amsterdam, 90-94, 233-44
 Bulgarian dial-up UUCP link, 271
 CWI (Centrum voor Wiskunde en Informatica), 233-34, 240
 NIKHEF (Nationaal Instituut voor Kernfysica en Hoge-Energie-fysica), 233, 235, 238, 292
 RIPE (Réseaux IP Européens), 233-39, 242-44, 250
Andrew File System (AFS), 37
Andrews, W. Clayton, 141-42
Appropriate Use Policy (AUP), 195
Ardis public data network, 62
ARPANET, 9, 88, 98, 252, 277-78, 280, 315, 352, 354-56, 359 ASN.1, 121-22
Association for Computing Machinery (ACM), 279
AT&T, 318
ATOMIC project, 313-15

Auckland, 182-84
 Wellington, 175-77
Auerbach, Karl, 31, 151
Australia:
 Adelaide, 198-201
 Australian AARNET, 193, 195, 245, 336
 Canberra, 193-97
 Melbourne, 184-87
 Sydney, 188-92
Australian Academic Research Network (AARNet), 193, 195, 245, 336
AUTOCAD, 23, 56

B

Bangkok, Thailand, 219-32
 general ledger system, 220-21
 Pantip Plaza, 230-31
 Stock Exchange of Thailand (SET), 220, 222-23
 Value Group, 226-28
Baobab, 284-85
Barad, Bob, 283-85
Bay Area Regional Research Network (BARRnet), 30, 86, 173-74 BBN, 88, 315, 357
Becker, Jordan, 152
Becker, Paul, 141
Behemoth, 161-64
 audio bus, 163
 chord keyboard, 162
 computers on, 162
 cost of, 164
 Global Positioning System (GPS), 164
 head mouse, 162-63
 helmet, 163
 power bus, 163
 security for, 164
Belgium, 260-68

Index

Bell, Gordon, 303
Bellcore, 304, 307
Berkeley, California, 157-60
Birkenbihl, Klaus, 255-56, 258
BITNET, 15, 38, 59, 68, 84, 86, 358
Bjelke-Petersen, Joh, 201
Blokzijl, Rob, 233-35, 237
Blue Book, The, 5, 11, 22-23, 124, 128,
   130, 272
  conversion of, 22-25
Bombay, India, 340-51
  Bureau of Indian Standards (BIS),
    351
  ERNET, 341-43
  NCST (National Center for Soft-
    ware Training), 340-45, 348, 351
  PTI (Press Trust of India), 349-51
  railway reservation system, 345-47
Bond, Alan, 201
Bonn, Germany, 254-59
Border Gateway Protocol (BGP), 88, 137
Bottorff, Norman, 225
Boulder, Colorado, 21-25, 153-54, 157,
   301-7, 361-66
Bratislava, Czechoslovakia, 15
Brim, Scott, 136-37
British Telecom, 71
Broadband ISDN (B-ISDN), 303, 315,
   321
Bruno, Giordano, 35
Bruno project, 35, 44, 116-17, 124-33,
   170, 302, 366
  applying to ISO world, 130
  ITU printing operation vs., 127-28
  termination of, 125, 153-54
Brussels, Belgium, 260-68
Bulletin board services, Minitel and, 20
Butterfield, Julie, 6
Butterfly, The, 174

C
California:
  Berkeley, 157-60
  Marina del Rey, 311-17
  Moffet Field, 171-74

  Mountain View, 161-65
  San Francisco, 166-70, 318-20
  San Jose, 22
CAMAC crates, 294-97
Canberra, Australia, 193-97
Carpenter, Brian, 18, 93
Casner, Stephen, 315-16
CCIR, 125
CCITT, 69, 125, 330
  recommendation D.1, 68
CDCNET, 186
Cedok, 13
Center for Telecommunications Re-
  search (CTR), 141-44
  Acorn project, 141-43
  operational nature of, 143
Centrum voor Wiskunde en Infor-
  matica (CWI), 233-34, 240
CERFnet, 105, 312, 329-30
Cerf, Vinton, 34, 84-85, 123, 151, 277-
  79, 343, 354
CERN, 18, 91, 172, 234, 236, 250, 257,
  271, 283, 292-93, 358
Chang, Michael, 60, 337
Chapin, Lyman, 123
Chatchi, General, 229
Chaundry, Chris, 185-86
Chen, Tommi, 67
CHEOPS satellite, 18
Cheung, Eric Lo Hing, 337
Chicago, 291-300
Chinese University (New Territories),
  60
Cho, Mr., 65-66
Chon, Kilnam, 329-32, 359
Cisco routers, 17, 102, 105, 194, 235,
  271, 275
CITI (Columbia Institute for Tele-Infor-
  mation), 143-44
  Private Networks and Public Objec-
    tives project, 144
City Lights bookstore, 159
Clark, David, 304-5
Clasper, Harry, 93-94
Cleveland, Ohio, 286-90
  Cleveland Free-Net, 286-89, 348
CLNS, 107

Index

CNET, 120
CNRS (Centre National de la Recherche Scientifique), 273
Cody's bookstore, 158
Cohen, Danny, 313
Colorado, Boulder, 21-25, 153-54
Colorado SuperNet, 270
Columbia University, New York:
    CITI (Columbia Institute for Tele-Information), 143-44
    CTR (Center for Telecommunications Research), 141-44
Comer, Douglas, 34, 357
Commercial Internet Exchange (CIX), 195, 312
Communications Week International, 108, 110, 131, 154, 302
Computer Literacy bookstore, 159-60
Computer Sciences Corporation (CSC), 318
Connection Oriented Network Service (CONS), 90
ConneXions journal, 3, 33, 165, 319
Cooper, Ann, 317
Copyright protection:
    of ITU documents, 129-31
    Value Group, 227-28
Cornell University, 136-40
    CUINFO, 138-39
    Gateway Daemon (*gated*), 137-38
    routing protocols, work on, 136
Corporation for National Research Initiatives (CNRI), 81, 277, 279, 303-4
COSINE project, 248-50, 261-64, 363
    budget, 249
    IXI (International X.25 Infrastructure), 249-50, 263
    origin of, 248
    Project Management Unit (PMU), 249
Crocker, Dave, 355
Crow, Trammel, 301
Crowcroft, Jon, 99
CTR, *See* Center for Telecommunications Research (CTR)
CSNET, 84, 354, 355-59

CUINFO, 138-39
Curtis, Kent, 354
CWI, *See* Centrum voor Wiskunde en Informatica (CWI)
Cypress network, 357
Czechoslovakia:
    Bratislava, 15
    Prague, 13-16
Czech Technical University, 13-14

D

DARPA, 268, 278, 280, 303, 311, 312, 315, 354, 364
Data Communications, 3
Datanet, 104-6
Datapak, 63
DEC LAT protocols, 213
DECnet, 17, 39, 40, 85, 92, 104, 105, 186, 257, 271, 293-94
DECnet Phase IV, 172
DECnet Phase V, 55, 110, 172
Deering, Stephen, 315
Delp, Gary, 305
Denning, Peter, 355
desJardins, Richard, 34-35
Develnet, 62
DFN (Deutsches Forschungsnetz) project, 257-58, 263, 274, 358
DG XIII, 89, 261-64, 267
Dial-up UUCP, 271, 343
Digital Equipment Corporation (DEC), 73, 150, 151, 295, 304, 358
    Western Research Laboratory, 357
Digital Resource Institute, 116
Directory assistance, Minitel and, 19
Directory User Agent, X.500, 96-97
DISH, 96
$Link, Singapore Network Services (SNS), 75
Domain Name System (DNS), 97-98, 147, 317
DSA, 95-98
Dublin, 83-89
Dunedin, New Zealand, 178-81
D Zero, 297-99

Index

E

EASInet, 93, 250, 256-57
EBCDIC character set, 24
EBONE (European Backbone), 89, 90-94, 240, 250, 257, 283
  contributions to, 92-93
  DECnet Phase IV traffic and, 92
  EBONE Action Team, 93, 250
  management committee, 93-94
  Memorandum of Understanding, 250-51
EDI, 74, 204
Eicher, Larry, 117, 130-31
Elamvazuthi, Chandron, 210, 212
Electronic mail, in outlying areas, 115
Elz, Robert, 186, 193
England, 95-99
ENIAC, 14
Epilogue Technology, 31, 198, 200
Eppenberger, Urs, 17
ERNET, 341-43
  floppy-based e-mail system, 342
  infrastructure, 342-43
ESnet (Energy Sciences network), 174
  HEPnet and, 293
Esprit, 262-64, 268
Estrada, Susan, 312
Ethernets, 17, 18, 54, 62, 73, 120, 126, 306, 324, 348
EUnet, 15, 45, 233, 239-42, 251, 257, 364
  EBONE consortium and, 242
Eureka group, COSINE project and, 248-49
European Academic Research Network (EARN), 15, 84, 247, 252, 256, 258, 271
European Academic Supercomputer Initiative (EASI), 256
European Commission, 268, 272, 276
  DG XIII, 261-64, 267
  RARE contributions, 247-48
European Council of Telecommunications User Associations (EC-TUA), 252
European Internet, 268
European Nervous System, 261
European Telecommunications Standards Institute (ETSI), 119, 252
European UNIX Users Group (EUUG), 240-42
European Workshop on Open Systems (EWOS), 252
EurOpen, 241-42
Exterior Gateway Protocol (EGP), 88, 137

F

Fair, Erik, 317
Farber, David, 84, 302-4, 306, 355
Faul, Stephanie, 280-81
FDDI, 18, 30, 40, 69, 73, 122, 197, 294, 333
Federal Emergency Management Agency (FEMA), 244
Federal Express, 62, 67, 231
Feist, Jerry, 138
Felderman, Robert, 313-14
Fermilab, 18, 291-97
  CAMAC crates, 294-97
  Linear Accelerator (LINAC), 294
  network architecture, 294
  networking at, 296
Fidonet, 284-85
Finland, 100-107
Finn, Gregory, 313-14
Firefighters, 4
FIX-East, 173
FIX-West, 38, 173, 195
Flaming, 4
Flat-rate pricing, 63, 70
Fluckiger, Francois, 18
Forrester, Ian, 178-81
Frame Relay, 32, 105-6
France:
  France Telecom, 19, 273-75
  Nice, 119-23
  Paris, 19-20, 108-15, 269-76
FRED, 96
Free-Net, 286-89, 348
Fry's, 160
FTAM, 17, 107, 264, 332

Index

FTP Software, 31, 34
Fuchs, Ira, 84, 303
Fujisawa, 38, 43-48
Fujitsu, Value Added Group, 41
Full duplex, definition of, 189
FUNET (Finnish University Network),
   104-5
Fuzzball, 88

G

Garg, Anil, 343
gated software, 137-38
Gates, Bill, 100
Gateway Daemon, 137
Geneva, 3-12, 18, 116-18, 124-33
Germany, Bonn, 254-59
Gigabit testbeds, rearch conducted in,
   307
GIPSI, 120
GMD, 255-58
   DFN (Deutsches Forschungsnetz)
      project, 257-58, 263, 274, 358
   EASInet, 93, 250, 256-57
GobNet, 306
Golden Shopping Center, 55-58, 231
   Macrosoft stall, 56-57
Goldstein, Steve, 281-82
GOSIP Institute, 35
Goto, Shigeki, 323
Graphics, standards and, 130
Gross, Phill, 149
Grundner, Tom, 286-89
Gruntorad, Jan, 13-15

H

Hackett, Simon, 198-201, 316
Haleiwa, 37
Halliday, Bob, 224-25, 231, 232
Hanafi, Waleed, 60-63
Happy Valley, 51-52, 63
Hardcastle-Kille, Steve, 95, 363
Harju, Raimo, 100
Hawaii, Honolulu, 36-37
HEAnet, 84

Hearn, Tony, 355
Heinanen, Juha, 103-6, 318, 363
Helsinki Free-Net, 289
HEPnet, 39, 172, 271, 292-93
   ESnet (Energy Sciences network)
      and, 293
   growth of, 293
Hermes project, 288
High technology, in outlying areas, 115
Hill, Robin, 200-201
Hitachi notebook, 49-50
Hoat, Ang Chong, 204
Hong, Yeo Ning, 74
Hong Kong, 51-64, 219, 337-39
   Golden Shopping Center, 55-58, 231
   Hong Kong University, 59-60
   Hutchinson Mobile Data, 60-62
   Jockey Club, 51-55, 62
Honig, Jeff, 136-37
Honolulu, 36-37
Huh, Moon-Haeng, 333
Huitema, Christian, 119-23, 278, 363
Huston, Geoff, 193-97, 363, 365
Hutchinson Mobile Data (Hong Kong),
   60-62

I

IBM 9000, 74-75
IBM, 93-94, 145, 256, 283, 304, 318, 358
   PARIS project, 304
IDNet, 79
IDPR/IDRP, 137
IETF, 128, 147-52, 196, 235, 278-79, 336
   certified protocol engineers board,
      proposal for, 148-49
   MIB (management information
      base), 150-51
   standards, 148
   Steering Group (IESG), 150, 196
   working groups, 148
India, Bombay, 340-51
Indian Institute of Technology (IIT), 343
INET, 278-79, 359
Infolan, 105-6
Infonet, 319

Index

Information Communication Institute
  of Singapore (ICIS), 69-70
Information Sciences Institute (ISI), 311-
  16
  ATOMIC Project, 313-15
  CERFnet, 312
  DARTnet, 312-13
  MOSIS service, 311
  multimedia conferencing, 315-16
  Terrestrial Wideband (TWB) net-
    work, 312-13, 315
Infrastructure, 365
Ingres, 56, 243
INMARSAT, 71-72
INRIA, 119-23, 255, 269-71, 273, 282
  ASN.1 benchmark, 122
  computer network project, 120-21
  MAVROS compiler, 121-22
  robotics projects, 119-20
  The Obviously Required Name
    Server (THORN), 121
  X.400 project, 121
Institut National de la Recherche en In-
    formatique et Automatique, See
    INRIA
Intercontinental Research Networking
    (CCIRN), 252
International Direct Dial (IDD) links, 72
International standards documents, 3-
    12
  availability of, 3-5
  copyright protection, lack of, 4
International X.25 Infrastructure (IXI),
    249-50, 263
Internet, 3-5, 8, 18, 97, 99, 109, 125- 26,
    128, 169, 177, 195-96
  Finland, 103
  France, 112
  installing at San Jose Convention
    Center, 29-35
  Internet Activities Board (IAB), 11,
    97, 149-51, 196, 277-78, 315
  Internet Assigned Numbers Author-
    ity (IANA), 315
  Internet Monthly Report, 317
  Japan, 39
  Managers Guide, 211

  in outlying areas, 115
  policy routing protocols, 106
  Request for Comments (RFCs), 3
  subnetwork support, 106
Internet Society, 196-97, 252, 278-79
Internode Systems, 198
INTEROP, 22, 25, 29-36, 130, 165, 198,
    352
Ireland, Dublin, 83-89
Irish Universities Network, 83-84
ISDN, 47, 77, 109, 235, 264-65, 303, 322,
    324
  Singapore, 71
ISDN Karaoke Machine, 323
Ishida, Haruhisa, 38-40
ISI, See Information Sciences Institute
ISODE (ISO Development Environ-
    ment), 95-96, 148, 248
ISO (International Organization for
    Standardization), 8-12, 130, 319-
    21
  standards, 332
IT2000, 77-78, 80-81
Ithaca, 134-40
ITU (International Telecommunication
    Union), 3-12, 20-25, 44, 116-18,
    124-25, 153-54, 170, 272, 330-31
  Blue Book, The, 5, 11, 22-25, 124,
    128, 130, 272
  Consultative Committee on Interna-
    tional Telephone and Telegraph,
    5
  copyright protection of documents,
    129-31
  Information Systems Steering
    Group, 124-25, 129
  lack of computer literacy at, 6-7
  mail system, 131-32
  printing department, 127-28

J
Jacobsen, Ole, 33, 165, 319-20
JAIN, 39
JANET Coloured Book protocols, 84, 96
Jansen, Peter, 225

Index

Japan:
  Akihabara, 49-50
  Fujisawa, 38, 43-48
  ISDN and, 47
  KEK, 292
  networks in, 38-39
  Tokyo, 38-42, 321-28
JARING network, 211
Jennings, Dennis, 83-90, 92-94, 122, 145
Jensen, Mike, 284
Jipguep, Mr., 117
Jockey Club (Hong Kong), 51-55, 62
  Customer Information Terminal
    (CIT), 53-54
  Telebet system, 53-54, 62
  vendor/technology policy, 54
Johnston, Peter, 261
Joint Network Team (JNT), 96, 282
JUNET, 39, 45-46
Junsec, 44, 48
JVNCnet, 335

K

Kahle, Brewster, 166-70
Kahn, Bob, 277, 280, 303-4, 315
Karrenberg, Daniel, 234
Keio University (Fujisawa campus), 39,
    43-48
Kent, Stephen, 123
Kerberos, 33
Kern, Bill, 355
Kim Il Sung University (Pyongyang),
    66
King, Ken, 139-40
Kirstein, Peter, 98-99, 358
Knowbots, 81
Knowles, Stev, 31, 148
Korea, 38, 329-34
Korea Telecom, 331-34
Kowack, Glenn, 239, 241-42, 363
Kowloon, 60
KREN (Korea Research Network), 330
KREOnet (Korea Research Environ-
    ment Open Network), 329-30
Kuala Lumpur, Malaysia, 209-18

MIMOS (Malaysian Institute of Mi-
    croelectronic Systems), 209-12,
    215
  Plus project, 212-13
  Tenaga Nasional Berhad, 215-17
Kummerfeld, Bob, 188-92, 197
Kundapur, Gourang, 349
Kuo, Frank, 85

L

Lambert, Carol, 134, 136, 139
Lambert, H. Dave, 134-36, 139
Landweber, Jean, 359-60
Landweber, Larry, 45, 84-85, 122, 278,
    352-54, 355, 358-60
Landweber Seminars, 358-59
Lanlink, 104-5
LANs (Local Area Networks), 305-6
Large Electron-Positron (LEP), 18
LAT, 73, 294
Lauck, Tony, 85, 150
Lauder, Piers, 188-90
Leased lines, 15, 17, 90, 101-2, 193
Le Guigner, Jean-Paul, 273-75
Leiner, Barry, 319-20
Linear Accelerator (LINAC), 294
Linear lightwave networks (LLNs), 142
Local Area VAX Clusters (LAVCs), 294
London, 95-99
Los Nettos network, 312
Lucas, Peter, 294, 296
Lynch, Cliff, 349
Lynch, Dan, 4, 123, 160

M

Macau, 65-66
McKenzie, 9-12
Madison, Wisconsin, 352-60
Malamud.COM, 270
Malaysia, 209-18
Management Information Base (MIB),
    34
Marina del Rey, California, 311-17

Index

Information Sciences Institute (ISI),
311
Markwell, John, 54
MBA Experiment, 135-36
MCI, 145
MCI Mail, 109, 270, 280
Medin, Milo, 171-74
Medinet, Singapore Network Services
(SNS), 75
Melbourne, Australia, 184-87, 193
Memnet, 307
Message Handling Systems, 190
MFEnet (MuffyNet), 85
MHSnet, 190-91
Michau, Christian, 273, 275
Michigan state network (Merit), 145
MicroGrafix Designer, 23
Microsoft Word for Windows, 23-24
Mikrokonsultit Oy, 100-102
Mills, David, 88
MILNET, 252, 335-36
MIMOS (Malaysian Institute of Mi-
croelectronic Systems), 209-15
Minitel, 19-20
Mobitex system, 62
Moccia, Mary Jo, 221-22
Mockapetris, Paul, 147, 305
Moffet Field, California, 171-74
Mohamed, B. Awang-Lah, 210, 212
Mosaic, 313-14
MOSIS service, 311
Motif, 56
Mountain View, California, 161-65, 171
Multichannel, definition of, 189
MultiMedia Data Switch (MMDS), 199
Mun Chun, Chew, 71
Murai, Jun, 39-48, 324-25, 328, 363
Murakami, Ken-Ichiro, 323

N
N-1net, 38
NACSIS, *See* National Center for Sci-
ence Information Systems (NAC-
SIS)
Naemura, Kenji, 321, 323

Narong, Khun, 226-28
NASA-Ames Research Center, 30, 171,
195
NASA Science Internet (NSI), 171-74,
244, 252
applications, 171-72
as Internet backbone, 173
links, ownership of, 173
Network Control Center, 172
SNMP and, 172
NASA Telephone Company, 173-74
Nationaal Instituut voor Kernfysica en
Hoge-Energiefysica (NIKHEF),
233, 235, 238, 292
National Center for Atmospheric Re-
search (NCAR), 87
National Center for Science Informa-
tion Systems (NACSIS), 38
National Center for Software Training
(NCST), 340-45, 348, 351
National Computer Board (NCB), 78-80
National Science and Technology
Board (NSTB), 67-68
National University of Singapore
(NUS), 67-69
Naylor, Chris, 175, 177
Naylor, Jeremy, 175
Naylor, Richard, 175-77, 289
Neggers, Kees, 90-94, 245-47, 251-53
NESTE system, 100
Netherlands:
Amsterdam, 90-94, 233-44
Utrecht, 245-53
NetPhone, 199-200
Network Information Center (NIC),
243-44
Network Interface Unit (NIU), 142
Networld, 29
Netzzentrum fuer die Wissenschaft, 255
Neuman, Clifford, 312
New Mexico, Santa Fe, 147-52
New Territories, 60
New York City, 141-44
Acorn project, 141-43
CITI (Columbia Institute for Tele-In-
formation), 143-44
New Zealand, 178-81

Index

World Communications Laboratory,
181
Ng, Nam, 59
Nice, France, 119-23
Nielsen, Torben, 36-37, 45
NiftyServe, 42
NIKHEF, See Nationaal Instituut voor
Kernfysica en Hoge-Energie-
fysica (NIKHEF)
Nippon Telegraph and Telephone
(NTT):
Kasumigaseki showroom, 323
vision, 321-23
Yokosuka research laboratories, 321
Ní Shúilleabháin, Aine M., 144
NJE, 15
Noam, Eli, 144
Nojima, Hisao, 323
Nomadic Research Labs, 164
NORDUnet, 93, 104-5, 234, 236, 240,
250, 282
Norwegian Telecom, 71
Novell, 12, 59, 105, 280
Nowlan, Michael, 242
NREN, 103
NSF, 38, 85-89, 122, 197, 281-83, 303,
354, 364
connections program, 146
NSFNET, 11, 30, 82, 83, 87-91, 137, 145-
46, 174, 195-197, 236, 243, 251-52,
256-57, 273, 281-83, 302, 312, 335,
364
NSTB, See National Science and Tech-
nology Board (NSTB)
NTT, 45
NUS, See National University of Singa-
pore (NUS)
Nynex, Minitel and, 20

O

OCR software, ISO standards and, 332
ODA (Office Document Architecture),
37, 98
Office of Technology Assessment, 146
Okado, Tomoo, 41-42, 326

Open Desktop (SCO), 56, 348
OrderLink, Singapore Network Services (SNS), 75
ORSTOM, 111-14, 119, 273
computer support, 112-13
functions of, 111-12
research centers, location of, 112
RIO network, 113-14
OSI IS-IS, 137
OSI (Open Systems Interconnection), 3,
12, 17, 45, 86-98, 191-93, 197, 235,
237, 246-48, 258, 276, 331, 361-62
OSPF, 137

P

PACCOM, 180, 330
PACE, 261
Packet Assembler/Disassembler, 356
Palalikit, Surat, 220-22
PARADISE ESPRIT project, 96
Paris, France, 19-20, 108-15, 269-76
CNRS (Centre National de la Re-
cherche Scientifique), 273
INRIA, 119-23, 255, 269-71, 273
Renater, 273-76
Parkkari, Vesa, 100-107
Partridge, Craig, 33
PBX, 33
PDP-11, 88
PDP, 53, 110, 292, 295-97
PeaceNet, 284
PERL code, 25
PhoneNet, 356, 358-59
Phone Shell Project, 46
Poireau, Gerard, 19-20
Port of Singapore Authority, 204-7
Postel, Jon, 3, 149-50, 311-12, 316
Prague, Czechoslovakia, 13-16
Prem, General, 229
Prestandardization research, 248
Privacy, 365
Programmers, memory and, 305
Protocols, basis of, 304-5
PSInet, 105
PTTs, 89, 91, 247, 256, 265-66, 318, 319

Index

Q

Quarterman, John, 170
Quipu, 95-96
    interfaces interacting with, 96

R

RACE (Research and Development in Advanced Communications Technolgies for Europe), 261, 264-66
Rahman Bin Shafi, Abdul, 215
Ramani, S., 340-45, 348-51
RARE, *See* Réseaux Associés pour la Recherche Européenne (RARE)
Rate arbitrage, 265-66
Recommendation D.1, CCITT, 68
Relevantum Oy, 100
Renang Group, 213-14
Renater (Réseau National de Télécommunications de la Recherche), 273-76
Renaud, Pascal, 111-13
Request for Comments (RFCs), 3, 311
    RFC 1181, 234
Réseaux Associés pour la Recherche Européenne (RARE), 91, 233, 234, 237, 242, 247-48, 250-51, 272
    contributions, sources of, 247
    Council of Administration, 238, 247, 252
    Operational Unit, proposed setup of, 251-52
Réseaux IP Européens (RIPE), 233-39, 242-44, 250
    Network Control Center (NCC), 237-38
Reynolds, Joyce, 316-17
Richter, Walter, 125-26
RIPE, *See* Réseaux IP Européens (RIPE)
Roberts, Steve, 161-65
Robotics projects, INRIA, 119-20
Rolnick, Harry, 65-66, 337-38
Romkey, John, 33-34
Rose, Marshall T., 34, 95, 111, 148, 196, 317, 363

Rosebud interface, 168
Rosenbaum, Jurgen, 268
ROSE project (Research Open Systems for Europe) , 264
Routing domains, reachability between, 137
RTF, 24, 25
Rutkowski, Tony, 3-8, 13, 22, 35, 44, 116-17, 124-25, 128-33, 154, 277-78

S

St. Silicon bulletin board, 286
San Diego Supercomputer Center, 312
    SDSCnet, 86-87
San Francisco, 166-70, 318-20
    SF Net, 166
    Wide Area Information Servers (WAIS), 167-69
San Jose, 22, 29-35
Santa Fe, 147-52
Schaumberger, Dean, 298-99
Schiller, Jeffrey, 33
Schooler, Eve, 315-16
Schrader, Bill, 87
Schwartz, Michael, 170, 302
Schwartz, Mischa, 141
SciTech, 299-300
SDSCnet (San Diego Supercomputer Center), 86-87
SEEDNET, 335-36
Seoul, Korea, 329-34
    Korea Telecom, 331-34
    KREN (Korea Research Network), 330
    KREOnet (Korea Research Environment Open Network), 329-30
SGML, 37, 332
Sham Shui Po, 55-58
Shaw, Robert, 153
Shein, Barry, 195
ShowNet, 31-32, 34, 166
Simple Book, The (Rose), 34
Singapore, 67-82, 202-8, 219
    IDNet, 79

Index

Information Communication Institute of Singapore (ICIS), 69-70
ISDN, cost of, 71
IT2000, 77-78, 80-81
National Computer Board (NCB), 78-80, 204
Port of Singapore Authority (PSA) systems, 204-7
Restricted Zone, 202, 204
SCATS system, 203-4
TECHnet, 67-69
Tradenet, 74-75, 81, 204
Singapore Network Services (SNS), 74-76
    $Link, 75
    Medinet, 75
    OrderLink, 75
    Tradenet EDI system, 74-75, 81
Singapore Telecom, 68, 70-72
    Skyphone, 71-72
    Teleview, 72-74
Singapore—The Next Lap (Times Editions), 78
Skilling, Peter, 225
Skyphone, 71-72
SMDS, 32, 67, 106
Smith, Mike, 117, 130
SMTP, 191
SNA, 92, 102
SNS, See Singapore Network Services (SNS)
SnailMAIL, 366
SNMP, 32, 33, 148, 198, 316
    NASA Science Internet (NSI) and, 172
Software Tool and Die, 195
Solutions Showcases, 32
Song, Joo-Young, 333
Song, Tay Eng, 80
Sons of Bruno, 35, 117
Sprint, 33
STACKS (Malamud), 45, 65-66, 67, 130, 323
Standards, free distribution of, 131
Standards haven concept, 330-31
Stanwyck, Don, 69-70
Sterba, Milan, 271-72, 302

Stern, Thomas, 142
Stock Exchange of Thailand (SET), 220, 222-23
Stockman, Bernhard, 93
Sun Microsystems, 23-25, 151, 161
SUN protocol suite, 188-90
    compared to TCP/IP, 189
    E-mail, 190
    messages/packets, architecture of, 190
    streaming protocol, 189
SURFnet, 90-92, 245-47, 257
    restrictions on content of traffic, 91
Swiss UNIX group (CHUUG), 243
SWITCH (Swiss Telecommunication System for Higher Education and Research), 17, 121, 242-43
Switzerland:
    Geneva, 3-12, 18, 116-18, 124-33
    Zurich, 17
Sydney, Australia, 188-92, 193
    SUN protocol suite, 188-90

T

T1 lines, 30, 256-57, 312
Taipei, 335-36
Taiwan, 38, 335-36
Tampere, 100-107
Tan, Rosli Md, 212
Tarjanne, Pekka, 7, 22, 35, 116-18, 132, 153-54, 302
Tarmidi, Ahmad, 214-15
TCP/IP, 15, 17, 34, 40, 45-46, 47, 68, 85-86, 90, 91, 95-96, 102, 106, 112, 122, 172, 186, 189, 200, 211, 233, 234, 237, 240, 248, 256-58, 268, 271, 274, 277, 294, 315, 329, 354, 363
    protocol suite, 9, 11, 12, 47, 85, 88, 114, 196, 311
    routing protocols, 137
TECHnet, 67-69
Telebet system, Jockey Club (Hong Kong), 53-54, 62
Telecom Finland, 104, 106, 117, 125

Index

Telekom Malaysia, 211, 213, 214
Telenet, 356
Teleview, Singapore Telecom, 72-74
Telnet, 139, 189, 316, 356
Tenaga Nasional Berhad, 215-17
   communications system, 216-17
   distributed systems project, 215-16
TeX, 37
Thailand, 219-32
Thinking Machines, WAIS and, 169
Thio Hoe Tong, Dr., 67-69
TIFF files, 23, 24
Time Engineering, 214
Todai International Science Network
   (TISN), 39
Tokyo, 38-42, 321-28
   Tokyo City Hall, 326-28
Top quarks, 297-98
TPS, 24, 25
Trademark protection, Thailand, 228-29
Tradenet EDI system, Singapore Net-
   work Services (SNS), 74-75, 81,
   204
Trade press, technical knowledge of,
   109-11
Transpac, 20
Tsim Sha Tsui, 58-59
Tymnet, 356

U
U.K. Coloured Book standards, 193, 358
Ultra networks, 18
United Nations Development Program
   (UNDP), 341
United States:
   Berkeley, California, 157-60
   Boulder, Colorado, 21-25, 153-54,
     157, 301-7, 361-66
   Chicago, Illinois, 291-300
   Cleveland, Ohio, 286-90
   Honolulu, Hawaii, 36-37
   Ithaca, New York, 134-40
   Madison, Wisconsin, 352-60
   Marina del Rey, California, 311-17
   Mountain View, California, 161-65

New York City, 141-44
San Francisco, California, 166-70
San Jose, California, 22
Washington, D.C., 145-46, 277-85
U.S. Defense Advanced Research Pro-
   jects Agency, See DARPA
University College London (UCL), 95-
   99
   networking at, 98-99
University of Hawaii network, 36
University of Melbourne network, 184-
   87
University of Sydney, 190
UNIX, 24, 47, 56, 241, 244, 339
   European UNIX Users Group
     (EUUG), 240-42
   Routing Information Protocol (RIP),
     137
   Swiss UNIX group (CHUUG), 243
USENET, 46, 239-40, 348, 364
UTP-based Ethernets, 40
Utrecht, 245-53
UUCP, 15, 39, 103, 122, 177, 189-90,
   211, 239, 355
   Dial-up UUCP, 271
   ORSTOM and, 113
UUnet, 45, 193, 211, 288, 341

V
Value Added Group, Fujitsu, 41
Value-Added Network (VAN), 266
VAX, 24, 53, 54, 61-62, 292-93, 303, 347,
   348
VAXen, 54, 73, 295-96, 298, 346
VME crates, 298-99
VTP, 17

W
Wah, Chew Keng, 204, 207
WAIS, See Wide Area Information Serv-
   ers (WAIS)
Waikiki (Hawaii), 37
Wanchai, 60

Index

WAN links, 18
WANs (Wide Area Networks), 306
Washington, D.C., 145-46, 277-85
Weird Stuff Warehouse, 160
Wellington, Auckland, 175-77
    City Net, 176-77
WHOIS database, 97, 237, 243
Wholebrain Technology, 153
Wide Area Information Servers
        (WAIS), 167-69, 186, 281, 348
    client interfaces, 168-69
    clients, 168
    document indexing, 167
    document storage, 168
    NeXT and, 169
    pieces of, 167
    servers on Internet, 169
    simple WAIS (SWAIS), 168
    Thinking Machines and, 169
    user requirements, 168
    WAIStation, 168-69
    XWAIS, 169
WIDE (Widely Integrated Distributed
        Environment), 39, 44-46
    ISDN module, 47
Williamson, Scott, 243
Wilson, Robert, 291
Wolff, Steve, 88-89, 145-46
Word Perfect, 24-25
World Communications Laboratory
        (New Zealand), 181
Worona, Steve, 13
Wurzel, 21-22

common schema for directory, de-
    velopment of, 97
directory structure, 95-96
Directory User Agent (DUA), 96-98
integration into ISODE, 95
name structuring, 97-98
performance, 98
relaying mechanism, 97
replication, 97
rigid hierarchy, 97-98
X.800, 23
Xerox Corporation, 304, 315
X Window System, 96, 198, 296
    kanji support for, 46

Y
Yap, Michael, 76-77, 80, 82
Yeung, Edwin, 51
Yii Der, Lew, 202-3
Yusoff, Rafee, 209, 212, 214-15

Z
Zakharov, Dr., 9-12
Zentec character set, 24
Zurich, 17

X
X.3, 356
X.25, 17, 41, 54, 62, 73, 83-84, 90, 101-2,
        112-13, 115, 120, 121, 190, 193,
        211, 246, 274-76, 318, 343, 356-57
    X.28, 84, 211, 264, 356
X.29, 84, 211, 264, 356
X.75, 113
X.400, 7, 17, 32, 95, 102, 121-22, 129, 153
X.500, 186, 317
    alternative hierarchies, 97-98